STO

WORK:
Pathway To
Independence

Bill G. Gooch
Lois Carrier
John Huck
Southern Illinois University-Carbondale

 American Technical Society

Contents

Acknowledgements ═══════

Dr. C. William Horrell, for the use of many fine photographs.
Daryl Littlefield, who took a number of photographs specifically for this book.
Terry Mauzy and Kathleen O'Mara who supplied more visual material.
Mrs. Jane Renfro, art teacher at Carbondale Community High School, who introduced us to some of her students and their work.

Daryl Meier, Vera Grosowsky, Richard Perry, James Stephan, John Coombs, Pat Smith, Somchai Thipkhosithkun, and George Nadaf for interviews which appear in this book.

Mr. Lawrence Keller for his assistance in investigating banking services and credit.

The staff of Carbondale Public Library for its cheerful assistance.

Preface

WORK: PATHWAY TO INDEPENDENCE is a lively, engaging textbook for the "related instruction" class in cooperative education and most vocational education programs. Sometimes humorous, but always positive, the text is designed to help young men and women gain self-reliance and independence. Its general philosophy is: "Use your own natural potential to build a future for yourself." The authors believe in people and their ability to shape their own lives. Step one on the "pathway to independence" is to know your rights and possibilities—step two is to know how and when to act.

Dealing with conditions in the world of work as they really are, WORK: PATHWAY TO INDEPENDENCE steers clear of the cut and dried and from behavioral cliches. It gives good, positive information and advice that explains *why* one course of action is better than another. It suggests actions, alternatives, and choices that will appeal to the adult in all young people.

There is nothing dull or condescending about this book. Its scope, sequence, and style are based on the authors' extensive research and their personal experience in the classroom. The interviews and narrative discussions present the required materials in an exciting, easy to read format that anyone can relate to.

WORK: PATHWAY TO INDEPENDENCE is divided into eleven parts. Each part represents an important but separate aspect of the book.

Part I, *On the Move Toward Independence,* is an overview of cooperative education. It explains what cooperative education is, what it hopes to accomplish, and how it works.

Part II, *Under the Big Umbrella,* is concerned with the sensitive subject of human relations on the job. The authors have approached topics like how to relate to your boss and your co-workers, conflict and tension on the job, sex, race, and self-assertion honestly and maturely.

Part III, *Occupational Safety and Health,* covers basic safety in a general way, and discusses the Occupational Safety and Health Act (and other related legislation) in detail.

Part IV, *Skills You Will Need,* is a special section designed to help students review the three R's independently. It introduces key concepts (including pride in craftsmanship) in the context of work-related instruction.

Part V, *Career Exploration,* concentrates on the possibilities within oneself. It recognizes the fact that job placement is not usually for life, and presents career information and job finding skills in a manner that attempts to plant seeds rather than convince.

Part VI, *Your First Job,* covers personal grooming and behavior. It is designed to help young people succeed on their first job and to avoid starting a pattern of job failures.

Part VII, *Understanding Economics,* explains the economic system in which we live, and how the young worker fits into it.

Part VIII, *You and Your Money,* is designed to help young people manage their resources and avoid unnecessary financial stress.

Part IX, *You and the Law,* explains how and why laws are made. It includes a survey of the lawmaking process and a practical discussion of how the law protects you.

Part X, *Habitat,* is designed to help develop concern for the community and environment in which we live. But not until we have solved our own problems.

Part XI, *Planning for the Future,* ends the book on an optimistic note about the future and how we can control it.

While there is a "general law" section, the authors have tried to maintain student interest and attention by also discussing laws in the sections where they have the most immediate meaning. For example, the OSHA legislation is discussed in the health and safety chapter, labor-management legislation is discussed in the chapter on the worker in our economic system, and environmental legislation and consumer legislation are discussed in their appropriate chapters. The same is true for consumer education.

There is a variety of student activities interspersed throughout the book. These activities vary from writing exercises to classroom participation. They include the following types of activities:

What Do You Think?   These are usually discussion questions on very real and sometimes controversial subjects. They could be adapted for individual use, students could respond to them in writing, or they could be used in small discussion groups or by the class as a whole.

Working Cooperatively   These are usually activities that take a number of people to do effectively. They may consist of games, bulletin boards, panel discussions, or role playing.

Checkpoint   These are little factual quizzes that are designed to reinforce terminology and other related materials.

Chapter Check   Chapter checks appear at the end of most chapters, except where they would be inappropriate. They are inappropriate when the chapter has dealt with attitude formation.

For a detailed discussion of this material, refer to the Instructor's Manual.

—THE PUBLISHER

 Part One

Daryl Littlefield

On the Move
Toward Independence

GETTING UNDERWAY

Human beings as infants are among the most dependent creatures on earth. Some species of animals can take care of themselves soon after birth. The more complex a creature is, the longer it takes. Humans stand at the top of the scale of complexity.

Being dependent implies that others exercise control over our lives. When children are young they need to depend on others. They can't do everything for themselves or make important decisions alone. Parents are often in a better position to judge what is good for them. Yet the journey toward independence begins almost at once. Even when it is quite small, a baby finds standing on its own two feet more satisfying than having someone hold it up.

At first your home and family are the most important influences in your life. Then the neighborhood comes into the picture. Soon school takes the center of the stage. Later still, work begins to compete with school. At last you become an adult, and work becomes a big part of your life. You establish a home and family, and the cycle begins again. This is not an exact pattern that everyone follows, but a general outline of the road to independence.

You are now at the stage where work and school are about equally important. Through your cooperative education program you are entering adult territory. Your teacher-coordinator will help you get the most out of your program. Some of the things you can expect to learn are:

- possible ways of earning a living
- how to find a job and apply for it
- how to make the most of relationships with others at work
- standards of occupational safety and health
- how the law affects your work and life
- how our economic system works
- how to manage your personal resources

Just as when you were learning to read, ride a bike, or drive a car, you will have to contribute time and effort. By the end of the year we hope you will find yourself much closer to independence.

Working Cooperatively

 Your teacher-coordinator wants to know more about you. A class survey will help. Three committees will be necessary.

Committee One makes up the questionnaire. It could consist of such questions as:

- What are your three favorite TV shows?
- What sports do you prefer to watch?
- What physical activities do you participate in?
- Who is your favorite female musician? Male? Musical group?

- What class have you benefited from the most?
- What subject have you disliked the most?
- If you could have any job in the world, which one would you choose?

You need not use these exact questions. Make up some of your own, thinking in terms of things it would be important or interesting for your teacher to know about you.

Committee Two is responsible for typing and duplicating the questionnaire.

Committee Three administers the questionnaire, explaining the procedure, distributing and collecting the papers, and tallying the results. Your teacher-coordinator will then have some record of your individual likes and the interests of the group as a whole. Such information will be useful in planning activities later in the year.

❀ Chapter One ❀

THE COOPERATIVE EDUCATION PROGRAM

Spincraft

WHY WORK?

A good and honest question you might ask is, "Why should I work?" Many quick answers come to mind: because I want to eat; everybody is doing it; that's the way life is; I might be able to do something for humanity; it's something to do. Let's look at the question from another point of view.

Whenever people decide to live together as a group instead of separately as hermits, they organize themselves. We have the family, the town, the state, the country, and international associations. For these groups to be worth living in, there has to be a lot of give and take. If the system is functioning properly, each individual receives companionship, protection, and the necessities of life. In return, each person contributes labor and talent.

We said *if* the system is functioning properly. Have you ever played on a ball team, acted in a play, belonged to a combo, or done anything else which required the cooperation of several people? If so, did you run into a player who wouldn't hustle, an actor who wouldn't learn his lines, or a musician who wouldn't practice? How did you feel toward that person? How did the rest of the group feel? Why? You were depending on that person, so the whole group suffered. The game was lost, the play flopped, or the music turned out lifeless.

In the world of work you will meet people who disappoint others. You will also meet many who do their part. These people realize that each of us receives the benefit of the work of others—food, shelter, transportation, clothing, entertainment. They do not want to be takers without being givers. Most of us feel that way. The problem is finding something we really want to work at, something we can feel good about contributing to.

SCHOOL AND WORK: HOW THEY RELATE TO EACH OTHER

Sometimes school seems an impractical place to be. What is it good for? Does it really prepare you to take your place in the adult world?

In the past, some people thought high school students should learn subjects such as literature, history, and algebra. Few practical courses were included. Such things could always be learned later, people reasoned. Then educators started looking at the results. High school graduates who could not go to college had few job skills. Often they ended up with the worst and lowest-paying jobs and then were unhappy because they felt they could be doing something better if only they had had the training. The situation is changing.

Various programs for developing work skills and giving students work experience have been started. In the last ten years, federal laws have been passed that help schools throughout the country get money and guidance for setting up vocational training programs.

Cooperative education means that you can have the best of both worlds. You can study academic subjects that interest you or that you need to graduate. You can also find out firsthand what the world of work is like. Interestingly enough, students in cooperative programs generally do better at their regular school subjects than before they entered the program. The job shows the importance of the subjects, and the subjects help a person do well on the job.

This isn't always true. Some subjects don't apply that directly, but even these can become more enjoyable. Once you feel you are getting a footing in the adult world, you can afford to have wider interests. You may take an art course or a dance course or photography, botany, or astronomy "just because."

Which is better? The cooperative education program, the regular academic program, or the college preparatory program? Not even the experts would like to answer that question! It isn't really a question of better or worse, but different. Having several types of programs available allows the high school student some alternatives.

Astronauts did not blast off into space with no preparation. They were in training a long time, getting used to both the idea and the feel of weightlessness, learning to be isolated from family and friends, finding out how they would eat, move, and work in space. Your cooperative education program tries to prepare you for another stage of independence. Education should be a matter of living as well as preparation. Getting out on the job for part of the day will make this more likely!

Astronautics Company

THE GIVE AND TAKE
OF COOPERATIVE EDUCATION PROGRAMS

Employers, students, teacher-coordinators, and parents all contribute to the cooperative education program. They all get something from it, too.

EMPLOYER	GIVES	Wages, On-the-job learning situation, Instruction and Encouragement
	TAKES	Your labor, Recognition in the community for willingness to help the young
STUDENT	GIVES	Hard work—brawn and brain Cooperation and enthusiasm, Skills
	TAKES	Knowledge of the world of work and how to succeed in it Wages, Increase in skills

In order to be sure that all parties who are going to cooperate in the program know what they are supposed to do, we depend on certain documents. These documents are something like contracts in that they get responsibilities and privileges down in writing so that everyone knows what's what. Otherwise things could get very fuzzy, and one party or another may end up feeling shortchanged and unhappy. Why not prevent such situations if we can? Let's look at the three documents that are important for the beginning cooperative student: the training agreement, the student agreement, and the training plan.

THE TRAINING AGREEMENT.   In cooperative education, the place where one works is called the training station. The training station is like a laboratory or shop class except that it is "downtown." Students learn by doing. Training agreements help assure that work done at the training station really is an educational experience. If a student thinks of his job only as a way to earn a little extra money, or if the employer thinks in terms of getting a little cheap labor, the whole purpose of the program is lost.

Even though training agreements are not legally binding, they are very useful in outlining the purposes of the program and defining the responsibilities of all parties involved. See the Sample Training Agreement for an idea of what items are usually included.

The student, the employer, the teacher-coordinator, and the parent all sign the agreement. All parties should read it carefully and make sure they understand everything before signing.

All the parties who sign the training agreement will find things running more smoothly if they keep in touch. Sometimes this will be done on a formal basis, as when your teacher-coordinator visits you at your training station. Informal contacts can also be highly valuable.

TEACHER-COORDINATOR	GIVES	Expert advice, Wide range of experience, Knowledge, Job skills Understanding and counseling
	TAKES	Satisfaction in doing a good and necessary job, Pleasure in helping others, Wages
PARENTS	GIVE	Encouragement and advice, if possible, Help with transportation and clothes, A home
	TAKES	A sense of relief at seeing one of their children become independent, A sense of pride

THE STUDENT AGREEMENT.   The cooperative education program gives you a start in accepting responsibility for yourself. The student agreement spells out the guidelines, listing the obligations you have to yourself, to your employer, and to your school. The wording of these agreements varies from school to school, but the ideas are much the same. (See the Sample Student Agreement.) We will discuss a few of the points in more detail below:

Students are expected to be regular in attendance at school and on the job.

Your employers agreed to become part of the program both because they wanted to provide opportunities for new workers to develop job skills and because they had work which needed to be done. What you do is an important and necessary part of the operation of your place of employment. If you do not show up, someone else must carry your load.

Your job is a regular part of the school curriculum, just as a science, math, or English class is. You receive credit toward graduation for work experience just as you do for other courses. Your job, your related class, and your other subjects are all vital parts of the grand design for your entry into the adult world of work. A good attendance record is necessary for continued participation in the program.

A student is expected to be on time at school and on the job.

Punctuality (being on time) is one way of showing that you are ready and able to accept responsibility for yourself. Many employers and teachers will judge you partly on your ability to be where you have to be at the time you are supposed to be there. If for some unavoidable reason you must be late, call your employer.

Notify your employer when circumstances force you to be absent from work.

Illness and emergency situations are bound to happen to all of us at one time or another. The sooner you let your employers know, the sooner they can arrange for a substitute. Notifying them is also a matter of courtesy. If, for example, you make arrangements to meet your friends at a downtown movie one evening and one of them gets sick and can't go, would you expect that person to call you and tell you so?

Notify your teacher-coordinator when you must be absent from school and work.

Very embarrassing situations can arise if teacher-coordinators don't know where you are. Suppose they turn up to visit you on the job and

SAMPLE TRAINING AGREEMENT

_____
(Program)

_____
(Date)

I. _____ will be permitted to enter
(student-learner)

_____ for the purpose of gaining
(training station)

knowledge, experience, and skill as _____ .
(occupation)

II. The course of training is designed to run for a two-year period with a minimum of 15 hours per week of on-the-job experience and at least one period in each school day for the supervised study of related and technical information.

III. The coordinator shall, with the assistance of the employer or someone delegated by the employer, prepare a schedule of skills and tasks to be learned on the job and an outline of technical and related information to be studied in school.

IV. Student-learners will be given the opportunity to gain well-rounded experience and to progress as their proficiency permits.

V. The student must not displace a regular worker.

VI. The employment of the student-learner must conform to all federal, state, and local laws and regulations.

VII. The teacher-coordinator will visit the training station to evaluate student-learner progress, to discuss training problems, and to coordinate related class work in school with the needs of the student-learner. By showing just cause, the coordinator may withdraw the student-learner at any time. The employer has the right to dismiss the trainee; however, the coordinator should be contacted at least two weeks in advance of termination, if possible.

VIII. The schedule of compensation to be paid the student-learner shall be fixed by the training agency and the coordinator. Such wages shall be comparable to the wages paid apprentices and other beginning employees in the same occupation. The beginning wage

of _____ at _____
(student-learner) (training station)

as of September _____ will be _____ per hour. Student-learners will be considered for wage increases, and if an increase is granted, it will be put into effect the first work week after the following dates: December 1, _____ and April 1, _____ Increases in the hourly rate will depend upon the progress of the student-learner and on business conditions.

IX. Safety instruction shall be given by the school and correlated with on-the-job safety training given by the employer.

X. All complaints shall be made to and adjusted by the teacher-coordinator.

This Training Agreement has been read and understood by the following:

_____
(student-learner)

_____
(teacher-coordinator)

_____
(employer)

_____
(parent or guardian)

you aren't there. It's not just a matter of keeping tabs on you, but a matter of getting everything to work out right for all parties concerned. If coordinators aren't in the know they can't help as much.

In most schools you are not permitted to work on the days you are absent from school.

While on the job, students must conduct themselves in a mature, acceptable, and positive manner.

Many situations must be considered under this point, and we will bring them up from time to time throughout the book. For right now, try to think in terms of behavior that presents *you at your best.* Try to dress so that you will look neat, be comfortable, and feel in step with others where you work. You will have to look the place over and see what is acceptable, because places of employment vary greatly.

A good rule is that if you find yourself wearing something or doing something that attracts a great deal of attention, it is probably not appropriate.

If you fail to perform responsibly at the training station, you affect your present and future employment opportunities, and also the opportunity of future students to work at that particular training station. If employers have several bad experiences with students, they may decide they've had enough.

Try to complete all job assignments promptly.

Doing a good job comes before doing a fast job. Still, new learners should be able to pick up speed as they go along. Training you costs your employer money, since you cannot at first do the job as well as an experienced employee. Employers are willing to spend a certain amount of time and money on training, but they will also expect to see progress.

Complete all assignments for the related class as best you can and on time.

The related class is designed to help you on the job. Try to take full advantage of it.

Avoid detentions, suspensions, and explusions.

Disciplinary problems are a head-ache for regular students, but for cooperative students they can be disastrous. Remember your cooperative education job is really the same as a school subject. If you are suspended or expelled from school you will have to give up your job, too. Your job may not be available after you have been readmitted to school. Your employer may have hired someone else meanwhile.

Try to understand as fully as you can the job of the teacher-coordinator.

Teacher-coordinators have a hard job! They have to keep everyone happy, including the student, the school, the employer, and the parents. They act as go-betweens, and they have the final authority and responsibility for all parts of the training program. They also have extensive experience for you to rely on when you need help.

You may not resign or change jobs unless you first discuss the situation with your coordinator.

On every job there are times when interest lags, frustrations come, and things just don't seem to be going right. Part of becoming an adult is learning to face and overcome problems and disappointments. Students are therefore discouraged from changing training stations. Three or four short periods of employment at different places are usually not as valuable as one long, steady period. In later life you may find that drifters are not the happiest of people. Your coordinator developed your training station assignment with great care, keeping in mind your particular career goal at the time you entered the program. In most cases it will prove worthwhile to stick it out. If this seems completely impossible, your teacher-coordinator is the person to consult.

Obey all traffic laws while traveling to and from the training station. Follow your employer's safety code.

Tickets and accidents could eventually mean that someone else would have to be responsible for getting you to your job. Since this someone else might not always be available, you may have to give up your job.

While at work, you may think some of the safety regulations are too much. Obey them anyway. Very often they resulted from bad accidents in the past.

Think about participating in the youth group most closely associated with your area of career interest.

Responsible individuals in a society must function in various roles. Some of these involve individual effort, but others require working effectively with others. The youth group associated with your program will help you develop group skills and will show you a great deal about organizing and running an organization. Why not look into one of the career clubs? If you don't like what you see, think in terms of how your participation could help to make it better.

The student agreement covers a lot of territory. We hope you will see not just the rules, but the thinking behind the rules. When children are quite small, it sometimes doesn't seem worthwhile to explain all the "whys" to them. One tends to say "just because" when they question a rule. We don't want to do that in this book. We want to explain things as well as we can so that following the rules will make sense.

___

What Do You Think?

Look again at the statements in the section on the student agreement. List them on a sheet of paper according to how much importance you would place on them. Put the statement you feel is most important at the top of the list. At the bottom put the statement you feel is least important. Rank the others in between.

___

THE TRAINING PLAN.   Imagine the training plan as a road map. You are already on your way toward occupational independence just by being in the cooperative program. Your training plan helps you move along smoothly, not missing anything and coming closer and closer to mastery of your job.

Why have a written training plan? There are different ways of learning things, and some ways are more efficient than others. If you put food at the end of a maze, then put a hungry little animal into the maze at the beginning, the animal will sniff the food and try to get it. How does it learn the way to the food? By trial and error. It bumps into walls, makes the wrong turns, turns back and tries again. After making plenty of mistakes, it is at last rewarded. It gets to the food, and will eventually learn to repeat the actions that brought it to the food with fewer trials—but only after a number of repetitions.

Some human beings choose that way of learning. They just bump along from one experience to the next, making the same old mistakes, doing things right once in a while just by accident. For most of us, that's just too frustrating. We prefer to look the situation over, decide where we want to go, then plan steps that lead in that direction. Go back to the map idea again. If you and two friends are going to motorcycle to Yellowstone National Park you will take a road map and plot your course on it, rather than just setting out down any old highway.

Your training plan helps assure that your on-the-job experiences will be directly related to your occupational goal, and that they are planned and progressive. One experience should lay the groundwork for the next.

The training plan also assures that you will be properly supervised. Let's talk for just a moment about supervision. We are not talking about discipline. We feel that if you are in the cooperative program you have been rated as mature enough to behave well without someone around to correct you all the time. In fact, recent studies suggest that many cooperative students are actually more mature in some ways than other students. Supervision is necessary because there are some things a young worker just couldn't know. For example, JoAnn works at a mail order company where some outgoing letters go through a postage meter while others are hand stamped. How is she supposed to know that without someone telling her? George is accustomed to using one kind of tool when he works on spark plugs, but his boss has discovered a much better one that is less likely to damage parts. So he shows George how it works. That's supervision.

Supervision is also necessary for safety reasons. Sometimes young people feel they are going to live forever. It's lucky for most of us that someone was around to prevent us from making mistakes that would have resulted in injury or death.

Training plans range from a few simple statements of what the student will do at the training station to a detailed description of every task. (Please see the Sample Training Plan.) Your training plan may be like this one, or it may be much more detailed.

One area we haven't gone into in this chapter is what the law says about young workers. You will find that in Chapter 27, and it might be a good idea to browse through that chapter now.

Working Cooperatively

A fairly common situation in co-operative education—and in a full-time job—is that people discuss their wages with each other. Sometimes this makes for problems. Discuss the following questions:

1. Why may one employer not be able to pay as much as another employer for the same kind of work?

2. How does the training agreement affect the question of wages?

3. How would you go about judging whether you are worth more than another person doing the same work you are doing?

4. How important is the matter of wages in the cooperative program?

5. If you were working full-time on a regular job, what could be the disadvantages of discussing your wages with a co-worker who makes less than you do? More than you do?

What Do You Think?

In each occupational field a person must learn certain basic tasks. After workers master these, they move on to the next stage. From the second stage there are more skills to reach for, if they wish to. At the top of the pyramid are special skills that would qualify them for a job involving more responsibility and having more rewards in terms of payment and prestige. It would usually take several years to get to the top of such a pyramid. (Please refer to the Sample Skills Pyramid.)

Do you think it is necessary to get to the top of the pyramid in order to be happy? Would there be room for everyone at the top? Suppose someone says, "I'm satisfied to stay at level two, but I'm going to do my best there." Someone else says, "I'd rather move on up to the top so that I can get more interesting assignments and make more money." Still another person decides, "I'm going to do well at level three, but then I'm going to stop so that I have some time and energy to devote to things I like to do outside work." Which of these three people is right? Could they all be right?

Chapter Check

1. What is the purpose of any written agreement?

2. Name the two written agreements most cooperative education programs use. Tell who the parties to each of these agreements are.

3. Why is a training plan important?

4. What do you see as the main goal of your cooperative program?

SAMPLE STUDENT AGREEMENT

The cooperative education program seeks to further the all-around development of the students, but especially to insure their ability to enter the world of work upon graduation and to be successful in it. In order to make the program fully effective, each student must agree to fulfill the following responsibilities:

1. To be regular in attendance in school and on the job.

2. To be on time at school and on the job.

3. To notify employer and teacher-coordinator when it is necessary to be absent from work and school.

4. To realize that being absent from school means not working either.

5. To carry out training on the job in such a manner that the student will be a credit to self and to the cooperative education program.

6. To do all assignments for the related class as well as possible.

7. To realize that cooperative education students are under the jurisdiction of the school throughout the day.

8. To behave maturely on the job as well as at school. Not to risk their jobs because of unacceptable behavior.

9. To pay all normal fees and charges necessary for class activities such as banquet, conferences, and field trips.

10. To avoid activities that would lead to detention, suspension, or expulsion.

11. To realize that if a student causes trouble at the training station, he/she might make it impossible for another student-learner to follow at that training station.

12. To accept the fact that students who are required to leave school for disciplinary reasons may not report to their training stations.

13. To register all cars that are being used to get to work. Infraction of traffic laws may cause termination of the job if the student then has no way to get to work.

14. To consult the teacher-coordinator about any difficulties on the job, and to make no changes without such consultation.

I fully understand the above statements and I agree to cooperate in carrying them out to the best of my ability.

Date _____

School year 19___ to 19___

_____
(student's signature)

_____
(parent's signature)

SAMPLE TRAINING PLAN

Name _____

Date _____

A. Title of Occupation _____

B. U.S. Office of Education Code Number: _____

C. Name and Address of Training Station _____

D. Name of Owner _____

E. Name of Training Sponsor _____

F. Broad Areas of On-the-Job Experience

1. _____
2. _____
3. _____
4. _____
5. _____
6. _____

G. Outline of On-the-Job Experiences:

1. _____

   a. _____
   b. _____
   c. _____
   d. _____

H. Individual Study References Available:
   Classroom — _____
   Training Station —

1. _____   1. _____
2. _____   2. _____
3. _____   3. _____
4. _____   4. _____

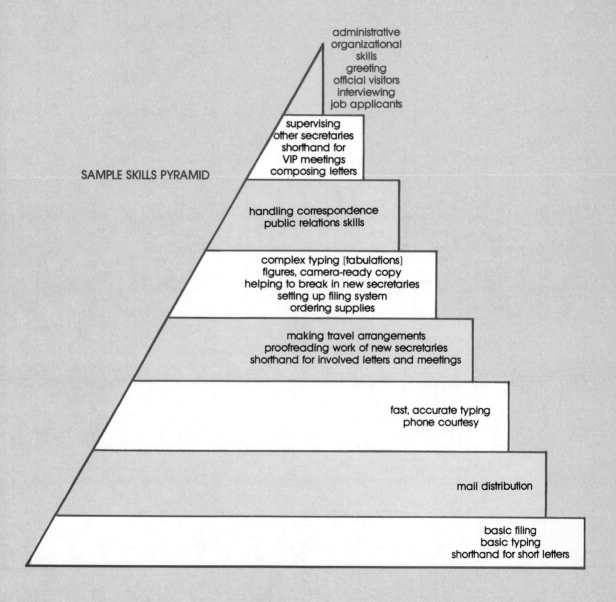

SAMPLE SKILLS PYRAMID

administrative
organizational
skills
greeting
official visitors
interviewing
job applicants

supervising
other secretaries
shorthand for
VIP meetings
composing letters

handling correspondence
public relations skills

complex typing [tabulations]
figures, camera-ready copy
helping to break in new secretaries
setting up filing system
ordering supplies

making travel arrangements
proofreading work of new secretaries
shorthand for involved letters and meetings

fast, accurate typing
phone courtesy

mail distribution

basic filing
basic typing
shorthand for short letters

 # Part Two

Under the Big Umbrella: Human Relationships

A WEEK OF MONDAYS

MONDAY I.   Josie worked at a rest home. She was supposed to report for work by 5 p.m. However, her boyfriend got off work at 4:30 and they liked to spend a few minutes together before she left for work. Those few minutes began to stretch out until Josie was late for work almost every day. This created an especially difficult situation because dinner was served at 5 p.m., and it was important that every worker be there to help out.

At first the supervisor was nice about it. She simply told Josie to be on time. As time went on, however, and Josie didn't improve, the supervisor became less pleasant. One day she said, "Josie, from now on you *must* be on time."

Josie was very defensive. Instead of admitting and facing up to the problem, she said angrily, "If you don't stop bugging me about being late, I'm going to quit."

The supervisor was surprised, but she had a lot of experience. She calmly said, "Well, think it over and let me know what you want to do."

By the end of the evening work shift, Josie wished she hadn't been so angry. She was now upset by the prospect of losing her job. She went back to her supervisor and apologized and promised she would be on time in the future. The supervisor was very understanding and didn't make a big issue out of it. It wasn't such a bad Monday after all!

MONDAY II.   John was a beginning draftsman in an engineering firm. He was not happy with his job because he was always fixing up or redoing other people's drawings instead of being given a project of his own. He should have talked the problem over with his immediate supervisor, Mr. Beard, but John thought Mr. Beard didn't like him. John had a talk with the division supervisor, Mrs. Grant, instead.

This is the response John got from Mrs. Grant: "I like your enthusiasm, John. In a few years we'll have plenty of important jobs for you to do. Incidentally, have you spoken to Mr. Beard about this?"

John said, "No." He was somewhat embarrassed. He now realized that he should have taken his problem directly to Mr. Beard.

"Well, I suggest you talk to him," Mrs. Grant said. "He is in a better position than I am to know when you're ready for a more difficult assignment. All new people are expected to be apprentices for a while."

If you were John, how would you feel about having to go back and talk to your immediate supervisor, especially after you had gone over his head? This Monday, however, didn't turn out so bad because Mrs. Grant did not mention John's visit to Mr. Beard.

MONDAY III.   Mary went into the restroom. Shortly after she entered, two other girls came in. One of them said, "Well, if you ask Mary to come along, then I'm not going to lunch with you."

"Well, that's childish," said the other voice.

"I don't care. She's not my type. I asked *you,* not *her.*"

"Okay. I'll ask her some other time. But I really think your attitude is dumb."

Mary knew that the voices belonged to Louise, her friend, and another girl named Sally. Mary's feelings were hurt because Sally didn't want to even give her a chance to be her friend. What was really confusing and aggravating, though, was that Sally acted friendly whenever they met.

After a few days Mary wasn't so upset about Sally.

In fact, later on Mary and Sally became friends. Mary told Sally she had overheard Sally's comments about her that day. Sally couldn't believe she had said such a thing, but they were both able to laugh about it.

MONDAY IV.   Harry joined a new religious movement. He really enjoyed going to meetings and working for the group. He then became interested in trying to get his co-workers to join. It wasn't long before he began to make a real pest of himself. He would go from one workman's bench to the next, explaining the beliefs of the religious group and trying to get his fellow workers to attend meetings with him.

Harry didn't realize that in addition to being annoying, he was actually stealing time from his employer, by not working himself and by keeping others from their work. His co-workers also got tired of listening to him. It was like having a high-pressure salesman at their side all day long.

Finally the boss was forced to ban the pushing of religious ideas during working hours. It was a blue Monday for Harry.

That night he told his girlfriend about it.

"Harry," she said, "your boss is right. He can't have everyone campaigning for his point of view during the work day. Why don't you invite a few of your work friends over here some evening?"

Harry looked thoughtful for a moment, then he laughed. "Why didn't I think of that?" he said.

MONDAY V.   Fern worked part-time in a public library. One night she got in an argument with a person returning an overdue book. Fern knew the fine was fifty cents, but the person insisted she only owed twenty-five. Fern finally got the person to pay the fifty cents.

After the person left, the supervisor came over and said, "I appreciate the fact that you want to do a good job, but that was a difficult situation. I would prefer that you turn the case over to me whenever there is a disagreement over fines."

Fern was angry. At first she pouted, then she went directly to the supervisor and said, "You don't trust me, do you? You don't think I can handle such situations."

"Well, that's not exactly true," said the supervisor. "But you must understand I have more experience in handling these situations than you do. It's only natural that I should be better able to represent the library."

Fern wasn't immediately satisfied. However, this was another case where time was able to help. About a year later, Fern saw a new girl do almost the same thing she had done. The new girl was right about the fine, but she was going about collecting it in the wrong way, and the supervisor had to speak to her, too.

Fern smiled and said to herself, "I think I've come a long way."

As you can see from our week of Mondays, all kinds of problems occur among people who work together. The "big umbrella" is the system of rules and privileges under which we operate. If it is a good umbrella, everyone should receive the same protection from it. Sometimes that doesn't happen. People don't care about each other as they should. The big umbrella shrinks or gets holes in it. Maybe if people knew more about what they should expect from their fellow workers, and what their fellow workers expect from them, everyone could keep the network of human relationships from getting damaged.

❋ Chapter Two ❋

MOSTLY ABOUT THE BOSS

Daryl Littlefield

WHAT IS A BOSS?

Perhaps it is best to describe bosses as coordinators. Bosses have to coordinate the workers and the work flow so that the job gets done and the business stays healthy. If the business doesn't do well, the boss won't be a boss very long. If the boss is running his/her own business, he or she may have to shut down, and that would mean a loss of available jobs.

We discuss stereotyping and the dangers of it in Chapters three and four. It may therefore seem strange to refer to *old style* bosses and *new style* bosses, but that is how a lot of workers view the people supervising their job performance.

Inland Container Corp / McGuire Studio, Inc.

Old style bosses give orders without providing explanations. They tend to be impersonal, which means they keep a certain distance between themselves and their workers and tend to operate on a highly businesslike level rather than on a personal basis. However, the so-called old style bosses don't have to be like four-star generals. They can be quite effective in getting the job done quickly and efficiently.

New style bosses try to provide a more human, personal touch. They explain things and make requests rather than issuing orders. They try to make sure their workers understand the whys behind a decision. Both types direct things from a wide point of view, as an air traffic controller in a tower can direct planes better than someone on the ground.

Age does not determine whether a boss is old style or new style. A younger person may operate in the more traditional way. An older person may work in the new style. Bosses are generally a combination of the new and old styles. There are occasions which call for understanding. There are also situations which require tough speedy decisions.

What kind of boss would you like to have? Some people don't like bosses who operate in the old style because they consider such bosses too difficult to work for. Other workers don't care for new style bosses because they think such bosses are too disorganized and don't provide enough direction and strong leadership.

When you look for a job, you should take into consideration the type of boss you can best work with. Such judgments are not easy to make. First impressions are not always true ones. Someone who appears friendly, encouraging, or understanding may prove to be a basically tough person. Someone else, who at first appears a little brusk or distant, may turn out to be very fair and considerate. You may not be able to find your idea of a perfect boss. You have to adapt to the situation. Hitters in a softball game don't always get the pitch that they want, yet they still go up to the plate trying to get a base hit. In a work situation, we have to be prepared to get along with all kinds of people and all kinds of bosses.

Most bosses do not like being parents or policemen. They don't relish the idea of babying workers along, constantly showing them how to do every single thing, every single day, patting them on the head every time they do something right. They don't like to spy on workers to make sure that nobody cheats on time cards, steals, or violates company rules. If bosses spent all day with such unpleasant business, they would have no time to coordinate and organize the workers and the work flow.

What kind of a boss do you think you would make?

CRITICISM

One of the most difficult aspects of a boss's job is giving good constructive criticism. If some parts of the work aren't being done right, it is up to the boss to change the procedure. When workers don't get along, the boss has to straighten out the situation. When customers are being turned off by the way certain things are handled, the supervisor has to inform the staff members what they are doing wrong.

Giving criticism usually doesn't make the boss the most popular person on the job. However, it is a poor boss who is primarily concerned with popularity. Criticism generally implies that the person giving it really cares about the job and the workers. Such a boss doesn't stand around and let the workers continue to repeat mistakes. If workers are allowed to use inefficient work habits or to be satisfied with insufficient work skills, they do not make good employees.

Applying What You Know

When we are quite young, we often dream of being a person in command. We would like to have authority over others since it seems so many people have authority over us. As we get older, we are more in control of our own lives, and the desire for power tends to fade. The more experience we have, the more we realize that having authority is having responsibility, too. We begin to realize that being boss is a hard job.

Suppose, for a moment, that *you* are the boss. Discuss what you would do in each of the following situations:

1. George comes to you and tells you that Betty is stealing tools. You know some tools are missing. You also know that George and Betty don't get along very well. Perhaps George is just trying to get Betty into trouble. Maybe Betty really is guilty. How would you go about solving this problem?

2. Ellen is a very attractive woman. She is a very good typist and does neat work. But there is a problem. Whenever an interesting young man comes into the office, Ellen spends too much time chatting and flirting with him. She sometimes makes clients wait or only gives them curt, half-hearted attention. If you were the boss, what would you say to Ellen?

3. You devise a new procedure for the packing of your product. The procedure involves attaching the address label on the box before it is sealed. You call your workers together and tell them, "From now on let's attach the address labels on the boxes *before* we seal them. If a mix-up occurs, we can quickly check the contents while the boxes are still open."

Mr. Adams, who has worked for the company for more than 30 years, objects. He says, "I've always done the job the other way and it worked okay. I don't think we'd have done it that way for so long if it wasn't the *best* way."

You realize Mr. Adams is objecting because he doesn't like changes in his work routine. He is basically a good and loyal worker who is older than you, and you don't want to upset him. How would you handle the situation?

CONSTRUCTIVE CRITICISM.   JoEllen landed a good job in the advertising department of a big city department store. She had taken several design and graphic arts courses in high school and was now taking some additional classes in the night school at the local community college.

She worked under the direction of a very talented layout man named

Mr. Brooks. He looked at her work as she finished it, made some suggestions, but generally praised the ads highly.

One day after finishing an ad for a set of pots and pans, JoEllen took it to Mr. Brooks for his review. He looked at it and said he didn't like it because it looked too "straight." He felt the photograph was ineffective, and the lead line for the ad ("All These—Only $42.95") made the cookware sound as if it were cheap in quality rather than price.

"Well, cookware *is* an everyday item," JoEllen said. "It's not something that's very exciting. Besides I worked hard on the ad."

"I know you did," replied Mr. Brooks. "However, the whole trick to an ad is to make everyday things *appear* exciting. Try again and show me what you come up with tomorrow."

JoEllen went back to her drawing board. She was upset because this was the first time Mr. Brooks had ever really criticized her. However, soon she started to page through the other materials she had gotten out of the files for possible use in this ad. Gradually, a new idea began to form in her mind. She pictured the pots and pans hung on a pegboard in an unusual way. The illustration would be placed on the left side, with a catchy lead line on the right, describing the variety of things one can cook with only eight pots and pans.

JoEllen had long since worked her way out of the bad mood. She really got involved. When she presented the finished idea to Mr. Brooks, he was quite pleased. He said, "Hey, you've really got something here! If you can do this well with everyday items, then you've got what it takes to be a fine ad person, JoEllen."

Naturally, JoEllen was pleased. She had learned something important —receiving criticism from a person like Mr. Brooks was a real plus, almost like getting a special bonus.

Let's reexamine some of the elements of this scene more closely. Note that Mr. Brooks' criticism first made JoEllen defensive. That means it made her try to defend herself and her ad instead of thinking about what Mr. Brooks was saying. However, defensiveness was not carried to an extreme in her case. Otherwise, she would not have developed a good idea on the second attempt. Soothing her hurt feelings would have absorbed all her time and energy.

Feeling somewhat hurt when someone criticizes you is very normal. If you didn't feel strongly about what you did, it would imply that you didn't really care about the quality of your work. However, being upset for a long time achieves nothing. JoEllen set to work and became so interested in the project, there was no room for hurt feelings.

DESTRUCTIVE CRITICISM. Most of you will not have to deal with bosses who constantly give bad or destructive criticism. After all, it is the boss's job to get people to cooperate together and work efficiently. A continuous stream of bad criticism creates nothing but bad will and dissatisfied workers. Also, as we said earlier, bosses who are not good, effective leaders will not be bosses very long. However, many of you will probably have to deal with bosses who are sometimes impatient or cranky.

Impatience often leads to sarcasm or sharp-tongued criticism. Anyone, even bosses, can have a bad day or be in a grumpy mood now and then. Impatience can also mean the boss has too big a load to carry at the moment. Criticisms made at times like these should be weighed carefully. An abrupt remark like "You never do anything right!" may really mean "You did this wrong." The worst thing a worker can do when he or she sees the boss is in a bad mood is to join in and get crabby, too.

GOOD (CONSTRUCTIVE) CRITICISM	BAD (DESTRUCTIVE) CRITICISM
— is given in a quiet, even tone of voice	— is shouted angrily
— centers on certain specific things that are wrong.	— shows general dissatisfaction and is not specific
— is clear and direct	— is sarcastic and humiliating
— refers to something that can be changed	— may refer to something a person can't help or change
— gives suggestions for improvement	— gives no idea of what a person might do to improve
— makes people cooperative	— makes people defensive

CONSTRUCTIVE — builds people up and helps them do a better job

DESTRUCTIVE — tears people down and makes it harder for them to do a good job

Applying What You Know

Below are two work situations involving problems on the job. In both cases the boss is forced to take action to solve the trouble. Following the description of the problem and the boss's action are three possible reactions of the worker involved. Write a short paragraph telling which response is the best. Why is it better than the other two?

1. Charles works in a muffler shop.

Whoever closes the shop at night is also responsible for putting away all tools and getting the shop in order for the next day's shift. Charles doesn't always get around to cleaning up, and the morning shift has been complaining about it to the boss, Mr. Williams. The boss calls Charles aside and reminds him that he is responsible for cleaning the shop before locking up for the night.

A. Charles gets angry and says, "Well, I think I work harder than all of those guys on the morning shift. Why are you bugging me to do more work?"

B. Charles says, "Yes, I know. I apologize. Sometimes when I start working on a job, I lose track of time. Suddenly, it's closing time. I'll try from now on to stop my regular work a little earlier so that I can clean up."

C. Charles shouts, "Look, Mr. Williams. I wasn't hired to be the janitor around here."

2. Susan makes deliveries for a pharmacy. She has received two traffic tickets in the past six months. The boss, Mrs. Bahr, is particularly concerned about the matter because the van Susan drives belongs to the pharmacy. She tells Susan, "I'm sorry, Susan, but if you receive one more traffic ticket, I'm afraid we'll have to let you go."

A. Susan replies, "Believe me, Mrs. Bahr, I will be more careful from now on. In the past I guess I just got carried away. I realize I could even lose my driver's license. I really don't want to lose my job or my license."

B. Susan gets huffy and snaps, "Well, I can't help it. It's not my fault. Driving fast is the only way I can make all the deliveries on my schedule."

C. Susan says, "The only reason I got those tickets is because the police are always watching out for me."

RESPECT

GENERAL RESPECT.   General respect can be applied to many types of people and things. For example, we generally respect other people simply because they are human beings. We also respect other living creatures. We respect life itself. We can even respect an efficient or complex machine. We show our respect for all of these things by the way we appreciate and treat them.

PERSONAL RESPECT.   Personal respect is a deeper kind of respect. It only comes after we get to know a person very well. Here's an example:

Barry's family moved when he was a junior. He had been top scorer on the basketball team. When he transferred to Centerville Community High, he hoped he would again be on the first string.

When he met his new coach he wasn't impressed. Coach Whitmore seemed so quiet. As the weeks went by, Barry learned that the coach almost never yelled at anyone. He had a plan worked out for each person for each practice session. Barry thought to himself, "Oh, man, this is grade school stuff." He had been used to practicing more on his own.

No one else seemed to be complaining, so Barry went along with the coach's ideas.

Gradually Barry came to understand that Coach Whitmore had a strategy. He was much more interested in developing a team than in promoting a few stars. Maybe Barry was a little disappointed, but he found he was enjoying membership on the team much more than he had in his previous school. Coach Whitmore was no fireball, but he was a nice guy to work with.

Then Barry got into academic trouble. He was about to fail algebra. He went to the coach and more or less asked him to bail him out. At his old school, special allowances had been made for athletes. So he was a little unhappy to hear Coach Whitmore say, "Sorry, Barry but I never ask a teacher to make a special deal for any of my boys. I have learned by experience that it isn't in your best interest or mine. You're smart enough to keep your grades up. I would just be encouraging you to miss out on something you may need later on. It would be much better for you to ask your teacher to spend a little extra time with you."

Barry reluctantly did so. He managed to get a C in the course, and he missed no practices and no games. Even though he never learned to like algebra, he knew Coach Whitmore had been right in his decision. Barry began to trust and admire him.

It came as a surprise to Barry when the Cougars started winning game after game. Coach Whitmore's "cool" seemed to unnerve the opponent more than a more razzle-dazzle approach would have. When they got into the state finals, Barry said to himself, "This guy really knows what he's doing."

At the end of the season, Coach Whitmore invited the whole team out to his house. He lived on a neat little farm. The house was a modified A-frame with many nice design touches. It brought a lot of comments from the group. Mrs. Whitmore said, "Eric designed it all himself, and he and I built most of it."

Barry respected his coach more. Where he had first judged Coach Whitmore as a meek person with a one-track mind, he now saw a highly competent many-sided man.

RESPECTING YOUR BOSS.   At first you might respect your boss in a general sort of way because of the position he has. That's what Barry did with his new coach. After a while you may notice how well he handles all his responsibilities, and your respect may grow. You might observe that he uses his authority well, not simply ordering employees around but enabling them to get the job done. Perhaps you may see him handling a touchy problem with understanding and compassion. Suddenly you realize that he is not only smart and knows his job, but he is a good person who cares about others.

Daryl Littlefield

EARNING RESPECT.   As a young worker or a new employee, you are entitled to respect from your fellow employees. However, when you are new on the job, the more experienced workers may be a little wary of you, mainly because you are inexperienced. After all, they can't respect your abilities and skills until you demonstrate them. They may also initially avoid you because of your race or sex.

If you go about your business as best you know how, people will soon see what sort of a person you are. They will discover characteristics they like and respect. Perhaps they respect how you treat an older, less popular, or handicapped person on the staff, or the patient way you talk to impatient customers. Maybe your sense of humor amuses and delights them, or they appreciate your interest in them. Over and above your skills on the job, showing your pleasant natural characteristics can help your co-workers respect you.

COURTESY.   Not all people merit respect in the deeper personal sense. Some people have personalities or characteristics which are difficult to approve of or like. Perhaps they talk too loud or spread rumors or don't bathe often enough. What should you do if you encounter an individual who is difficult to deal with? First, you should treat them with courtesy. It costs nothing to be courteous, and it can do so much good. Besides, maybe such people don't know they have unappreciated characteristics. Perhaps they are doing the best they can, or they may have a special problem you know nothing about. Courtesy is something like oil in a car. It helps things move more smoothly. Courtesy means being polite and avoiding arguments. You can seldom change a person by arguing.

DISRESPECT

Showing disrespect is not the same as not respecting someone. Not respecting someone can be a quiet matter. You may never make a point saying, "I don't respect you," but you won't pattern your life after that person's. You may choose not to respect a crooked politician. Rather than throwing rotten tomatoes, which would be disrespectful, you might not vote for that candidate. That would not involve disrespect, and it would be a much more effective way of making your feelings known. To avoid those who cheat or steal is not disrespectful. It simply means you don't want to be involved with people you can't respect.

Disrespect is often an open display of feeling. Usually it doesn't get at the real issues at all. Say an old bum is shuffling along First Street downtown. His clothes are filthy and barely hanging together. His hair and beard are full of disgusting things. He seems to be hunting for a cigarette butt. You probably won't have deep respect for him. However, you may pity him and still see him as a human being. If you shouldered him off the sidewalk and made him walk in the gutter you would be showing him disrespect. What would that do for him? Would it change his life? Would he get the point? What would it do for you? Would you be a better person for having shown your strength in such an uneven contest?

Let's take an example closer to home. Do students ever behave disrespectfully towards each other at school? Rudy's brother got picked up on a drug charge. The word got around. One day in consumer's ed, the subject was saving money. Students were telling what they would save for. Suddenly Tony popped up with, "Hey, Rudy, you better save up to bail your brother out of jail." Maybe Tony just thought he was being funny, but he was also showing disrespect for Rudy's feelings. He was making Rudy appear less respectable to his classmates.

All of you have heard others make disrespectful comments *about* teachers or parents, or even *to* them. Sometimes people believe that the only way they can make their point is to be disrespectful. Such people draw attention to themselves, but do they accomplish much? Would a strong, logical presentation of their complaint be more likely to bring about change?

Sometimes disrespect is a matter of carelessness or ignorance. A litterbug might fall into such a category. Let's try to keep in mind that disrespect is often nothing more than an immature or egotistical display which makes more problems than it solves.

HUD

What Do You Think?

Let's look at the "Week of Mondays" in terms of respect and disrespect.

Do you think Josie was disrespectful to her boss? What did she do about it afterward? What about John and his decision to go over the head of his immediate supervisor? What about Sally and her unkind remarks about Mary, when she thought Mary could not hear them? Did Harry show respect toward his fellow workers by hounding them with his religious beliefs? What was wrong with Fern's attitude toward the person who misunderstood the fines on overdue books?

Working Cooperatively

You have probably heard of Dr. Benjamin Spock. (He is not to be confused with Mr. Spock of *Star Trek*.) Dr. Spock was frequently in the news during the Vietnam War. He was one of the leaders of those who opposed the war. He didn't oppose it simply to get into the news. Dr. Spock has long opposed war and the violence man does to his fellow human beings.

Dr. Spock, however, is best known for his contributions in the field of child development. In fact, his name has come to be a household word. His most famous and still highly popular book is called *Baby and Child Care* (New York: Pocket Books, Inc., 1946). Maybe your mom and dad used it to raise you. Who knows, you might even use it some day to rear your own children.

Dr. Spock's book outlines the various stages of growth and development in a baby. It tells parents what they can expect of the child at these various stages and makes suggestions how they can cope with problems along the way.

Using what you have learned in this chapter, along with a good deal of common sense, make a booklet called *Everything You Ever Wanted to Know about Getting Along with the Boss,* or, if you prefer shorter titles, you could simply call it *The Boss Book.* Maybe you can come up with an even better title!

Here are some steps to follow:

1. Decide on format. Format means such details as how the book is to be laid out, how large the pages should be, what design the cover should have, and what illustrations, if any, should appear on the pages.

2. Divide the class into four committees. Committee one takes down the various suggestions made by the class. Committee two edits (that is, corrects and cleans up items such as language and spelling). Committee three does the typing and proofreading. Committee four puts the book together by laying out the pages, placing the illustrations, and designing the cover.

3. Now you are ready to begin. The class should think about and make suggestions on the following situations (you may make up additional situations). What if:

The boss seems to be ignoring you.

The boss asks you out to lunch.

You don't know whether or not you can use your boss's first name.

The boss pronounces your name incorrectly or gets your first name wrong.

The boss forgets about an appointment and leaves the office. A short time later the person who has the appointment shows up.

The boss asks you to tell a person on the telephone that he or she isn't in.

The boss asks you to do something you don't know how to do.

The boss blames you for something you didn't do.

The boss trusts you with some confidential or private information.

The boss asks you questions about one of your co-workers.

The boss tells you to be punctual for work.

The boss asks you why a certain piece of work hasn't been finished yet.

The boss asks you to work on his or her car during regular work hours.

You go out on a date with the boss's son or daughter.

The boss doesn't send you a get-well card when you are in the hospital.

The boss sends you a get-well card when you are in the hospital.

It is the boss's birthday.

Applying What You Know

Write a page or so on one of the following topics:

1. A person in public office whom I respect.

2. A younger person whom I respect.

3. An older person whom I respect.

4. The type of person I cannot respect.

❧ Chapter Three ❧

YOU AND
YOUR CO-WORKERS

C. William Horrell

UTOPIAS

Have you heard the word *utopia*? A utopia is an imaginary world invented by people. They give this imaginary world all the features they want in the world they'd most like to live in. People have written many stories and essays about such worlds. A number of science fiction stories deal with them. Utopias intrigue us because, at least on paper, they are perfect worlds.

Utopias, like other daydreams, have a purpose. Dreaming gives us ideas and opens up possibilities we hadn't thought of before. However, utopias don't work out so well in real life.

First of all, everything is pre-planned and regulated in a utopia. Life would be smooth and secure, but it would lack surprises, novelty, and variety. Someone would invent the rules or patterns for living, and everyone would have to fit into the scheme. Of course, this is true to some extent of all societies. If people are going to live harmoniously together, a certain amount of organization is necessary. In a utopia, however, almost all areas of life are prearranged. Very little is left up to the individual. That would be all right if most people desired and valued the same things and wanted a similar life style. However, that doesn't seem to be the case. People are as different as plants. Just as one climate isn't suitable for both tropical and arctic plants or animals, no one set of rules and prescriptions fits all kinds of people. The following activity will give you an idea of the problems involved in setting up a perfect world that would satisfy everyone.

Develop a mini-utopia of your own. Think of three conditions you'd like to have in your home. Think of three such features you'd like to have at school, then three at work. Here's an example:

My name is John Swenson. I'm 15 and a sophomore in high school. Here are the conditions I'd prefer.

At home:
1. I'd like my parents to make my little brothers and sisters stay out of my stuff.
2. I'd like to have the use of the family car two nights a week, no questions asked.
3. I'd like to feel free to bring friends home more often.

At school:
1. I'd like to spend less time at school.
2. I'd like to stop worrying about grades all the time.
3. I'd like to have a girlfriend.

At work:
1. I'd like everyone to like me.
2. I'd like a promotion every few years.
3. I'd like to be involved in making advance models of cars.

Have you written down your nine choices? Divide into small groups, four or five people to a group. Read your choices to each other.

Did everyone in your group want the same things? How many similar ideas did you come up with? Can you see how difficult it would be to design a perfect world that would please everyone?

Let's go back to John's list. A year

from now he might drop some of the items and put others in their places. That brings up another problem with utopias: they might seem to be perfect worlds to begin with, but we change and the world changes. Utopias don't allow for change.

As we mature we come to realize that we can't have a perfectly safe, unchanging, utopian world. Many of us feel that the price for such a world would be too much to pay even if it were possible. It would involve casting people in certain roles, enforcing rigid rules, and eliminating differences among us. Instead, we can search for ways of having both order and freedom. By learning to tolerate differences between ourselves and others we can make our world more flexible and interesting, and we can protect our own right to be different. Let's look, then, at what tolerance means and what it can do to improve the world we live and work in.

TOLERATING DIFFERENCES

Some people think that tolerance means giving up something—*putting aside their own likes and dislikes in order to make room for somebody else's.* This isn't really the case. Think of tolerance as peaceful coexistence. You can be as different as you want from me, as long as you don't hurt me or take advantage of me. I can be as different as I want from you, as long as I don't hurt you or take advantage of you. It's an unwritten contract to which we both become parties. When your wishes and mine conflict, then we must compromise. Each of us gives in to the other, working toward a solution that we can both accept.

A story follows which shows how people react to differences. Decide for yourself which of these people you'd most want to be like.

THE STRANGER.   Stan came to this country from Yugoslavia two years ago. He's been trying to learn English, but still has a heavy accent. He's a machinist and works at the bench next to Dave's.

Dave thinks Stan is an interesting person and would like to see Stan's country someday. He tries to help him whenever he can, but Stan knows as much or more about the occupation than Dave does. It's just that he has language problems and doesn't know much about American customs yet. He's a little touchy, because he can't tell for sure when someone is kidding him or being unpleasant.

On Stan's other side is an older man named Pete. Pete isn't very interested in other ways of life. Unlike Dave, he has no desire to see Yugoslavia. He really doesn't like to travel at all, although someday he wants to go to Florida. Pete quietly minds his own business and does his job. Once in a while he watches Stan for a minute or so. He never talks to him much, but he does say hello and goodbye.

Ben works in the same aisle. He has always lived in the same city. His life hasn't been easy. He often feels as if someone is trying to put something over on him. Dave has always gotten along with Ben, and has talked to him enough to know that Ben has some good points under his rather gruff exterior.

One day Ben comes up to Dave and says, "What are you always hanging around with that foreigner for? He doesn't even speak our language."

At first Dave thinks Ben must be kidding. "Oh, Stan's okay," he says.

"If he can't even speak English then he should shut up," says Ben.

"What's bugging you?" Dave asks. "He's not hurting you, is he?"

"Darn right he is," shouts Ben. "I wish he'd go back where he came from. There's not enough jobs here now, without these guys coming in and taking over."

Dave is surprised by Ben's outburst and doesn't know just how to interpret it. He's glad Stan isn't around at the moment. Although he'd like to defend Stan, he doesn't know how to go about it without upsetting Ben further. He decides to end the conversation for now.

"Well, Ben," he says, "you certainly have a right to your opinion. Maybe we can talk about it sometime at lunch. But right now I'd better get back to my bench."

What Do You Think?

What are some of the reasons Ben might feel the way he does? Do you think he might feel threatened in some way by Stan?

For the young worker, handling people like Ben can be a problem. He sounds like a trouble-maker, and to some extent he is. He's narrow-minded and rigid (unable to change easily). He may be unhappy and insecure in his personal life. Somehow we've got to make allowances for people with problems without letting them make other people miserable.

Do you think Dave did the right thing? Would he have accomplished much if he had argued with Ben then and there?

What about Pete? Does he have a right to keep his distance if he wishes?

1. Make a list of all the religions to which people you know belong.

2. Make a list of all the foreign countries from which you know people.

3. Make a list of all the languages you have ever heard spoken. (Don't forget the bits and pieces you've heard in the movies or on television.)

STEREOTYPES

All sports car drivers drive fast and recklessly.
All cute girls are stuck up.
All black people speak poor English.
All Frenchmen are sexy.
All professors are stuffy.
All football heroes are dumb slobs.
All redheads have short tempers.

These are all stereotypes. The word *stereotype* originally comes from the printing trade. If you had something you wanted to print many copies of exactly alike, you went to a printer. The printer made a mold, poured metal into the mold, and made a good, long-lasting metal plate. From it he could print as many copies as you needed, each one just like every other one. The plate was called a stereotype.

Later the word began to be used in the area of human relationships. To have a stereotype of a group of people means that you see them all alike as if they were all printed with the same plate or made from the same mold.

What a stereotype really says is, "I'm not interested in you, because I already know all about you. I know your kind." The person who has a stereotype of a group refuses to look at the individuals in that group. Can you think of some problems that arise when people have stereotypes of others?

TONY: A STEREOTYPE IN ACTION.   Tony, an Italian, applied for a job at a warehouse on the Seattle waterfront. Mr. Buck, the employer, noticed his name, asked a few questions, and terminated the interview. Tony didn't get the job, and he never found out why.

Mr. Buck told his assistant, "I'm afraid he wouldn't have worked out. He looked okay, but you know how those guys are. He'd probably end up fighting all the time. Those guys are tough. Junior mafia." He laughed at what he considered to be his little joke.

The sad part of it is that Mr. Buck didn't even bother to look at Tony's record. Tony has never been dismissed from any job for fighting.

He applied for this job because he has a lot of experience with warehousing of fresh fruits, vegetables, and flowers. He didn't get the job, so he suffered because of Mr. Buck's stereotyped idea of Italians. Mr. Buck didn't do himself a favor either. He needed a good man, and he blew it.

ALICE: ANOTHER STEREOTYPE IN ACTION.   Alice wasn't happy at work. She'd been employed by the magazine *Photosports* for two years. When she came to work she had been promised that as time went by she would be taught some layout and editing skills and would become more involved with the actual making of the magazine. Instead, she had spent most of her time answering the telephone and serving as receptionist. She considered talking to her supervisor about it. Then she changed her mind, saying to herself, "What's the use of talking to Mr. Barnett? He's just like all bosses. He'll think I'm one of those kids with more ambition than brains. He'll probably just pat me on the head and send me back to the reception desk." So she didn't go talk to her boss. She is still sitting unhappily at her station.

MORAL OF THE STEREOTYPE STORIES:

GIVE THE OTHER PERSON A CHANCE.

Applying What You Know

Is there some truth in a stereotype? Try this experiment and find out.

Think of someone you know fairly well, who is a member of another ethnic group but with whom you've never eaten. Make a list of things you think that person eats most often. Then ask three days in a row what that person had for dinner.

How does it compare with what you thought?

THE CLUCK-CLUCK CLAN.   The Cluck-Cluck Clan meets almost every working day. The members go off in a corner and talk and exchange gossip. Sometimes they make a lot of noise, even during working hours. The supervisor feels on edge, realizing that she will probably have to step in and quiet them down. That's a part of her job she doesn't particularly enjoy.

The disturbance the Cluck-Cluck Clanners make is only part of the problem. The other part is that the Clan excludes others. In your school you probably call such groups cliques (clicks). Some people feel more secure if they belong to a group of "select" people. They like feeling that they have been invited to belong while others have not. Sometimes they don't give much thought to what it is they have been chosen to belong to.

The Cluck-Cluck Clan can also be the nerve center for gossip. Members might be heard saying such things as:

"Say, did you know Georgia's pregnant? Well, I don't know if it's true, but that's what I heard."

"Boy, is Tom mad. Bill got promoted to chief salesman. It's just because he's a friend of the boss. If I were Tom, I'd quit."

"Did you hear that Jim and Erica are separated? I don't blame Jim at all. Why, Josie told me that Erica. . . ."

"Nancy's missing two dollars from her desk drawer. I don't want to say anything, but Barbara's the only one who worked late last night."

Almost everyone likes to talk about others some of the time. What we have to avoid is gossip that is meant to cast shadows on others or hurt them. Most of us do not want to be part of that kind of talk anyway. But another kind of gossip can also cause trouble: thoughtless gossip. People who think they are just passing the time of day may be failing to foresee some possible consequences of what they are repeating. When they spread rumors, they seldom know what problems the person they are talking about already has. The gossip can be the final straw that makes the person break down. Rumors can also ruin friendships and even marriages, or cause people to lose their jobs. No one has the right to endanger a person's job, reputation, or relationships, even if the gossip is true.

It is often much easier to gossip when one has the protection of a group such as the Cluck-Cluck Clan. Gossip is almost sure to be appreciated, maybe even expected. Furthermore, by belonging to the group you are somewhat safe from being gossiped about yourself. This protection is often temporary, however. You could end up on the outside sooner or later. Even if that doesn't happen, you may become more and more insensitive and unaware of the problems you are causing by gossiping. You may come to accept the group's standard of behavior in respect to gossip rather than developing your own.

Some people would prefer to be loners than to belong to a group such as the Cluck-Cluck Clan. Luckily, you don't have to choose between two such extremes. You can have different circles of friends and move between them. You may have a group of friends you eat lunch with, another group you play cards with, still another group you go swimming at the "Y" with evenings. You can be friends with almost everyone at work on a casual, everyday basis. From among these many friends, you can choose a few persons who are special to you, people you can trust and confide in.

You can do several things to combat groups such as the Cluck-Cluck Clan. First of all, you don't have to belong to groups that exclude others. That is, you can try to see to it that anyone is welcome. Avoid vicious or thoughtless gossip. Last, ignore the Cluck-Cluck Clan if there is one where you work. If you think they are talking about you, don't be angry or hurt. Consider the source. Are they the kind of people whose opinion you should value highly? Or are they thoughtless people who have some growing up to do? The more they are ignored, the less power over others they have.

We asked a sampling of people why they gossiped. Here are their answers:

"I like to be the first one with the news. I like the attention I get when I pass it on."

"It makes my day more exciting. Things get so hum-drum. Gossip livens things up."

"I think that if people do certain things, they are just begging to be talked about. If they don't like people talking about them, they should watch what they do."

"I just happen to like watching people. I talk about them because I think they're interesting. I don't really want to hurt anybody. But they never hear what I say about them, so how can it hurt them?"

What would you say about these answers?

HANDLING COMPETITION

The Green Bay Packers try to win a championship game against the Miami Dolphins.

General Motors attempts to design a better-looking compact than American Motors.

Jess tries to sell more vacuum cleaners than any other salesperson in his district so that he will become district manager.

Is competition good or bad? That's a controversial question. It is hard to reply with a simple *yes* or *no*.

Competition can be healthy and exciting. If you are running the hundred-yard dash against people as good or better than you, you're forced to try your best, inflate those lungs, stretch out those legs, keep that eye and mind keen. Even if you don't win, you will gain a lot by trying.

In school or on the job, competition can help you to do the best possible job and get you to test your real limits. Quite often you find your limits are further out than you thought. Competition can also teach

you to be a good loser. It can show you that your whole life doesn't hinge on one failure. You have many chances to try again.

However, competition carried to its extreme can make people do themselves in. Several years ago, it was reported that elementary school children were having to compete so much they were showing an alarming increase in ulcers! Or take the example of the teenager who is small for his age and insists on playing contact football to prove himself. He could end up dead.

On the job, people compete for pay raises and promotions. All of us want to have our services appreciated, and quite often rewards take the form of higher wages and better positions. Nothing is wrong with trying to better oneself. Several points should be kept in mind, however.

When competition comes to mean a lifelong struggle to get ahead of the next guy or to have more than one's neighbors, it becomes a good way of wasting one's life. More and more, young people are being turned off by this kind of competition and are looking for alternative ways of living.

Competition is hard on people if they have no sense of their upper limit. We all have fantasies about becoming millionaires, presidents, or the most loved teacher of the century. For most of us, though, it would be only frustrating to pursue such ideas. We have to have some sense of realism in what we want. Many people force themselves on toward impossible goals. They make themselves nervous, irritable, and continuously dissatisfied. Sometimes they are tempted to cheat, lie, or gossip to advance themselves, and they end up in trouble. The story that follows gives an idea of how people can get to thinking in unwholesome patterns when they are overly concerned about getting ahead.

A BUSY LIBRARY?   Ms. Schofeld worked as head librarian of a branch library in a big city. Every month, each librarian had to fill out a statistics sheet which showed how many books had been checked out that month and what special activities had been offered. These reports were used to give the taxpayers some idea of what their library dollars were accomplishing and as a basis for setting up budgets.

Ms. Schofeld wanted to be considered the best librarian in town. She hoped to move into a higher administrative position. She began to think that the surest way to make herself look good was to have a good statistical report. She wanted to show that a great many books had been circulated so that it would look as if she had done a great job of selling the public library.

Each month she found a way to pad the circulation figures. She'd add a figure of 25 for people who took books home without checking them out. She'd add another 100 for people who borrowed books and then loaned them to others to read. She used any excuse she could think of to doctor her figures and make them look better than those of the other branches.

At first, nobody noticed. After a while, however, because her figures were so out of proportion with those of other branches, she was asked for an explanation. You can imagine her embarrassment. Her competition with other branch librarians was without meaning. In no way did it indicate that she was a better librarian or that she would be a more suitable choice for a higher position. Padding her statistics hurt her more than anybody. She didn't lose her job, but from then on people didn't trust her reports. Ms. Schofeld lost an important part of her good reputation.

BEING A GOOD WINNER

Suppose you compete squarely and fairly by doing the best possible job you can, and you come up the winner. You may find good wishes coming in from all sides. You may also run into some resentment. Perhaps you got a raise and someone who was hired at the same time didn't get one. Or you got promoted and a person who had been on the job longer than you did not. Naturally, their feelings toward you may be ambivalent. That means, on the one hand they might feel happy for you; on the other, they might be a bit envious, too.

Accept any congratulations or compliments gracefully with a simple "thank you." Then go quietly about your work. In a week or so, people will have accepted you as the winner, especially if you haven't changed your friendly behavior toward them.

Winning involves a special problem for people who have experienced a lot of failure and who have come to expect it. Maybe people around them made them doubt themselves. Maybe the world seemed so big and difficult to them. Then, suddenly, they experience success. They feel happy at first, then uneasy. "Do I really have a right to succeed?" they ask themselves. "Is this success just a mistake that will soon be followed by more failures?"

If you find yourself thinking like this, fight it. Concentrate on your success and what made it possible. Try to pick out elements that you could repeat in another situation. Look at yourself in the mirror and say, "I did it!" You have a right to succeed if you do it honestly and fairly.

For most of us, successes are not strung together like Christmas tree lights. In between successes there may be several failures, near-misses, or neutral events. Thinking about your past failures is okay if you are trying to learn to avoid them in the future. However, thinking about your successes as well as your failures gives you a much more balanced picture of yourself.

What Do You Think?

Did you know that being unable to get along with other people is one of the most common reasons employees are fired? Tell what effect the following situations could have on co-workers, on the business, and on the public:

1. A worker shouts, swears, and makes a scene when he doesn't get his way.

2. A worker does her job but refuses to help anyone else, even in an emergency.

3. Two employees argue in front of a patient or customer.

Working Cooperatively

Many of you no doubt have enjoyed reading "Dear Abby," "Ann Landers," or some other advice column in the newspapers. Here's a chance for you to try doing their job.

Choose partners by drawing names out of a hat. Each person writes a "Dear Abby" letter (or "Dear Abner" if your partner is male) describing an on-the-job situation and asking for advice. The next day each person composes an answer to his/her partner's letter. A sample exchange of letters follows:

Dear Abner:

    I just started my first office job. It took me a long time to find it, and I want very much to do everything right. My problem is an older woman who has worked here a long time. Almost every morning, she comes to my desk and hangs around for 15 or 20 minutes, talking and keeping me from my work. I found out that she has done this from time to time to many of the other women in the office. I don't find her particularly interesting, and I don't like the kinds of things she says about other people. I don't want to come right out and tell her to shut up. But I do want to keep my job. How should I go about telling her to stop bothering me.

                                    —Worried

Dear Worried,

    Don't be too worried. Surely everyone around knows what your problem woman is like, so no one will blame you unless you contribute a lot to the conversation.

    You are perfectly within your rights to say, ''Excuse me, but I don't have time to talk today. This letter is needed right away.''

    After a few such comments she's pretty sure to give up and hunt for another victim. If this doesn't work, have a private talk with your supervisor about the situation.

                            Yours truly,
                            Abner

❧ Chapter Four ❧

TWO SPECIAL AREAS OF INTERPERSONAL RELATIONSHIPS

Southern Illinois University
Photographic Services

THE CHANGING WORLD OF HIS AND HERS

Who has the best deal in life—men or women? That's a good question to ask if you want to start a lively discussion. In recent years a great deal has been said and written about the sensitive topic of masculinity and femininity. In this chapter we are going to look at some of the aspects of the sexual revolution which affect people in the world of work.

Stereotypes of male and female roles have developed over a very long period of time. If asked what characteristics they expect to find in a woman, many people would respond by saying that a woman should be pretty, motherly, sexy, helpful, and lovable. Asked the same question about men, they might include such attributes as handsome, sexy, strong, successful, and independent. Certain tasks have been thought of as specifically male or female. Some occupations, too, have been considered women's work or men's work. Now many of these ideas are being challenged. Women, especially, are insisting on a new definition of femininity. Let's try to gain some perspective on what today's woman wants in terms of educational and working rights.

A quick historical review will help get us started. Before 1920, women in this country did not have the right to vote. In fact, they had very few legal rights at all. When a girl married, her husband was allowed by law to take over the management of any money or property she brought into the marriage, whether she wanted him to or not. Women of the upper classes were taught that it was beneath their dignity to earn a living outside the home. Middle and lower class women were allowed to enter only a limited number of occupations. They were often required to work very long hours at low pay. Certain professions were difficult or impossible for women to enter. For example, it was all right for a woman to be a nurse, but a doctor? That was something else!

The 19th Amendment to the Constitution gave women the right to vote. It was a big step forward, but it took years of struggle to bring it about. Now, new laws are being passed which are designed to give women job and educational opportunities equal to those of men.

Demands for such equality have often been met with jokes and smart remarks. "Oh, you mean you'd like to be a big husky he-woman? How about a nice pair of baggy overalls?" Or, "You'd better develop those biceps!"

Jobs in heavy industry have been closed to women. The fine arts have also often been considered outside the woman's realm. Women who wrote novels or poetry sometimes kept their writings to themselves or used male names in order to get their work published and read. Women who painted, sculpted, or worked in other art media did not recieve much encouragement or public recognition. Go to almost any art museum and count the number of paintings by men and then count those by women. You will find a great many more by men. Why? Is it because women have had no experiences to share through art? Have they consistently lacked the necessary brains, coordination, or creative vision? Women have been proving more and more that this is not the case. The reason they have been denied recognition in many fields is simply that such participation was at odds with the old stereotype of women.

Some women's rights movement leaders feel deeply and bitterly that men exploit (take advantage of) women. They say men are threatened by

INTERESTING DATES
IN THE WOMEN'S MOVEMENT

1848 Seneca Falls Convention: Lucretia Mott, Elizabeth Cady Stanton, and others make a "Declaration of Sentiments," which was the first public protest in America against the social, political, and economic inequalities between men and women.

1849 Elizabeth Blackwell completes her medical training and becomes the first woman doctor in America.

1917 Jeannette Rankin becomes the first woman to serve in the Congress of the United States.

1920 The 19th Amendment to the Constitution, giving women the right to vote, is ratified.

1963 Congress passes the Equal Pay Act.

1974 Girls are allowed to play Little League Baseball.

1976 Military academies admit women.

strong-willed, able women who can compete with them. This is probably true of some men but not all. Some actually prefer to be around intelligent and competent women and do not regard them as unfeminine. If a girl prefers to do some very active work or to work outdoors, not all men will think she couldn't possibly be a good lover, wife, friend, or mother.

What about men's liberation? Men certainly have had some difficult things thrust on them, too. For example, men are supposed to be tough and unemotional. They are not supposed to cry. In some circles it isn't considered masculine to be able to cook, sew, or weave. Men have also traditionally shouldered heavy responsibilities in terms of supporting a family. In spite of the fact that there are always some fathers and husbands who don't take good care of their families, there are a great many men who do. Men begin their working lives in their late teens or early twenties and stay on the job day after day, year after year. It is often harder for them to quit a job than it is for a working wife, since the man is basically expected to be the provider.

Today, both male and female roles are changing. More women are working outside the home than ever before. Men are sharing domestic tasks that were formerly assigned to the women. Why shouldn't a man help with the dishes or laundry? Why shouldn't a woman wash the car now and then or help with home repairs? There need not be two lists of tasks to be done, one labeled *male* and the other *female*. Both men and women need liberation from the old stereotypes.

Women today want more options. Some still want to be wives,

mothers, and homemakers. Others want to have careers. Still others want to combine homemaking and a career. In the world of work, women want to be free to pursue any occupation in which they feel they can do a good job. They also want to receive the same wages as men for doing the same work. Do these seem like fair demands?

Being one of the first to break through old boundaries can be very difficult. Women often encounter problems when they enter occupations that have traditionally been considered the male's domain. Men also have problems if they choose jobs which have long been thought of as women's work. The two stories that follow show what can happen when career choices conflict with the traditional ideas of male and female roles.

SALLY.   Sally's father had been handicapped by a war injury but had, nevertheless, established a good small appliance repair shop. Ever since she could remember, Sally had enjoyed watching him work. As she got older she liked taking things apart to see how they worked and putting them back together again. When she took typing in high school, she soon realized that she was more interested in the typewriter as a machine than in learning to type. She made some inquiries and was accepted into a typewriter repair training program after she graduated from high school. She did very well. Most of the people in the program were men. They teased her a little, but none of them did anything to discourage her.

However, once she was on the job, she attracted a great deal of attention. Most of the workers in the offices where she serviced machines had not seen a woman doing that kind of work. People made little jokes about the "woman repair*man*" and about her clean little hands working on that great big, bad, old machine. At first she didn't mind too much, but it started getting on her nerves after a while. She thought it would never stop. On some occasions she even found it difficult to concentrate on her work. Then one day a customer called in a complaint about her work, and when another repair person was sent to check it out, he found absolutely nothing wrong with the machine Sally had worked on. Sally felt that the customer had not been able to believe that a woman could repair something as complicated as an electric typewriter, and that upset her.

She decided to talk to her supervisor. He listened calmly, then he smiled and said, "That's what it's like to be a pioneer, Sally." He advised her to stick it out a little longer. "Once your customers are used to seeing you, your visits will cause less of a sensation, and you will be able to do your work without so much hassle."

Was he right? Yes. People can often learn to tolerate change if they are not preached to or badgered. Time also helps. What seemed strange and unnatural soon got to be quite ordinary. In less than a year, Sally's visits to the offices on her route got to be routine.

MIKE.   Mike accepted a secretarial position in a bank which employed a large number of men. He didn't expect any problem with his job. He figured the guys would understand that a male secretary doesn't have to be an oddball or freak. In general Mike was right. But there was one person, named Barry, who decided to give Mike a bad time.

On the first day, Barry walked up to Mike and kidded him about taking a "squaw's job." Mike didn't care. He'd heard that kind of thing before. He figured a little teasing never hurt anybody.

Things got less than funny in a hurry. A few days later someone erased a dictaphone belt Mike had on his desk to transcribe. It turned out that Barry had not only erased it, but he came and told Mike he had done so, more or less daring him to do anything about it. "Are you going to tell mama?" he asked as he walked away.

Mike was very angry. His first thought was to use his fists. Although he was small in build, he was strong. He had had a reputation for fighting at school, and it had gotten him in lots of trouble. He realized that if he lost his job for punching Barry he'd have trouble landing another. So he overlooked this, too, even though it meant he had to tell his supervisor that he had erased the tape accidentally.

Barry just wouldn't give up. He continued making crude remarks that would anger anyone. He continuously made cracks about Mike having a girl's job. Mike began to feel that since he couldn't afford to get into a fight with Barry, he only had one other alternative, and that was to quietly begin looking for a different job.

Fortunately, that didn't happen. The bank hired another male secretary for Mike's department. The new man, George, had more experience. Barry tried a similar routine on him, but it didn't work. So one day when George and Mike were having lunch, Mike mentioned his problem and asked George how he had gotten Barry off his back. George said, "Look, man, don't let a guy like that know he's getting to you. If you look around you'll see that he doesn't get much support around here. Forget him."

Mike followed George's advice. Rather than being visibly upset, he just laughed or returned a pointed or humorous comment. Sure enough, Barry lost interest. The game had lost its point.

Why do you suppose Barry behaved the way he did? That would be hard to say without knowing him better. However, social changes such as we have been talking about in relation to male and female roles can be confusing and upsetting to some people. Maybe Barry's own insecurities as a male made him try to challenge other people's masculinity. In any case Mike was able to keep his job and be comfortable in it. He was grateful for George's help.

What Do You Think?

Discuss the following occupations in terms of what women can contribute to them. Feel free to say that you believe certain occupations should be for men only or for women only. But be prepared to defend your position.

- Industrial physician in a steel mill
- Switchboard operator
- Criminal investigation detective
- Animal trainer in a zoo
- Railroad engineer

- Automobile mechanic
- Nurse
- Bulldozer operator
- President of the United States
- Trainer for a hockey team
- Nursery school teacher
- Clothes designer

Write a short essay on one of the following topics. If none of them interest you, pick out a related topic you would prefer to work with.

1. Should the man always pay for everything on a date?

2. If you were the boss, would you hire a man for a secretarial position?

3. Does it make any difference to you whether the doctor or dentist you go to is male or female?

Many good career materials are available for men and women seeking occupations. You will find out about them as you continue through the book. Here, however, we want to mention a few sources of information for women who want to expand their career horizons. We will begin with a book that explores some occupations that have previously been more or less closed to women.

SATURDAY'S CHILD: 36 WOMEN TALK ABOUT THEIR JOBS
by Suzanne Seed; J. Philip O'Hara, Inc., Chicago, 1973.

Thirty-six good career ideas for women. Many of them are within the reach of an average woman with a strong will to make it on her own. Excellent photographs and interviews.

A WORKING WOMAN'S GUIDE TO HER JOB RIGHTS
Prepared by Rose Terlin for the U.S. Dept. of Labor (Women's Bureau, Leaflet #55)

Available from the Superintendent of Documents, U.S. Government Printing Office, Washington, D.C. 20402.

This pamphlet outlines the legal rights women now have in regard to their occupations. Information is also available from these two agencies: The U.S. Department of Labor, Employment Standards Administration, Women's Bureau, Washington, D.C. 20210, and the U.S. Equal Employment Opportunity Commission, Washington, D.C. 20506.

MELTING POT OR NOT?

The United States has often been called the "melting pot" of the world. Even before the Revolutionary War, colonists came from many countries—England, France, Holland, Sweden, Spain, and others. In the 19th and 20th centuries waves of immigrants came from Ireland, Germany, eastern and southern Europe, and the Far East. The great hope was that all these people would melt together into a richly varied society where peace, plenty, and freedom would be possible for everyone.

To some extent, that is what happened. Many Americans have learned to live in harmony with each other. The average standard of living is higher here than in many other countries, and we have freedoms that are not available in some other parts of the world. But, unfortunately, the whole picture was not that simple. Fears and jealousies cropped up. Some groups of people were looked down upon because they were poor or spoke another language or had different customs. Prejudice and discrimination took root. Today we still face many serious problems in living together, but we are making progress.

Terry Mauzy

Many modern Americans have come to accept the idea of peaceful coexistence. They want to retain their own way of life, but they respect other people's ways of living as well. They may not want to eat the same foods as their neighbors up the block, but they don't think of those neighbors as weird or dangerous. While they may choose to stay apart from other ethnic groups, they do not try to keep others from getting equal protection under the law or equal educational and occupational opportunities.

Some Americans have gone one step further. They have discovered that contacts with people of different backgrounds enrich their lives. They don't simply tolerate differences; they enjoy them. They appreciate the music, foods, and clothing that come to them via other cultures. Do you like silver and turquoise jewelry? How about tacos? Have you ever played chess or backgammon? These are just a few of the things that have been borrowed from other cultures. Ideas, thoughts, and various art forms have also been exchanged and assimilated. By *assimilated* we mean they have become a genuine, well-integrated part of our culture. Our national heritage is richer for all the ethnic groups that have contributed to it.

Working Cooperatively

The English language has a great number of interesting words which it has borrowed from other languages. These words have made the language more expressive than it otherwise would have been. Can you think of some of them?

Try starting with foods. Or musical terms. What about the names of different dances?

Make a blackboard list. Keep adding to it for several days. Can you come up with 100 such words?

A RIGHT TO RIGHTS

Appreciating other ways of life is a good start towards learning to live together in the practical, everyday world. But we have also come to realize that the protection of personal rights can't depend entirely on the good will of people. No one can really force people to feel a certain way about other people. Nor can anyone demand that people get along together. What we can do is insist on good laws being made and enforced, laws that can stop one group of people from taking advantage of another group. In Chapter 30 we will go into more detail on what part

Maytag Co.

individuals can play in the law-making process. For now we will concentrate on a law that has to do with your rights in the world of work.

Let's first look at the term *equality*. Do you believe that being equal is the same as having equal opportunity? The fact is, people aren't any more equal in terms of abilities and talents than they are in terms of height or weight. Some people are smarter than others; some have more sex appeal; others can run faster or jump higher. The same is true in the world of work. Not all people have the ability to reach the same level of success. Rewards differ according to performance. Most of us can understand that.

But equality of opportunity is something else. If people are not given the opportunity to try to succeed at a certain occupation, then, of course, they feel deprived and mistreated. The law we are going to discuss now is designed to protect this right.

The Civil Rights Act became law in 1964. Title VII of that Act was amended in 1972. This amendment prohibits discrimination in all employment practices, including hiring, firing, lay-offs, wages, promotions, and training. The lawmakers realized that to write such prohibitions into the law was not enough. There had to be some way of seeing to it that the law would be obeyed. So part of the law consists of a provision for setting up the Equal Employment Opportunity Commission, often called the EEOC.

The EEOC receives and evaluates charges of racial, religious, sexual, and other forms of discrimination. In order to have your case reviewed, you must make a specific complaint in writing and send it to the EEOC. You must do that within 180 days of the time the incident which you believe was in violation of your rights occurred. The EEOC has 120 days to reply. It can either work out an agreement between you and your employer, or it can refer the matter to the courts.

Someday you may feel you have been discriminated against. Before taking action, however, a young worker would be wise to keep the following in mind. General dissatisfaction with a situation is not enough. All of us feel from time to time that we have been treated badly or unfairly. This can even happen between friends or within a family. You would want to be very careful about bringing a discrimination charge in such an instance. A situation can be unpleasant or even unfair without being discriminatory in the legal sense. The person filing the complaint would have to be able to prove that he or she has been denied employment or advancement because of prejudice on the part of the employer. Also, the person would have to be able to show that he or she was truly qualified for that job or that promotion.

If you have thought a situation over carefully and objectively and have come to the conclusion that you were indeed discriminated against, what would you do? You have the right to go to your employer and ask for an explanation. Not getting a particular job or promotion is not automatically a case of discrimination. Your supervisor may have had reasons for what was done. Also, there is always the possibility that something you did or said or failed to do played a part in the decision. Keep an open mind when you approach your employer. Being calm and rational will get you much farther than if you are emotional and belligerent. If under these circumstances you are still not satisfied that the decision was a fair one, you can contact the EEOC and ask for help.

Finding Out for Yourself

If you want to know exactly how the Equal Employment Opportunity Commission works, write for the booklet entitled *EEOC at a Glance*. This booklet explains the procedures and lists regional offices where you can get further information and help. To get the booklet write to:
U.S. Equal Employment
Opportunity Commission
Washington, D.C. 20506

SENSITIVITY

Sensitivity is a word frequently used today. Being sensitive means being responsive to the world around you. Sensitive people can have their feelings hurt or can be moved by something beautiful. Sensitivity encompasses a whole range of feelings which a human being can experience. The sensitive person is often very much aware of the feelings and needs of others.

Insensitive people are not as much in touch with life as sensitive people. They don't experience as much, appreciate beauty to the same degree, or feel as deeply with or for people. They are often unaware of how they affect others. They seldom think about such things. Usually their feelings are not easily hurt because they are so unaware. Their lives may be less painful, but, on the other hand, they miss a great deal.

Most of us would prefer to think of ourselves as sensitive people. However, there is such a thing as being *too* sensitive. A touchy person can be just as difficult to be around as an insensitive person. Often oversensitive people think they are being abused or insulted or ignored. If you've ever known people like that, you may have felt you had to tiptoe around them or leave them alone entirely.

If you have been deeply hurt by prejudice or discrimination or if you have something in your past you don't want others to know about, you may be over-sensitive. You may misjudge people's intentions and hurt yourself even more. It is one thing for a person to advise you, "Don't be so sensitive." It is another to try to change your feelings, but it can be done. It takes patience, experience, and courage. The story that follows is about a young man who was over-sensitive about his past.

PRISONER OF THE PAST.   After two years in prison, Fred found it hard to get a job. Finally he landed one as a janitor in an office building. He came to work at 4 p.m. each day and stayed until midnight, cleaning up after everyone was gone. After a few weeks, he really liked his job. It gave him enough (but not too much) contact with others. He had time to think and plan for the future, and he was left pretty much on his own as long as he did his job well.

One evening Fred went into one of the salesman's offices to clean. He noticed a little pile of coins on the desk. He felt very uncomfortable. He hurriedly dusted around the money, quickly cleaned the rest of the room, and left.

A few nights later the same thing happened. This time more money was left on the typewriter table, including some bills. Fred felt angry. "Someone is testing me," he thought.

After this had happened a few more times, Fred felt very suspicious. He thought that because he had been in prison someone was trying to find out if he could be trusted. He left a note on that salesman's desk which said, "I know you are testing me. You don't need to. You want to see if I will take the money. Well I won't. Yours truly, Fred."

When John, the salesman, found the note, he was puzzled. In fact, he at first thought it had been placed on his desk by mistake. As he worked through his mail, however, he discovered the little pile of money. Suddenly, it occurred to him what had happened. "Fred must think I laid a trap for him!" he said to himself.

That afternoon John waited for Fred so they could talk it over. John said, "Look, I know you've got a problem. People really don't know yet whether or not they can trust you. You're very sensitive about it, and I don't blame you. But that doesn't change the fact that I wasn't testing you. It just happens that I'm a little careless with my money and some-times I lay it down and forget about it when I come back from lunch or coffee."

They talked some more, and they both felt better. Fred told John, "I really thought you were testing me. Next time something like this comes up, I'll remember today."

John replied, "I'm going to be working late now and then in the next few weeks. Stop in and talk when you have time."

Fred did so. They found plenty to talk about, including their common interest in boats. Fred began to feel less and less touchy about his past. Other people in the office where he worked began to feel more comfortable with him, too. Before, he had seemed to them to have a chip on his shoulder. Now he seemed more open and friendly.

A CLOSING NOTE

Rising above prejudice has a great deal to do with how you feel about yourself. People who feel good about themselves don't need to downgrade anyone else. People who feel good about themselves also rebound better when they are the victims of prejudice.

People who find their way into an occupation that gives them a decent living and other rewards as well tend to have a much better opinion of themselves. That gives them a head start in protecting themselves from prejudice and in treating others as they want to be treated.

Transition, as you may know, means a gradual change. There have been many transitional periods in history during which change gradually occurred. Americans may be in such a transitional period right now, as far as human relationships are concerned. We are slowly moving toward understanding and acceptance and a new era of opportunity for all. It takes time, of course. Modern laws help speed up the process. But a great deal depends on how each of us responds to the challenge on an individual basis.

Working Cooperatively

Imagine that the class has been commissioned to set up a beautiful restaurant on the grounds of the next World's Fair. You want the menu to appeal to many different ethnic backgrounds—and to those gastronomic adventurers who like to try new and different foods. Such a menu could include:

appetizers	poultry
breads	fish
soups	vegetables and fruits
salads	desserts
meats	beverages

Everyone in the class may contribute five food ideas from their ethnic background, or from any ethnic foods they particularly enjoy.

Choose a committee of four or five to design the menu layout. The cover should carry out the international theme of the restaurant.

Chapter Five

WAR AND PEACE: COPING WITH STRESS AND CONFLICT

PROS AND CONS OF STRESS

Psychologists interested in evaluating the effects of stress on living organisms studied young rats. The rats were divided into three groups. One group was given daily stress in the form of mild electric shocks. The second group received a small amount of handling each day. The third group was given food and water, but otherwise left alone in the nest. These rats were not stressed or handled.

Which group do you think grew up the strongest? The psychologists thought that the unstressed rats (group three) would have the advantage. The psychologists were surprised. The rats that encountered stress (group one) or were handled (group two) grew faster, opened their eyes sooner, and their brains developed more quickly. They even developed greater resistance to some diseases.

Of course, competent psychologists don't apply what they learn from studying animals directly to human beings. The animal behavior data are only used as a starting place. Further studies using human subjects have to be made before any of the knowledge can be applied to human situations. In this case, psychologists have observed in a number of studies that human babies who are simply given basic care but are never played with, challenged, or put under any kind of stress grow very slowly. They often lose ground in terms of weight, skills, and alertness. Some tend to develop personality problems while they are still young.

Learning to cope with stress is part of the growing process. For example, compare your first date with a more recent date, or your first sports performance with one after you were more experienced. For many of us, the stress doesn't actually lessen or disappear, but we learn to cope with it. So many magazine articles and books have appeared on stress in modern life that it seems like a modern phenomenon. But even the earliest people on earth probably suffered stress. Would you agree that stress is a normal part of life?

Southern Illinois University / Photographic Service

Bob McCullough / Inland Steel Company

Some stress has survival value. It helps build stamina. For instance, if you decide to build your body by weight-lifting, you put it under stress. Gradually you are able to lift more and hold it longer. Emotional and mental stress also build us up and make us better able to handle problems and difficult situations. Beyond a certain point, however, stress can be destructive. Too much of it can cause physical illness, emotional disturbance, even death. One prediction says that 57% of the next generation of Americans could die of heart disease. Diet, exercise patterns, and heredity all influence such diseases. If stress on the job helps tip the scales toward death, we must try to understand it and minimize its effects. First we will be looking at stress that we more or less bring on ourselves. Then we will turn to stress and conflict that result from living and working closely with others.

What Do You Think?

Every occupation has its own kinds of stress. Name several potential sources of mental stress and tension on your job.

?

BEING YOUR OWN WORST ENEMY

As you move around in the world of work you can't help noticing that many people have almost destroyed themselves trying to get ahead. They live in a constant state of tension about holding on to their jobs, getting promotions, and impressing their bosses and fellow employees. They often have their eye on the next rung of the ladder of success, and therefore they get little day-to-day satisfaction from their work.

Part of this kind of tension is brought on by the fact that we live in a society where success is highly valued. We put ourselves under pressure to be charming, beautiful, rich, smart, marriageable. Concentrating on the idea of success rather than on definite steps toward a goal can bring about almost unbearable tension. In the story that follows, Joseph is an example of a person who put himself under too much pressure.

IN OVER HIS HEAD.   Although Joseph had only a small amount of layout experience, he took a job as staff artist for a big school district. When he was interviewed for the job, he had a feeling that he wouldn't be able to handle it with his limited background. He was to make bulletin board layouts for teachers and principals, design small publications such as school play or concert programs, and do any other such tasks that came up. The job paid well. There wasn't another applicant for it, so he got it.

At first Joseph was able to keep up with the few easy jobs which came in. But he soon became overwhelmed. Being inexperienced, he was slow. When he saw that he was getting farther and farther behind, he began to panic. Instead of finishing any one project, he dabbled at many. After he missed several deadlines, people began complaining. He worried about his job all the time, even at night. He couldn't sleep very well and started having stomach problems. Rather than admitting temporary defeat until he could learn more about this kind of work, Joseph kept pushing himself. He didn't want to lose his job, even though he knew he couldn't handle it. The more he pushed, the more tense he became and the less he was able to do. He was in over his head.

An even greater problem arose. He wanted to be considered an artist. It was a matter of status to him. He started playing the role as he saw it, wearing off-beat clothes and being high-handed with people. What do you think happened to Joseph? You're right. He was fired.

Joseph was crushed. For the first few days he thought he was going to have a nervous breakdown. But he made it through this crisis. The relief from the constant on-the-job tension was so great it almost made up for everything. Food started tasting good again. He began sleeping better.

What could Joseph have done to avoid the painful situation described above? He could have taken some aptitude tests in high school to help him find out if this was a good occupation for him. He could have quickly enrolled in a graphic arts course in a community college evening division. If Joe had forced himself to concentrate on his work rather than on his problems he might have improved enough to feel at least somewhat secure. Joe could have gone to his boss and asked to be transferred to a less demanding job. (That would be hard for most of us to do, but, when you think about it, it would have been a sensible approach under the circumstances.)

Ambition (the desire to achieve) is a good and useful quality when it is based on self-knowledge and realistic goals. Ambition which only amounts to wishful thinking creates unproductive stress.

What Do You Think?

Another common source of stress which you at least partially impose on yourself is financial stress. It is hard to avoid financial crunches altogether. You can control how often they occur by being realistic about your material wishes and getting them in line with other goals and values in your life. Here are a few sample situations to consider:

If you thought working a lot of hours overtime was going to destroy your marriage, would you work fewer hours?

If you found a job you liked very much but it paid less than another job you didn't like as well, which job would you take?

Would you be satisfied to drive a Volkswagen if several of your friends had Porsches or Alpha Romeos?

No one can answer such questions for you, and it is legitimate to say you'd prefer a Porsche or that you would take the job that offered the most money. But, remember, in order to have some things you give up others. You build into your life a certain amount of stress and tension which would not otherwise be there. Each of us must set an upper limit on the amount of preventable tension we can allow in our lives.

Write a story about a time when you felt yourself to be under great stress. Tell what happened, and whether it was good or bad for you. Here are some possibilities, but you may use other ideas.

1. You had a fight with your girlfriend or boyfriend.

2. You had an argument with the coach because you had to sit out a good part of an important game.

3. You got arrested by the police.

4. Someone in your family was seriously ill or injured.

5. You were accused of something you didn't do.

6. You were accused of something you did do.

7. You lost your part-time job.

THE TENSIONS OF SOCIAL LIVING

In nature, some species are social and some are not. The loners come together for a few very basic purposes such as reproduction and occasional physical protection. They don't come together to build houses and communities, hunt food, or share tasks. The social animals do. They work out details of their daily lives on a give-and-take basis.

People are, generally speaking, social animals. They are interdependent, which means they depend on each other for basic needs. They have complex systems of give-and-take in which power is assigned and regulated. Over and above purely practical concerns, people need people for emotional reasons. They need love, companionship, trust, and esteem. Living close to other human beings gives us comfort, support, and joy. But, as we said in the previous chapter, human beings vary greatly, and there are bound to be conflicting ideas, needs, desires, and attitudes.

Much tension in the world of work results from these differences. Conflict between people is not an altogether negative feature of social living. It can stimulate us, put some zing in life, and lead toward broader understanding. Of course, it can also destroy trust and friendship and make life miserable. How can we use conflict creatively rather than allowing it to be a destructive force?

First of all, you must develop a strong sense of when a conflict is worth mentioning. You may prefer to overlook minor irritations simply because they don't matter that much to you. For example, a co-worker may speak sharply to you when he is in a bad mood. He doesn't do it regularly, so you might not see any point in getting into an argument about it. Or someone has an annoying habit, but it doesn't affect your efficiency, well-being, or happiness. You may decide to put up with it. However, some issues may be a lot more important to you, and if you don't try to straighten them out, you may suffer a great deal of tension as a result.

Let's pause here to consider two kinds of tension: covert and overt. Covert tension is kept hidden inside the person. Tom thinks George is always trying to make a fool out of him, but he never mentions it to George. Shirley believes that JoAnn doesn't do her fair share of the work, but she doesn't discuss it with her. Overt tension, on the other hand, is tension that comes to the surface. Tom goes to George and says, "Why are you always trying to put me down?" Shirley tells JoAnn how she feels.

You can probably imagine what kinds of problems arise when covert tension exists. Ignoring temporary problems may often be a good policy, but ignoring stubborn problems that go on and on solves nothing. People who feel they have been wronged feel less and less able to do anything about it, and frustration sets in. A tense climate develops, allowing mistrust and dislike to flourish. Some people who don't feel free to air their grievances begin doing mean, petty little things to get at those who have supposedly offended them. Or, little by little, they become sour, difficult people who make others feel uneasy around them.

Bringing problems out into the open can be difficult, too. The boss can't have people fighting, arguing, and carrying on feuds on the job. Such actions keep people from working efficiently, pull down the morale of the workers, and make a bad impression on customers, clients, or visitors. Most places of employment regard physical fighting as grounds for immediate dismissal, and you can probably see why.

However, openly expressing your feelings, needs, or wishes does not have to involve fighting or loud arguments. You can learn to make your point effectively without turning people off by what you say or do. You can open up lines of communication and get others to discuss the problem with you. Chapter Six, "The Art of Self-Assertion," suggests some techniques for doing so. Understanding other points of view is a good way to begin, and we are going to concentrate on that now.

SUBJECTIVE AND OBJECTIVE POINTS OF VIEW

Have you ever heard someone say about a painting, "I may not know much about art, but I know what I like"? That is a good example of a *subjective* point of view. People who say that judge a painting by whether or not it appeals to them. Their opinions are based mainly on their feelings about the work of art and how it happens to fit their personal ideas of what a nice painting is.

Artists, art critics, and informed laymen study many kinds of paintings. When they look at a new work for the first time they, too, make an emotional response to it. Either they like it or they don't like it. But they don't stop there. They go on to explore the form, color, balance, variety —all of the elements that they have learned contribute to a good painting. They try to understand and appreciate it for what it is, on its own terms. To do that they must look at it *objectively* as well as subjectively. Are you beginning to understand the difference between these two basic points of view?

Let's stop for a moment to define these two important terms. The subjective point of view is one's own personal point of view. It reflects a specific individual's mind, emotions, interests, prejudices, and background. From it we can learn how that particular person responds to situations or how he or she feels about things. The objective point of view is almost the opposite. It is free from purely personal feelings, opinions, and responses, and it takes into consideration the world outside the individual. It relies more on thought than on emotion and on sifting through the evidence on both sides of a question. Perhaps the chart below will help make this clearer.

SUBJECTIVE	OBJECTIVE
My world	The world
My feelings	People's feelings
My ideas	What others think or say
Holding my one point of view	Exploring many possibilities
Looking inside myself for answers	Looking outside myself for answers
Often approaching problems in an emotional way	Often approaching problems in a rational way (using reasoning)

Both viewpoints are valuable, and many stressful situations can be straightened out if you can move between subjective and objective ways of looking at things when the need arises. The story that follows will give you an idea what we mean.

A CLEAN SWEEP.   Todd works in a machine shop. The boss comes to him one afternoon and tells him to stop what he is doing and sweep the floor. Todd's first thought is, "Why should I have to do it?" He doesn't like being torn away from his project just when everything is starting to fall into place. Besides, clean-up work isn't his favorite thing to do. These are his subjective reactions.

Now let's say he quickly calms down and puts the whole thing in perspective. He realizes that somebody has to do the job. Remembering that the boss has asked a different person to do it each day, he realizes that each worker is taking a turn. Besides, sweeping the floor is no big deal. It only takes a few minutes. Todd knows that a clean floor is not only a safety factor, but it provides a much more pleasant workplace. He gets the push broom and sweeping compound out of the locker and starts to work. He has moved from a purely subjective point of view to a more objective one.

Being able to look at a situation objectively doesn't mean that we have to give up our subjective point of view. In the story, Todd might not enjoy cleaning up even after he decides to do it. What we must try to do is compare our point of view with other points of view and base our actions and words on what we discover. When we do that, various things can happen:

1.   We may completely change our minds on an issue.

2.   The other party may change his or her position entirely.

3.   We may expand our point of view to include an idea or reason we hadn't thought of before.

4.   We may reject the other person's point of view, giving reasons.

5.   We may simply agree to disagree. If the question does not have anything to do with getting the job done, it may not need a resolution.

6.   If two parties cannot arrive at a necessary compromise, a third party might be asked to listen and make suggestions.

Applying What You Know

Three situations are given below. Each is presented from two different points of view. See how easily you can move from one point of view to the other. It will take some imagination!

RULES FOR TOOLS.   You have a friend at

work who lets you use his tools. Once in a while you forget to return them. However, you're always very careful not to damage any of them because you know your friend takes pride in his tools. One day he suddenly tells you that he doesn't want to lend you his tools anymore because you don't bring them back promptly. He says that sometimes he even has to go looking for them. What would you say?

You have your own set of tools in the shop where you work. Your co-worker Larry often asks to borrow them. You like him, so you share your tools with him. After a while, though, you see that he frequently forgets to bring them back, and you have to spend too much time rounding them up. How would you try to straighten things out with Larry?

SUPPLY LINE. Patrick is in charge of the office supplies at Cleves Printing Plant. He takes his work seriously and gives everyone the third degree whenever they ask for even so much as a pencil. He'll ask, "What do you want it for?" or "Didn't I just give you one yesterday?" You and your co-workers are becoming resentful. You don't like being treated like children, and you feel you should be able to get a ballpoint pen without being hassled. How would you deal with Patrick? At what point would you go to the boss?

You have been given the responsibility of running the supply room at Cleves Printing Plant. You think lots of people try to rip the company off, and you are going to put a stop to it, at least in terms of the office supplies for which you are responsible. One day your boss comes to you in private and says there have been some complaints about the way you control supplies. He tells you that he appreciates your concern, but that you need not be quite so tight with them. Would you feel sold out? What would you say to the boss?

GREAT BUT LATE. Geraldine is a good worker, once she gets down to business. But four out of five days she is 10 to 20 minutes late. Other girls in the typing pool begin resenting her being late. Then they start following her pattern. You are the supervisor of the typing pool, so it is up to you to tell her to be on time. How would you phrase it?

You are quite often late for work. You don't worry about it because you always finish your day's work, even if it means staying a few minutes after closing time. One day your supervisor tells you that you must start getting to work on time. She explains that your frequent tardiness makes the other girls feel you are receiving special privileges. What would you say?

YOU AND OTHER PEOPLE'S PROBLEMS

Maybe this scene is familiar to you. A family sits down at the dinner table. Jack, the second youngest, is in a bad mood. He begins by objecting to the food, then he starts teasing his little sister. His father tells him to stop. Jack protests, "I'm not doing anything!" He turns to his little sister and says, "Cry-baby. See, she's going to cry."

"One more time, Jack, and you'll go to your room," the father says.

That probably would have settled Jack down. But his older brother puts in his two cents' worth. "That little brat ought to go to his room right now."

Jack sticks out his tongue with a lot of chewed up food on it.

"Shut your mouth!" yells his horrified older sister.

"Yeah," pipes up the little one.

"Can't we have any peace and quiet around here?" says the mother.

It turns into a free-for-all until the father shouts, "Everybody, shut up!"

A gloomy silence descends over the dinner table. Everyone is glad when the meal is over.

Let's carry this situation over into the world of work. Most likely, there will be some arguments between people who work together. The people who disagree can talk it over or even argue about it. Once the matter is settled, they can go on from there. It doesn't have to be an earth-shaking event.

However, here's what sometimes happens. Two workers are arguing. A friend of one of them decides to help. So now it's two against one. Several other people gather around, and soon everyone is talking at once, making remarks, and giving advice. All kinds of unrelated issues are dragged in. Before long, it's a free-for-all like the one we saw at the dinnertable. Little progress is made toward solving the basic problem, and now there is a lot more confusion and argument than there was to begin with.

You may have heard or seen the word *escalation.* In war time it means the enlarging of the battle area or increasing the intensity of the fighting. That's what can happen when people get into arguments that are really none of their business. Before entering into an argument which is not your own it would be well to consider these points:

- Do you really know and understand what the argument is all about?

- Does the person whose side you're on really need and want your help?

- Will what you say escalate the tension or calm things down?

- If you were the one having the argument, would you want others to interfere?

RESOLVING CONFLICTS

Can you see what the following words have in common: settlement, contract, armistice, compromise, agreement, treaty? If you said that all of them have something to do with negotiating a peace, you are correct. In his book, *When I Say No I Feel Guilty,* Manuel Smith says that primitive creatures have two responses to trouble—fight or flight. That is, they can try using physical force or they can run away. But, he adds, human beings have a third way of dealing with conflict. They can approach others verbally. They can come to a settlement, make an agreement, or decide on a compromise.

Let's briefly review what we have learned in this chapter about solving conflicts. First of all, we know that tensions can complicate our relationships with others. They can build up into fear, dislike, or hate. But we also realize that relieving our own tensions by attacking others verbally or otherwise won't help matters much. If we want to resolve conflicts successfully, we have to take into consideration other people's points of view. We have to be able to move between subjective and objective ways of looking at problems.

In the next chapter we will be talking about useful techniques for approaching others in conflict situations. Before we turn to that, let's look at the flow chart below. Some procedures are more effective than others in solving conflicts. For example, if your immediate supervisor does something you feel is unfair, it is usually better to talk it over with him or her before going to the next person up the line. Or suppose a co-worker does something that bothers or wrongs you. If you tell the boss before trying to discuss it with that person, you may make a permanent enemy. The flow chart will help you develop some good plans for working out problems between yourself and others.

For a little practice, pick one of the following conflicts and make a list of four or five steps you would follow to resolve it.

1. Roxanne often asks you to help her with her typing load. You are her friend, so you say okay. Then she starts jazzing around while you do her work. You are being taken advantage of, and you know it. How will you go about solving the problem?

2. You and Debby open the restaurant where you work three mornings a week. You agreed to divide the tasks. Debby is to take care of the salad set-ups and you are going to do the grill set-ups. Sometimes Debby is late. Sometimes she has a cup of coffee or sits and reads the morning paper before she gets to work. Several times the boss has come in and been upset to find that the salad bar isn't ready or isn't very attractively put together. He speaks to you about it, since you have been working there a long time. He assumes it is your responsibility. How could you straighten out this problem?

3. You and Caesar take turns guiding groups through the factory where you work. Each tour group is shown a short film. Caesar often forgets to rewind the film and is generally careless with the projector. Twice in one week you have had to rewind and focus while your group sits there and waits. It's happened before. What steps could you take to keep it from happening again?

4. Boris likes to talk about other people in the office. Several times he has quoted you as saying something you did not say, and it has gotten back to you. On one occasion the person about whom you supposedly said something bad got very angry. You calmed him down, but then you decided you had better do something about Boris. What would you do?

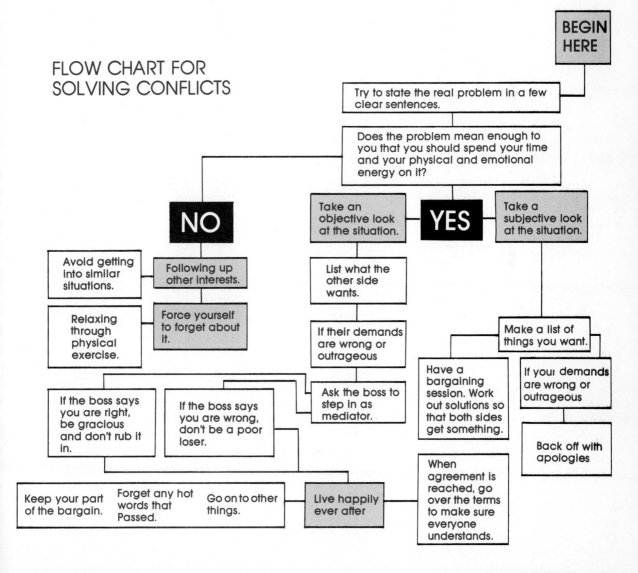

FLOW CHART FOR SOLVING CONFLICTS

Checkpoint

We've used some new words in this chapter. Check yourself to see if you know what they mean. Match the words with their definitions.

1. overt

2. escalate

3. negotiate

4. covert

5. subjective

6. objective

a. under cover

b. to work out a settlement

c. your own personal point of view

d. open, easy to see

e. to enlarge or make more intense

f. a broad outlook that takes into account many points of view

❧ Chapter Six ❧

THE ART OF SELF-ASSERTION

Circus World Museum

WHAT IS SELF-ASSERTION?

Self-assertion is the basic skill of letting others know how you feel, what you think, what you like and dislike, and what kind of a person you are. In the story that follows, Stanley could respond to the situation in different ways. We have supplied two endings to the story. As you read, try to determine which ending shows self-assertiveness and which does not.

Stanley works for M & H Hardware Store. One Saturday morning he is helping a customer find a repair kit for a toilet tank. Stan takes one out of the box to show the customer and to give the customer a few pointers on how to replace the old fittings with this new set. Just then Mr. McGrundy comes hurrying up. Ignoring the customer, he storms: "I thought I told you to put the trash out first thing this morning. Now we've missed the pick-up. What's the matter with you anyhow? Guess I'll do it myself next week." And off he goes to his office.

Stanley is upset. He feels badly enough about forgetting the trash. He is also very angry at having been shouted at in front of a customer. He feels red in the face and shaky. He finishes with his customer, then—

Ending One: Stanley becomes very quiet and goes about his business as if nothing had happened. He waits on customers politely enough, but not very warmly. He is distant and preoccupied and is quietly getting more and more angry. He begins thinking up nasty things to say to his boss, but he knows he will never say them. At the end of the day, he counts the money, cleans up, says, "Good-bye, have a nice weekend," and goes home. But he is in a bad mood and can't stop thinking about this morning's crisis. Sunday morning he wakes up still thinking about things to say to Mr. McGrundy.

Ending Two: Stanley waits until the store is not busy, then goes into the office where Mr. McGrundy is going over some purchase orders.

"Excuse me, Mr. McGrundy," says Stan. Mr. McGrundy looks up from his work. "I just wanted to say that I'm sorry I forgot the trash. But I don't like being corrected in front of a customer. It ruins what I am doing with him and makes me feel small. Next time I'd prefer if you'd tell me in private."

"I didn't mean to embarrass you, Stan. But I was angry when I saw that truck going down the street without our trash. It makes such a mess for the next few days. I hope you won't forget it again. But you are right. I shouldn't have said anything to you in front of your customer."

As far as both Mr. McGrundy and Stan are concerned, the matter is over. Each can go about his business with no hard feelings. Stan will try not to forget the trash again. Mr. McGrundy will make a point of talking problems over with Stan in private from now on.

Do you see the difference between assertive and non-assertive behavior? The second ending, of course, shows an assertive response. Stan's approach was good. Notice what he did and did not do:

1. He did *not* accuse, abuse, or shout at Mr. McGrundy.

2. He did *not* make a scene in front of another customer.

3. He did *not* try to avoid the fact that he *had* forgotten about the trash.

4. He did *not* threaten to quit.

5. He did wait for a good time to see Mr. McGrundy (after he had calmed down and the store wasn't busy).

6. He did choose a good place (the office) to talk to his boss.

7. He did apologize for his mistake.

8. He did state exactly how he felt in a direct manner.

9. He did suggest what he would like to see happen in the future.

INEFFECTIVE SELF-ASSERTION

In our mass society a person can feel lost in the crowd, like a nobody. In order to feel more important than that, some people try to assert themselves by showing off. They draw attention to themselves by wearing inappropriate clothing, telling people off, being loud, and making crude jokes. They seem to be afraid no one will notice them if they don't put on a show, but much of what they do turns out to be obnoxious or childish. People back off from them. Show-offs discourage others from getting to know, like, and respect them. Such superficial self-assertion is not very effective.

Aggressiveness is another form of self-assertion that often turns out to be ineffective. Aggressive is an adjective we apply to people who are often ready to attack. They are quick to start arguments or fights. (Aggressive can also mean to be full of initiative and bold. That is not the meaning we have in mind here.) Imagine for a moment that Stan had been very aggressive with Mr. McGrundy, starting a loud argument. Here are some of the consequences that might have ensued:

1. Stan may not have taken the time to figure out exactly what he wanted to say or how he could best say it. He might easily have given Mr. McGrundy the idea that he was objecting to having to take care of the trash rather than that he was objecting to being corrected in front of a customer. In the heat of the moment, such things frequently happen.

2. While forgetting the trash wouldn't have been grounds for dismissal, talking back and shouting might have been. Mr. McGrundy doesn't really have to put up with employees who do that sort of thing. He could have fired Stan under such circumstances.

3. Stan might have gotten angry enough to shout, "I quit!" Later he might regret it, yet it would be hard to back down. Or Mr. McGrundy could immediately take him up on his offer to quit.

This is just a sampling of the kinds of bad situations that can develop when people use aggressive behavior as a means of self-assertion. None of the above provides a very happy ending to the story.

Let's move on to some basic principles of effective self-assertion.

SELF-ASSERTION AND
HOW YOU VIEW YOURSELF

People can waste a lot of time stomping their feet and shaking their fists over things that don't matter to them much in a long run. They act upon feelings of general dissatisfaction. Sometimes they haven't stopped to think what they really want or need. Knowing oneself is an important step towards effective self-assertion. You must sort out what is and what is not important to you so that your self-assertion has a real and specific purpose.

How people feel about themselves also comes into the picture. Those who look back on a lot of failures and shortcomings may not feel good about themselves. They may feel they do not deserve to be heard or to have what they say acted upon. Or, if people feel that they have never done anything really bad yet haven't done anything good either, they may consider themselves dull and uninteresting. Such a person may think, "I really don't have much to offer." People who lack self-respect for these or other reasons are almost bound to have problems with self-assertion. What can they do about it?

No one can change the way you feel about yourself by simply saying, "You *ought* to feel better." It is true, though, that you can gain respect for yourself with every little success you experience, whether it is getting a person to go out on a date with you, receiving a compliment from one of your teachers, pleasing your parents in some small way, or doing a task at work well. As you begin feeling better about yourself, you will find it easier to assert yourself. Once you learn to assert yourself effectively, you will begin having more self-respect. Your attitudes and actions dovetail into each other.

SELF-ASSERTION:
LETTING OTHERS KNOW YOU

Self-assertion doesn't apply only to conflict situations. Letting others know you is another form of self-assertion. In our modern society, where so many things seem impersonal, this kind of self-assertion becomes particularly important.

Terry Mauzy

We have ways of introducing people to each other, conducting meetings, making business phone calls, and writing business letters. Most societies develop such patterns, making it easier to conduct business and carry on social activities. While these patterns are very useful, they have their limits. Over and above daily contacts, most people desire deeper relationships with others. In order to have them, they must assert themselves.

For example, if Jack would like to know Barry better, he could go beyond the usual hello/good-bye routine. He could let Barry know that they share a common interest if that is the case. Or he could offer to help Barry with a task that requires skills he has. Little by little they could get to know each other's likes, interests, dislikes, needs, and wants. By asserting themselves they could be finding out enough about each other to form a close friendship. If they had merely continued to say "hi" and "good-bye" and "how's the weather?", they would have laid no such groundwork.

Letting others know you can also be important in such situations as the job interview. We'll be talking about job interviews at length in Chapter 15, but here let's just briefly compare an assertive and a nonassertive person in an interview situation.

Mary Ann was interviewing for a job as a lab technician's aid. She had not held a job in a lab before, but she had completed a junior college program to prepare her for such a position. So had Doris, another girl interviewing for the job. Doris' grades were a little higher, but not enough to matter. She had had no job experience either. Mrs. Smith, the personnel manager, interviewed the girls separately.

Let's compare their behavior.

Mrs. Smith said, "Mary Ann, did you participate in any clubs or sports while you were in school?"

Mary Ann said, "A few," without going into any detail.

Later when Mrs. Smith asked Doris the same question, Doris said, "Oh, yes. I used to belong to the skating club. I also belonged to the debate club for a while until I realized public speaking wasn't really my line. I was especially interested in a club for students planning to go into medical careers."

Which girl is Mrs. Smith getting to know better?

Mrs. Smith asks Mary Ann, "Do you plan to take more courses?"

Mary Ann: "I don't know."

Doris: "I really don't know yet. I can't afford any more schooling right now, and I am anxious to get some work experience first so I know what I really want. Someday I might like to be a social welfare nurse."

Which girl seems more interesting to Mrs. Smith?

Mrs. Smith asked each girl if they knew how to do different lab jobs, such as taking care of bacteria cultures, keeping records, and cleaning fragile equipment. Mary Ann answered each question with a simple "yes" or "no." Doris answered yes to some of the questions. To others she said, "Well, I haven't done that yet, but I've had some practice in doing . . . (and she would mention a similar task). I think I could learn it easily."

If you were Mrs. Smith, which girl would you hire?

Let's look at these interviews a little more closely. Mary Ann might do just as good a job as Doris. Mrs. Smith had very little to go on because Mary Ann didn't assert herself like Doris did. Perhaps Mary Ann had just as much talent and interest, perhaps she would have been a steadier worker than Doris, and maybe she would have stayed with the company longer. However, she responded so quietly and unassertively that Mrs. Smith didn't know what her potential was.

CASEBOOK

The following three stories show people in different work situations that called for self-assertiveness. As you read them, test your own responses. See if you know more about self-assertion now than you did at the beginning of this chapter.

CASE 1: THE PAPER CAPER.   Ricardo was the purchasing agent for a lighting fixture company in Houston. He was young, but very good at his job. Whenever he ordered supplies or materials, he made very careful cost and quality comparisons. He made it a practice to consult with people who had used the products.

One day, he ordered heat-sensitive paper for the photocopy machine. The machine being older, it was a little more bother to operate than more recent machines. The paper was the critical factor. If the paper was old, the reproduction would be poor.

Ricardo usually ordered paper for the machine once a month. The last shipment had to be sent back because the supplier sent old paper. Several days went by before a replacement shipment came. When the time came for the usual monthly order to arrive, Ricardo assumed that the same thing wouldn't happen again. But it did. Complaints streamed in from everyone who used the machine. Ricardo went down to check it out, and, sure enough, the paper was old again. He felt disgusted. He went back to his office and called the supplier.

"Oh, I'm really sorry," said Tom Burns, the supplier, after Ricardo had told him about the paper.

"I am, too," said Ricardo. "It really gets us bogged down when we can't use the photocopy machine. Both our design and sales departments depend on it."

Tom Burns said, "Well, I'll have our man pick up the paper and deliver a new batch on Friday."

Ricardo felt that the supplier knew he was young and was therefore not giving him the quality of service he would have given an older, more experienced buyer. He didn't say anything like that to Tom Burns, though. He insisted on getting the paper sooner.

"Look, we really can't wait that long. We need that paper today," said Ricardo.

"Well, can you send someone over to pick it up?" said the supplier.

"No, I'm sorry, our trucks are busy. And we feel it is up to you to bring it to us, since this is the second time we have been inconvenienced by you."

"I'll see what we can do, but I doubt that it will be before Wednesday," replied Tom.

Ricardo repeated, "I'm sorry, but we need the paper today. We are completely out, and we can't use the paper you sent us."

"That's a problem all right," agreed Tom, "but I just don't know if I can arrange to get more paper over there today or not."

"We will expect the paper today. Otherwise we will cancel the order and go to a different supplier," said Ricardo.

"That'll be hard to do. Everyone's low on this paper right now," came the answer. Ricardo knows better, because he has previously checked several other suppliers. He didn't make an issue of it, because he wanted to solve the immediate problem as soon and as efficiently as possible.

"Well, can we expect our paper today?" asked Ricardo.

"We'll give it a try," said Tom. The phone call ended.

The paper was delivered that afternoon. The immediate problem was solved. Then Ricardo could concentrate on a long-range solution. He began by getting himself lined up with another supplier. After that, he planned to discuss the possibility of getting a new machine with his boss.

NOTICE: Ricardo had to keep quietly insisting, repeating himself over and over again. "We need the paper. We need the paper." He could have told the supplier off, but then he might not have gotten the paper, and his main goal was to get the paper.

Ricardo didn't verbalize all his thoughts, such as, "You are taking advantage of me because I'm young and fairly new on the job. You are taking advantage of me because my name sounds foreign to you." These thoughts went through Ricardo's mind, but he knew they wouldn't be very useful put into words.

Ricardo used a threat he was prepared to go through with, since he had checked other suppliers beforehand. That put him in a better position to deal with the negligent supplier.

After the immediate crisis was over, Ricardo looked for ways to keep it from happening again.

CASE 2: MONEY MATTERS.   Everyone liked Tommy. He was always cheerful and sensitive to other people's problems. It felt good to be around him. However, Tommy was a bit careless with his money, so much so that he never had any in his pocket.

Jim worked in the customer relations office with Tommy. Almost every other day, Tommy asked Jim for coffee money. "Hey, old buddy, here I am without a dime for coffee again. Can I borrow one from you?"

Jim hated to say no because he liked Tommy. Besides, Tommy brought so much life to the place that buying his coffee seemed a small price to pay. Then Tommy began borrowing lunch money from him. He usually didn't remember to pay it back, either.

At last Jim decided things had gotten out of hand, and he knew he would have to do something about it. Jim couldn't afford to keep lending money without getting it back. Tension was quietly building up. Jim started to resent Tommy, and he didn't want to let that continue.

So one Friday morning Tommy said, "Hey, listen, pal, I'm broke and I want to take Jill out for tacos at noon. Can I borrow a few bucks? I'll be getting paid on Monday and I'll give it to you then."

This time Jim said, "I'm sorry, Tommy. I'm a little short myself today." He didn't lend Tommy the money.

But did Jim solve anything? Not really. He didn't tell Tommy how he felt. He didn't assert himself with Tommy. A week or so later the same old problem was back again.

This time Jim saw that he would have to be more honest and straightforward. When Tommy asked for money, Jim said, "Tommy, I can't afford to lend you any more money because you don't pay it back. It makes me feel bad when I say yes and give you the money even though I really don't want to. It also makes me feel bad to say no to you, but there's a good chance I'll never see my money again. I hope you will understand why I don't want to lend you any more money."

Tommy looked surprised, but he bounced back in a hurry. "I don't blame you," he said. "I'm not very good about paying it back."

Tommy was so nice about it that Jim had the urge to say, "Oh, well, it really doesn't matter. Here's the money." But he didn't do it. He realized that the situation might very well go back to what it had been.

NOTICE: It's sometimes very hard to be assertive with people you like or love. But, like Jim, you have to realize that it may be necessary if you want love or friendship to grow. Otherwise things are put on a false basis and little troubles become big troubles.

When Jim told Tommy he was a little short of money, he still didn't give Tommy any idea of how he felt about the situation. It often seems easier to make up an excuse rather than telling the person the truth. But it's not easier in the long run. The same problem will no doubt come up again.

You usually don't lose friends by being assertive in such situations as this story described. If you tell someone politely and calmly how you feel about a problem that concerns both of you, chances are you will come to an agreement or compromise. If the other person decides not to be friends anymore, the friendship may not have been a healthy one in the first place. If a person expects other people to completely give up or ignore their feelings or needs, the relationship may very well wither and die.

CASE 3: TOO MANY BOSSES. Sherry worked as a junior secretary in a big law firm. Several more-experienced legal secretaries handled the most demanding work including tasks given them by the senior partners of the firm. Sherry was assigned to handle the secretarial work for five of the young lawyers.

These five lawyers were new on the job and had little idea how much time each secretarial task took. All of them thought their work should have first priority. Sometimes Sherry had work in her typewriter and one of them would come into her office and ask her to stop what she was working on and do something for them. If she refused, they would be angry. If she agreed to do it, others would be angry.

At first Sherry thought she could please everyone, but she soon learned that there weren't enough hours in the working day to do so. If someone said a job was rush, she took his or her word for it and put it ahead of other work she already had on her desk. Then some people complained that their work wasn't getting done fast enough. Sherry tried to hurry. Her percentage of typing errors went up. She felt tense and pushed. Things went from bad to worse.

One day Sherry had lunch with Polly, one of the older secretaries. She ate her food in less than ten minutes and got up to leave the lunchroom. "What's your hurry?" asked Polly.

"I've got to get back to work," said Sherry. "I'm swamped."

"Yes, but this is your lunch hour," replied Polly. "You shouldn't spend it working. You need a break."

Sherry had gotten so tired and upset that she began to cry. "I just can't keep up," she told Polly.

"Wait a minute," said Polly. "I've seen your work. You have a lot to do, and yet you do a better job than a lot of new secretaries we've had. So what's the problem?"

Sherry described what had been happening. Putting it into words helped her understand it better. "I just don't know whose work to do first so I end up making mistakes and wasting a lot of time."

"Oh, I know all about that!" said Polly sympathetically. "People get awfully pushy if you let them. Sometimes they don't even realize it. Once when I had that problem here's what I did. I put an IN basket on my desk and explained what it was for. I told my bosses I would do the jobs in the order in which they came in. I marked each job as it was put in the basket. It worked very well."

"That sounds easy," said Sherry. "But it's hard to say no when someone comes rushing in and wants a job done right away. I'm afraid someone will get mad at me."

"They might when you're first setting up a system," said Polly. "But in the long run they'll understand it and get used to it. Right now they are used to pressuring you and they probably don't even know they're doing it. You can still make exceptions now and then. After you're here longer you'll have a better idea when to do so. Be sure you let the person know you are making an exception. If the same person keeps having emergencies, stop making exceptions."

Sherry decided to try Polly's idea. Everyone took it pretty well. Some people even kidded her about it a little. When problems came up she said something like, "I'm sorry I can't get to that right now, but I'll do it the first chance I get."

After a few weeks, people liked the new system much better than the old way. Only one lawyer was unpleasant about it, but the other lawyers got on his case and straightened him out.

NOTICE: Sherry got help from someone in the know. Although in her case it happened by chance, any of us could seek out a more experienced person to help us. With Polly's help, Sherry worked out a way of getting things done without so much confusion and stress. It paid off. If Sherry had not been self-assertive enough to try Polly's system, her reputation for being a good, fast worker might have suffered. Maybe her tension would have made her unpleasant to be around and caused even more problems. If things had not worked out so well, Sherry could have talked the problem over with her supervisor.

❋❋ Part Three

American Red Cross,
photo by Rocco Morabito

Occupational Safety and Health

CAUTION!
WORKING MAY BE HAZARDOUS TO YOUR HEALTH!

If Joe cried out for help, Irma didn't hear him. Looking up, she happened to see him slumped over his machine. His head and shirt were bloody. She called to him and received no answer. She ran to find the foreman. Other workers gathered around. One man covered Joe with a jacket. The foreman ran up and began calling out directions. He tied a tourniquet around Joe's left arm to stop the bleeding. Irma and the others saw with horror that four of Joe's fingers were lying on the other side of the press. Within minutes Joe had been rushed to the emergency room at St. Anthony's hospital. At first everyone was too stunned to think about Joe's future. Then little by little they began to realize what this accident would mean to Joe's life.

Jane worked in a chemical plant. She became pregnant, but had a miscarriage. After a short time off she returned to her old job. She became pregnant again, and again lost the child. Numerous tests were made by her doctor. She was even sent to a special clinic. It began to appear that a chemical used in a product her company made might be at fault. However, not enough scientific data had been gathered to prove this conclusively. Still Jane felt she had no choice but to quit her job because she and her husband wanted children.

Job-related accidents and diseases ruin many lives each year. Does it have to be that way? It depends on how much effort employers, employees, and safety officials are willing to put into getting at the root of occupational safety and health hazards and stopping them. Safety-engineered plants have shown dramatic reductions in serious accidents. Conscientious control of dangerous substances has also resulted in good control over certain occupational diseases.

Our first step will be to see what some of the major hazards are. Then we will look at some recent legislation designed to improve our nation's occupational safety and health record.

Chapter Seven

HAZARDS IN THE WORK ENVIRONMENT

Duo-Fast

DANGER FACTORS

When the same person kept having accidents, people used to say, "He's just an accident looking for a place to happen." That statement was partly meant to be funny, but behind it lay the belief that certain people are more likely than others to have accidents. Sometimes this is called being accident-prone.

Are some people really accident-prone? Several research studies at first concluded that this was so. Researchers noted that in the factories studied just a few people were involved in most of the accidents that happened. In other words, Mary turned her ankle one day. Another day she cut her finger. Still another day, she slipped on a wet floor and hurt her back. Meanwhile, nothing happened to Dick, Gerry, and Gene. It seemed as if people like Mary might actually be accident-prone. So these researchers decided to study people like Mary and see if they had similar personality characteristics that might help cause accidents. If so, perhaps these characteristics could be changed, or the behavior resulting from them could be modified.

However, when the researchers began studying workers with high accident rates, they couldn't identify any particular characteristics they all seemed to have in common. Furthermore, as time went on some subjects became accident-free while people who had been accident-free became accident-prone. As far as the researchers could tell, no one person is consistently accident-prone throughout his or her life. The studies suggested that almost all of us at one time or another are accidents looking for places to happen.

If accident-proneness doesn't cause accidents, then what does? Safety engineers have identified five major problem areas:

1. inadequate knowledge

2. insufficient skill

3. environmental hazards

4. improper habits and attitudes

5. unsafe behavior

Let's look at each of these in more detail.

INADEQUATE KNOWLEDGE

"What you don't know can kill you!" Severe words, but true. Until recently few of us were aware that lead, mercury, asbestos, silicone, rayon, and a multitude of other fairly common materials could cause disease or even death. Cases of chemical-related occupational illnesses have frequently been in the news, and we are becoming more conscious of the hazards.

Technology has advanced rapidly in our century. Fast and powerful equipment and machinery have been invented and new sources of energy have been discovered. Sometimes new knowledge is put into use before all of its effects are adequately understood on a practical level. A machine that was thought to be safe in design turns out not to be because some human factor was overlooked. Perhaps the designer took into consideration the time it takes a worker to do a certain operation, but then failed to realize that the worker couldn't work at that pace on a continuous basis. The machine could turn out to be a hazard. Nuclear energy might be another case in point. While scientists know how to set up nuclear plants with a good degree of safety, some problems in relation to the generation of nuclear power haven't been adequately solved.

What can workers do to protect themselves? First of all, they can understand that inadequate knowledge on *their* part is also hazardous. Everyone should know as much as possible about the machines and materials with which they work. Co-workers can give some tips and warnings, and employers are obligated to instruct workers when there is a clear and present danger.

Another important way to protect yourself is to take your own lack of knowledge seriously. Treat an unfamiliar substance as if it were dangerous until you find out more about it. Stay away from unfamiliar machinery and equipment until someone explains and demonstrates how to operate them.

You can also try to be a well-informed person. Watch for news items and documentaries on television that have to do with occupational accidents, work safety laws, new inventions and discoveries that could influence your work life. If you read a news magazine once a week, you will certainly run across articles on such subjects. For information on a specific health or safety problem which you feel you should know more about, you could check your public library.

INSUFFICIENT SKILL

John's little sister Doris was always bugging him to let her ride his bike. "No," he would keep saying. "You'll break your neck or wreck my bike or both." But one day she got on the bike anyway and found herself careening down the driveway and right out across the highway. She had no idea how to stop the bike and so she ran into a fence. That stopped her. She was bruised and scratched and had broken her arm. Even at that, her family felt very lucky when they considered what might have happened!

Doris was only seven at the time of her accident. She did not yet have enough experience with bikes to realize her danger. She had neither the strength nor the skill necessary to ride a large boy's bike safely. People much older than she have a similar problem. New workers as well as workers who have been on the job for a number of years sometimes try to perform tasks which are beyond the present level of their skills.

You can develop new skills with a minimum of risk to yourself and others. Safety experts often recommend these four steps:

1. Observe a skilled person who is safety-conscious perform the task.

2. Have the skilled person show you step-by-step how to do it.

3. Perform the task slowly while the skilled person watches.

4. Practice the task under supervision until you feel you can do it safely and efficiently.

ENVIRONMENTAL HAZARDS

It is unrealistic to believe that you will ever work in a completely safe place. A properly lighted and ventilated room with padded walls and sterilized air would probably be somewhat safe, but most of us wouldn't care to work in that kind of atmosphere!

The American National Standards Institute developed the following list of mechanical hazards. Are any of these present at your workplace?

Type of Hazard	Examples
Prime Movers	Fans, Pumps, Compressors, Blowers
Power Driven Machines	Saws, Drills, Meat Slicers, Lathes
Elevators	Passenger or Freight, Electric, Steam, Hydraulic, Hand-Operated
Hoisting apparatus	Jacks, Lifts, Cranes, Derricks
Conveyors	Belts, Chains, Pulleys, Sprockets

Boilers and Pressure Vessels	Piping System, Hot Water Heaters, Steam Boilers, Condensers
Vehicles Mechanical Power Transmission Systems	Motor Driven Pushcarts, Dollies, Trucks, Axles, Shafts, Bearings, Pulleys
Electrical Apparatus	Motors, Generators, Transformers, Lines, Lights
Hand Tools	Hammers, Knives, Files, Axes, Crowbars
Chemicals	Explosives, Vapors, Fumes, Corrosives
Highly Inflammable and Hot Substances	Lacquers, Gas, Oil, Plastic, Steam, Hot Water
Dusts	Explosives, Organic, Inorganic
Working Surfaces	Floors, Ramps, Stairs, Ladders
Radiation	Radium, Ultraviolet Rays, X-rays
Miscellaneous	Pits, Tanks, Windows, Shelves

Employers are placing more and more emphasis on minimizing the danger from the equipment and materials listed above. Despite their efforts you must use good judgment. Responsibility for a good health and safety program at work has to be shared by both the employers and the employees. If you are supposed to use goggles, safety shoes, hard hats, aprons, shields, gloves, leggings, etc., don't be without them. Respect all warning signs.

IMPROPER HABITS OR ATTITUDES

"Seat belts restrict my movement."

"I'm too hot with these blooming goggles on."

"I can't get the feel of the work with these heavy gloves on."

Attitudes such as these are based on a small element of truth. Some safety equipment isn't comfortable, at least not while you're getting used

C. William Horell

to it. Force yourself to develop good habits right from the beginning. Don't wait until after an accident happens.

"I could do this job a lot easier if that guard on the machine was removed."

"I don't need to reset that safety guard just for these last few items. I'll just let it go and reset it when I start a whole new batch."

"If I taped down this safety switch I wouldn't have to keep turning this machine off and on."

These attitudes all cancel out important things that have been done to insure your safety. Safety rules and equipment are developed using the best and newest knowledge about human capacities and limitations. You may at times be able to go beyond those limits. For example, you may be able to work safely without a guard on your machine some of the time. But making such exceptions for yourself can easily become a habit. Then you may make an exception on a day when you can't afford to. Perhaps you're tired or not as alert as usual. You've got the guard off. See what a vulnerable position you could get yourself into!

"I always follow the rules, so I'm sure nothing will happen to me."

No matter how careful you are, you still have to watch out for the careless worker who doesn't follow rules or take safety seriously. Just as in drivers' education most people learn about defensive driving, so you will have to learn to use some defensive tactics on the job. For example, if you are helping to repair an electrical connection you may run into a co-worker who thinks it is silly to turn the power off. Don't let such an attitude put you in danger. Check the current yourself to make sure you can do the job safely.

UNSAFE BEHAVIOR

All of the factors discussed so far—inadequate knowledge, insufficient skill, environmental hazards, improper attitudes and habits—can cause unsafe behavior. There are additional causes.

Everyone enjoys talking or kidding around once in a while. But some people pick the wrong time and place. Distracting others while they are performing potentially dangerous tasks could cause the loss of fingers or eyes or even worse injuries.

Emotional states also influence on-the-job safety. Beware of extremes. Studies have shown that workers who are extremely happy or high and those who are very depressed (low) run the greatest risk of accidents. You can, no doubt, see why. Depressed persons might be concentrating on personal problems rather than paying full attention to the work. The new father or the person who just won the sweepstakes might also find it hard to concentrate on the job at hand. An angry person could easily make a thoughtless and dangerous mistake. It is wise to wait until you are in control of your emotions before you perform tasks which involve a high degree of risk. Exercising self-control pays safety dividends.

You have probably already had plenty of advice about drugs and alcohol. In addition to all the usual hazards of substances that lessen your hold on reality or slow down your responses, you may do yourself grave harm on the job. You may be unable to react quickly or accurately enough in a dangerous situation. Or a routine job that would not be very dangerous for an alert worker could become hazardous if the worker could not concentrate properly or coordinate movements well. Please refer to the spiderweb photos. These resulted from a controlled scientific study. The webs show the effect of drugs on the spider's ability to spin a web.

Department of Mental Health Research Division Raleigh, N.C.

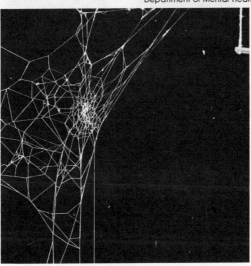

Looking back at the list of potential hazards, choose one that is present at your workplace. Make a warning sign or poster that you would display in the danger area if you were the supervisor.

C. William Horrell

THE ANCIENT ART OF SELF-DEFENSE

A body in good condition is one of the most valuable assets you can have. Good health is at the very heart of happiness and productivity. It colors your relations with others and your view of yourself. It helps determine your physical and mental stamina. Good health can mean the difference between merely existing and loving life.

What kind of health standards do you have? Answer the following questions on a sheet of paper and see if you are satisfied with the answers:

1. How many times in the last week did you eat a well-balanced meal?

2. How many days in the last week did you eat mainly hot dogs, hamburgers, french fries, and other fast foods?

3. List the sweets you ate yesterday.

4. How many nights in the last seven did you get at least seven hours of sleep?

5. Do you smoke cigarettes?

6. How many colds did you have during the past year?

7. Which of the following physical activities have you participated in during the last week?

a. jogging

b. taking a walk

c. dancing

d. swimming

e. weight lifting

f. exercise routines

g. bowling

h. team sport

8. How many days were you sick during the last month?

9. How many days during the last week would you say you felt "up"? How many "down"?

Finding Out for Yourself

Which health problems can you handle yourself and which do you need help with? A good book to help you answer these questions is

Take Care of Yourself:
A Consumer's Guide to Medical Care
by Donald M. Vickery and James F. Fries
(Addison/Wesley Publishing Co., 1976)

The authors, who are both medical doctors, feel that an individual can do a great deal to live a fuller, healthier life and to avoid high medical costs. They offer advice on finding a good doctor, avoiding medical fraud, practicing preventative medicine, stocking your medicine cabinet properly, etc. The last half of the book covers health problems ranging from appendicitis to acne, telling what you can do for yourself and when you should go for help.

Working Cooperatively

High blood pressure is a serious health problem in the United States. You can easily monitor your own blood pressure to make sure it stays in the safe normal range. The instrument used to take blood pressure is called a sphygmomanometer (sfig-mo-ma-NOM-ah-ter).

Several companies market kits for home use.

Have your school nurse or teacher demonstrate how to take someone's blood pressure. Working in pairs, practice taking each other's.

FIRST AID

American Red Cross.

photo by Rudolph Vetter

Have you ever wondered what you would do if someone in your home or workplace suffered a heart attack or stopped breathing? What would you do if someone at work broke an arm or leg? If you were the first to arrive at the scene of an accident and someone was bleeding profusely, would you know what first aid to administer? Would you know what *not* to do?

First aid experts generally say that the first thing to do in an emergency situation is to run to the telephone. Call the police or the fire department and state the problem as best you can and as briefly as you can. You may think you are wasting precious seconds since in the case of severe injuries or heart attacks there is so little time to prevent irreparable damage or death. If you don't summon help at once you may be unable to do so once you have started first aid procedures. If you are trying to get someone's heart going again or attempting to help them start breathing regularly you may tire out before anyone finds you and can assist you.

What you can do after that phone call depends on what kind of first aid training you have had. Would you feel insecure in an emergency situation where first aid was needed? If so, you could check with the American Red Cross office nearest you. Perhaps you will decide to enroll in a first aid class.

What Do You Think?

Sometimes untrained persons trying to give first aid can do more harm than good. Families have sued such people after the death of a loved one, claiming that the victim died as a result of the first aid rather than from the accident itself. Persons giving first aid are only trying to help. Does it seem fair that they should be sued?

Some states have "Good Samaritan" laws. In the Bible the Good Samaritan was the only person who would stop and help the man who had been robbed and beaten. The modern "Good Samaritan" laws protect people who provide help in an emergency situations. Under such laws, people administering first aid cannot be sued if they were following standard first aid procedures. This implies that such a person would have had some kind of first aid training. Does this seem like a good solution to the problem?

Working Cooperatively I

Make a life-sized cardboard dummy. Clothe it with all the safety equipment you can think of, making objects out of paper, cloth, or other available materials. These might include goggles, hard hat, mask, non-skid shoes, knee guards, etc.

Working Cooperatively II

Choose one of the following tasks and prepare a short presentation that will emphasis some of the safety factors connected with it. Write your name and the task you have chosen on a piece of paper and give it to your teacher. Be ready to give the class clear instructions on how to do the task safely. If possible, demonstrate the task as you tell about it.

1. jogging

2. putting in a new electric light switch

3. changing a worn-out cord on an iron

4. putting on eye make-up

5. using a Bunsen burner

6. changing the bit on an electric drill

7. lifting a heavy object from the floor to a table

8. cleaning motorcycle parts with carbon tetrachloride

9. jacking up a car to change a tire

10. loading a staple gun

Chapter Check

1. Give five examples of occupational accidents.

2. What is an occupational disease?

3. Name five main factors that cause occupational accidents.

4. List some of the mechanical hazards that are present in many work places.

5. What steps would you follow if you had to teach a new worker a dangerous task?

6. What are some of the things you can do to keep yourself in top physical condition?

Match the following words or phrases with their definitions:

1. hazard   a. poisonous material

2. resuscitation   b. breathe in

3. Good Samaritan Laws   c. substance that can chemically burn

4. toxic substance   d. danger

5. inhale   e. getting someone who has stopped breathing to breathe again

6. caustic   f. has the possibility of being dangerous

7. potentially dangerous   g. protection for those who give first aid

❋ Chapter Eight ❋

THE
OCCUPATIONAL
SAFETY
AND
HEALTH ACT

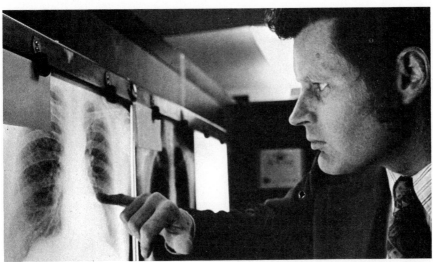

National Institute for Occupational Safety and Health

THE PURPOSE OF THE ACT

On April 28, 1971, a law went into effect that protects more than 60 million workers in over 5 million workplaces: The Occupational Safety and Health Act of 1970. It is designed "to assure so far as possible every man and woman in the nation safe and healthful working conditions and to preserve our human resources."

The Occupational Safety and Health Act provided for the setting up of the Occupational Safety and Health Administration under the jurisdiction of the U.S. Department of Labor. From now on we will refer to this agency as OSHA, and you will see it referred to that way in newspapers and magazines as well.

OSHA is responsible for determining safety and health standards for various kinds of workplaces. It also enforces these standards. OSHA has ten regional offices and more than 100 smaller field offices. These offices schedule and conduct inspections. If safety and/or health violations are found, citations are issued. (A *citation* is a notice that a company is in violation of the law.) The company is told what the penalties will be if it doesn't remedy the situation within a given amount of time. If the company doesn't comply, OSHA legal personnel can begin action against it in federal court.

The Occupational Safety and Health Act also established the National Institute for Occupational Safety and Health (NIOSH). Working under the U.S. Department of Health, Education, and Welfare, NIOSH conducts research on various phases of occupational health and safety. Rules and enforcement aren't enough. We need new knowledge as well. NIOSH helps provide it.

What Do You Think?

In time of war, governments have often been accused of "using people as cannon fodder." What do you think the expression means?

Industry has sometimes been accused of using workers in a similar manner. That is, if workers got sick or died, so what? There were always more people to fill up the ranks. If people were injured on the job, there were always other people with which to replace them. How would such an attitude on the part of an owner or employer affect the safety and health practices in a workplace? Would such employers be likely to go out of their way to provide a safe and healthful environment?

Not all owners or employers were or are negligent and hard-hearted. Many have tried to provide good, safe, and even beautiful working environments for their employees.

Other employers have not done so. They have put profits before people and have refused to take the necessary measures to protect employees. If this were not true, the creation of OSHA would not have been necessary.

How much of a role do you think the government should play in maintaining safety and health standards in workplaces? That's a very complex question. Rather than trying to answer it now, think about it as you move through this chapter.

QUESTIONS AND ANSWERS ABOUT OSHA

Q. Who is protected by the Occupational Safety and Health Act?

A. All people who work in private industry, except for those in special fields already covered by other laws before this Act was passed (e.g., mining and atomic energy). Government employees are also protected by other laws, so they do not come under the jurisdiction of the Occupational Safety and Health Act, either.

Q. Will my workplace be inspected by OSHA?

A. It depends. At this time not all workplaces can be inspected on a regular basis. OSHA has had to set priorities. Industries with high injury and illness rates are inspected more often than those with low rates. Industries involving potentially harmful substances such as asbestos and lead are inspected more frequently. Imminent danger situations are also high priority.

Q. What is an imminent danger situation?

A. An imminent danger situation is one in which some hazard is present that could at any time cause injury, disease, or death. The hazard is the result of neglect. For instance, some electrical wires are so worn that the insulation on them is gone. People are working nearby on concrete floors that are sometimes wet. Or a company is supposed to have a dampening system so that a certain kind of chemical dust is kept from floating about and getting into the ventilation system. The system has malfunctioned on several occasions, but only a half-hearted attempt is ever made to keep it in working order. In such cases a regular OSHA inspection may not be scheduled. But if OSHA is notified, that workplace will go on the high priority list and OSHA officials will inspect it as soon as possible.

Q. How will I know what health and safety standards apply to my workplace?

A. Your employer should have copies of the OSHA standards that apply to your workplace. You can also write to the OSHA office nearest you, stating your line of work and asking them to help you obtain a copy of the applicable standards.

Q. Can OSHA answer my questions about the possible dangers of various materials?

A. The National Institute for Occupational Safety and Health (NIOSH) takes care of this. See the sample request form included. You can get copies of these forms by writing to:

> The National Institute for Occupational Safety and Health
> Hazard Evaluation Services Branch
> U.S. Department of Health, Education, and Welfare
> Cincinnati, Ohio 45202

Q. May I register a complaint if I feel that a standard is being violated at my workplace?

A. Yes. If possible, discuss the situation with your supervisor first. If that doesn't help, make a written request for an inspection and send it to the OSHA office nearest you. As a protection for you, your name may be withheld from your employer so that you won't suffer any consequences for drawing attention to the problem.

Q. Are there any rules for making requests for inspection?

A. Such a request must be made in writing. You may not do it by telephone. The most important rule is that you must be exact and specific. You must zero in on exactly what the problem is and not just make a general statement that conditions are lousy. You must name the hazard.

Q. Will I ever hear what happens if I request an inspection?

A. Yes. You will be advised of what OSHA plans to do about your complaint. It may decide that your case isn't strong enough or that it is not a high priority case. If OSHA decides not to make an inspection, you can request a review of that decision. You would, of course, want to be sure of your ground. If your workplace is inspected and your employer receives a citation saying that he is in violation, your employer is required to post that citation in the danger area or where workers threatened by the hazard will see it.

Q. If I have a bright idea regarding a standard, would OSHA be interested in hearing about it?

A. Yes. All workers are welcome to submit information, comments, and suggestions to OSHA in writing.

REGIONAL OSHA OFFICES

OSHA REGION I
18 Oliver Street
Boston, MA 02110

OSHA REGION II
Room 3445, 1 Astor Plaza
1515 Broadway
New York, NY 10036

OSHA REGION III
15220 Gateway Center
3535 Market Street
Philadelphia, PA 19104

OSHA REGION IV
1375 Peachtree Street, N.E.
Suite 587
Atlanta, GA 30309

OSHA REGION V
300 South Wacker Drive
Room 1201
Chicago, IL 60606

OSHA REGION VI
Texaco Bldg., 7th Floor
1512 Commerce Street
Dallas, TX 75201

OSHA REGION VII
911 Walnut Street, Room 3000
Kansas City, MO 64106

OSHA REGION VIII
Room 15010 Federal Bldg.
1961 Stout Street
Denver, CO 80202

OSHA REGION IX
Box 36017
450 Golden Gate Avenue
San Francisco, CA 94102

OSHA REGION X
Smith Tower Bldg., Room 1808
506 Second Avenue
Seattle, WA 98104

U.S. DEPARTMENT OF HEALTH, EDUCATION, AND WELFARE
NATIONAL INSTITUTE FOR OCCUPATIONAL SAFETY AND HEALTH

REQUEST FOR HEALTH HAZARD EVALUATION

This form is provided to assist in registering a request for a health hazard evaluation with the U.S.
Department of Health, Education, and Welfare as provided in Section 20(a)(6) of the Occupational
Safety and Health Act of 1970 and 42 CFR Part 85. (See Statement of Authority on Reverse Side.)
*The provisions of this section provide for evaluation of health hazards resulting from exposure to
chemical substances only: Physical agents (noise, heat, etc.) and safety are not covered by this
section.*

The

HEALTH HAZARD EVALUATION PROGRAM

of the

NATIONAL INSTITUTE FOR OCCUPATIONAL SAFETY AND HEALTH

U. S. DEPARTMENT OF HEALTH, EDUCATION, AND WELFARE
Public Health Service
Center for Disease Control
National Institute for Occupational Safety and Health

LAWS THAT HELP THE SICK OR INJURED WORKER

The laws we will be discussing here do not actually come under the Occupational Safety and Health Act. We are putting them here in case you have wondered, "Yes, but what happens if, in spite of all these precautions, I still have a serious accident?"

Social Security is usually thought of as a way of providing income for retired people, but there are other phases of the program. If you are permanently disabled, you may receive social security benefits. To be eligible, workers must have worked 20 quarters out of the last 40. (We'll explain this in detail in the chapter on social security, Chapter 29.) If a worker is young and hasn't had time to work that many quarters, other rules apply. Social security laws are often updated and procedures are changed, so it is best to check with your local social security office if you encounter a problem. Many people don't know what benefits they are entitled to receive, so they become totally dependent on their families.

Almost every state has its own labor laws, including laws covering workman's compensation. While federal laws made in Washington, D.C., can cover many things, they cannot take care of all the different needs of different workers in different states. Workers' needs in North Dakota may be quite different from workers' needs in South Carolina!

The idea that employers have responsiblity for injuries which occur at their places of business was not always accepted. Even up into this century injured workers had to prove that the company was at fault, but this was difficult to do. Many workers could not afford lawyers. Even when cases got to court, the employer usually won. The reasons given were that the employer had not been negligent, that the injured person or other employees had contributed to the accident, that the person had been aware of the hazards and had agreed to work there anyway. Death and disabling injuries came to be accepted as risks one had to take on the job.

For many years, owners and employers were strong enough politically to keep workman's compensation laws from being passed. Finally in 1911, the first workman's compensation law was passed in New Jersey. It was soon tested in the courts and declared constitutional. After that, one state after another began passing such laws. These state laws differ in detail, but they all share one basic premise: workers injured on the job do not have to prove their case in court. They can receive all or some of the benefits below:

1. Payment of a major part of the medical expense.

2. Subsistence income if unable to work.

3. Continuing payments for permanent disabilities either for a specified amount of time or for as long as necessary.

4. Payment to dependents (spouses and children) if death results from a work-related injury.

These various state laws helped focus much more attention on job safety. Because employers were held financially responsible for on-the-job injuries, they began to feel the truth of the idea that safety pays.

There is a chance that some workers in your state are not covered by workman's compensation laws. All young people entering the work force should find out from their state department of labor what the workman's compensation laws cover and what benefits are available.

Chapter Check

1. Which of the ten regional OSHA offices is located nearest you? For what reasons might you want to contact it?

2. Give an example of a general complaint. Give an example of a specific complaint. Which is more effective?

3. Explain what a citation is. What is the main reason an employer is required to post a citation he receives?

4. How can an employer or employee find out whether or not the company is in violation of OSHA standards?

5. What kinds of workplaces have high priority when it comes to OSHA inspection scheduling?

6. What do the initials NIOSH stand for? Why might you want to contact NIOSH?

7. Can an employer fire you for reporting a violation of OSHA standards? How are you protected?

8. What is the purpose of state workman's compensation laws?

 # Part Four

C. William Horrell

Skills You Will Need

DOES EDUCATION PAY?

A 1976 study of poverty in the United States was described in *U.S. News and World Report* (November 8, 1976, p. 57-58). Researchers found that among heads of households over 25 years of age those with more education were better off financially than those with less education. In the following figures notice how the percentage of poor people goes down as the years of education go up!

1 to 8 years of schooling	41.8% were poor
9 to 11 years	24.3% were poor
high school diploma	23.7% were poor
college, 1 year or more	10.25% were poor

People with very little education are often not qualified for interesting jobs that pay well. They end up with jobs nobody wants, jobs that are monotonous and pay poor wages. Moreover, these low-level jobs are being phased out. Machines are doing more and more of them. In one sense, that's all to the good. It keeps human beings from doing heavy or meaningless tasks. But where does it leave the person with no job skills and no special knowledge or training?

Education gives people more choices, more options. It's easier for an educated person to find out about new occupations and to keep up with what's going on in the world of work. It's easier for them to write resumes and application letters. If they are trained for one kind of work, they usually find it easier to re-train for a related kind of work that offers more opportunity.

A few other factors also seem to be indirectly involved. More research must be done before facts can be established, but right now it appears that less educated people tend to have larger families. So here's a person doomed to a low income job with more mouths to feed than someone who is better educated and has a higher-paying job. Not only that, but the divorce and separation rate among low income families is high. When a person can't get a good job, supporting a large family is so hard that it creates fighting, tension, and discouragement. Statistics show that the break-up of a home quite often leads to poverty, especially for women left alone with responsibility for supporting a family.

How valuable is a high school diploma? It depends on what kind of education is behind it. In any case, it's a good piece of paper to have in the world of today. It can open some doors for you. A high school diploma means that you have mastered certain basic skills. The more you know and the more you are able to do, the better chance you have to control your own life.

Do you feel that your education up to this point has not been everything it should have been? Many people feel that way. It doesn't do much good to look back and figure out whose fault it is or to say, "If only. . ." Look ahead and try to take over the responsibility for your own education. Be ready to accept suggestions and advice from others, but in the end, decide what *you* think you need to know. Once you have gotten that far, you will have to plan steps that will help you get the knowledge you want. Take advantage of whatever your school has to offer, but remember that not all education takes place in schools.

What Do You Think?

A civil service employment office sends out a bulletin listing available jobs. One of the positions is described as follows:

Building Service Worker I   Minimum salary is $4.28 per hour.
There are no formal requirements for this position.

"No formal requirements" means you don't have to have any special skills or training to apply for this job. Sound good? Yes, but here's the rest of the ad:

At present time, there are approximately 700 candidates for this position.

What do you think of those odds? You could be the lucky one. But if you were at a race track, would you bet against such odds?

❧ Chapter Nine ❧

FACTS ON
THE LOOSE

C. William Horrell

FINDING OUT HOW TO FIND OUT

Living in the 20th century, we could go to school all of our lives and
still not learn a fraction of what there is to know. Over the centuries, and
especially during the last two centuries, man has made a great many discoveries, developed complex systems of thought, and accumulated a vast
store of facts. It's an overwhelming situation for the individual. What facts
are really important to learn? What knowledge is the most valuable?

Most of us don't think about it much, but the first facts we master are usually facts which have to do with survival. In addition to these basic facts we may desire to know things which would improve or enrich our daily lives. We try to find out as much as possible about the things we are really interested in. And sometimes facts are interesting in themselves, even when they have no practical or immediate use.

How many facts can you carry around in your head? Quite a few—but never enough. This chapter will show you what you can do about it. The first step is to realize that it is much more important to learn *how to find out* what you want to know than it is to try to become a walking encyclopedia.

People are a valuable information resource which we often overlook. If you wanted to learn how to use a certain tool or what a certain word means you could go to a person who might know. How do you feel about showing someone else how to do something you are good at? Most of us really like the feeling. The persons you ask for help will very likely be pleased to share their knowledge with you. People can sometimes show you tricks of the trade or give you problem-solving ideas that would be hard to find in books.

Organizations and agencies can also help you answer questions. Someday you may need legal help or you may want to find out what your rights are. There might be a legal aid society in your community. The need for help with a drug problem or venereal disease may arise. County Health Departments have trained workers to help in these areas. You may want to learn how to play tennis or soccer. Try your city or neighborhood park. Most of these organizations or agencies are listed in the telephone book. If you can't find what you want, the clerk at the city hall or county courthouse may be able to direct you. Some types of services may not be available in smaller cities or rural areas. In such cases, you could ask your public librarian to help you find the address of the agency.

Working Cooperatively

A neighborhood in a big city set up an information center. One woman did most of the work at first. She kept a file on people who had certain kinds of information or skills. Maybe they could speak a foreign language or fix stock cars. An advertisement was put in the community newspaper, asking people to call the information center if they had a special skill or if they needed to get in touch with someone else who had a special skill. After a few months, the center had more than 250 names on file representing quite a number of skills. A group of six volunteers was kept busy answering phone calls and helping people find each other.

Your class can set up an information sharing system. The system that follows is very simple and should give you a beginning idea of how computer coding and sorting works. You will need a one-hole punch, 4″ × 6″ file cards, scissors, and pens.

First, study Sample Card 1. Then, as a group, decide what items you want to include on your cards. The holes from 1 through 10 stand for special interests, such as 1-music, 2-sports, 3-cars, 4-cooking, etc. (Your class doesn't have to use these specific categories, but everyone has to use the categories the class decides upon.) Down the left side the holes could indicate different types of cooperative programs. Down the right side might be favorite subjects, favorite foods, or another group of items the class agrees to use.

Now have one person mark off one card according to the sample in your book. Have that person punch holes where the circles are. Next, pass that sample card around so that everyone can use it as a pattern for punching a card. (This is important so that when the cards are stacked in a pile the holes in them will be uniform.)

Meanwhile, have two people draw a large card on the blackboard, using the categories the class has decided upon. Each person can then transfer the details onto a card. Now everyone should have a card with their name on it and holes punched around the sides and top. What those holes stand for should be clearly indicated on the card.

Now look at Sample Card 2 in your book. With your scissors cut little wedges into each hole that applies to you. For example, if you like to cook you will cut a wedge up to that punched hole. If geography is your favorite subject you will cut a wedge up to that punched hole.

After everyone is finished, place all the cards in a pile, facing the same way. If you want to quickly find out who in your class is in Distributive Education, stick a spindle or screwdriver into the hole beside "DE." Shake the cards. The cards of those who are in "DE" will have wedges cut at these holes and their cards will fall out of the pile. The cards of those who are not in "DE" will stay on the spindle.

If you wanted to find out who likes to build things you would stick the spindle through that hole, shake, and see which cards fall out.

We have used this information retrieval system more or less for fun, and it may have helped you find out more about some of the members of your class. Such systems have much wider and more complex application in industry, government, and many other fields. When they are used on a massive scale, many of the operations you did by hand would be done by machine.

	1	2	3	4	5	6	7	8	9	10	

SAMPLE CARD ONE

SAMPLE CARD TWO

	1	2	3	4	5	6	7	8	9	10	
	Office Occupations			1 Music				Math			
	Distributive Educ.			2 Sports				Science			
	Home Ec. Related			3 Travel				Art			
	Manufacturing			4 Cars				Shop			
	Personal Services			5 Dancing				Communications			
	Inter-Related			6 Cooking				Music			

4 Cars
5 Dancing
6 Cooking
7 Building Things
8 Sewing
9 Movies & Theater
10 Stamp & Coin Collecting

THE PUBLIC LIBRARY
AS AN INFORMATION RETRIEVAL SYSTEM

You can find out many things by watching TV and movies, especially if you choose carefully what you watch. The trouble is that TV can't help you when you want to know a certain fact right now. It can't respond to your needs on an individual basis. For example, you might watch a debate between two presidential candidates. Suppose that both candidates had previously been in the United States Senate. You want to know how each of them voted on civil rights issues. It could happen that the program you are watching would give some background information including such facts. But it is also likely that this would not be the case. If you really want to know, you'll have to try another source.

How about the public library? It's full of books, and books can often fulfill your particular information needs. (Besides, you are or will soon be paying taxes to help support the public library, so why not get some use out of it!) Let's look at a few of the tools in the library.

THE CARD CATALOG.   The card catalog is the key to the library. It lists all the books the library owns by title, author, and subject. The cards in the card catalog have numbers in the upper lefthand corner. The number on each card is known as the call number. If you want to find a certain book, look under the author's name. If you want to find a certain subject, look under it in the card catalog. Once you have spotted a book you want in the card catalog, copy down the call number. That number corresponds to the number on the spine of the book and will help you find it on the shelf. Can't find what you want? Ask the librarian, who is there to help you.

THE DEWEY DECIMAL SYSTEM.   If books were stacked on the shelves any old way, you'd have a rough time finding what you want. Instead, the books are organized into categories, and each category is given a number.

Fiction books are in one large category, and are usually arranged on the shelf alphabetically according to the author's last name. This category includes science fiction, romance, westerns, mysteries, historical novels, and many other kinds of stories.

The following numbers are the numbers given to the categories of non-fiction (factual) books:

000-099	General works (encyclopedias, etc.)		
100-199	Philosophy and Psychology		
200-299	Religion	600-699	Applied Science, and Technology
300-399	Social Sciences	700-799	The Arts
400-499	Languages	800-899	Literature
500-599	Pure Science	900-999	History, Geography, and Biography

This way of organizing books is called the *Dewey Decimal System* after the man who invented it, Melvil Dewey. There are other systems, too, but this is the most popular.

MAGAZINE AND NEWSPAPER RACK.   Most of us can't afford to buy every magazine we'd like to look at or read. The library can help here, too. You'll probably find such magazines as *Redbook, Ebony, Hot Rod, Vogue, Sailing, Time, Newsweek,* etc. *Toad Claw?* Probably not.

THE REFERENCE SHELVES.   These shelves are reserved for books that can help you find facts fast. In many libraries these books cannot be checked out but must be used there. The reason for this is to make sure that library users have access to these books when they need them rather than having to wait a week or two until someone else returns them. You will find dictionaries and encyclopedias, medical books, sports' records, fact books, travel guides, how-to manuals, etc.

Checkpoint

Below is a list of reference books. Your public library may not have these exact books, but it will have similar ones. Following the list of books is a series of twelve problems. Which book would you use to solve each of the problems?

Books
a. Scott Standard Postage Stamp Catalog
b. The Toll-Free Digest: A Directory of over 14,700 Toll-Free Telephone Numbers
c. World Almanac and Book of Facts
d. Ulrich's International Periodicals Directory
e. Dictionary of Scientific and Technical Terms
f. Auto Repair Manual
g. Congressional Quarterly's Washington Information Directory
h. Book of Etiquette and Good Manners
i. Famous First Facts
j. Consumer Complaint Guide
k. Comparative Guide to Two-Year Colleges and Career Programs
l. Baseball Encyclopedia

Problems
1. Melissa wants to subscribe to Popular Mechanics. Her friend tells her it is no longer being published. Melissa checks in _____ and finds it is still being printed. She also finds an address to write to.
2. John is curious about how many American soldiers died in World War I compared to the number who died in World War II. Where does he look? _____.
3. Greg collects stamps. He wants to know what an old stamp from Brazil is worth. He looks in _____.
4. Pete and Sally want to make a motel reservation in Florida. They would prefer to do it by phone, so they look in _____.
5. Renee looked up the word "ionization" in a regular dictionary. The definition wasn't exact enough, so she looked in another kind of dictionary. Which one? _____.
6. Shelly and her boyfriend are going to try to clean the spark-plugs in her car. They get a manual from the library to help them. It is called _____.
7. Maurice is concerned about the right-to-work law. He wants to write his senator

about one aspect of it. He can find out the name of his senator by looking in _____.

8. Dale bought a power tool that turned out to be faulty. He took it back to the store, and they wouldn't do anything about it. They didn't think he would do anything about it. He went to the library and found the address of the Better Business Bureau, as well as the addresses of several consumer protection agencies. Where did he find these addresses? _____.

9. Earl and Mary Ann are planning to be married. They want a small but formal wedding. Mary Ann wants to do everything just right. She consults _____.

10. When was the first babysitters' insurance policy issued? (For this and other fascinating first facts you could look in _____.)

11. Tim bet Arthur that Stan Musial hit more home runs than Jackie Robinson. They went to the library to check. They looked in _____.

12. Randy is thinking about enrolling in a junior college with an emphasis on vocational education. He pages through _____.

Working Cooperatively

Your telephone book is also a valuable resource. Round up as many phone books as you can for this activity. Find someone you could call in each of the following situations:

1. You bought your girlfriend (boyfriend) an identification bracelet. Now you want to have it engraved with both of your names. If you look in the phone book and can't find anything under *Engravers,* what else could you look under?

2. The child upstairs has accidentally swallowed some cleaning fluid. His mother comes rushing down to your apartment for help. You get out the phone book. Where do you look? Whom do you call?

3. Whom do you call to find out the airmail rate to Canada?

4. You need a new muffler for your car and want to get the best deal you can.

5. You need a tow truck to pull your car out of a ditch.

6. You want to register to vote and don't know what office to go to.

7. You have to meet someone at the airport and want to find out if the plane is on time.

JUDGING WHAT YOU READ OR HEAR

You know that you cannot believe everything you read or hear. Think back to the last political campaign. Was everything that was said on both sides actually true? Ads in magazines and on TV make a lot of big claims for products. Can all these claims be proven?

People can be manipulated by books, magazines, teachers, politicians, friends, TV, and movies. To manipulate means to manage the facts in such a way that people are led to believe or accept an idea, product, or theory. The manipulators often exclude facts that don't enhance what is being said. Facts may be misquoted or used out of context. Manipulation also involves appealing to people's sense of pride or worth or their wish to be popular or good-looking. There are many manipulative techniques, and you can learn to recognize them. Then you will be better equipped to evaluate the truth of what you see or hear.

One problem is that many of us tend to believe what we want to believe. A person who is a Republican probably thinks the Democratic candidate told more lies than the Republican candidate. A Democrat would tend to think just the opposite.

Scientists studying this question of whether or not we tend to believe what we want to believe did some interesting research. They questioned fans who had gone to a college football game in which the opposing teams were bitter rivals and traditional enemies. These fans were shown replays of the game and asked which team they saw commit more fouls. For the most part, fans from each school thought their team had played a good, clean game compared to the game the other team had played. Very few of the spectators gave an objective judgment of the situation.

Sometimes we see, hear, or think what we expect to see, hear or think. Here's an example of such a situation:

> The 11th president of the United States was
> James Polk, pronounced P-O-K-E.
> Another word for people is folk,
> pronounced F-O-K-E.

The white of an egg is the _____.

Did you think Y-O-L-K? See how easy it is to slip into expecting something to be a certain way and therefore reading, seeing, or hearing it that way?

A manipulator takes advantage of the tendencies people have to believe what they want to believe and to see and hear what they expect to see and hear. You can protect yourself by being objective. Try to take an alert and questioning attitude.

Some of the techniques used by manipulators are discussed in Chapter 25. You may want to refer to them now.

Working Cooperatively

Sometimes in a group discussion one person makes a case for the unpopular side of the question. Such a person is often called the devil's advocate.

Suppose your American government class is debating the question, "Should the draft system for the armed services be resumed?" Most of the class argues against resuming the draft.

Then one person, Dennis, raises his hand and argues that the draft should be resumed. He becomes the devil's advocate. He chooses the wrong or unpopular side of the question and gives some sensible reasons for reinstating the draft.

What purpose does a devil's advocate serve? Dennis may not actually be in favor of resuming the draft. He wants to shake people up a little and make them think more carefully about the position they have taken. He's really saying, "Wait a minute. It's not as simple as that. Look at all these other factors."

Look at the issues below and decide which one you would like to discuss as a class.

1. Should women in the army be assigned to combat duty?

2. Should people serving prison terms for first degree murder be allowed parole?

3. Should apartment owners be allowed to refuse to rent to families with children?

Give everyone a day to think about the issue the class has chosen. Then have each person write a pro (for) or con (against) statement one sentence long on a slip of paper.

Choose one person to read the statements out loud. Did most of the people in the class feel the same way about the question? If so, ask three people to be devil's advocates.

Chapter Check

1. Name at least three good sources of information that are easily available to most people.

2. Library Know-how:
   a. What is the card catalog used for?
   b. Why do libraries arrange the books according to a system such as the Dewey Decimal System?
   c. How are books of fiction arranged?
   d. What kind of books will you find on the reference shelf?

3. What does the word *manipulation* mean?

4. What is a devil's advocate?

❀ Chapter Ten ❀

COMMUNICATING

Daryl Littlefield

VERBAL AND NON-VERBAL

Human beings have many ways of communicating with each other.
The first way most of us think of is speech. People also have non-verbal
ways to communicate, such as facial expressions, posture, touching,
kissing, or smacking someone. Sometimes verbal and non-verbal communication are used at the same time. Your face as well as your words tell
others that you are happy, angry, afraid, or bored.

In modern times, people use mass media to communicate. The word *media* is the plural of the word *medium.* Medium often means "in the middle of" or "in between." A substance or object through which a message passes is a medium; that is, it goes between the communicating parties. For example, television conveys the message of a newscaster, a president, a musician, or an actor to the audience. The message passes through it.

Working Cooperatively

In addition to television, can you think of at least five other media? Divide into groups of four or five and have each group make a media collage.

Some of you will have seen or even made collages before. A collage is a design made up of appropriate bits and pieces of materials pasted on a background. Some pieces stand out from the background to give a three-dimensional effect. When artists make collages they use different kinds of paper, various fabrics, labels, dried flowers, all kinds of things. For your collages, try to get items that suggest the different media. You could use news clippings, pictures of movie stars and rock singers, book jackets if you can get them, T.V. program schedules, or an old roll of film looped in an interesting manner and attached to the background.

What Do You Think?

Looking back on your life so far, from which media do you think you have learned the most? Why? What are some of the features of the electronic media (television, movies, stereo, etc.) that you especially like?

Checkpoint

Keep a TV journal for one week. Each morning when you come to class record the shows you watched the night before. Your journal might be set up something like this:

Program		
Time Slot _____		
Type of Program _____		Liked _____
Don't Watch Regularly _____ Watch Regularly _____		Didn't Like _____

When a week is up, compare notes with other members of your class.

Which five shows did most of the class watch?

What categories did these shows fall into?

Were they detective, comedy, soap opera, talk shows, variety, news, other?

Did anyone watch a program nobody else watched?

Discuss some of the characteristics of a good show. It would be best to talk about one kind of show at a time. For instance, what makes a good news show? a good talk show? variety show? soap opera?

THE PRINTED WORD

Is reading going out of date? Sometimes that appears to be the case. Statistics show that many people now rely more heavily on television and movies for information and entertainment than they do on the printed word. Studies also show that many Americans don't know how to read very well.

Mutual of Omaha

Yet few people would say that reading and writing are no longer necessary. The more ways people have of getting information, the better. For example, people who like car racing might enjoy watching the Indianapolis 500 on television. But suppose they want to know who the winners for the last five years were. They may have to look it up in a sports encyclopedia or almanac. Or if they wanted to know more about a certain Ferrari engine, they'd have to consult a technical book on engines. They would be extremely limited if they had to rely solely on television for the information they wanted.

Young people entering the world of work still need basic communication skills. The person who tries to tell you that reading isn't very important is not doing you a favor. Here's a true story that will show you why.

A cooperative education student got a good job as an auto mechanic. Several months later he was out of work. The teacher-coordinator who had helped him get the job was very concerned. She called the employer and asked what had happened.

"Well," said the employer, "Brian was the best mechanic I ever had. But he couldn't read the orders for servicing each car. He couldn't order supplies. We are so busy that no one could spend time giving him verbal directions. Several times he fixed things on people's cars that they didn't ask to have fixed, and we had to foot the bill. I'm really sorry to lose him, but I need someone who can read."

Do you think that was fair? What would you have done if you had been the employer? What would you have done if you had been Brian? Do you agree that everyone needs some basic language skills?

You don't have to be a speed reader. When you apply for a job, no one is going to ask you how many words you can read a minute. No one is going to give you a reading comprehension test. From what we have seen of the world of work, however, we would be putting you on if we tried to say that reading doesn't matter. Executives, when asked to list the qualifications they most desire in their employees, often put the ability to get along with others first, the skills to do a good job second, and communication skills third. Reading and writing are extremely important when it comes to communication. But do you also see that people with these skills might be better at getting along with others and doing a good job? They will probably think more highly of themselves which often makes it easier for them to work with others. They also tend to be their own teachers, picking up skills on their own.

What Do You Think?

Herbert Kohl, in his book *Reading, How To,* gives another important reason why people should have at least some basic language skills. He says, "It is possible that through the development of control over language, people can come to understand their own capacity to free themselves."

What do you think he means?

CAN PEOPLE TEACH THEMSELVES TO READ?

Yes! Many people have done so, and under very bad conditions. Some time ago the following true story appeared in a magazine.

An unmarried man abandoned his pregnant girlfriend. The woman came from a very conservative family. She knew her folks would be angry and humiliated by this situation, so she didn't mention a word of it to them. She went away for a while, gave birth to the child, then came home again. What did she do with the baby? While she was in the hospital a supposedly reputable person told her that she could put the baby in an institution where it would have good care for a certain number of dollars a month. The woman was in such a panic that she agreed to this arrangement. She didn't try to find out much about the institution. She just assumed it was an orphanage, but in reality it was a home for severely retarded children. This perfectly normal child had no playmates who were not retarded. He got no formal schooling and very little attention. Does he seem like a likely candidate for learning how to read?

The boy grew up. When he was in his late teens, some psychologists were sent by the state accreditation board to evaluate the institution. Numerous violations of the code for running such a place were found, and the people operating it were told they would be closed down unless they could come up to the standards in a specified amount of time. But meanwhile one of the psychologists noticed this young man taking a keen interest in the work of the evaluation team. The psychologist decided to test him. He got definite clues that this person was not retarded. On return visits the psychologist talked with the young man and did more testing of different kinds. Before long, he found out the young man could read!

The young man was asked how he had learned to read in such an environment. He explained some of the things he had done. He had followed, watched, and listened to janitors, kitchen employees, and visitors. Occasionally an old magazine or newspaper came his way. He had plenty of time to look at them, and little by little he matched a few objects in the pictures with some of the words underneath. When he had found several pictures with the same word under them, he could be reasonably sure what the word said. Once in a while he had a chance to point to a word when an adult was present and say it with a question in his voice. "Car?" "Girl?" and so on. At some point he figured out that letters have sounds, and began sounding out words. His was a slow, difficult way to learn, but learn he did.

Few of us have had to learn under such conditions. Yet even under improved conditions many Americans don't learn to read well. They think of reading as a very complicated business that not everyone can master. The truth is, though, almost anyone can master it. Over the past fifty years the process of learning how to read has been made to seem much more complicated than it really is. Any of the things we do with our brains and muscles and nerves are all amazingly complex when studied in detail. For example, if you study eye movements, visual stimulation, memory, thought processes, and all the other things that go into reading a sentence, it is extremely complicated. And there is so much that isn't yet known about the reading process. But people don't need to know all the detailed information in order to read, anymore than a child needs to know about its pharynx and larynx and vocal cords when it it learning how to talk.

In improving your reading ability on your own, the first thing to keep in mind is that written words are just spoken words put down on paper. A written word you are trying to figure out may be a word you've heard many times on television or in conversation.

How do you change sounds into marks on a paper? That's where the alphabet comes in. Each letter of the alphabet stands for a sound, or more often, for several sounds. Your little brother is getting on your nerves and you tell him to be quiet. "Shhhh," you say. If you wanted to write it down you would do so by putting down the letters that make the sound.

You probably know that not all words are spelled exactly as they sound. Why isn't "fight" spelled "fite"? Why isn't "tough" spelled "tuff"? Sometimes the reason is that the word in question originally came from another language and the spelling follows the rules of that language. Other times the word is very old and is spelled according to ancient spelling rules that are no longer in effect. And sometimes the reason why a word is spelled a certain way is a mystery to almost everyone. When you run into these kinds of words you have to memorize each of them. This might sound like quite a chore, but actually there are many more words in the English language that obey the rules than words that don't. That makes life a little easier.

Most letters of the alphabet have more than one sound. How do you know which sound is meant? Look at the difference in the g in George and the g in give. When you run into such problems, try the trial-and-error method. Try it one way, and if that turns out not to make sense, try it the other. The more intelligent guessing you do, the better you get at it. Often you can get hints from the words that surround the problem word.

Applying What You Know

Alphabets were quite an invention! Not only did they make written communication possible, they became an art form in themselves. If you want to make posters, brochures, programs, or your own greeting cards, the lettering you use will be very important to the success of your design.

Try to find several books on lettering in your school or public library. (You may have to look under the word *calligraphy* in the card catalog. Calligraphy means "beautiful writing" and it is the term often used to refer to writing when it is used as an art form.)

After all members of the class have had a chance to look at the books, let each person design one of the following, using a style of lettering he or she especially likes:

1. A record jacket for a hit rock group

2. A valentine or birthday greeting card

3. A baseball score card

4. The front page of a school newspaper

5. A candy bar wrapper

Some members of the class who have had mechanical drawing may prefer to draw a floor plan for a small shop or office using the special lettering drafters use to mark their drawings.

When everyone has had a week to complete the design, display them attractively around the classroom.

USING STANDARD ENGLISH ON THE JOB

If you were invited to a day-time beach party would you wear the same clothes as if you were going to a fancy discotheque at night? If you were writing a letter to a company asking about a job opening would your letter sound the same as if you were writing to your closest friend?

Just as we use different clothes for different occasions, we also use different language patterns for different occasions. When speaking or writing to friends our speech is informal, lively, spontaneous. By spontaneous we mean that we don't think much about it, we just use the words and patterns we are used to. Sometimes, however, a more formal language is appropriate. This more formal language is often referred to as standard English.

Standard English is a must for success on the job in many cases. It is used because it is more uniform than other forms of English. Being more uniform it is easier to use it for conducting business. Misunderstandings can be kept to a minimum. Time can be saved. Things run more smoothly and efficiently. The person who uses the correct, standardized form of English on the job comes across as a well-educated, competent person.

Well, then, does that mean that you should give up your own patterns of speech if they are not the same as those of standard English? We'll answer that question with another question. Why choose one kind of language when you can so easily have both? You can have your own individualized, informal, spontaneous way of speaking and writing. You can also develop skill at using a more businesslike, standard form of English. You can do this by paying close attention to standard English patterns when you hear them. Many TV shows use standard English patterns. So do many books and magazines. You will run across people in the world of work who talk clearly and correctly. Just by listening attentively you can pick up many good language habits.

Flexibility is one of the keys to survival. Flexibility means that a person can change easily as the situation changes. People can develop a feel for when one kind of language is more appropriate than another, just as they can develop a feel for what kind of clothes to wear on various occasions. Developing such understanding and flexibility in the use of language adds another dimension to you as a person.

LANGUAGE SKILLS PORTFOLIO

The exercises in this section are designed to help you find out where you are, what you know, and what you need to know. The idea is to find out about your skills, not to compete for a grade. The answers are given at the end of the book so you can check yourself.

All of the games are based on a study of reading problems in high schools today. Some of the games will be simple for you. Work through those rapidly. Others are more difficult and you may have to spend more time on them. It would be better to spread the games out over several days rather than doing them all at once.

You will find ways to improve your reading and writing skills on your own. You will also find suggestions for continuing your language growth outside of your classroom.

GAME ONE:
THE THOUSANDS OF WORDS YOU ALREADY KNOW

You know more words than you think you do! That's because you meet words everywhere—on television, in newspaper headlines, on the street, on cans, bottles, and cartons, in comic books.

Mark or fold a piece of paper so that it has four columns. Put the following headings at the top of the columns:

DRINKS	DEODORANTS	VEHICLES	MAGAZINES

Now put the words listed below in their proper columns. They are probably all words that you have seen many times before. Allow yourself about five minutes to do this one.

Mad	Seven-Up	V-8	Pinto
Right Guard	Corvette	Dr. Pepper	Dial
Honda	Secret	Newsweek	Playboy
Seventeen	Time	Sanka	Kool-Aid
Ford	Bud	Yamaha	Arrid
Harley Davidson	Sure	Fresh	Reader's Digest
Coke	Ebony	Folger's	Rabbit
Ban	BMW	People	Mum

GAME TWO:
MUSCLE BUILDING

Take three pieces of paper and label them 1, 2, and 3. On the first page write all the words you can think of. Don't worry about spelling right now. Time yourself (or have someone else time you) for exactly three minutes. Repeat the exercise on the second and then the third sheet, using only three minutes each time.

When you have finished all three sheets, count the number of words you wrote each time. Did your score increase? Did you "loosen up" as you did the second and third sheets?

One of the big problems with writing is that people freeze up when they try to put words down on paper. Sometimes it's hard for people to realize that the words they use in writing are the same words they use in everyday speech.

Spoken words drift away and are often soon forgotten. Writing is for when you want your words to go farther or last longer.

GAME THREE:
DON'T LET THE BIG ONES GET AWAY!

antidisestablishmentarianism

That's one of the longest words in the English language. Trying to get it all at once would be like trying to eat a submarine sandwich in one bite. So try to pick it apart. Is there a word in it you already know? How about *establishment?*

antidis-*establishment*-arianism

Attack the part of the word you know first. Then break the rest up into little pieces or syllables.

an-ti-dis-establishment-ar-i-an-ism

Now the word is almost manageable. If you learn to pronounce it, you will be one of the few people who know one of the longest words in our language. You won't have a lot of chances to use it in conversation, though!

Below is a list of words. Copy them on a sheet of paper, then underline the smaller word (or words) that are in the big words. If you know part of the word but not all of it, see if you can sound out or guess at the part you don't know.

injustice	homemade	intersection
sexist	enrage	stereotype
disgraceful	earrings	stepbrother
fearful	landmark	resentment
nightmare	conformity	
unthinking	beekeeper	
lollipop	uphold	
threatening	courageous	
innermost	freeway	

GAME FOUR:
THE COMPANY THEY KEEP

Words seldom stand alone. They are usually surrounded by other words. If you don't know what a certain word means, look at the company it keeps.

For example, you may not have been sure of all the words in Game Three. Look at some of them again in the sentences below. Take a good guess at the meanings. Then see how close you came by looking up the words in a dictionary.

1. Two Yamahas just missed crashing into each other at the **intersection** of Main and Roosevelt.

2. John's idea that all pretty girls are conceited is a **stereotype**.

3. Do you think Mary's idea that the man should pay for everything on a date is **sexist?**

4. The lion tamer only teased the animals, trying to **enrage** them with cracks of his whip.

5. The dog snarled and made a **threatening** move toward me; so I took off.

6. When presidents are sworn into office, they promise to **uphold** the Constitution of the United States.

7. Though dying of leukemia, Jenny made a **courageous** effort to remain cheerful and active.

8. Some of the Supreme Court's decisions on civil rights were **landmark** decisions.

9. She hummed a little tune which sounded happy, but in her **innermost** heart she was hurt and angry.

GAME FIVE:
ALPHABET SOUP

Sometimes when you are writing a rough draft of a letter or paper you may want to write fast so you don't lose any of your ideas. For the moment, your thoughts will be more important than the way you spell. But when the time comes to recopy whatever you are working on in its final form, you will want to have every word spelled correctly. You may also need to look up a few definitions to make sure you are using the right word. So you will have to use a dictionary.

You know how to use a dictionary. This game is designed to help you use it faster and more efficiently. Then it won't seem like such a hassle to look up a word. You will need fifty index cards (they could be used on one side) or fifty pieces of paper cut to about that size.

Fill your fifty cards with any fifty words you choose, one word to a card. Try to have at least one word for each letter of the alphabet.

When you get them made, trade packs with the person next to you. Put the pack you get in alphabetical order as fast as you can. Then check each other's work.

If you think you are pretty good at this, try putting together 3 or 4 packs. Maybe even more!

This exercise should help you find the part of the dictionary you need much more quickly. But what if you don't know how to spell a word you want to look up? Again, smart guessing goes a long way. Try your first idea, then think in terms of how else the word could possibly be spelled. If you're really stuck, ask someone.

GAME SIX:
THE ROOTS GAME

Sometimes a whole family of words is based on one root word. Take *bio-* for example. *Bio-* is from the Greek language and means *life*. So whenever you see *bio-* as part of a word, it is most likely related to the word *life*.

biology: the study of living things   **biography:** the story of someone's life

bionic: a mechanical imitation of a living person

bioluminescence: light that a living creature naturally gives off, as in the case of the lightning bug

biopsy: an operation in which a doctor removes a piece of living tissue from a person so he can study it to see if it is diseased

What do these words mean?

graph (to write)	lumin (light)	tele (far off)
autograph	illumination	television
biography	luminous	telegraph
graphite		telescope

Check the answer page and see how close you came to getting the meanings of any of these words you didn't already know.

GAME SEVEN:
GETTING IT DOWN ON PAPER

Pick one of the following subjects:

1. Hard Rock
2. Blues
3. Bach and Beethoven
4. Progressive Jazz
5. Country and Western
6. Some other kind of music you like or dislike

Make a short statement about your subject out loud. Write down the words you said. Check and see if you remembered to put down all the words. Now add to what you said. Think of something else you could say, but instead of saying it, write it down. Try to write one complete page. Read it over and see if it really sounds like you.

GAME EIGHT:
SENTENCE SURGERY

Copy over the page you wrote for Game Seven, improving it as you go along. *Improving it* means fixing something that doesn't sound quite right to you or adding an idea that you didn't think of the first time around.

You must be the doctor. Look at what you have written and read it out loud. Does it say what you want it to say? Does it have power? Is it correct?

Here are some checkpoints for sentences:

1. Have you used *enough* words to make your idea clear?

2. Have you used unnecessary words that don't add to the meaning or power of your sentence? Weed them out.

3. Have you used tired words? These are words that people use over and over again till they mean almost nothing at all. Give your sentence vitamins—bright, fresh words—words from the language you speak every day.

Finding Out for Yourself

Interested in doing more on your own to develop your communication know-how? Buy your own copy of this paperback:

How to Read Better and Faster by Norman Lewis (T. Y. Crowell)

This book has been around for awhile and has helped thousands of adults learn to read with more understanding, speed, and pleasure. Maybe it will help you, too. You keep track of your progress, and the things the author has you do are interesting. You might also like to try his *30 Days to a More Powerful Vocabulary*.

❧ Chapter Eleven ❧

MATH FOR
EVERYDAY USE

Terry Mauzy

PLUS AND MINUS

In this, the age of the computer and the calculator, it would be easy to think, "Why do I need math skills?" It's true that these machines have taken a lot of the drudgery out of mental work, just as other types of machines have taken much of the drudgery out of physical labor. But what about these operations?

understanding your paycheck
writing bills
understanding a contract that involves money
making change
checking the change you are given
weighing things
measuring things
inventory control

Many small tasks that we still do without machines require basic math skills. Also, a computer can do nothing without man. Someone has to program it, know how to get information from it, correct it, and repair it.

In this chapter we are going to give you examples of ways you can use math in everyday life. In the not-too-distant future we are going to be using the metric system instead of our present systems of measurement, so let's get a headstart on it, too.

YOUR PAYCHECK

You want to know exactly what your paycheck is all about. No big trick, right? You work 40 hours for $4.00 per hour. So just multiply:

$$\begin{array}{r} \$4.00 \text{ per hour} \\ \times 40 \text{ hours} \\ \hline \$160.00 \end{array}$$

$160.00 is your *gross* pay. *Gross* means everything you have earned for that pay period. But don't expect to get $160.00. Your employer is required by law to withhold (take out) a certain amount from your gross earnings. The amount you have left after all the deductions are made is called your *net* pay. Some people also refer to it as *take-home* pay.

How much money will be withheld from your earnings? Two deductions will be made for sure: federal income tax and social security tax. Some states also have a state income tax, which is usually quite a bit less than federal income tax. Does your state have one?

Your employers will ask you to fill out a tax form so they can calculate your federal income tax. (See the sample form).

You can claim one *exemption* for each person who is dependent on you. *You* are dependent on you, so you are one exemption. If you have a husband or wife who doesn't work and depends on you, you have two exemptions. Say you also have two children. Then you have four exemptions. The more exemptions you have, the less tax will be withheld from your check.

Read this paragraph very carefully, or it may confuse you. If you want to, you can claim no exemptions. Why would anyone want to do that, when they could claim more and have less tax taken out per month? People sometimes claim no exemptions so that when income tax time rolls around they won't have to cough up any more money for taxes. Sometimes your employers may not take out enough tax, even though they use tax tables and try to be as accurate as possible. If you claim no exemptions, or one fewer than you actually could claim, your employers read their tax tables and take out a little more from each paycheck. Then when tax paying time comes, your withholding will more than cover what you owe. Maybe you will even have paid in too much, and you will have some money returned to you by the federal government.

Your employers usually use prepared tables in order to tell how much income tax and social security they should withhold. The amount withheld for social security will show on your check as a deduction for F.I.C.A. These initials refer to the Federal Insurance Contributions Act.

What other deductions might there be? Many companies have a retirement plan. You contribute a certain amount of each paycheck, and the employer matches that amount. All of the money goes into a fund for your retirement, and during all the years you work that fund is earning interest. Having such a plan is better than relying entirely on social security for your retirement income.

Voluntary deductions might include union dues, savings bonds, donations to charities, and insurance premiums. Employers cannot make such deductions unless you say so. There will be forms for you to fill out and sign so that your employers have your consent in writing before they make any of these deductions.

After all these deductions have been made, what you have left is called your *net* pay.

Example: Larry earns $4.00 per hour at the stationery store. Last week he worked 32 hours. He has no dependents and claims no exemptions. His employer withholds $10.40 for federal income tax and $3.50 for social security. Larry has also requested that $6.25 a week be withheld for a savings bond, and $1.00 for the United Fund. What will his gross pay be? What will his net pay be?

$4.00 × 32 hours = $128.00

$10.40 federal income tax
  3.50 social security
  6.25 savings bond
  1.00 United Fund
_____

$21.15 total amount of deductions

$128.00 (gross pay)
− 21.15 (total amount of deductions)
_____

106.85 net pay, or take-home pay

As you know, employers must prepare a payroll. So for each employee they must calculate gross earnings, deductions, and net earnings. They must see to it that the withheld amounts get where they are supposed to go—to the federal government if it's federal income tax, to the social security administration if it is social security money, etc. Then checks have to be prepared and distributed. So you can see that many job opportunities are related to payroll preparation!

If you don't understand something on your check, think about it, try to figure it out if you can. If you cannot, politely ask for an explanation. If you work for a big company, a payroll clerk could help you. In a small place of business you could go directly to your employer.

Checkpoint 1

How important do you think it is to understand what your paycheck is all about? Can you think of a good reason to save your check stubs? If you save them, you can compare each paycheck with the one before to see if everything makes sense. And you can always check figures as we did in the preceding example. Try these for practice.

1. Tanya makes $11 per hour as a typewriter repair woman. She works 20 hours a week. Her weekly paycheck shows that $38.00 has been withheld for federal income tax. $8.25 was withheld for social security. She has $5.20 per week deducted for health insurance, and $7.50 for union dues. How much is her take-home pay?

2. Skip worked 24 hours at $4.30 per hour. $22.00 was withheld for federal income tax, and $2.80 was withheld for state income tax. Also, there was $7.60

for social security. How much money does he actually get?

3. Richard drives a delivery truck and gets paid $3.80 per hour. In a two-week period he worked 44 hours. Deduct $10.50 federal income tax, $2.35 social security, $1.50 United Fund, and $5.00 for a savings bond. What's his net pay?

Checkpoint 2

Are you sure of these important terms having to do with your paycheck? Try matching terms and definitions.

1. gross

2. net

3. exemption

4. deductions

5. withholding

6. dependent

a. money held back to pay for taxes

b. total amount of money earned, before deductions

c. someone you take care of financially

d. take-home pay

e. an allowance made for you or your dependents

f. money taken out of your gross pay for taxes, retirement insurance, etc.

FIGURING BILLS AND MAKING CHANGE

Don't be in a hurry when you are writing up someone's bill or making change for them. Accuracy comes first because making a mistake can leave a bad impression, suggesting that you are careless or dishonest. However, when you do make a mistake, a simple apology and correction is all that is necessary. The best policy is to perfect your math skills so that you will make very few mistakes.

RULES FOR MAKING CHANGE. Count out the change carefully as you look into the register. Count it again out loud for the customers, placing it in their hands or on the counter. If someone gives you a big bill, lay it across the till as you are getting out the change. Check yourself, then put the bill where it belongs and count out the change to the customer. This may save embarrassing mistakes.

Below are some practice cases. Use actual sales slips if possible. Otherwise, use your own paper.

1. Joe took his girl out for dinner. They each had steak at $3.75 per person. Joe had a coke at $ .35, and his girl had coffee at $ .40. Joe had Boston cream pie at $ .75. His girl couldn't eat another bite, so she had no dessert.

You are the waiter. Write up a neat sales slip for them. Include 5 percent sales tax. If Joe gives you a $10 bill, how much change does he have coming? If he gives you $20, how much?

2. Carrie is going to make Christmas dresses for her two little girls. She buys 3 yards of blue fabric at $2.95 per yard. She buys 3 yards of red fabric at the same price. She gets 2 zippers at $ .75 each, 2 spools of thread at $ .25 each, and 6 yards of trim at $ .39 a yard. The sales tax where she lives is 5 percent.

Write up a sales slip and figure out how much Carrie owes you.

3. John had his car tuned up for $42.50. He got a special deal on an oil change, $7.00. He replaced one windshield wiper blade at $3.75. How much did he owe the service station?

Working Cooperatively

Split into two groups and make up some sales problems for each other. For each, write up a sales slip. Make your figures neat and legible and check them before you hand them to your partner-customer.

INVENTORY CONTROL

Have you ever gone into a store to buy some special item and found the shelf empty where the item should be? Were you disappointed? Angry even? There may have been a breakdown in inventory control.

Inventory means what you have on hand. You may be involved in taking inventory where you work. You count and count and count. Inventory control means keeping an up-to-date record of how many items you ordered and received from your supplier, how many have been sold, and how many are left. Larger retail businesses now have mechanical ways of controlling inventory. As the customer checks out, the inventory numbers are recorded on the special cash register calculators. But in many places, inventory and inventory control still have to be done by hand.

Assume you are in charge of the department that sells hammers, nails, and bandages. How will you make sure your shelf never gets empty? You could buy a very large supply of everything, right? Just as sure as you do, a new type of "can't miss" hammer will be made, and you

Mutual of Omaha

will be stuck with 10,000 Thumbsmashers that you can't give away. Buying a very large supply is also very expensive. You would need a great deal of storage space.

If you had some basic information you could solve your problem. Here are some questions you would need to answer:

1. How many hammers, nails, and bandages are sold each month, on the average?

2. Do you ever need to have more than a month's supply on hand?

3. How long after you have placed an order does it usually take to receive more?

You would need to keep accurate records, too. Here's a sample page from an inventory control notebook.

Manufacturer: **Thumbsmasher, Inc.** 239 Penny Street Recess, IL 60000		Catalog No. 321562	
		Item: Thumbsmasher Hammers.	

Month	Number on Hand on first of month	Number Ordered on first of month	Number Received during month	Number Sold during month
Jan.	4	25	0	4
Feb.	0	0	25	8
March	17	0	0	6
April	11	25	25	6
May	30	0	0	8

Looking at this chart you can tell that the situation in January was not good. Some customers probably had to be turned away. The situation at the end of March was a little too close for comfort, too, especially if you know you generally sell six or seven Thumbsmashers each month. Luckily the April order came in very fast.

The inventory record gives you a good idea of where you stand. If carefully analyzed it can give you a reasonably safe buying pattern. Every so often you would also go and count the physical objects to make sure the number on your shelves agrees with your record book.

ORDERING

You look in your inventory control book and find that you need to order more hammers. What basic information would you need?

1. The number of hammers you want

2. The price per hammer

3. The name and address of the manufacturer or distributor

Most orders are written on an order form. Occasionally, however, there is a rush for the item, and you call in an order. In most places it is the practice to then write up a confirming order and send it on by mail. Such a follow-up order should always be marked **Confirming,** otherwise you could end up getting two shipments. Find out exactly how such things are handled in your company. Make notes for yourself on things that are tricky and don't come up every day. Basically, though, writing up an order is not difficult. Here is a typical order form.

ORDER FORM		ORDER NO. 5284	
VENDOR: THUMBSMASHER INC. **239 Penny St. Recess, IL 60000**	**PURCHASER:** Your Store, Inc. 1825 N. West St. Carbondale, IL 62028		
Quantity	Catalog number & Description	Unit Price	Total Price
15	321562 ball peen hammer	$5.27	$79.05
		TOTAL:	$79.05

When you receive the bill for this order of hammers, it will probably include sales tax and shipping charges.

In the upper right corner there is an order number. This is so that you and the vendor can identify this particular order, in case there is a problem with it. If you have to call him about it, you can simply say, "I'm calling in reference to order no. 5284," and he can quickly pull it out of his file. Your address appears on the order so the Thumbsmasher Company knows where to send the items.

The catalog number can be obtained directly from Thumbsmasher's catalog, but, in this case, you had recorded it in your inventory record book, and that saved having to look it up.

To determine what your order will cost, you must multiply the number of items times the unit price (price per item).

15 hammers × $5.27 per hammer = $79.05

It is also wise to check where the price breaks occur. A price break is a lower price per item if you order a larger number of items. For example, if you had ordered from 25-50 hammers, each one would have cost you $5.15. If you ordered 51-150, the price break would be even more of an advantage. You would pay only $5.05 per hammer. You always want to take advantage of a price break if you can sell the items, and you have the funds and the storage space.

Checkpoint 4

1. If you order 150 spools of thread at a wholesale price of $ .09 each, how much will your order cost?

2. If you order 15 lures at $2.50 each, 25 boxes of hooks at $2.00 each, and 10 tackle boxes at $5.50 each, how much will you have to pay?

THE METRIC SYSTEM

One kind of measurement all of us learn early in life is money measurement. Basically, our money system is a matter of 10's:

one dime = ten pennies
one dollar = ten dimes
ten $1 bills = one $10 bill

ten $10 bills = one $100 bill
ten $100 bills = one $1000 bill

Don't you agree that this is a fairly simple system? Soon other measuring systems in our country will be simplified, too. The metric system, which is also based on tens, will be our system of measuring, as it has been in Europe and other countries for some time. The way we tell time and count money won't change. But we will have new units for measuring length, weight, volume, and temperature.

Kind of Measurement	Units in Our Present System	Basic Units in the Metric System
length	inch, foot, yard, mile	meter
weight	ounce, pound	gram
volume	pint, quart, gallon	liter
temperature	°F (Fahrenheit)	°C (Celsius)

One of the first important things to learn about the metric system is the list of prefixes. Here are the prefixes you will find in the metric system:

kilo = thousand (1000)

hecto = hundred (100)

deka = ten (10)

deci = tenth (1/10 or 0.1)

centi = hundredth (1/100 or 0.01)

milli = thousandth (1/1000 or 0.001)

micro = millionth (1/1,000,000 or 0.000001)

Now let's put the basic metric units with these prefixes:

meter
kilometer = 1000 meters
hectometer = 100 meters
dekameter = 10 meters
decimeter = 1/10 meter
centimeter = 1/100 meter
millimeter = 1/1000 meter
micrometer = 1/1,000,000 meter

liter
kiloliter = 1000 liters
hectoliter = 100 liters
dekaliter = 10 liters
deciliter = 1/10 liter
centiliter = 1/100 liter
milliliter = 1/1000 liter
microliter = 1/1,000,000 liter

gram
kilogram = 1000 grams
hectogram = 100 grams
dekagram = 10 grams
decigram = 1/10 grams
centigram = 1/100 grams
milligram = 1/1000 grams
microgram = 1/1,000,000 gram

°C
0° Celsius—freezing point of water
100° Celsius—boiling point of water

There are formulas for converting yards into meters, miles into kilometers, quarts into liters, etc. For example, 1 yard = 0.91 meters. One centimeter = 0.39 inches. But do you see how slow and complicated converting from one system to the other could be? For most purposes it would be better to start thinking in metric terms rather than translating from our present system to the metric system everytime you measure something.

If you should, however, feel a need to be able to convert from one system to the other, the best plan would be to buy one of the many good and inexpensive pamphlets on metrics. *Metrics Made Easy,* put out by Barron's Educational Series, Inc., is a useful, pocket-sized metrics manual.

The metric system is based on tens. Since you will want to multiply by tens frequently, we are now going to show you a short-cut method of doing so and of keeping track of the totals.

TABLE FOR MULTIPLYING BY 10s

mega	= million	$= 1,000,000 = 10 \times 10 \times 10 \times 10 \times 10 \times 10 = 10^6$
kilo	= thousand	$= 1,000 = 10 \times 10 \times 10 = 10^3$
hecto	= hundred	$= 100 = 10 \times 10 = 10^2$
deka	= ten	$= 10 = 10^1$
dece	= tenth	$= 0.1 = 1/10 = 10^{-1}$
centi	= hundredth	$= 0.01 = \dfrac{1}{10 \times 10} = 10^{-2}$
milli	= thousandth	$= 0.001 = .001 = \dfrac{1}{10 \times 10 \times 10} = 10^{-3}$
micro	= millionth	$= 0.000001 = \dfrac{1}{10 \times 10 \times 10 \times 10 \times 10 \times 10} = 10^{-6}$

If you studied the table closely, you noticed that 10^3 meant 10 times itself three times—$10 \times 10 = 100 \times 10 = 1000$. If the number was a decimal such as 10^{-3}, it meant that 1 was *divided* by 10 times itself three times. So one thousand = 1,000 = $10 \times 10, \times 10$ and one-thousandth =

$$0.001 = \frac{1}{10 \times 10 \times 10}$$

Knowing how to work with tens this way can help make you an instant expert on metrics. For example:

1. To multiply $100 \times 1,000$
($100 = 10^2$, $1,000 = 10^3$)
Write $10^2 \times 10^3$
Add the number of times 10 is multiplied, so
$10 (2 + 3) = 10^5$
$10^5 = 100,000$ (1 and 5 zeros)

2. To divide $1,000,000 \div 100$
Write $10^6 \div 10^2$

Subtract the number of times 10 is multiplied, so

$10^{(6-2)} = 10^4$
$10^4 = 10,000$ (1 and 4 zeros)

Place a Celsius thermometer and a Fahrenheit thermometer in your classroom. Record readings on both for two weeks. If you can, hang them outside a window some of the days.

By the end of two weeks you should have a feel for degrees Celsius. What temperature C is comfortable for you?

At what point on the C scale do you begin feeling too warm? Too cold? If you were taking a child's temperature, at what point would you start being a little concerned?

After two weeks, put the F thermometer away. Rely only on your Celsius readings.

Checkpoint 5

A. Match the prefixes with their numerical equivalents:

1. micro

2. hecto

3. kilo

4. centi

5. deka

6. milli

7. deci

a. thousand (1000)

b. millionth (1/1,000,000 or 0.000001)

c. ten (10)

d. hundredth (1/100 or 0.01)

e. hundred (100)

f. tenth (1/10 or 0.1)

g. thousandth (1/1000 or 0.001)

Check your answers at the end of the book. Do this exercise over until you get it fast and perfect.

Applying What You Know

When we adopt the metric system, some changes in our vocabularies will occur. For instance:

1. When you weigh yourself, your weight will be in _____.

2. If you want to tell friends how far you drove between Los Angeles and Houston, you will tell them how many _____ you travelled.

3. If you need new linoleum in your kitchen, you will measure to find out how many _____ your floor is long and how many wide.

4. If you have a cold and are running a temperature, the doctor will tell you what your temperature is in _____.

5. Instead of buying a quart of milk, you will buy a _____ of it.

6. If you buy a bag of potato chips, the weight stamped on the package will be so many _____.

7. The wrenches you use to fix your car will be sized by _____ rather than in fractions of inches.

❧ Chapter Twelve ❧

THE AMERICAN CRAFTSMAN

C. William Horrell

AN ENDANGERED SPECIES?

So far in this section we have covered communication and math skills. Now let's move on to manual skills. Manual skills are skills involving the hands. But that doesn't mean they don't also involve the mind. Manual skills are closely related to a person's ability to think and plan and figure things out. They require a great deal of coordination between mind and body.

Do you believe that people value manual skills less than they do other skills? This often appears to be the case, and it is unfortunate. Even in a highly industrialized society such as ours there is a great need for craftsmen—people with a high level of manual skills. All of us could benefit by learning to do some tasks that require good manual skills.

For example, when an appliance breaks down or the car stops running, many people immediately call a service person. They don't know much about handling tools or making the simplest repairs. They wouldn't know how to begin building a fence or making a toybox or sewing a top or shirt. Think of the money they could save if they had some of these skills.

You may have heard about urban homesteading, a special government program for rebuilding the inner cities of large urban areas. Older houses that have been abandoned sometimes become the property of the city. (This usually happens because no one pays the taxes on them.) Quite often these dwellings are still structurally sound, but they are run down. The urban homesteading program allows such homes to be given away to people who will fix them up and bring them up to current building code standards. You can imagine how many applicants there are for these free homes! Just think, people can own a house without making payments on it for 20 or 30 years as many others have to do. They can spend some of the money they would have had to use for rent to help renovate the house they get. What do you think is one of the decisive factors when city governments are choosing people to receive these homes? Their manual skills. The thinking behind this is that it wouldn't work to give the houses to those who don't know how to handle tools, repair plumbing, or paint. But if they are given to people with the know-how to fix them up, both the individuals and the community will benefit.

In addition to the practical side of having some manual skills, our sense of beauty is also involved. Our pleasure in the well-made, the human and warm, finds an outlet both when we make something we can be proud of and when we own or use something a craftsman has made.

The factory system almost wiped out the craftsman. Skills became less and less important. Many workers who had done satisfying and exacting work before became mere tenders of machines. If skills aren't needed or valued, they tend to disappear. That happened in our country for a number of years. In recent decades, however, the services of craftsmen have again been much in demand. Many people turn to hand-made things to get away from the oppressive feel of mass production in a mass society.

Maybe you will be satisfied to gain only a minimum of manual skills for practical, everyday use. Or perhaps you will want to develop a particular manual skill as a leisure-time activity. Some of you may even want to perfect certain manual skills and make a living using them.

We looked around our comparatively small city to see if crafts were making a comeback here. We are pleased to report that many of them are alive and well. We found many kinds of craftsmen, all of them enthusiastic about their work. We asked three of them what they thought young persons' chances of success were if they chose to follow a craft for a living. Let's take a look at what they said.

A MORNING IN A BLACKSMITH'S SHOP.   We turn right at the old barn and follow the rutted road to the long, rectangular building. When we enter, we have to give our eyes a chance to adjust to the half-light inside. A smell that reminds us of a campfire floats up from a bright spot at the far end.

We make our way through piles of tools, pieces of metal, and a small trunk waiting perhaps for a new lock. The place has a crowded, busy look.

Daryl Meier is just heating some pieces of metal which he must not lay aside just yet. We watch as he pounds them to the shape he wants. He tells us a little about the forge he is using. It has an air blower on one side and looks something like a barbecue oven.

"We use special coal from Georgia, a very low sulphur coal. If you don't use good coal, you can get impurities which contaminate the metal you are working with. Sometimes even newspaper that you use to light the fire can be troublesome because of the ink."

He gets to a stopping place, and we walk to the other end of the building. It's chilly. Doors are left open at both ends of the structure for ventilation. A haze cuts across the sunbeams sliding in at the front door.

First I ask Daryl to tell us a little about his background. "I come from a background of teachers," he begins. "My mother taught school for 50 years. I was an education major in college. Then I went into business administration."

"There seems to be quite a gap between those interests and blacksmithing."

"Yes, in a way. You might call me a dropout. I wanted to get out of the mainstream of the success pattern that is so common in our country today. I wanted to succeed in a different, more satisfying way."

"Can you remember when you began feeling this way?"

"Not exactly. I became interested in a group called the National Muzzleloading Rifle Association. In their spare time they get together and shoot muzzleloaders. Conversation is mostly about another way of life, the pioneer way. Many of the weapons, tools, and implements talked about and used have to do with blacksmithing. I started out with a hobby and ended up changing my goals and style of living."

"Did you also want to be on your own?"

"Yes, something like that. I admit that I felt some satisfaction at the end of the day when I was in the business world. I had completed a good transaction, done something to benefit the company. But I learned that I am the kind of a person who needs a more physical sense of accomplishment. Somewhere along the line I had experienced the satisfaction of holding a real, material object in my hand which I had made myself and saying, 'This is what I did today. I made this.'"

"How would you account for the renewed interest in blacksmithing today?"

"A blacksmith's services are still needed and valued, for example, for the repair of all kinds of farm implements and household items."

"So a modern blacksmith would focus on repair work?"

"Not necessarily. For example, my first love is making beautiful damascus steel knives. By the way, do you know the difference between a *blacksmith* and a *whitesmith?*"

"I didn't even know there was such a thing as a whitesmith!"

"Those are old names based on the color of the metal. The blacksmith worked with iron. It turned black in the fire, and he left it black. The whitesmith worked in tin, a white metal. Or he worked with iron, too, but didn't leave it black. If he wanted to smooth it out, make a finer surface, he rubbed off the black in the process. He wasn't really trying to change the color but to enhance a blade or other surface of an object."

"What other items do you make?"

"I'm interested in making reproductions of pieces blacksmiths of the 18th century would have made, both household items and items you might carry about your person, such as a pocket knife. There's a good market for these things today."

"Why is that?"

"For some people, it's a matter of wanting to get back to a simpler way of life. They idealize pioneer days and want to surround themselves with things that help them get back there. For other people, it's different. They have to buy so many modern, mass-manufactured items void of any human touch. They are tired of it and want the things they use everyday to have that man-made touch, where personal involvement shows in the finished product."

"Is the quality also better?"

"Not necessarily. No, it's not just a matter of quality. Machine-made items can be high quality, too. It's the warm, personal feel of things made by hand that people want. You might say people are seeking personal, human contact through commerce."

"What about shoeing horses?"

"I'm not qualified to do that," he answered.

"Is it especially difficult?"

"The *farrier* shoes horses. He's a special kind of a blacksmith and has to have a special license. Why? Well, in the old days there happened to be some poorly trained blacksmiths around. Bad shoeing can lame a horse and cause accidents. So a law was passed saying that a farrier had to be tested and licensed. Farriers were required to have licenses in this state before doctors were!"

"I hadn't thought of horseshoeing as very complex."

"Farriers have to know about horse anatomy. They can even correct the gait of a horse by the way they shoe it."

"Let's turn now to a little about the business side of your craft. Do you feel you had to give up a lot to begin as a blacksmith? Did you have to rethink your goals, especially your financial hopes?"

"Yes, I suppose I did, although for me the overriding satisfaction of making things counted for a great deal."

"How hard do you think it would be for a young person to make a go of it at blacksmithing?"

"It's not easy. You would have to give up the usual success pattern. The first few years are the hardest. You could probably not make as much money as you would in a factory. If you could continue to live at home for two or three years, working at your trade with considerable concentration, you could probably be independent in that amount of time."

"Do you think women could be blacksmiths? It's not too heavy for them?"

"Traditionally, blacksmithing was a man's world. But there's no reason women can't be blacksmiths. A puny woman couldn't do it. Neither could a puny man. A healthy, strong person, male or female, could."

"What do you believe is the most difficult part of starting out as a blacksmith?"

"You have all the same problems of any small business. The biggest problem is that you want to make, to manufacture. But you have to find outlets for your work. That takes time, and a different kind of energy. I wish I didn't have to do it. But I do have to."

"What are some of your outlets?"

"I sell some items, such as tomahawks, on a wholesale basis to different outlets in various parts of the country. I also show my work at various fairs and shows. For example, I just got back from the Great Western Fair in California. Have you ever heard of a blanket trader?"

"No. What's that?"

"You throw a blanket down on the floor, on the grass—wherever the show is—and spread your wares out on it."

"Like the old-time peddler almost."

"Yes."

"How do you find out about shows and fairs?"

"I belong to the Illinois Craftsman's Guild and am listed in their directory. I subscribe to trade magazines such as *American Blade,* a magazine of special interest to knife makers and collectors. Sometimes I see announcements in these. Someone who is organizing a fair uses a mailing list from one of these, and I get a brochure. Once you've begun showing, you more or less keep in touch. You know about annual events and you hear from people."

"You teach blacksmithing, too, don't you?"

"Yes. Last summer I had nine students."

"Could you describe a few of them? What kind of people take blacksmithing courses?"

"You'd be surprised at the range of needs and interests. One of my students was an elementary school art teacher. She likes to work with metal. She wanted to learn something about blacksmithing so she could make her own tools."

"Why would she make them? Why not just buy them?"

"They're expensive, for one thing. But the other problem is that out of the thousands of possible shapes and sizes for stake tools (tools you use for forming metal), you probably can't buy more than a dozen or so today. If you work in metal, you would like to have more possibilities than that."

"Did she learn enough to make her tools?"

"Yes. Another man who had been a tuckpointer for many years decided to set up a blacksmith shop. He was interested in manufacturing rather than repairing. He accomplished quite a bit, and he did open a shop afterwards."

"Did you have anybody with absolutely no experience with tools and crafts?"

"Yes, one young man. He didn't want to go into the family business. He had been to college and had a good academic background, but now he wanted to do something with his hands. Considering where he began, he · made quite good progress."

"Is he working as a blacksmith now?"

"I think he works a regular job part-time and works at his blacksmithing the rest of the time."

"That seems like another good solution to the financial problems of someone who wants to get started in a craft."

"Yes, it is."

"Do you think the crafts are encouraged in our high schools today? For example, are shop classes valuable?"

"I really don't know what's being done in shop classes today. From my own experience, I would say they don't emphasize crafts as such in shop. They tend to have an orientation toward skills you can use in industry. However, the first really significant thing I ever made with my own hands was a wooden chest. It was just a kit job, and I assembled it in shop class. I didn't make the parts. Still, I distinctly remember the pleasure I took in the finished product. It was a special moment for me. If a student gets that out of a shop class, the class has been valuable."

"What about other subjects? Were there others that contributed to your development?"

"Others? All of them! Everything you learn is useful. Mathematics, without a doubt. You need it for almost every kind of work, from papering a kitchen to building a whole house. English. Well, I tend not to be very verbal. My English classes taught me to put my thoughts into words."

He paused a moment. "I like understanding the *whys* of things, how things work. Do you know I can predict the future because I know something about chemistry and physics. For instance, I know that if I put something at the top of an inclined plane it will slide down. Without that knowledge, I'd have only trial-and-error to learn by. I still learn much by experimentation, but I have some place to begin, some degree of prediction of outcomes."

Many times since this interview with Daryl I have found myself thinking about that blacksmithing class next summer!

AN AFTERNOON WITH A WEAVER.   We have a weaving by Vera Grosowsky hanging in our dining room. Sometimes the shapes remind me of cross sections of seed pods. Other times I see heads of animals talking to each other. The texture is rich and varied, the colors earthy.

Vera has stopped by today because I asked her to share some of her experiences as a craftswoman with us. She is a weaver and a teacher of arts and crafts at a local community college.

Vera Grosowsky: One of the most appealing things about a craft is that it is one of the few things you can do that is totally self-determined. You decide what you want to do and how you want to do it. You are completely involved in the whole process from beginning to end. And you always know that the next piece you do is going to be the *best.*

Lois Carrier: How do you account for the comeback the crafts are making?

V. G.: I think it is a reaction to the mechanical kind of world most of us live in. People complain about this, and they have a significant complaint. They want to feel a sense of life around them.

L. C.: How did you happen to get into weaving?

V. G.: I had a degree in fine arts. When I came here with my husband, I felt restless at first. I decided to take a weaving class. My teacher encouraged me to continue and I did.

L. C.: How do you market your work?

V. G.: That can be a problem. Two galleries handle my work. One is a commercial gallery and one is an artists' co-op. You can also have an agent who sells your work for you. I'm thinking about doing that.

L. C.: What would be the advantage?

V. G.: Greater exposure, for one thing. As a weaver, you have to establish a reputation just as an artist does. You can do that better if an agent sells things all over the country, and to businesses or individuals who can use them in more prominent places. Another advantage is that when people wander into a crafts shop, they usually aren't prepared to spend much more than $50, if that. Your larger weavings have to cost much more than that, as do the more intricate one-of-a-kind things you make.

L. C.: Do you ever work on commission? That is, does anyone ever say, "Make me this or that kind of weaving to put in this or that spot?"

V. G.: Yes, I've worked that way a few times. It's all right, but I guess I'd rather have someone see a weaving I made and like it and buy it. You always have to worry about whether the person who commissions you to do something will like it when it's done.

L. C.: Let's talk about a young person's chance of making a living at a craft such as weaving.

V. G.: First you have to establish a reputation. While you're doing that, you would probably have to hold another job, at least part-time. Also you can do what we call *production weaving.* You could make a comfortable living doing that.

L. C.: What is production weaving?

V. G.: You design a piece and you make several just alike. If you are the kind of weaver who makes one of a kind only, it would be much harder to survive financially. There's so much time involved.

L. C.: You could combine the two, couldn't you? Make enough production pieces to earn a living, then spend the rest of the time on special one-of-a-kind pieces?

V. G.: Yes, that would be a good solution.

L. C.: How much equipment would you need to begin with?

V. G.: Very little. The Navajo Indians historically only used sticks. Some weaving can be done without a loom and much can be done on a simple loom you could make yourself. If you were going into production weaving, you would have to have a mechanical loom. That saves you all the time of picking up the yarns by hand.

L. C.: What is the largest weaving you ever saw?

V. G.: I'm not sure about the exact size, but I've seen people working high up on scaffolding to complete a piece.

L. C.: Do you like teaching along with your weaving?

V. G.: Yes, I find it exciting.

L. C.: Do most of your students come to you with fairly good art and craft backgrounds?

V. G.: I get all kinds of students. I think the most difficult ones are those who were praised too much when they were able to copy well as children. They seem to have missed out on the playfulness and individuality of the art experience. They have to give up things they were praised for in the past. That's hard.

I also believe that most students have had far too little three-dimensional art experience as children. In grade school, for example, the art periods are confined mostly to drawing and painting. This lack of exposure to other crafts, such as pottery and weaving, affects what students on the college level are able to do.

L. C.: What do you think is the best preparation for a student who wants to go into the arts and crafts?

V. G.: Anything that teaches you to observe closely. Biology. Gardening. Anything that teaches you about the environment. Things that help you develop a sensory repertoire. Things that give you an awareness of how things feel, smell, sound, look.

When our son was little we took him to the junkyard. We found treasures. We had fun. The element of fun is basic to the art experience.

Making anything is good preparation.

L. C.: Do you think the government could do more to encourage the crafts?

V. G.: The National Endowment for the Arts is doing some good things now. So is CETA (Comprehensive Employment Training Act). But I believe the government could help much more by funding better art programs in the elementary and secondary schools. I think they could help establish and maintain specialized schools, too.

L. C.: Thank you for coming by, Vera. Talking with you has made me aware of how much each of us can do just on our own to satisfy our need for making things, creating things. The junkyard idea intrigues me!

Daryl Littlefield

AN EVENING AT THE MUSEUM. The museum in which Richard Perry works is an unusual one. It is darker than most museums. Around the wall you find windows to peer through—windows into the past. Each is a scene in miniature from our pioneer heritage: house-raising, pig slaughtering, furniture making, a neat little cabin. Every implement, tool, piece of furniture is made to scale and looks as if it could be picked up and used by a miniature person.

Turning away from these dioramas, you can look at some of the items full-scale. You can walk by the broom maker's, the cooper's (barrel maker's) shop, the cabinetmaker's, the pioneer kitchen. Some days you will find someone demonstrating spinning or weaving, shingle making, or turning on a lathe. Best of all, you can try operating some of these antique machines yourself.

Richard Perry is the preparator. His job is to set up the displays and improve them, maintain all the museum pieces in top condition, and restore antique tools and implements which the museum acquires. He builds all sorts of things. The day we talked to him, he had a spinning wheel under construction.

"When did you become interested in the crafts you are now using in your work?" I asked. "Did you always enjoy making things with your hands?"

"Well, not exactly. That is, I didn't start making and restoring furniture until I was in college. However, I have enjoyed drawing and painting as long as I can remember."

"Your background is mainly in the fine arts then?"

"Yes."

"Being a preparator and a furniture maker as well as an artist is a rather unusual combination, isn't it?"

"I don't know. I think it's a good one for me. My first love is still painting. I can't do that for a living at this time. A job such as I have here allows me to use my knowledge and talents. I find plenty of challenge here."

"How did you learn all the crafts you know? You can restore or repair almost anything."

"You might say I'm self-taught. I used books. I tried things. And of course my background in art made me familiar with some principles and techniques which I put to good use here."

"You have a small furniture making business on the side, don't you?"

"Yes, I'm not very busy there, though. I have my name in the yellow pages, but I haven't had many calls."

"Why?"

"Partly because I'm not there much. Also, I've not put much time into it yet. To make a living at it, you'd have to plan in detail how to let others know where you are and what you can do."

"I was just going to ask you about that. Do you think people can still make a living following a craft?"

"Absolutely. No doubt about it. There's a real revival of interest in the past and in handmade things. No reason why young persons shouldn't succeed if they manage well."

"Do you think one has to scale down one's material goals to be a craftsman?"

"No. In fact I think I've scaled mine up. I find I like beautiful things, and I admit I want to be able to afford them. To be able to do so, a craftsman has to excel in his work. He has to become known. When that happens he often ends up having more work than he can handle. Little by little he can create an environment for himself that reflects his love of beauty."

"How do you become known?"

"By word-of-mouth, for one thing. If you make a beautiful piece of furniture or restore an antique properly, the word gets out. You can also submit pieces for shows, of course."

"Do you know many successful craftsmen?"

"Oh, yes. There are lots of them around here. One young married couple makes nothing but African thumb pianos. They make a living at it. One of my friends has a custom-made jewelry business with two other people. I also know an extremely fine cabinetmaker. His father and grandfather followed the same trade. He's so good that he was asked to come to a city in the South to help restore some of the beautiful old houses and their furnishings."

"That would take a lot of historical knowledge as well as practical skills."

"That's true. You learn a lot as you go along. You get into it and find books about it. You meet people who know much more than you do and you learn from them. I wanted to apprentice myself to the cabinetmaker I told you about, but I didn't do it for a number of reasons."

"How would you have gone about it?"

"Well, there's a federal program that is designed to aid young craftsmen. The person finds a master craftsman to whom he'd like to apprentice himself. If that craftsman accepts him, he can apply to the government for a kind of scholarship. The National Endowment for the Arts pays his teacher, the master craftsman, and gives the student a stipend to live on. The master gets help, and the young craftsman gets a living wage while he is learning."

"Would it take a lot of money to start out as a craftsman?"

"I wouldn't say a lot. I think you could get enough tools and equipment together to be a cabinetmaker for about $800 to $1000. And, of course, you'd have to have some way to sustain yourself financially until you are established."

We can think of Richard as someone who has several goals. He wants to paint and teach someday. He has had to compromise and do something else to earn a living now. But he chose a job—and prepared himself for it—that would allow him to use his skills and bring him the satisfaction of creating something with his hands. Maybe someday you will see one of his paintings hanging in a gallery.

 Part Five

Inland Steel Company

Career Exploration

BUT THERE ARE SO MANY!

If your teacher-coordinator offered you a new American car of your choice free, how would you react? Excited? You bet! But you'd probably ask, "What's the catch?" That's a smart question, and there is a catch. You would have to choose a particular one above all others and tell why you picked it—all within a month's time.

That might sound easy enough. But, there are four major car manufacturers in the United States. Each of them produces a station wagon, a full-size, a middle-size, and a compact car. Four companies times four types equals 16 cars. Now then, each car can have different features or options that the buyer can choose. The car could be one color or two, have a vinyl top or a plain top, a radio and/or tape deck, air conditioning, backseat speakers, special hubcaps. Let your imagination run wild, and you will see that there may well be over 100,000 possible combinations of these options. Choosing one particular car out of all these possibilities has become a much more complex matter than it first seemed!

How would you go about deciding? You could list the cars you know something about, and the features you like or dislike about them. Maybe you don't like or need a station wagon, and that would eliminate a number of cars. Maybe you would consider how big a car you could afford to operate and maintain, and that would cross off more possibilities. After that, you might make an options table something like this:

OPTIONS I FEEL I MUST HAVE	OPTIONS I WOULD LIKE TO HAVE IF POSSIBLE	OPTIONS I DEFINITELY DON'T WANT

Now you are on your way toward making a good choice. From here you can narrow it down to five cars, then try to see or drive those five and compare them. One will win out over all the others.

Union Pacific Railroad Photo

But you know and I know that even though your teacher-coordinator is rich and famous, you'd better not hold your breath waiting for the free car. Your teacher-coordinators have a different offer to make. They will give you all the help you need to find out what occupational options are open to you. Coordinators do not make occupational choices for you. They help you get practical work experience so that you will have a better idea of what you want to do when you choose an occupation.

Just as the car you might have chosen might not meet your needs several years from now, so the first occupation you choose might not be your lifetime choice. (We'll talk more about that later.) Choosing the wrong car wouldn't be a great tragedy. The car would still get you where you wanted to go, and you could take care of it so that in a few years it would bring a good price as a used car. You could then move up to something you like better. Choosing the wrong occupation may not be a matter of life and death, but it is much more serious than choosing the wrong car. Years of a person's life can be wasted.

One reason people make mistakes when choosing an occupation is that they just don't know what opportunities are available. Sometimes people know certain occupations exist, but they still can't enter them for one reason or another. People who have wanted to become doctors haven't had the money to pay for the years of schooling they would need, so they compromise and become paramedics or medical technicians. People who dream of becoming commercial pilots sometimes find they have a physical disability that makes that occupation impossible for them, so they take another job in the airlines industry. Many people have to make such choices. Knowing that shouldn't keep people from trying to reach an occupational goal, however. If occupational goals are realistic, there is a good chance that people will reach them. But if they don't get all the way there, at least they are likely to be involved in a field which interests them.

The job of choosing the best possible occupation for yourself is a lot harder than picking a car. Luckily, you don't have a 30-day time limit!

Have each person write down ten occupations on ten small slips of paper. Each person tries to pick five that are fairly common and five that are a little out of the ordinary. Clerking in a store would be a fairly common occupation. You probably know several people who do it. Being a dog catcher would be more unusual.

Choose a committee of four to alphabetize the slips, eliminating duplicates. Write the occupations on the blackboard. How many did you come up with? Are there some that sound more exciting to you than those you suggested?

SHOULD YOU FIT THE JOB OR SHOULD THE JOB FIT YOU?

In the past, vocational educators have been accused—and sometimes rightly so—of trying to shape students to fit certain jobs, rather than helping students find jobs that fit their needs and talents. This situation is not ideal. Ideally a person's interests and abilities should be the major factor in occupational choice.

But there is a very real problem here. Vocational education teachers try to find out what kinds of jobs are available in the world of work and what the manpower needs are in their communities. Then they help students train for these occupations. Otherwise they are afraid that students will end up training for jobs that don't exist. People may be jobless, lose self-respect and hope, and not know where to turn. A conscientious teacher is naturally going to be very concerned about such possibilities.

Always keep in mind that your teacher-coordinators want you to succeed in the world of work. They are more experienced, and therefore more realistic. Whatever work experience they help you to obtain will be useful even if it does not turn out to be in an occupation you want to follow for life. But their help and their presence should not keep you from doing a little career exploration—and a little self-exploration—on your own.

The decision about what you are going to do with your life is a personal one. Other people can help you, but in the end you are the one who has to make the final decision.

The first step is to find out about as many interesting careers as possible. The *Dictionary of Occupational Titles* (Available from the Superintendent of Documents, U. S. Government Printing Office, Washington, D. C. 20402) lists and describes over 21,000 occupations. Looking into it, you may be overwhelmed by possibilities. It will help you realize that you aren't limited to just a few kinds of jobs. Career exploration can be an adventure.

❀ Chapter Thirteen ❀

CAREER
PORTFOLIO

Terry Mauzy

AGRIBUSINESS

People working in agribusiness provide food and other agricultural products for the rest of us. Farmers fit into this category. They have to know a great deal about *agri*culture *and* about *business*. Farmers have their share of problems. They have to struggle with nature. They can't decide to take off for a few days and leave their crops and animals to shift for themselves. Sometimes in good years more food is raised than can be used, and they may not get fair prices for their crops. Farmers will tell you, though, that there are great satisfactions in living an active, outdoor life, close to nature, and in being somewhat independent. Many farmers are becoming more active politically and trying to get laws passed that would protect and help them

The raising of plants and animals has become much more scientific than it used to be. Many careers involving laboratory and experimental work are related to agribusiness. Government and private agencies have programs for the improvement of agricultural products. In the future there will have to be more advisors and planners to insure the national and world food supply. Most of these scientific jobs in agriculture require more than a high school education. Remember, though, there are ways of getting more education if you want it.

There are also many people who do not own farms, but are hired to work on the land. They are called migrant workers because they move with their families from place to place as the crops ripen. Many migrant workers do not get good food, a decent education, adequate health care, or financial security. Automation is coming to the orchard, too. In the past, people thought a machine could never be made which could handle delicate fruits carefully enough. A mechanical fruit picker is being designed now which can. The migrant workers are becoming obsolete.

Logging falls under agribusiness, too. Jobs in it range from tree cutting to truck driving to smoke jumping to replanting. As a nation, we are becoming more and more aware that we can't just march in and cut down a lot of trees time after time without paying the price for it someday. Also, when trees are cut, many other parts of the forest ecology are affected. Soil is more prone to erosion, animal life is disturbed, and streams are sometimes polluted. Both governmental agencies and private lumber companies have an interest in protecting the forest ecology. They employ people in their laboratories to study soil, to test ways of growing trees faster, and to design new products that can be made from the waste materials and leftovers. Some of the larger lumber companies are experimenting with setting up public recreational facilities on the forest land they use. Several have had good campgrounds and hiking trails on their tracts of land for many years. They hire people to plan, maintain, and supervise such facilities.

It may have occurred to you by this time that if you choose a career in agribusiness you have to consider geographical location. Certain crops and forest resources are found in particular areas. You may have to relocate in order to engage in some of these agribusiness occupations.

Did you hear about the professor who is experimenting with the growing of certain plants which can be processed to make oil? If he succeeds, he will have made a contribution to solving the energy crisis, at least on a small scale. Does he fit in the agribusiness cluster? Well, partly anyway.

Terry Mauzy

TRANSPORTATION

Many of us are fascinated by tele-transportation such as we've seen in science fiction films and TV shows. You simply beam yourself to wherever you please. No waiting for buses, driving in traffic, or paying for an airline ticket. One generation's science fiction can become the next generation's reality! But for the present we will have to rely on the more ordinary ways of getting places.

When you think of careers in transportation you no doubt think of drivers, pilots, and engineers. Considering the distances Americans travel both for business and pleasure, these occupations will be important for a long time to come. Because of the energy crunch, public transportation might become even more vital than it was in the past.

If you could go behind the scenes at an international airport, you would see how many workers it takes to keep traffic flowing. Schedules have to be drawn up, tickets sold, traffic controlled, and food services provided.

With so many people traveling for pleasure now, the occupation of travel agent has been gaining importance. To be a travel agent, you would have to be able to work well with people. You would also have to be good at reading and correlating detailed schedules and making accurate travel arrangements. Any background in geography or foreign languages you have would no doubt prove useful, as would any traveling you have done.

Transportation includes moving goods and materials, as well as people. Independent truckers own their own rigs and arrange their own pickups and deliveries. Other truckers work for big transit companies. In either case, the long-distance truckers are often loners to some extent. Their way of life takes them away from home and family more than many other occupations would.

The same might be said for the merchant marine. The merchant marine is our fleet of ships carrying cargo all over the world. Many people feel that our country's merchant marine has been badly neglected and that our carrying capacity has fallen below that of many other countries. Steps are being taken to correct that. Young people who want to see a bit of the world and are willing to work hard and put up with some periods of monotony might enjoy several years in the merchant marine. Be careful, though. People in the merchant marine tell us that the sea gets in your blood!

No matter what means of transportation we talk about, a fleet of mechanics and safety inspectors stands behind it. These people are the "doctors" of their occupational cluster. No trucking company, bus, train, or airline could operate without them.

BUILDING TRADES

You have seen people operating all kinds of modern equipment, demolishing old buildings and structures and constructing new ones. Learning to handle a piece of equipment that is many times your size and

Terry Mauzy

weight takes time and practice. For your own safety and that of people around you, you really have to know what you're doing! Many people prefer outdoor construction work to sitting in an office all day.

But a construction-related job can also be an indoor, less physically active occupation. Before a building is begun, much groundwork has to be laid. Architects, designers, cost estimators, drafters, secretaries, consultants, purchasing agents, and many others are involved.

In the building industry you will find many specialties. You might be a carpenter, plumber, flooring installer, electrician, cabinetmaker, etc. Many of these take special training, but many skills can be learned on the job or in apprenticeship programs. If new construction slows down, as it does from time to time, people with special skills may find it easier than non-skilled laborers to make it on their own for a while. They can use their skills for repair and renovation jobs.

Notice how many jobs in construction take brain as well as brawn. Notice also how, if you had to, you could move from one specialty to another within this cluster. The fact is, you can do that in most clusters if you are alert and continue to learn whatever there might be to learn in your work environment.

Be ready for many innovations in the construction field! We have to come up with new ways of solving problems, such as shortages of materials and energy. Not so very long ago, solar heating seemed to belong to science fiction. Now it is coming into greater and greater use. Occupations dealing with solar heating are on the rise. If an occupation in such a field interests you, you might find that a conventional heating and cooling company might be a good place to begin. Community colleges and technical schools offer courses in such new fields.

Some old problems never seem to go away. Termites, rats, roaches— who needs them? Some companies specialize in pest control. It's a more scientific field than it used to be. The need for exterminators is likely to exist for some time to come.

When you choose an occupation, you have to take into consideration what you are like as a person. Some of us like an element of danger in what we do for a living. That doesn't mean that we like to take foolish chances, but rather that we can face danger calmly with common sense, and perhaps with a bit of pleasure even. Others of us prefer a more peaceful environment in which we can do an exacting job with pride and satisfaction. What kind of an environment is best for you?

SERVICE OCCUPATIONS

All of us should try to master as many everyday skills as we can. If I ride a bike to work everyday, I should be able to patch a tire or make a simple brake adjustment. If my washing machine goes on the fritz, I should be able to check a few simple possibilities for what may be wrong with it. If I have a small accident with my car, I should be able to replace a back-up light or pound out a small dent in the fender.

Still, there comes a time when people can't do everything for themselves. Either they don't have the time or the skills. They call in an expert. Mechanics and repair people offer services rather than products.

Nowadays, more and more occupations involve service. People need and want many services, and they are becoming more and more able to afford them. The girl in the photo who trains dogs is highly skilled. Her

Terry Mauzy

services may be a matter of life or death for the dog, especially if it is a city dog. For example, a dog that cannot respond to voice commands is a good candidate for getting hit by a car. Some people raise show dogs. They hire a trainer or handler who is experienced and knows what the judges in a dog show will be looking for. If you like animals and would enjoy working with them, a pet shop might be a good place to get some know-how. (Three students in the psychology department of a big university even started their own pet consultation service. People with emotionally disturbed pets call them for help!)

Hair styling, manicuring, figure improvement—these and other such services are often referred to as personal service. Cosmetology is the more formal name for the science (or art) of giving permanents, straightening hair, coloring it, doing facials, applying make-up, etc. You can see how important it is that people who use chemicals on other people's skin and hair should know what they are doing. Most states therefore require cosmetologists to have licenses. Looking good is big business today. Most people feel better when they look their best.

Providing services is a good way to earn a living. For some people it is much more than that. Nuns, priests, rabbis, and ministers find joy in helping others overcome their problems and in giving them help, encouragement, and guidance. In modern times, many people in religious careers have been active in movements designed to help solve social problems.

Public service jobs include postal carriers, police personnel, firefighters, city sanitation workers, and many others. Many jobs in environmental control are classified as public service jobs and involve planning, inspection, and enforcement activities. Your city hall might be a good place to track down more information on some of these jobs.

Doctors spend many years preparing for their professions. They have their college years, several years in medical school, and a period of internship at a hospital. It costs a great deal of money, and when doctors complete their education, they have to have still more money for offices and equipment. Many young doctors have to postpone having families and homes until they can get over these financial hurdles.

Maybe you can't afford a long medical education or don't feel that you would want to stay in school that long, yet you are extremely interested in a medical career. Today, there are various medical paraprofessions you can enter. Being a paraprofessional means that you have had some medical training, but not as much as a doctor. You assist the doctor in skilled tasks that you have learned to do, thus releasing more of the doctor's time for such things as difficult surgeries, special highly-skilled treatments, and consultations.

Paraprofessional careers exist in many other fields, too—engineering, urban planning, teaching, law, librarianship, and mental health. Most of them involve training over and above what you have had in high school but not as much as a full professional in those fields would have to have.

OCCUPATIONS IN RECREATION

In the good old days, many people worked 12 or more hours a day. Eventually the 40 hour work-week became standard. Looking into the future we can be fairly certain that the work-week will keep getting

Cincinnati Milacron

shorter. People will have more leisure time, and more men and women will be finding careers in recreation and entertainment.

If you feel you have the talent to become a singer, dancer, actor, or magician, try it! Move toward it by participating in school or community programs or form your own group. Competition in the field of entertainment is keen, and it takes a great deal of determination to succeed. Many entertainers have to start out working another job in order to have a little financial security. Eventually some of them become full-time entertainers. Others don't, but they have the satisfaction of having given it a try. They may also be able to find a related job in recreation.

Competent people are needed in the recreation area, people who can plan and supervise leisure time activities for young and old people. If you are good at games and sports and enjoy teaching them to others, this may be a field for you to investigate. People with backgrounds in various crafts also work in recreation. For example, park departments hire them to run specific workshops and classes for children and adults.

City and state governments, as well as the federal government, hire many people to keep our outdoor facilities and wilderness areas beautiful and safe for those of us who want to use them for recreation and leisure.

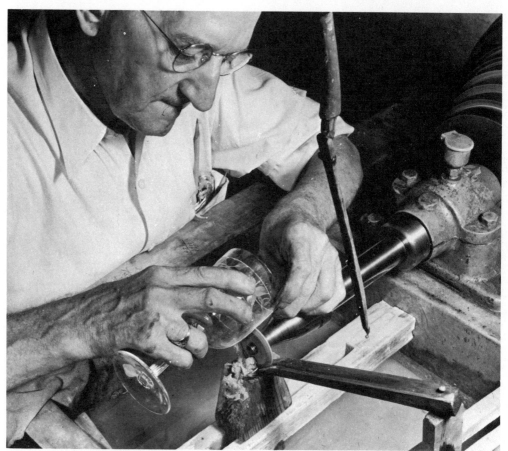

Lennox Industries, Inc.

THE FINE ARTS

Sometimes we want more than just entertainment. We want to be caught up in drama, moved. We want to experience anguish and joy. We want to come to new understandings, to a clearer vision of ourselves and our universe. For some of us this means attending a musical performance. For others, it might be a night at the theater or ballet, or an afternoon at the art museum.

Some gifted people spend their lives giving us these deeper pleasures and insights. You could be one of them! However, not everyone can be a musician or an actress or painter or sculptor or novelist on a professional basis. Yet there are many occupations that relate to the arts.

Theater-related occupations would include business managers, make-up artists, light technicians, and set builders, for example. Museums hire people to help prepare exhibits, guards, sales personnel, librarians, and secretaries. People who are interested in writing often find their way into careers in publishing companies. Not all such people are frustrated artists, of course. But many of them want to be in touch with the arts. They enjoy the stimulation they get from their work environments, and they derive satisfaction from being part of a team that produces something memorable.

C. William Horrell

COMMUNICATIONS

In the last fifty years, there have been big happenings in the field of communications. The printing press is of course a much older invention than the various electronic media. However, it is only in this century that so much printed material has become available to so many people. We have access to a great many books, magazines, and newspapers.

Even at that, people don't read nearly as much as they watch television and listen to the radio. A great many careers have been created by the demand for news, information, and entertainment via electronic media. Let's list just a few communication careers: disc jockey, typesetter, camera crew, copy reader, editor, reporter, in-studio technician, photo journalist, computer operator, public survey team, advertising agent.

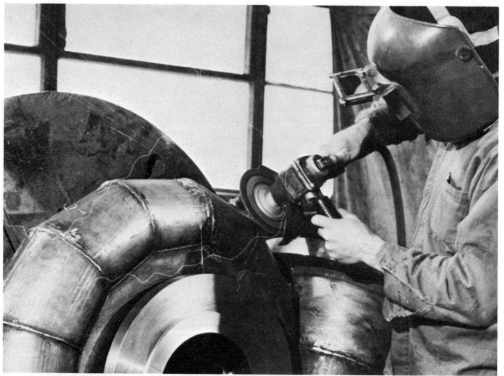

Allis-Chalmers Corp.

OCCUPATIONS IN MANUFACTURING

Americans have one of the highest standards of living in the world. That means they have many products available to them. Our factories manufacture all kinds of things, from mouse traps to huge cranes for construction work. Many factories use the assembly line technique of making a product. Each person along the line does some small part toward putting whatever it is together. Most car manufacturers produce cars this way. Other factories (often smaller ones) hire skilled workers who do a series of operations connected with the making of the product.

DoAll

SALES CAREERS

Once products have been manufactured, they have to be made available to consumers. They are sent to wholesalers or distributors, then to the retail stores where we buy them.

If you like handling good-quality merchandise, selling clothing can be exciting. It takes imagination, too. Many people appreciate sincere, knowledgeable comments and suggestions. If you are interested in such a career, you would want to find out as much as possible about new materials, famous designers, measuring for alterations, new styles, and other related things. You may even want to take some junior college courses in merchandising. What seems at first glance to be a simple job has the possibility of becoming much more. Many jobs are what *you* make them.

Some people who sell in department stores become buyers for their departments. Suppose someone working in the shoe department is promoted to buyer. That person will go to New York, Chicago, or other cities where the latest in shoes is being shown. Buyers are responsible for selecting high-quality merchandise and for knowing what their customers want and can afford.

Specialty shops put an emphasis on one group of products. In our city, for example, we have a mountaineering store which sells hiking and climbing boots, parkas, dehydrated camping foods, and sleeping bags. If you have a hobby or a special interest, you might want to think in terms of getting a job where you could sell merchandise in that field. You may have special knowledge which you could put to good use.

Our three basic physical needs are food, clothing, and shelter. The person who sells shelter is called a *realtor*. Realtors must take a course and pass a real estate exam in order to be licensed. One requirement of their job is that they must enjoy meeting people. As one realtor put it, "It's like putting a complicated puzzle together to get just the right house and the right buyer together. When I can do that, I'm happy."

We have barely scratched the surface of opportunities in buying and selling. We might also mention purchasing agents. Some are in charge of buying raw materials for factories. Designers of products specify the type and quality of materials. The purchasing agent then works hard to find the best possible price for the best possible material. Purchasing agents can also be in charge of buying office supplies and business machines.

Another selling career is that of manufacturer's representative. Maybe your company makes diagnostic instruments for medical doctors. Your job would be to take the instruments out to clinics and doctors' offices and demonstrate them. Or your employer could be a furniture manufacturing company. You would take colorful brochures and sometimes samples around to furniture dealers to see if they would carry them in their stores.

We don't want to forget door-to-door salespersons. A great many jokes have been made about them, but they can be very good ambassadors for their companies if they have common sense and tact. If the company is a good one, there is no need for fast talk and hard sell. Good salespersons like people and enjoy selling worthwhile products.

OFFICE AND BUSINESS CAREERS

Office jobs for men and women can be found in banks, insurance companies, clinics, government agencies, courts, city schools, law offices, investment firms, universities, and many other places. The range is so wide that we can cover only a few of the possibilities.

Good secretaries are always in demand. Some basic skills are necessary to enter this field: typing, shorthand, good language skills, a working knowledge of business machines, telephone skills, etc. If you have some of these, you can always learn others on the job. Business courses are offered at night school in many places, too.

Computers are being used much more widely in the business world now. Key punch operators, programmers, repair personnel, and statisticians are just a few of the occupations that are open. Some of these jobs are highly skilled and require a good knowledge of math. A person who likes detailed work, demanding a high level of accuracy, would be good in this field. There are other computer-related jobs that require less skill. Some business schools offer short programs of instruction for these jobs.

C. William Horrell

MINING AND HEAVY INDUSTRY

In sharp contrast to careers in business and office work are those occupations in mining and heavy industry. Our country is rich in natural resources, and many people work at mining iron ore and coal, drilling for oil, or quarrying stone.

They go deep into the earth through narrow shafts, noticing the warning signs and signals on the way down, testing the air with their special devices to see if the concentration of gas is low enough to make their work place safe. Only then do they set to work with modern tools. Workers and ponies are no longer harnessed to cars to get the coal out to the main shaft. Still, they often work in cramped positions and there is always an element of fear. Do miners feel a surge of joy once they emerge into sunshine and fresh air at the end of the day?

By *heavy industry*, we usually mean iron and steel plants and large fabrication mills that make things such as structural steel and large machinery. But iron and steel workers were also partly responsible for the large sculpture in Chicago which was designed by the famous artist, Pablo Picasso. They fabricated it according to his plan. The labor of iron and steel workers is evident in many parts of our lives!

C. William Horrell

FOOD PROCESSING AND DISTRIBUTION

It's hard to figure out why we left food processing till last, since all of us like to eat!

As consumers, we don't buy wheat: we buy flour. Most of us don't buy a steer: we buy hamburger, steak, or roast beef. Food processors get food ready for our tables and package it.

Many food processing plants have several home economics experts to test and improve their products and to demonstrate various uses of processed foods. New techniques of food preservation, such as the freeze-dry process, are constantly being developed. More research is being done to find substitutes for chemical preservatives which appear to be harmful.

Related occupations range from delivery personnel who truck the foods to retail outlets to government inspectors who periodically check to make sure that the foods are safe and clearly labeled so that consumers know what they are getting.

Terry Mauzy

MILITARY SERVICE

Did you know that it is possible to learn an occupation in the Armed Forces? Each branch of the service needs people with occupational specialties, so it trains people for them. Here are some occupations for which you could be trained while in the service: welder, drafter, electrical repairer, nurse, cook, aircraft mechanic, meat cutter, office manager, photographer, helicopter pilot.

What requirements would you have to meet to get into the Armed Forces? What educational opportunities would you have? How much would you be paid, and what other benefits would you receive? How many years would you have to serve? Could you be married? These are the questions you might want to ask at the Army, Navy, Air Force, or Coast Guard recruitment office nearest you. All big cities have them, and they would be listed in the telephone directory under *United States Government*.

You could also write to: Selective Service System
1724 F Street, N. W.
Washington, DC 20435

1. The assembly line concept has enabled us to produce more goods at a faster rate, but there have been many problems connected with it. What about the worker who must do the same small operation over and over again, at a regular pace, day after day, year after year? It can turn workers into robots.

In recent years much effort has been made to modify the assembly line system. Experiments have been made in which four or five workers put a whole car together. This means the workers have to have much more skill, but they are much less bored and can take pride in what they are making.

Another plan that has been successful is to train workers to do five or six different operations each and let them change off among these.

Do you have any other ideas how assembly line work might be made better for the workers?

2. "I don't want to sit around and type all day," a high school senior said to a secretary in a wholesale beauty supply company.

"Oh, but typing is only a small part of my job," answered the secretary, who had held her job for four years. "I arrange meetings, supervise new secretaries, write letters, announcements or memos for my boss. I meet people. I represent our company on the phone. I do product research. I do some bookkeeping. And there's more!"

Have you heard people speak of secretarial work as something anybody could do? Do you believe it? What qualities do you think a boss would value highly in a secretary?

3. How do you feel about homemaking as a career? Do you think it is demeaning (degrading) to be a homemaker? That is, do you think it makes you less of a person?

What skills should a good homemaker have?

What do you think about being a homemaker and having a career, too? Can you think of some of the problems that might result? How could a husband and wife work them out?

Do you think a husband and wife could successfully reverse the usual roles, the man staying home and keeping house and the woman going out to work?

Working Cooperatively

"What's My Line?" That's the name of a well-known TV game show. A panel of four tries to guess what line of work each contestant is in. The panel members can ask only questions that can be answered with a *yes* or a *no*.

Choose a panel of four from your class. Let three other people pretend to belong to three different occupations which the panel must guess. The panel can ask only yes or no questions.

Change panels and contestants until everyone has had a chance to participate.

We will end this chapter with a list of addresses where good career materials are available. All of these addresses have been carefully checked, and the pamphlets mentioned are worth having.

Go through the list and choose an occupation you would like to know more about. (Not all occupations could be covered in this list, of course. If you are interested in an occupation that is not represented here, ask your teacher-coordinator or librarian for help in finding an address to write to.)

Write to the company or office and request career information. Your letter should be simple and to the point.

RED PAGES FOR
CAREER EXPLORERS

American Industrial Hygiene Association
66 So. Miller Road
Akron, Ohio 44313
(Industrial hygienists are being hired by many large companies. These people are trained to recognize and correct health and safety hazards on the job.) Ask for: "Industrial Hygiene: the Key to Occupational Health"

Amalgamated Meat Cutters and Butcher

2800 N. Sheridan Road
Chicago, Illinois 60657
Ask for one of these:
"Occupational Brief: Packinghouse Worker"
"Occupational Brief: Retail Meat Cutter"

American Academy of Physicians' Assistants
2341 Jefferson Davis Highway, Suite 700
Arlington, Virginia 22202
Ask for:
"Physician's Assistant—Questions and Answers"

American Bankers Association
1120 Connecticut Avenue, N.W.
Washington, D.C. 20036
Ask for: "Banking: Horizons of Promise"

American Dental Hygienists' Association
211 East Chicago Avenue
Chicago, Illinois 60611
Ask for pamphlets on dental hygienist or dental technician as careers

American Foundrymen's Society
Golf and Wolf Roads
Des Plaines, Illinois 60016
Ask for: "Metal Casting . . . an Art . . . A Science . . . a Career"

American Hospital Association
840 North Lake Shore Drive
Chicago, Illinois 60611
Ask for one of these:
"Today's Hospital: Career Center for America's Youth"
"Careers that Count"
"Look into Social Work Jobs in Health Care Settings"

American Institute for Design and Drafting
3119 Price Road
Bartlesville, Oklahoma 74003
Ask for: "Drafting as a Career"

American Petroleum Institute
Division of Marketing
1801 K Street, N.W.
Washington, D.C. 20006
Ask for: "Basics for Service Station Salesmen"

American Society of Landscape Architects
1750 Old Meadow Road
McLean, Virginia 22101
Ask for one of these:
"Landscape Architecture: a Career"
"Women in Landscape Architecture"

American Textile Manufacturers Institute, Inc.
400 S. Tryon Street
Charlotte, North Carolina 28285
Ask for one of these:
"There's a Career for You in Textile Manufacturing"
"There's a Career for You in Textile Marketing and Merchandising"
"There's a Career for You in Textile Research and Development"
"There's a Career for You in Textile Environmental Sciences"

Association for Computing Machinery
1133 Avenue of the Americas
New York, New York 10036
Ask for: "Facts on Computer Careers"

The Associated General Contractors of America
1957 E Street, N.W.
Washington, D.C. 20006
Ask for one of these:
"Construction"
"Construction: Opportunities Unlimited"

Automotive Information Council
28333 Telegraph Road
Southfield, Michigan 48034
Ask for:
"Automotive Mechanics—a Career Opportunity"

Cessna Aircraft Co.
Air Age Education Department
P.O. Box 1521
Wichita, Kansas 67201
Ask for:
"Air Transportation"
"Come Fly with Us"
"What Are You Going to Do with the Next Half Century?"

Committee on Careers in Retailing
National Retail Merchants Association
100 West 31st Street
New York, New York 10001
Ask for: "Your Opportunities in Retailing"

Department of Transportation
Federal Aviation Administration
Washington, D.C. 20591
Ask for: "Air Traffic Control" or ask for general pamphlets on aviation careers

Direct Selling Association
1730 M Street, N.W.
Washington, D.C. 20036
(Direct selling is door-to-door selling, or in-the-home selling) Ask for: "An Appealing Alternative"
"Who's Who in Direct Selling"

Life Insurance Marketing and Research Association
170 Sigourney Street
Hartford, Connecticut 06105
Ask for: "The Life Insurance Career"

Harry Lundeberg School (Merchant Marine)
Piney Point, Maryland 20674
Ask for:
"Training for Careers in the Towing Industry"
"The Harry Lundeberg School—Bulletin"

National Association for Practical Nurse Education
122 East 42nd Street
New York, New York 10017
Ask for information on practical nursing as an occupation. They have material for both men and women.

National Association of Broadcasters
1771 N Street, N.W.
Washington, D.C. 20036
Ask for one of these:
"Careers in Radio"
"Careers in Television"

National Association of Letter Carriers (AFL-CIO)
100 Indiana Avenue, N.W.
Washington, D.C. 20001
Ask for one of these:
"So You Want to Carry the Mail!"
"The Mail Man"

National Association of Plumbing, Heating, Cooling Contractors
1016 20th Street, N.W.
Washington, D.C. 20036
Ask for:
"Your Future in the Plumbing-Heating-Cooling Industy"

National Association of Realtors
Department of Education
430 North Michigan Avenue
Chicago, Illinois 60611
Ask for: "Careers in Real Estate"

National Career Center

3839 White Plains Road
Bronx, New York 10467
Ask for one of these:
"A Profitable Career in Barbering and Men's
Hairstyling Awaits You"
"Picture Yourself as a Professional Hairstylist and
Beautician"

National Career Center

3839 White Plains Road
Bronx, New York 10467
Ask for: "An Exciting Business Career Awaits You"

The National Executive Housekeepers Assoc., Inc.

Business and Professional Bldg.
Second Avenue
Gallipolis, Ohio 45631
Ask for: "Futures in Executive Housekeeping"

National FFA Center

P.O. Box 15160
Alexandria, Virginia 22309
Ask for: "Careers in Agriculture and Natural
Resources"

National Fire Protection Association

470 Atlantic Avenue
Boston, Massachusetts 02210
(fire-fighting information)
Ask for: "It's a Job to Save a City"

National Hairdressers and Cosmetologists Assoc., Inc.

3510 Olive Street
St. Louis, Missouri 63103
Ask for: "Cosmetology as a Career"

National Pest Control Association, Inc.

8150 Leesburg Pike
Suite 1100
Vienna, Virginia 22180
Ask for: "Career Opportunities in the Pest Control
Industry"

New York Life Insurance Company

Careers
Box 51
Madison Square Station
New York, New York 10010
Ask for one of these: "Careers for a Changing
World: The Arts"
"Careers for a Changing World: Business and
Office"
"Careers for a Changing World: Communications
& Media"
"Careers for a Changing World: Construction"
"Careers for a Changing World: Health Care"
"Careers for a Changing World: Hospitality &
Recreation"
"Careers for a Changing World: Manufacturing"
"Careers for a Changing World: Natural Resources
and the Environment"
"Careers for a Changing World: Transportation"

Shoe Service Institute of America

222 West Adams Street
Chicago, Illinois 60606
Ask for: "How Your Gifted Hands Can Put You on
Your Own Two Feet. Fast!"

United Brotherhood of Carpenters and Joiners of America

101 Constitution Ave., N.W.
Washington, D.C. 20001
Ask for: "Carpentry as a Career"

United States Department of Justice

Federal Bureau of Investigation
Washington, D.C. 20537
Ask for: "FBI: Career Opportunities"

U.S. Department of Commerce

Maritime Administration
Washington, D.C. 20230
Ask for: "Information Regarding Employment in the
U.S. Merchant Marine"

Chapter Fourteen

WHO, ME?

Self-portrait, Julie Carman   Self-portrait, Tina Smith

HOW WELL DO YOU KNOW *YOU?*

You now have an idea of the many opportunities that exist for you in the world of work. The next step will be to investigate a very interesting and complex subject—you!

"Who, me?" you say. "I've known me all my life."

Quite often we are so busy living day by day that we don't take the time to analyze ourselves. That's healthy, to some extent. However, just as a store owner needs to take inventory every so often, so we need to take an inventory of ourselves. That's what you will be doing in this chapter. It will help you decide if you are heading in the best possible direction *for you*.

Edward Smith

One of the best things you could do for yourself right now is to take advantage of any testing programs available at your school. The word *test* means trouble to most of us, especially in the context of school. It shouldn't. The tests we are talking about are not given with the idea of assigning you a grade. They are designed as inventories to help you take stock of your assets. No one claims that these tests are 100 percent accurate, but they can give you some good hints about what you might be able to do well, what your personality traits are, what interests you have, and how all these might work together with your abilities. Tests can measure many things.

Determining how you see yourself is not an easy task. Your opinion of yourself changes from time to time. Analyzing yourself isn't as simple as looking in a mirror and describing your physical features. You piece together a self-concept by looking inside yourself and by observing how other people see you and react to you.

In this chapter we are going to try to help you make an informal inventory of your own assets. We hope to call attention to the things you have going for you and to suggest how you might coordinate them with your occupational choice.

NEEDS WE ALL SHARE

All of us have certain basic needs. One way in which we try to satisfy some of them is through work. What are these needs? A well-known psychologist, Dr. Abraham Maslow, has studied the subject. In his book *Motivation and Personality* (New York: Harper, 1954) he outlines five categories of needs: physiological needs, safety needs, belongingness needs, esteem needs, and self-actualization needs. Let's look at these categories of needs in a little more detail.

PHYSIOLOGICAL NEEDS.   We need certain things just to stay alive—air, water, food, shelter, and rest. These are basic survival needs.

SAFETY NEEDS.   Once we are able to stay alive, we begin feeling the need for safety. We want to be as safe as we can from physical danger such as being eaten by a lion or struck by lightning. We want to be safe from physical assault. We also want psychological safety. That is, we want the *feeling* of being safe, of feeling secure.

BELONGINGNESS NEEDS.   Once our physiological needs and our needs for safety have been taken care of, we have time to begin feeling the need to belong. We want to be part of a group, a culture, a society—to have close contact with others of our kind.

ESTEEM NEEDS.   If people esteem us, they have a good opinion of us and value us. Once we have satisfied our need to belong, then we begin needing to be liked and respected in the group to which we belong.

SELF-ACTUALIZATION NEEDS.   After we have satisfied all the above needs, we become aware of wanting to be fully ourselves, individuals. We want to express ourselves in action. We want to do things that give us a sense of self-fulfillment and accomplishment. We need to do things which reveal our thoughts, feelings, abilities, and insights.

Self-portrait

Greg Lancaster

Dr. Maslow feels that people always try to meet these needs in the above order. *Always* is always a strong word to use. You could probably find many exceptions in this case. For example, for some people the need to belong may at a given moment be put before the need for safety. Or an artist may put the need for self-actualization ahead of the need to be held in esteem. A person may give up his need for safety in order to save a loved one. Dr. Maslow's scheme is, however, a good general idea of how people structure their needs on a day-to-day basis. Let's look at some examples of how these needs we've talked about can be satisfied through work.

1. People want to have food, clothing, and shelter. They work so they will have the money to satisfy these *physiological* (physical) needs.

2. People need to feel secure. They satisfy their *safety* needs by planning ahead, putting money into retirement and insurance plans. They try to do good work so they won't lose their jobs.

3. People need to be around others, to have friends. Work provides some of the chances people have to satisfy their need to *belong.*

4. People want others to see that they have ability, knowledge, skill, and likeable traits. At work they can partially satisfy their need for *esteem.*

5. If people have the type of job they want, they may even move toward *self-actualization* on the job. They may be able to express themselves through their work.

PERSONAL INVENTORY, STEP I

For this chapter you will need a manila folder with 10 or 15 sheets of paper in it. Keep it until you complete your inventory. The first part of your inventory will have to do with your needs.

Do you agree with Dr. Maslow's ideas on needs? Do your needs follow his general pattern? Write one paragraph (or more, if you like) defining the needs you believe you can someday satisfy through your work.

YOUR STRONG POINTS.   Next you need to inventory the resources you have to bring to your job. What abilities do you have? What kinds of things are you best at doing?

Don't let wishful thinking enter into your self-analysis at this point. Deep inside you may wish you could be a brigadier general or an opera prima donna. But now is the time when you will have to say, "I don't think I can really achieve that," or "Yes, I can achieve this, but I will have to find out how to go about it." If you aren't honest with yourself, you may push yourself into an occupation you can't handle or keep yourself out of an occupation from which you would have gotten great satisfaction.

We will give you a few ideas for assessing your abilities. If, however, you really feel lost or unsure, go for help. Asking for help when you need it is another sign of maturity. Even the President of the United States seeks help from his advisors. Your teacher-coordinator or your counselor often know just the kinds of questions to ask you so that you can think effectively about yourself. To think effectively about yourself you must be able to see yourself from different points of view and to be somewhat objective about it.

It's hard to classify skills into mental and physical. It's too easy to make an artificial division. For example, writing a letter takes physical coordination and skill, as well as the ability to think and develop sentences. Repairing a washing machine takes a lot of mental ability in addition to physical strength and agility. Robert M. Pirsig, author of *Zen and the Art of Motorcycle Maintenance* (New York: William Morrow and Company, 1974) has something to say about this. In reference to mechanics he writes: "An untrained observer will see only physical labor and often gets the idea that physical labor is mainly what the mechanic does. Actually, the physical labor is the smallest and easiest part of what the mechanic does. By far the greatest part of his work is careful observation and precise thinking."

When you think about it like that, you will see that there isn't a category of physical jobs for dumb people and another category of mental jobs for smart people. Keep that in mind when you do the following exercise. Try not to answer according to what you think would put you in a better light. If you really want to find out something about yourself, you will have to be as honest as you can.

PERSONAL INVENTORY, STEP II

Select one from each of the following pairs that best fits you, and copy it into your self-inventory folder.

1.a.   If someone shows me how to do an arithmetic problem, I catch on quickly.

1.b. It takes me a while to learn how to do a new kind of arithmetic problem.

2.a. I could learn how to do a gymnastics routine on the parallel bars fairly easily.

2.b. I don't think I have the physical strength or coordination to go into gymnastics much.

3.a. If the gears on my bike started acting up, I would first try to fix them myself.

3.b. If I had trouble with the gears on my bike, I would take it straight to a repair shop.

4.a. I could write a business letter if I had to, but it would take me a long time.

4.b. I can put a business letter together fairly easily.

5.a. I am good at showing other people how to do something step by step.

5.b. I don't explain things very well, so I don't think I'd be good at teaching others how to do something.

6.a. I am physically quite strong for my size.

6.b. Physical strength is not one of my big assets.

7.a. I think I could have a calming influence on a tense situation between people.

7.b. If I get into a situation where people are arguing or disagreeing, I get nervous and uneasy.

8.a. I don't feel uneasy when I meet new people.

8.b. I get tense when I meet new people.

9.a. I find it very hard to speak in front of a group of people.

9.b. I have a bit of the ham in me and I like public speaking.

10.a. I like to develop ideas for doing things such as organizing a yard sale or designing a school yearbook.

10.b. I am good at carrying out ideas, but I don't particularly like to plan things.

11.a. If I had to decide which of three job applicants to hire, I feel I could make a wise choice.

11.b. I wouldn't really know how to go about choosing the best of three job applicants.

12.a. If I buy a model to put together or a pattern to make a dress, I have little trouble following the directions.

12.b. If I buy something that has to be put together by following written directions, I have problems assembling it.

Have you made your choices? Now comes the hard part. Write a paragraph or two describing the kind of person you believe yourself to be on the basis of the choices you made. Below is an example of how a young man named Joe Green described himself:

"I'm a little impatient when it comes to learning things. I seem to learn something more easily if physical skills are involved. I like fixing things and can take care of my bike and car pretty well. I can follow written directions okay when it comes to mechanical things. I have no trouble using repair manuals.

"I don't have much letter-writing ability. I wouldn't like public speaking because I'd be too self-conscious about what I had to say.

"I'm good at basketball and have taught others how to play the game. I enjoy showing others how to do things I can do well.

"I'm pretty easygoing and like being around people. I can remain calm during a dispute, and several times I've been asked to help settle an argument. I think I am usually tactful. But I wouldn't like to be in a position where I'd have to hire or fire anybody.

"I don't especially like to plan or design things. I'm just as happy being asked to do something and then doing a good job of it."

After you have written your paragraph or paragraphs, make a simple list of things you think you do well. Are there certain kinds of things people often ask you to help them with? Do you receive compliments for some things you do and not for others? Have you done particularly well in any of your school courses? If so, can you figure out what abilities were involved? Do you excel in some leisure-time activities?

After you have made a list of at least ten things you can do well, put a plus sign in front of each that you think you could use in a job situation someday.

YOUR LIKES AND DISLIKES.   Did you notice something interesting in the last section? When we think of our abilities we often think about them in terms of our likes and dislikes. Sometimes there is a relationship between what people like and what they are good at, but not always. You may enjoy doing something and still not be particularly good at it.

What would you do if you discovered that your likes or interests and your abilities didn't match very well? What do you think about the following alternatives?

a. You could realize that you can't do a certain thing well and turn to something else.

b. You could choose that activity as a leisure-time activity instead of choosing it for your life's work.

c. You could learn more about it so that you could get better at it. This might involve more education, an apprenticeship program, or self-education through books.

PERSONAL INVENTORY, STEP III

Look at the list of activities which follows:
Stamp or coin collecting
Listening to music
Making music (playing instruments and/or singing)
Camping, hiking
Participating in team sports such as volleyball, football, soccer
Participating in individual sports such as tennis, golf, swimming
Acting in plays
Helping other people (Candy Stripers, Scouts, etc.)
Building something such as a piece of furniture
Working at crafts such as leatherwork, knitting, macrame
Working on cars
Drawing or painting
Taking photographs
Attending plays or concerts
Dancing
Traveling
Pick out those you like to do and copy them into your folder. Add other activities you enjoy. Now go back and score each item. Use a scale of 1 to 10. If you like the activity only a little, give it a 1. If it is your favorite activity, give it a 10.

PERSONAL INVENTORY, STEP IV

The likes and dislikes we have talked about so far deal mostly with your interests. We want to draw your attention to some other likes and dislikes that will help you determine what occupation to follow.

Here, again, pick one of each pair of statements and copy it into your folder.

1.a. I like to work outdoors.

1.b. I prefer to work indoors.

2.a. I like to work with people (have contact with patients, customers, clients, etc.)

2.b. I like to work with things.

3.a. I like to work on my own without much supervision.

3.b. I feel more comfortable working under supervision.

4.a. I prefer a job which involves a lot of physical activity.

4.b. I am satisfied to do work that doesn't involve a great deal of physical activity.

5.a. I work best at a steady pace with no deadlines to meet.

5.b. I can work well under pressure if I have to.

6.a. I need peace and quiet in order to concentrate.

6.b. I can work with lots of other activities going on around me.

7.a. I like to work as part of a team.

7.b. I like to work alone.

WHERE YOU HAVE BEEN. If you have had a job before, your experience could be a big help in choosing your career. Many of you have been involved in such work as cutting grass, waiting on tables, selling papers, bagging in a grocery store, selling, or babysitting. Next you will be asked to analyze any work experience you have had so far.

PERSONAL INVENTORY, STEP V

First at the top of your page, write the name of a job you have had. Then record the following information about it:
Responsibilities I had
Things I liked about the job
Things I disliked about the job
Skills I used on the job
Skills I learned on the job

PERSONALITY AND CHARACTER TRAITS. In Part II, *Under the Big Umbrella,* we talked about personality traits that can mean success or failure on the job. As the last step in your Personal Inventory, think about your personality and character traits.

PERSONAL INVENTORY, STEP VI

As a group, make a blackboard list of adjectives that describe workers. Include both positive and negative traits. Here are a few to get you started: friendly, courteous, kind, tactless, tactful, loud, honest, loyal, neat, funny, quiet.

After all the adjectives the class can think of have been written on the board, pick out those that you think apply to you right now and add them to your folder. Then make a list of characteristics you would like to acquire, words that you would like to be able to apply to yourself in a few months or a year or a few years.

MOVING AHEAD

Now that you have taken a brief look at yourself, you are closer to being able to make a wise occupational choice. Remember the story about choosing a car that began this section? You narrowed the field down by deciding which options mean the most to you. Since you can't work at all the 20,000 plus occupations listed in the *Dictionary of Occupational Titles,* you will have to follow a similar procedure in choosing an occupation. You will have to compare your interests, abilities, and needs with a description of the occupation you select. The *Dictionary of Occupational Titles,* put out by the U.S. Department of Labor, is an excellent reference for this task because the occupations listed in it are described in terms of general duties involved and in terms of worker characteristics necessary for the job. Another good reference is the *Encyclopedia of Careers and Vocational Guidance,* edited by William Hopke (New York: Doubleday, 1975). Your school or public library probably has both of these.

Once you have been able to identify a few specific occupations which interest you, you can explore these more thoroughly. Talk with someone in the occupation; visit the worksite; talk to employers; work at a part-time job in that area of work; participate in a volunteer activity connected with the occupation. Remember, too, that your teacher-coordinator can help you.

 **Part Six**

Your First Job

CONQUERING THE FIRST DAY BLUES

You may be very glad you have landed a job and yet feel somewhat uneasy about your first day. First days are hard work even though you probably won't work very hard!

Young workers were asked what problems they encountered the first day. Most of them said they didn't really have problems, but they felt uncomfortable. The two main sources of discomfort were that they didn't know anybody and that they didn't know what to do.

Getting to know people is a matter of time. We'll talk about that in Chapter 18. As far as not knowing what to do, keep in mind that most employers try not to press you too hard the first day. They realize that you are faced with a whole new situation and need some time to get used to all the new faces and circumstances. They also realize that while you can be shown some things about your job, you might be too excited to concentrate and remember things that first day. The second day and the days thereafter more will be expected of you. You will really have to concentrate to learn the routines. Many new employees find it helpful to jot down instructions if there are so many details that it is hard to remember them all. In any case, your first day is a little like being lost. That feeling won't last long. You will soon find new friends and have plenty of chances to learn and to grow.

❈ Chapter Fifteen ❈

JOB
ACQUIRING
SKILLS

American Telephone and Telegraph Company

FINDING JOB OPENINGS

By now you have had a survey of job possibilities. You have considered your personal assets: your experience, abilities, interests, and aptitudes. You probably have some ideas about what kind of work you would like to do.

Now the question is, how do you go about getting the job you want? If you were merely looking for any kind of work, you could run your finger down the want ads column and see if there is anything you are qualified to do. This is different than making a special effort to get a job doing what you really want to do.

Upon graduation, you may not be able to walk right into the exact job you have in mind. You could, however, follow up some leads that would put you closer to your occupational goals. First we are going to suggest some good sources of job information.

COOPERATIVE EDUCATION PROGRAMS.   You are presently in an excellent position to discover job openings of the type you seek. In fact, over 60% of students in cooperative education programs are hired by their cooperating employers. While you are working, your employer has the opportunity to evaluate your potential as a full-time employee, and you can evaluate the opportunities available to you with that company. Does it have openings in the type of job you want in the long run? Is there opportunity for advancement in your chosen field or will the opportunities be limited?

Your teacher-coordinators can also be an excellent source of job opening information. If your abilities, needs, and desires are made known to them, they can be watching for appropriate opportunities. Since they are constantly in touch with employers in your community and are interested in you, they can be very helpful.

PEOPLE YOU KNOW.   For many years, surveys have indicated that young people often get their first job with the assistance of people they know. These people don't always have jobs to offer, but they might know about available openings and pass the word along. Since you are seeking independence you may be concerned with thoughts such as, "Maybe I'll only be hired because of someone's pull and not for what I can do." That really isn't much of a problem. At this stage, you are looking for a specific job for which you know you are qualified. You can make a reasonably realistic judgment about your qualifications, regardless of how you hear about a job. Besides, most employers are more hard-headed than to hire someone just to please a friend. After all, they are running a business.

EMPLOYMENT OR PLACEMENT OFFICES.   Recent legislation (Education Amendments of 1976, Title Two, P.L. 94-482) places greater pressure on schools to provide placement services. Until now, guidance counselors and teacher-coordinators have tried to help students find permanent jobs when they could spare time from their regular duties. Soon schools may be able to take more responsibility for helping students locate jobs. Ask your teacher-coordinator if any placement services are available through your school.

Your state also has employment offices. They will be known by such names as the Texas State Employment Service, the Maine State Employment Office, etc. The basic purpose of these agencies is to help the unemployed find jobs, and their services include both job counseling and placement. They are public agencies and their services are free.

Private employment agencies are licensed by the state. They keep in touch with employers to find out what kinds of workers they need. If you contact such an agency, a member of the staff will interview you and try to help you land a job that might meet your needs. Many agencies specialize in certain kinds of jobs, such as technical occupations, data processing sales, engineering, or iron workers. The yellow pages in the phone book list private employment agencies in your area.

Private employment agencies are not free. Either you or the employer must pay a fee. Before accepting any job through such an agency, be sure you understand who is to pay the fee and how much that fee will be if you have to pay it. Don't sign anything until you know for sure what the terms are.

Sometimes employment agencies are classified according to the way fees are handled: EPF (Employer Pays Fee), APF (Applicant Pays Fee), or a combination of EPF and APF. Some agencies also make special arrangements. For instance, an agreement can be made in which the employers pay the fee if they are satisfied with the work you do. If they don't like your work and have to let you go, you pay it. Occasionally this sort of arrangement leads to misunderstandings and trouble. For the new worker, it would probably be better not to get involved with these special arrangements but to stick to a straight EPF or APF arrangement.

How large a fee should you be willing to pay? Generally, if you are expected to pay the fee you will be allowed to do so over two or three months' time, because the fees are generally high. After all, the agency is in business to make money. We can't suggest a fair rate that would apply all over the country in all situations. Perhaps you could check with your teacher-coordinator or your state employment office. Be cautious in dealing with an employment agency, just as you would be cautious in buying a stereo. The same rules apply to both situations: one, read the fine print before signing anything; two, ask questions; three, if you have any doubts ask some knowledgeable persons for their opinion.

TRADE PUBLICATIONS.   If your occupation has an association or a union, there may well be a trade magazine. Frequently these publications provide job leads or listings. For these jobs you would usually have to be willing to move to another city, because the publications are national in scope.

WANT ADS.   The Sunday edition of your local newspaper generally has more classified ads than the weekday editions. In the classified ads section you will find the help wanted ads. These can be valuable to you if you know how to use them.

The help wanted ad can be an open ad or a blind ad. An open ad includes the name and address of the firm, type of business it is, and a brief description of the job. It is the best ad in one sense because it provides so much information. These ads often attract many applicants, so act quickly if you see something you are interested in.

A blind ad doesn't give the name and address of the company. You reply to a box number. It may not give you adequate information about the job requirements. The advertiser uses the blind ad to avoid the flood of applicants that would result from an open ad. If you respond to a blind ad, you will probably need a resumé. We'll discuss resumés later in this chapter.

Checkpoint

Bring the Sunday help wanted ads to class. Circle three ads that could be of interest to you. Answer the following questions about each:

What skills are required?

Which of these required skills do you have?

How close does it come to fitting into your occupational plans?

Where is the job located?

Is the rate of pay given? If so, is it reasonable? (If you don't know whether or not it is reasonable, ask your teacher-coordinator or compare it with rates given for similar jobs.)

STEPS IN APPLYING FOR A JOB

Suppose you have spotted a job that sounds good to you. Your next step will be to develop a sales plan. You must sell yourself to your prospective employer. How do you sell yourself? In most cases you will have to make an appointment to be interviewed. (If you go through an agency someone there will make the appointment for you.) You will have to fill out an application form, and you may have to provide a resumé and references. Your sales job will depend on how well you do these things. It may all sound a bit overwhelming to you right now, but we will be going over each step in detail. You will find that it is not such an ordeal to apply for a job after all. Each time you do it, you gain a little more know-how even if you don't get the job.

You or your employment agency have called to make an interview appointment, and an interview is now scheduled. Nervous? If so, understand that most people are nervous in an interview situation, especially the first time. As people mature, they learn to admit, accept, and overcome nervousness, at least to some extent. To overcome nervousness doesn't mean that you no longer feel nervous. It means that you

Daryl Littlefield

have learned to cope with it and control it well enough so that you can present yourself. It helps to remember that others have faced similar situations and done well. So can you. Also, the person who appears not to be the least bit nervous can sometimes give the impression of not caring very much. The prospective employer expects you to be somewhat nervous, but not so much so that you can't make a good case for yourself.

An excellent strategy for coping with nervousness is to be thoroughly prepared. You will be more confident and better able to concentrate on the business at hand. Being prepared involves finding out as much as you can about the company and the job, and thinking in advance about just how you might fit into the job. Also consider how the job might meet your long-range occupational plans.

If you are answering a want ad in the newspaper, you may not have a chance to find out much about the company in advance. But if you do have a chance to study the company, here are some questions you might want to answer for yourself:

1. What is the expected future demand for the products or services the industry provides?

2. Does the company have a good reputation in the industry?

3. Does the company:
   a. have a history of discrimination?

   b. rank high, low, or average in wages?

   c. have a great deal of employee turnover?

   d. provide fringe benefits?

4. Are there opportunities for advancement?

You may be saying to yourself, "Such information would be pretty hard to find." You're right, especially in regard to your first job. If it is a big company, some of this information might be available through its employment office. Business magazines such as *Fortune* have articles on various companies from time to time. If you know someone who works for the company, that person might be a good source of information. Even though you can't answer all the above questions, get together as much information as you can.

The big day arrives. You are going for your interview. How can you make the best possible impression? Your appearance is vitally important, because the interviewers don't have much else to go on when they first meet you. Groom yourself neatly and wear appropriate clothes. Appropriate means right for a particular situation. We'll be discussing appropriate dress in more detail in Chapter 17. The interviewers have to consider what kind of an impression you will make on the public if the job involves contact with clients or customers. They must think about what kind of an influence you will have on your co-workers. Your personal appearance is the biggest hint they get.

Other hints: Take some basics with you—personal data sheet (we'll discuss this later in this chapter), social security card, pen, and pencil.

Don't smoke or chew gum during the interview.

Plan to arrive five to ten minutes before the scheduled appointment time. Allow extra time for travel. The 8:15 freight train, the morning rush hour traffic, getting lost can all delay you, and this is one appointment for which you *must* be punctual.

Approach the interview with a positive attitude. Expect to get the job. Any salesman who doesn't expect to make a sale probably won't. Expecting to get the job and feeling that it is yours by right are not the same. Expecting to get the job is confidence based on thorough preparation. Feeling that the job is yours by right is foolishness and will probably show in cocky behavior.

When you arrive for the interview, you will need to inform the receptionist or secretary of your name and appointment. The secretary will probably ask you to have a seat until the interviewer is ready. When you are shown into the office, the interviewer will no doubt introduce him/herself. You may simply respond with, "Pleased to meet you." And how about a friendly smile?

If the interviewer extends a hand, shake it firmly. Your handshake should be neither a bone crusher or a wet dish cloth. In all probability the interviewer won't know how to give you five or any variations of the newer greetings. It would also put the interviewer on the defensive, and you don't need that now.

Stand until you are invited to sit down. Don't slip into the old TV slouch that makes you appear too informal, careless, and unalert. If you carried a purse or portfolio with you, hold it on your lap or place it on the floor near your chair. The desk is for the interviewer's work, not for your belongings.

Have you ever spoken with someone who didn't look you in the eye? Did it make you feel uneasy? Would you buy something from such a person? If the prospective employer is to buy your personal sales program, now is the time to give your best. Look at the interviewer, confident that you can do the job for which you are applying.

You may be asked specific questions about yourself and why you want the job, or you may simply be asked to talk about yourself. In any case, try to be self-assertive. Remember that term? Turn back to Chapter Six briefly and look at the sample interview situations there.

An interview is a two-way conversation. The employer wants to find out as much about you as possible. On the other hand, you, too, need to find out as much as possible about the company and the job. You may want to ask questions about the business, the wages, vacations, and insurance. Write down your questions in advance so you will have them clearly in mind. Take them with you so you can refer to them if you need to. Think about the best order for asking them. Would you ask about wages and vacations first?

If no job offer has been made by the end of the interview, it is appropriate to ask, "May I call back in a few days after you've had time to consider my application?" This gives the interviewer the opportunity to tell you that a) you have the job; b) you don't have the job; c) other applicants must be interviewed before a decision is made. Thank the interviewer and leave.

Can you think of reasons why you or any other young applicant might not be hired? Here are some that are commonly given:

Employer preferred another applicant. You can't do much about that. Don't let it upset you. There are other jobs in the world.

Your personal appearance was inappropriate or careless.

You were late for the interview.

Your attitude was poor. You may have been too cocky or not courteous enough.

You smelled too much. You may have worn too much perfume, or you may have neglected to shower, use deodorant and/or mouth wash.

You may not have projected the image of a positive, confident, interested applicant.

You may have asked too much about wages and fringe benefits and not enough about the company and the job.

You may have expected too much, been too demanding, asked for too high a starting salary or too high a position in the company.

Get some interview practice by dividing into groups of three. Each group then prepares an interview situation to present to the class.

Draw straws for which of the three of you is going to be the prospective employer, which the applicant who gets the job, and which the job applicant who

is not chosen.

Invent a name for the company and decide what job the applicants are applying for. Plan what each of you will say or do during the interview that will turn the employer on—or off. When you are ready, present your interview before the whole class.

PERSONAL DATA SHEET

Either before or after your interview you will be asked to fill out an application form. For some jobs you may also be asked to provide a resumé. We will be coming to these items soon. Meanwhile, let's look at a very basic document you should have. We will call it a Personal Data Sheet.

A Personal Data Sheet is simply an informal record of your personal information, job experience, and education. You won't be giving it or showing it to a prospective employer. It is just for your own use. Keep it among your personal papers at home where you can refer to it when you need to. From it you can get the information you will need for filling out an application or writing a resumé.

Look at the sample Personal Data Sheet. If there is anything on it you don't understand, ask your teacher-coordinator to explain it. Then make your own Personal Data Sheet. Do not write in this book. Your teacher may be able to provide you with a copy you can write on. If

not, you could copy it on your own paper and fill it in.

Now you will have the "raw materials" for some of the other exercises in this chapter. You also have a document that will be useful to you outside of school!

PERSONAL DATA SHEET

NAME _____
 Last   First   Middle

ADDRESS _____

TELEPHONE NO. _____ SOCIAL SECURITY NO. _____

DATE OF BIRTH _____

HEIGHT _____ WEIGHT _____ HEALTH _____

PHYSICAL HANDICAPS _____

Education

High School

Name of High School: _____

Address: _____

Dates attended: From _____ To _____ Did you graduate? _____

Grade Completed: _____

Junior High School

Name: _____

Address: _____

Dates attended: From _____ To _____ Grade completed: _____

Elementary School

Name: _____

Address: _____

Dates attended: From _____ To _____ Grade completed: _____

Other Educational Experiences (Trade School, Beauty College, Armed Forces School, etc.)

School: _____

Address: _____

Dates attended: From _____ To _____ Courses Taken: _____

Work History

(List the jobs you have held, beginning with the most recent)

1. Employer's Name: _____ Dates of Employment: _____

   Address: _____

   Kind of work performed: _____

   _____

   Immediate Supervisor: _____

   Highest Wage: _____ Reason for Leaving _____

2.

3.

4.

Activities

(List sports, plays, yearbook or newspaper preparation, student council, clubs, volunteer work, etc.)

Personal References

(Generally speaking, these should not be relatives or any of the supervisors you listed above in your work history.)

1. Name: _____
   Position: _____
   Address: _____
   Telephone No.: _____
   Permission obtained to use this person as a reference:
   Yes _____ No _____
2.
3.
4.

LETTERS OF APPLICATION AND APPLICATION FORMS

A situation may arise in which you will want to contact a prospective employer by mail first. Perhaps you are responding to a blind ad or applying for a job in another city or state.

The letter you write will have to be brief, to the point, and neat. You should, in most cases, enclose a resumé. (We'll talk about resumés next.) Three elements are essential in your cover letter. First, mention how you found out about the job. Second, suggest what educational or work experiences you have that are appropriate for the job. Third, express your willingness to meet with the employer. A copy of the letter a young man named Ryan Schaake wrote to a prospective employer, Mrs. Keller, follows:

Some companies will send an application form to you in response to such a letter or in response to a phone call. In most cases, however, you will be asked to fill out an application form at the time of your interview. Please see the sample application form so that you will have some advance warning of the kinds of questions it will include.

Naturally, you will want to take your time and do as neat a job as possible. Read the questions carefully before beginning to write. Can you see the advantage of having your Personal Data Sheet along with you? You would have the information at your fingertips and would therefore feel less pressured. Sometimes it's difficult to remember dates or think of people who could serve as personal references for you. With your Personal Data Sheet in hand you would have all those details with you.

January 21, 19

Mrs. Karen Keller, Director
Rectangle Bank
408 South Main Street
Hamel, Illinois 62059

Dear Mrs. Keller:
    Mr. Bruce Williams, president of Williams
Construction Company, informed me of the records
clerk opening in your bank. Since I am
interested in a career in banking services, I
would like to be considered for the position.
    As my resumé indicates, I have had jobs
requiring record keeping and accounting for cash
and credit. I feel I can learn the duties and
perform well in the records clerk position.
    I look forward to the opportunity of
discussing the position and my qualifications
further with you. I am available for an
interview at your convenience.

                        Yours truly,

                        Ryan O. Schaake

Working Cooperatively

Have each person in the class get an application form from some company in town and bring it to class. You could ask one of your parents to bring home one from where they work, or you could go to a store, office, or factory and ask for one, explaining why you need it.

Compare the forms. Discuss words you aren't sure of or questions that don't make sense to you. Keep in mind the kinds of information you might want to write down ahead of time and bring with you to an interview.

RECTANGLE BANK
Hamel, Illinois
APPLICATION FOR EMPLOYMENT

NAME: _____ DATE: _____
     (Last)   (First)   (Middle)   SOCIAL SECURITY NO.: _____

ADDRESS: _____
     (Street)   (City)   (State)   (Zip)

Telephone No.: _____ How long have you lived at above address? _____

Position applied for: _____ Would you work full-time? _____ Part-time? _____

     If part-time, how many days and hours? _____

List any friends or relatives working for us: _____

Date available for work: _____ 19__ Rate of pay expected: $ _____ per week

Do you have any physical defects? _____ If yes, describe: _____

Have you had a major illness in the past 5 years? _____ If yes, describe: _____

Have you ever been convicted of a crime? _____ If yes, describe: _____

Education:

Last school attended: _____ Dates attended: _____ Graduated? _____

Previous schools: _____ Dates attended: _____

    _____ Dates attended: _____

    _____ Dates attended: _____

Qualifications you feel you possess for this job: _____

_____

Work Experience: List the jobs you have held in the last ten years, beginning with the most recent:

Company Dates   Supervisor   Duties Pay   Reason for Leaving

_____

_____

_____

_____

Personal References:

Name _____ Name _____

Address _____ Address _____

Telephone _____ Telephone _____

Position _____ Position _____

Name _____ Name _____

Address _____ Address _____

Telephone _____ Telephone _____

Position _____ Position _____

THE RESUMÉ

A resumé (pronounced reh-zoo-MAY) is a summary of your personal data, education, and work experience. Very few young workers will need to prepare a resumé when applying for their first jobs. Still it is a valuable skill to have at your fingertips, and later on it may help you get a better job.

In preparing your resumé you will again find your Personal Data Sheet extremely useful. Most of the information you will need will be on it. Your resumé is a more formal document, of course, and you will want it to be neatly typed or printed in ink. Remember, the resumé can be a part of your sales campaign.

There are three basic sections to a resumé: personal data, education, and employment history. Usually personal data will appear first. That will include such things as your name and address, your age, and health. Next, you will briefly summarize your education. Then, list your work experience. If you have experience which prepared you for the job but have had no directly related education, *stress* the work experience by placing it *ahead* of the education. Describe those parts of your experience that are directly related to the job for which you are applying. How would you handle it if you had education for the job but no work experience?

The education section should list the schools you have attended, how long you attended them, and whether or not you completed the course. The last school you attended should be first on the list. If your grade average was good, list it. If not, don't include it. If you had scholarships or were engaged in extracurricular activities, list them. If you received education or training outside of regular schooling, list it. You should stress your positive achievements, but be careful—do not exaggerate them. It goes without saying that everything you put in your resumé must be honest. You would be doing yourself a disservice to put anything in that isn't true.

Most young job applicants will have very little work experience to put in the employment history section. You, as a cooperative education student, will have an advantage. List the jobs you have had, starting with the one you have now. For each job, state the name of the company, the dates you worked there, and the duties you had, stressing especially those duties and skills which relate to the job which you are seeking. With each job indicate your reason for leaving. Don't put down personal gripes. If you didn't like the company or didn't get along with someone, forget about it. That's history. Your reason for leaving will often be something like "accepted a position providing opportunity for advancement," or "accepted a position with an opportunity for job growth." You can also list volunteer activities, such as scouts or candy stripers, if they relate to the job you are seeking. For example, your experience as a candy striper might be valuable if you are applying for a job as a nurse's aide. If you are applying for a job in outdoor recreation your experience as a scout could be important.

Another item should be included in the resumé—personal references. A personal reference should come from someone in a responsible position who can tell the employer a little about you. If you wish someone to do that for you, you should always talk to them first, getting their permission to list them as a reference. Another acceptable practice is to simply say on the resumé, "References furnished upon request."

After you have drafted your resumé, polish it up. Make it an effective, attractive sales tool. Check your grammar. Check all spelling. Check all dates. Type it or get it typed. When it's complete, it should be neat and *one* page long. Why only one page? Remember, the purpose of the resumé is to get you into the employer's office for an interview, not to tell your entire life history. So it should be brief but make the employer want to know more about you.

Remember Ryan Schaake's letter to Mrs. Keller? This is a copy of the resumé he sent along with the letter.

```
            Ryan O. Schaake        Telephone:  549-3786
            906 Diamond Lane
            Hamel, Illinois 62059


Personal:   Age: 17              Single
            Height: 5'9"   Weight: 162 lbs.
Education:  Hamel High School. Graduation Date,
            June, 1981.
            Captain of the baseball team.
            Two years in the Cooperative
            Education Program:
            Company: Z-Town Discount Store,
            Hamel, Illinois
Experience: Z-Town Discount Store, Hamel,
            Illinois.
            9/19 to Present: Shelf stocker,
            cashier, office worker.
            Duties: Responsible for maintaining
            shelf stock in sports department,
            including monthly inventory and
            purchase recommendations. Respon-
            sible for accurate record of sales,
            including cash and charge.
            Responsible for checking and re-
            cording sales receipts of cashiers,
```

cashing checks, and some customer
relations work.
Reason for leaving: Seeking a
career in banking services.

Southwestern Register, Hamel,
Illinois
3/1978-9/1981: Newspaper delivery
Duties: Responsible for delivery of
daily paper to 98 customers.
Seventy-five customers were in the
downtown business section.
Reason for leaving: Took a job with
Z-Town Discount
Store offering opportunity for
greater experience and
responsibility.

Applying What You Know

Prepare a resumé for yourself. Select whatever information you need from your personal data sheet. If you are making a resumé for a job in a particular company, you would want to pick out the information on your personal data sheet which best applies to that job. For another type of job you might want to write a different resumé because other facts might be more important or you might have a reason for putting the facts in a different order. For now, prepare a simple resumé that gives a good all-around picture of you and your abilities and experience. Remember, one page only!

What Do You Think?

Do you think it is honest to stress your good points which are related to the job you are applying for and not mention others? Why?

What impression would you get of persons who emphasize their bad points?

Chapter Check

1. List five possible resources for locating job vacancies. Which do you think would be best?

2. What are the common reasons people aren't hired?

3. Discuss the three types of private employment agencies. Which kind of arrangement would you prefer? Why?

4. What is a personal data sheet good for?

5. What is the purpose of a resumé? How long should it be? Why?

6. True or false? When completing an application form or resumé, a person usually lists education and work experience beginning with the most recent and working back in time to the earliest experience.

❧ Chapter Sixteen ❧

SMALL BUSINESS CASEBOOK

Alan Carrier

SUCCEEDING ON YOUR OWN

Do you want to get rich fast? Owning your own business probably isn't the way to do it. Many people who have small businesses think that isn't really the point of it all anyway. They do want financial security, but they also want independence of a special kind. They want to organize and run things, to be their own bosses and use their own ideas. They want to create something and watch it grow. They want to do the things they feel they are most skilled at doing. Let's look at four case histories of small business owners.

SERIOUS CLOWNING

Meet James Stephan, Jamie-O—The Clown. He has a very successful small business in entertainment.

Lois Carrier: When did you begin clowning?

Jamie-O: A long time ago. In elementary school I developed my own magician's show. Then I was on a telethon. Afterwards a man contacted me and said he thought I was a natural clown. I hadn't thought about it before. He offered to teach me all about it, and he did.

L. C.: Did you have a distant career goal in mind that far back?

Jamie-O: No, not really. I love entertaining people. But later on I decided to study cinema-photography. Clowning totally supported me all the time I was in school. And even now, if I want to spend the next few years finding a permanent career, I can afford to. I can always fall back on clowning.

L. C.: Are there many clowns in the United States who can make a living at it?

Jamie-O:	I don't know exactly how many professionals there are. There's an organization called *Clowns of America.* I believe they have about 5000 members, but these range from people clowning for a few hours here and there to professionals. There are probably at least 5000 more who don't belong to *Clowns of America.*
L. C.:	What do people get out of clowning?
Jamie-O:	I see it as a form of personal expression. People can act out a whole side of their personality that may not otherwise come to life. That's what I like about teaching clowning, too.
L. C.:	Oh, you've taught clowning, too. Where?
Jamie-O:	A number of places. I taught for the Continuing Education Department here. I taught classes at the YMCA. I also taught a few classes in Florida.
L. C.:	Isn't there a special school for clowns in Florida?
Jamie-O:	Yes. It's really a training school for people who want to work for Ringling Brothers, Barnum & Bailey. The trouble is, it's very competitive. Out of some 2000 applicants, probably only 50 or so will be chosen to attend. And only a few of them will end up in the circus. So it's just not designed for people who want to find out more about clowning or try it out.
L. C.:	Are there other schools for clowns?
Jamie-O:	Several universities offer courses in clowning and circus performance. One in Pennsylvania. One in Kentucky. Probably others, too. You could find out more from Clowns of America. I'd also like to mention Circus Kirk. It's a special summer program especially for high school students. They go to school to learn various aspects of the circus. At the end of the summer they put on quite a production. They do everything themselves, from the business end to working out the acts.
L. C.:	Would you ever like to teach either in a university that has a clowning class or a place like Circus Kirk?
Jamie-O:	I'd love to. It's one of my long-range ambitions.
L. C.:	But what field of work will you go into meantime?
Jamie-O:	Well, I've thought in terms of some kind of public relations work. I like meeting people, being a kind of middleman between a company and the public. Clowning itself is a kind of public relations.
L. C.	When you started clowning professionally, how did you get customers? How did people know about you?
Jamie-O:	Word-of-mouth is the main way. You do a party or help

open a new business. People like you. Your name comes up when people are looking for someone to entertain them. The word spreads. Also, when I first came here I ran an ad in the newspaper for a while. Now I don't have to do that anymore. I have plenty of work.

L. C.: Do you travel a lot in your business?

Jamie-O: I put about 17,000 miles on my car in a year's time. I make many fairly short trips. My territory, so to speak, takes me across and up and down most of the state of Illinois.

L. C.: Do you like traveling?

Jamie-O: As a matter of fact, I do. I go to a lot of small towns. Maybe some people would be bored, but I'm not. I find plenty to do. I get a kick out of playing tricks on motel attendants. I like meeting all kinds of people. I like it when people enjoy my show.

L. C.: Do you have several routines? How do you set up your shows?

Jamie-O: First, I have what I call my suitcase show. I carry one suitcase, and out of it I can get two to three hours of entertainment. This is for impromptu engagements when I need to be flexible. An entertainer has to respond to his audience. He has to be spontaneous, engaged. The other type of show I do is more elaborate. When the stage is available and I know ahead of time what kind of a group it will be, then I do more detailed planning and a more involved set of routines.

L. C.: Where did you get all your acts and routines? Do they just come to you kind of naturally?

Jamie-O: Yes, and often in response to an audience. Also, I've been in this business for close to 15 years and have developed quite a repertoire. You develop a feeling for the right thing at the right time.

L. C.: Your kind of work isn't too dependable financially speaking, is it?

Jamie-O: Depends on what you mean. I've made plenty of money. Enough to get through school and live very comfortably, too. But you do have dry periods when business is slow.

L. C.: What do you do about them?

Jamie-O: Well, you can establish a kind of cycle. You can anticipate to some extent when business will be good and when it will be slow. January's not much good, for example. But spring is, and the Christmas holidays are full of parties and other engagements. In the fall I do a lot of car dealer

	shows. You have to know when the slow periods are and put enough money aside to tide yourself over. You can't just spend everything you make. It takes some planning.
L. C.:	Are there any special expenses connected with your work?
Jamie-O:	Yes, some. For example, last year I spent about $2000 on balloons and so forth.
L. C.:	Do you do any free shows, any benefits for organizations?
Jamie-O:	Yes. But I'm a bit cautious about it now. There are some organizations I wouldn't work with again. They don't even have the courtesy to say thank you, and they can be cold and presumptuous. Sort of like you owe it to them. I don't like that.
L. C.:	What kind of benefits have you done?
Jamie-O:	I have my pet charities. I go to two nursing homes in town several times a year. I also go to a state operated school for retarded children. I'd say I do about 18 benefits a year.
L. C.:	Does working with sick or retarded people take a special talent?
Jamie-O:	There are several things I've learned. One is that sometimes with groups like this you don't get the response you do elsewhere. At least not the immediate response. You might think you aren't getting through. But then you come back and they remember you. They ask for something you did before. So you have to learn not to judge by the immediate situation. Also, retarded children in particular like to do a lot of touching. You have to be ready for closer contact than you might have elsewhere.
L. C.:	You are recently married, aren't you? Do you think life as an entertainer makes marriage difficult?
Jamie-O:	Not in my case. I travel, but I'm not away for days and days at a time. My wife is an opera singer. We each have our own interests. Entertaining isn't a problem in our lives, because both of us understand it as a way of life.
L. C.:	Your clowning is a unique small business, and we certainly appreciate having had this chance to talk to you about it.

Finding Out for Yourself

For further reference:

CLOWNS OF AMERICA
2715 East Fayette St.
Baltimore, MD 21224

CIRCUS KIRK
Dr. Charles W. Boas
P.O. Box 181
East Berlin, PA 17316

Daryl Littlefield

THE BEST PANCAKES IN TOWN

Ten years ago John Combes started in the restaurant business. Since then, he has opened two John's Original Pancake Houses.

Lois Carrier: How did you get into the restaurant business? Did you work in a restaurant while you were in high school?

John: No. It's funny how I happened to. I thought I wanted to be a lawyer so I enrolled in prelaw. My best friend was in the food business, and I got interested. First I went into business with him. Then I went to work for a big restaurant chain.

L. C.: And from there you began your own business?

John: That's right.

L. C.: Did you have a large amount of capital to put into your business when you began?

John: No. I had excellent credit, though. I had a bank that was willing to back me. You know how I got my good credit rating? When I got out of the army I had about $1000 saved. I wanted to buy a car. So I went to the bank and talked about a loan. I paid that loan back very fast. The next time I wanted to borrow, there was no question. Now the bank knows I will make good on any loan. I'm a good business risk.

L. C.: Do you think anyone can establish good credit?

John: Sure. But, of course, in terms of business backing, you have to have contacts. Friends. People that know you and will tell others that you are reliable and a good businessman.

L. C.: What is the biggest problem you've faced in your business so far?

John: I haven't really had any big problems. I like challenge. I like overcoming obstacles. Something else. I take care of little problems *before* they become big. Neglect a small problem, and it gets out of hand. Then you've got trouble.

L. C.: You seem to be a very positive and self-confident person. How did you develop those traits?

John: A lot had to do with my parents. They always took the attitude that we children could do anything we wanted to do if we got the training. We never learned to think in terms of failure. I'm handling my own children the same way. I want them to be independent, enthusiastic, sure of themselves. I want them to have good judgment.

L. C.: Does your family help you in your business?

John: My wife helps very much. She does a lot of the administrative work. Running your own restaurant takes an enormous number of hours a day. I appreciate the fact that my wife is able to help.

L. C.: What about the children?

John: They're too little yet. But I'll tell you, they are my best critics. They come in here and tell me this or that isn't quite right. They notice a lot!

L. C.: I had breakfast here the other day. I had eaten here a few times before you took over. You've made some good changes. I noticed two things especially. One was an attention to detail that was missing before. Clean salt and pepper shakers. Hot syrup for the pancakes. That kind of thing. The other was a big difference in the service. The waitresses seem more competent.

John: When I worked for a big chain I tried to notice everything. I tried to make mental notes of things people liked and didn't like. I developed a feel for little special

	attentions. I like to receive those little attentions when I eat out, and I want to see that my customers get them, too.
L. C.:	What do you look for when you hire a hostess or waitress?
John:	Well, there's a difference. In a hostess I want someone with a beautiful personality. I want them to be neat and sharp. Classy. I'd rather have an ugly lady with these qualities than a beautiful young lady without them. Generally I like to hire someone around 40 years old for the hostess jobs. A hostess should be mature, love people, and she has to be a bit of a diplomat, too.
L. C.:	What about waitresses?
John:	Here again, personality comes first. They have to be friendly. Positive in their approach to people. And of course they have to be neat and clean.
L. C.:	Do you have a training program for your waitresses?
John:	Yes, they work with someone who's been here a while. There are certain ways we do things. Those special little touches we talked about before. And when we're busy, they have to be quite efficient. It takes time and practice.
L. C.:	Do your people stay with you a long time?
John:	The average turn-over of employees in most restaurants is 60% every 6 months. In some of the fast food chains the turnover can run 100% each year! My rate is 40-45%. That's a good rate. Especially since this is a college town and people don't stay around forever.
L. C.:	You attended college. What do you think it contributed to your success?
John:	Actually, I feel I learned a great deal by experience, on the job. That's education, too. As to my formal education, it added other dimensions. Take the speech classes I had. Extremely valuable in terms of meeting people, formulating ideas, listening to others, responding fully. My law courses I've used in real estate dealings. I own several apartments now. I have a realtor's license. Yes, I've used those courses, too.
L. C.:	Did you make any mistakes in starting your business, things you would do differently if you had to do it over again?
John:	I made millions of mistakes. That's how you learn. But here's the thing. Don't let anything continue. You make a mistake. You analyze it immediately. You attack the problem and correct it.

L. C.:	Like a builder. If he is off in his measurements for the foundation, the whole structure could suffer. What you're saying is that you can't build very well on a mistake.
John:	Yes.
L. C.:	Do you think the restaurant business is fairly stable? After all, people always have to eat.
John:	I think this kind of restaurant is. We serve good food at reasonable prices. Our suppliers are all good companies. We don't have just the fast foods. I make a fantastic spaghetti sauce. I do it myself. And I offer spaghetti dinners at a reasonable price. Even during the Great Depression little restaurants that managed to have nourishing food at a reasonable price got by okay.
L. C.:	Do you think it's true that people fail in small businesses because they over-expand? That is, they try too much too soon, and don't build carefully enough?
John:	That certainly is a problem. I'd say expansion in the wrong area is a big problem. Before you start a business—or expand it—you should get a market forecast. There are market analysts in most big cities. You contact them, tell them what you want to do. They collect all kinds of statistics and other data and make predictions. They tell you, "On the basis of our research, we think you will do well," or "This isn't the right time or place for what you want to do." Such an analysis costs you money, but it can save you money too! The predictions by these analysts are about 75% accurate. In any case, you have to find out if your community needs and wants what you want to offer.
L. C.:	Have you gotten any help from the Small Business Administration?
John:	No. I don't feel the government helps the small businessman enough. Small businesses should be given a better tax break. Cash flow is tough enough in the beginning, but then you're hit with taxes. The tax people can come and chain your door shut if you are even one day late with your taxes. In addition to subsidizing small businesses, the government should make a few changes in the tax structure. That could be more beneficial in the long run.
L. C.:	Do you ever wish you didn't have so much responsiblity?
John:	Oh, yes. I spend so many hours on my business. I enjoy it, but it does get heavy. And I don't see my family enough. There are other things I like to do.
L. C.:	You mean recreational activities?

John:	Yes, partly. I like boating. Also tennis and racketball. I make time for such activities.
L. C.:	You said, "Partly." Did you have somthing else in mind?
John:	Yes. I have a long-standing interest in politics. I'd like to go into politics someday. Politicians should be like doctors. Making the diagnosis, prescribing the cure. But today so many senators and representatives who are supposed to be leaders are actually just followers.
L. C.:	Would you like to be a senator or representative?
John:	Yes, I believe I could make a good contribution. I believe I would enjoy it and find it challenging. Someday.

Daryl Littlefield

GOING TO WORK AT HOME

"I started with one chair, one shampoo sink, and one hair dryer," said Pat Smith. She has had a beauty shop in her home for almost thirteen years. At the time she opened her business, she had three small children to support. She wanted to find an occupation that would allow her to spend time at home and yet earn money. She decided to take cosmetology courses to earn her certificate and license.

"It wasn't easy," she said. "My father was very kind to us. We moved in with him, and he paid the bills that year I was in school. He also helped the first year I was open. I don't see how I could have done it without him."

We talked about zoning laws. If you start a small business in a residential area you have to obey special rules so that your business won't detract from the neighborhood as a living place. Pat can't, for example, put up a big sign on her lawn. The only sign she can have must be on the house itself, and it cannot be bigger than the size specified in the city code. She can't hire a second beauty operator to work in the shop, unless that second person is a relative who also lives in the house. She can't sell retail cosmetics. That would mean delivery trucks would be coming and going, which isn't very pleasant in a quiet neighborhood where children are playing.

Pat works about 35-40 hours a week at hair cutting and styling, and about one hour a week at such tasks as checking her inventory, paying bills, ordering supplies, taking care of taxes, insurance, and licensing.

Pat keeps up with new fashions in hair design, new materials, and new techniques by attending classes whenever she can. She has taken an advanced course, plus three semesters of work over the years. "Hair stylists today take courses in such things as art, psychology, and bookkeeping, not only in how to work with hair," she told me.

"Another way of keeping in touch with what's new is by attending shows," she said. "Shows are sponsored by dealers and manufacturers of beauty products. There are demonstrations, lectures, and fellowship with people who have similar interests. You can become part of a special group of demonstrators, and you can compete for prizes. From the state level you can move up to the national. The best hair designers even go to a big show in Europe which is the 'Olympics' of the hair design world. You have to be on the top level of your profession to compete in this."

Pat, and many men and women like her, decide to build up a good neighborhood clientele, to do as good a job as they can, and to keep up with new ideas. They may not have time or money to compete in the shows. Also, as Pat points out, it takes a special flair. People that go into design have to concentrate more on their careers, and that often means sacrificing other activities. Some people are satisfied to do a good job and have time for their families and things they like to do. Others prefer to move into the more competitive and demanding design aspects of the occupation. Pat said that these two groups are necessary to each other. The one creates the new and beautiful hair designs. The other puts these designs to work in everyday life. Each group depends on and benefits from the other.

Pat's clientele is less than 10 percent male. Until a year ago, women in this state could style men's hair, although they were not allowed to cut it. Also, men were more secretive in the past about getting permanents, having their hair colored, and so forth. Things are now opening up a little.

I asked Pat what she thought was the main reason many small businesses fail. She said, "One thing nobody tells you is that you can't take any money out of the business the first year. All money received must be plowed right back in. You have to calculate how much money you would need to live on for one year. When you have saved that amount you are ready to open your business. You will have enough to get by on while your business takes root."

Daryl Littlefield

CYCLE STOP

A bicentennial cyclist stopped at Somchai's bicycle shop. Later he wrote to Somchai, "I've travelled about 40,000 miles on my bike, and your shop is the best I found in all of the United States." If you asked Somchai, maybe he would show you his packet of postcards from all over the country, many with similar messages.

How did Somchai Thipkhosithkun get such a good reputation? I walked through the rows of bikes, some 20 to 30 repaired bikes waiting to be picked up plus several rows of new bikes. We went back to his little counter and talked.

Somchai came to the United States from Thailand about twelve years ago. He wanted to attend architecture school, but first he had to learn the language. He entered a special program designed to help people learn English as a second language as quickly as possible. Then he took other courses. Meanwhile a friend of his told him about an opening for a bicycle mechanic in a sporting goods store. He applied and got the job.

What did he know about bikes then? A lot. His father had owned a bicycle shop in Thailand. Somchai said, "When I was a child, I took apart every toy I had. Other kids pushed or pulled their toy trains around. Not me. I took it apart. That was the way I played. My parents thought I was a very destructive child. They stopped buying me toys." Now he's using that love of knowing how things work in his business.

After he had been at the sporting goods store two or three years, he and a friend formed a partnership. They opened a bike repair shop where they could keep the overhead low. In the beginning they concentrated on building up a good inventory of parts so they could give better service. Soon they had a lot of customers and a growing reputation. They broke up into two separate bike shops. Both are doing well.

"How did you decide about going on your own?"

"Well, I felt a need. That's how any business should start—in response to a need in the community. When I began thinking about it, the bicycle boom was just getting underway. Bikes to counteract environmental problems. Bikes for health. Bikes to help out the energy crisis."

"I realized that the selling of bikes would soon come to a peak. The demand for them would reach a high point, then level off and go down. After that, service would be the bigger factor. A community can get saturated with bikes. But the service need goes on and on. I sell bikes, but my emphasis is on service."

I asked if he had had courses in business management, accounting, and so forth. He had had a few. He found them a bit cold, lacking in human considerations, too much emphasizing the fast buck. He learned some useful things, but realized that he must combine them with his own feeling for his particular business. For example, you may find a formula for calculating what percentage of your income you can afford to spend for rent. But you cannot follow such rules blindly. Every situation is different.

The first year Somchai had an accounting firm keep his books. They provided a valuable service. They kept him from missing deadlines, such as the deadline for monthly sales tax reports. They set up a good, workable system of books for him. They knew about forms, and legal issues that he had no knowledge of. After the first year he was in a much better position to keep his own books, and that is what he does now.

"Many people are afraid of the Internal Revenue Service or the state tax people," said Somchai. "They shouldn't be. Those people are there to help. They were a lot of help to me. I kept making a mistake in estimating my taxes. Finally I called them. They took one of the forms and wrote on it in red ink, showing me exactly how to do it. From then on, no problem. That sample helped a lot."

Next I asked if he advertised much.

"No," he said. "You can overadvertise."

"What do you mean by that?" I asked.

"Well, you don't need it. It's an unnecessary expenditure. You see, the best kind of advertisement is what your customers say about you. You have to do top quality work. It gets around. People tell their friends, 'Don't take your bike any place but there.'"

"People want to be respected. Hard sell tactics aren't respectful. It's like telling a customer that you know everything, that they'd just better take your word for it. The first rule is to listen. Listen before you speak."

"As each customer comes in, I try to see that particular person. I try to guess what they would be happiest with. If a man comes in the shop with a good knowledge of bikes, he doesn't want to be shown a less-than-the-best product. The salesperson should be well informed so that he can discuss the best points of different bikes intelligently with this kind of customer. Then, if a person comes in and has less money than he needs to buy the best, you have to comfort him and help him compromise. You can point out to him what extras he really doesn't need. You can help him that way."

While we were talking, several customers came in. Some of them called Somchai by name. One girl wanted something done right away, by that afternoon. Somchai didn't just say, "Okay." He went outside and looked at her bike to see if he could estimate how much time was involved in the repair. He didn't want to promise something he couldn't deliver. Another person came in to show Somchai a badly warped hub and to ask if Somchai could build him a replacement. The conversation was lively. This man knew something about the mechanics of bikes, and he and Somchai had that in common. Another man came in and wanted an unusual size tire. Somchai didn't have one, but referred him to another bike shop that probably would have it.

Somchai's business is seasonal, as are several of our other small businesses. He is open during winter, but very few customers come in. "It's a good time, though," he says. "For one thing, you can assess what you have done the past year, what the future holds, what changes or improvements you could make. You don't have time for that kind of thinking and planning during the rush periods. Also, I love this time because I can do other hobby-type things here. No bikes to repair, so I spend my time doing things I don't have time to do other seasons."

Somchai has a good education. He likes to learn. Now he wants to take more courses in the humanities—literature, music, art, philosophy. He works hard at his business, but he also has deep interest in many other areas of life.

My last question is the same one I've asked all our small business people. What suggestions can you offer young people who might want to start a business of their own? Here are some of Somchai's suggestions:

1. "Don't be too optimistic. Don't think in terms of making a fast fortune. Having your own business takes a great deal of time and effort. You don't usually make big money. You make a comfortable living. But the big thing is, you are independent. You can take pride. You are doing something you really like doing."

2. "Running a small business is something like gambling. Only in gambling you make a mistake, and it's final, right then and there. With a small business, you have to be willing to take risks. But not foolish risks. If you make a mistake, you have a year or so to set it straight. You don't usually go out of business overnight. But you have to keep assessing your performance, seeing what went wrong, planning on the basis of your experience."

3. "One of the best investments I made was subscribing to the trade journal in my field. It costs maybe five dollars a year, but it is an important way of finding out who deals with certain parts, who knows about this or that angle of the business. I know people who won't read trade journals. They say the people that put out the journals tend to undercut small dealers. That's not the way to look at it. You read these journals to keep pace, to find things out. You are the loser if you don't take advantage of the information they offer."

4. "How you view people will be a big factor in your success. People have to be able to trust you, first of all. Honesty is not just a matter of not cheating someone. Honesty is also knowing your product, not selling a person more—or less—than he really needs. There's so much jargon nowadays. So many people trying to snow others with big words and an appearance of knowing what they are talking about. People have a right to directness, to the truth. You may be able to snow people for a while. But if you want to stay in business, you can't afford it. Another thing. It is unpleasant to take bad feelings about something you did at work home with you at night."

It was raining when I left Somchai's shop. I felt good because I had met an important person—a person deeply involved in living. I smiled to myself about something he had said. He had told me that in terms of work and energy, a bike is more efficient than a jet, and only slightly less efficient than a bird.

Based on these interviews, what qualities do you think it takes to run your own business? Make a blackboard chart with these columns:

Now suggest qualities that might fit in each column.

MOST IMPORTANT	FAIRLY IMPORTANT	NICE, BUT NOT NECESSARY

Finding Out for Yourself

The Small Business Administration (SBA) is a government agency designed to help people who want to start small businesses. It can provide you with much valuable information. It grants loans to some small businesses. It sponsors workshops in management, as poor management accounts for many small business failures.

We found the following pamphlets particularly helpful:

1. Starting and Managing a Small Business of Your Own, available (at a reasonable price) from the Superintendent of Documents, U.S. Government Printing Office, Washington, D.C. 20402.

2. SBA: What It Does (free)
3. Checklist for Going into Business (free)
4. Economic Opportunity Loan Program (free)

For these free materials, write to: SBA, 219 South Dearborn St., Chicago, Illinois 60604.

The Occupational Safety and Health Administration of the U.S. Labor Department has a good pamphlet on small business safety:
OSHA Handbook for Small Businesses (OSHA 2209)

To get it, write to the OSHA office nearest you. (The addresses of the regional offices can be found in Chapter 8.)

❧ Chapter Seventeen ❧

"MIRROR, MIRROR, ON THE WALL...."

Daryl Littlefield

WHAT GOOD GROOMING IS AND ISN'T

If you have ever been to the racetrack or watched the Kentucky Derby on television, you will remember how sleek and beautiful the horses looked as they came up to the gate. They aren't like that by nature. If they were wild horses, they would be beautiful in a different way. The typical racehorse is very well groomed—washed, brushed, and combed, the whole works. Why? Will it help the horse win the race? We'd have to ask an animal psychologist about that! From the horse lover's point of view, though, grooming emphasizes everything about the horse that is beautiful. The ripple of strong muscles under a shining sleek coat, a combed tail feathering out behind a speeding horse. Grooming a horse calls attention to all its finest points.

The same might be said of us! Good grooming brings out our best physical characteristics. The big difference is, of course, that the horse is more or less unaware of how it looks and makes little effort to groom itself, whereas people have to take matters into their own hands.

Is grooming just for girls? You would think so, looking at the shelves of library books on grooming for women and comparing them with the two or three modern books on grooming for men. But if you look around you, you will see that many men are paying quite a bit of attention to how they look. Men are wearing a greater variety of clothing. Men's clothes are more colorful than they used to be. Men are having their hair styled, colored, and permanented. And why not? That's part of the sexual revolution too. You feel better when you look better regardless of whether you are male or female.

Let's admit right from the start that some of this business about how you look is hocus-pocus. It's not true that clothes make the man, or that the ideal woman measures 36-26-36. It's not true that you can always tell what people are like just by looking at the way they dress and groom. You can't pick out a criminal from a good citizen just on the basis of personal appearance. The shifty-looking character might be the good guy, and the clean, upright-looking one might be the thief or killer.

Now comes the problem. You may believe you have the right to dress in any fashion you desire. You do have that right. But employers also have the right to choose people whose attire fits in and gives a positive image of the company. Employers have more to consider than just their personal ideas of dress and good taste. Their businesses are strongly influenced by how employees get along, and many employers feel that way-out clothing or sloppy grooming creates problems. Employers also have to think of the impression their people are going to make on customers, patients, clients, and the general public.

Your chances for landing and keeping a good job can be drastically reduced if you don't conform at least to some extent to current patterns of acceptable appearance. Fortunately, rigid dress codes are almost a thing of the past, except in very exclusive places. Most employers will not insist on business suits and ties for salesmen or only dresses for women employees. They just want neat, low-keyed people who make a good impression. For most workers, then, adequate standards of dress and grooming are not that difficult to maintain. Young people want to appear neat and mature, therefore they are willing to go along with dress standards as long as there is some room for self-expression. Generally speaking, employers do allow for that.

From time to time you hear a lot of talk about being "natural." If that means not applying too much makeup, not wearing girdles or corsets, or not putting on a white shirt and tie everyday, fine. If it simply means being too lazy or unimaginative to do anything to bring out your good features, then naturalness can be a negative factor. Sometimes being natural reflects a kind of wishful thinking about the good old days before deodorants, toothpaste, and mouthwash. Were the good old days all that good, though? Geri, Lois, and Pauline don't think so anymore!

NATURE BOY.   Geri and Lois worked together in a small newspaper office. Their boss, Foss, was a nice guy, but he was always jumping on some bandwagon or other.

One day Foss announced that he was going to "go natural." An alarming thought! What he meant was that he was tired of all the gimmicks of civilization—soap, aftershave, and deodorant. It was a fateful August for the rest of his staff. The days were hot, even as early as ten o'clock in the morning. Sure enough, Foss meant business. He started coming to work without having used any deodorant. The first few hours weren't so bad. But by noon, the smell was unpleasant. By midafternoon, the whole office had an offensive odor.

"Funny," said Lois. "When I'm in here all the time and get a little used to it, it doesn't bother me so much. But if I leave the room and come back, it's almost overwhelming!" Geri, on the other hand, said it bothered her all the time, almost giving her a headache.

After a week of this, the girls cornered Foss. They said that being natural was fine for hermits, but he should have mercy on them in that small room. He laughed and agreed to "go civilized" again. The girls suspected that he was getting pretty tired of smelling bad just for the sake of an idea anyway.

THE BASICS

Can you improve on nature as far as your appearance is concerned? What are the basics on which you can build? The rest of this chapter will be devoted to general suggestions. For more detailed ideas you may want to consult some of the books listed at the end of the chapter.

YOUR HAIR, YOUR CROWN.   Many hair styles are acceptable nowadays—longer hair for men, shorter hair for women, curly or straight for both men and women, afros and semi-afros, and ponytails. But *no* hair style is acceptable if the hair is dirty, stringy, or dull.

Almost any good book on grooming will give you some idea how to choose a hair style that's right for you, taking into consideration the shape of your face and the type of hair you have. If you are the kind of person who does not like to be bothered too much about such things, you would do best to keep your hair style short and simple. For some people, simplicity can be more elegant than an elaborate style. If you want to try something more unusual and exotic, be sure you have the time and know-how to keep it up.

Dandruff is a plague almost everyone suffers from at one time or another. To fight it, use a good dandruff shampoo or a regular shampoo for three or four nights in a row. Be sure to rinse well and get all the shampoo out each time, otherwise you may find your hair dull and lifeless. It's a good idea not to wear dark clothing when you're having a "snowflake" problem.

Most beauticians will tell you that too much shampooing is bad for the hair. For most people once or twice a week should be enough. Beauticians are almost as insistent that people brush their hair as dentists are that people brush their teeth.

Having your hair styled by a beautician is a nice luxury to afford now and then. Again, though, don't have your hair done in such a way that you can't keep it looking nice by yourself. Choose your hair dresser with care. Don't take chances with an amateur. The many chemicals used to straighten, color, and curl hair today can damage your skin and hair if improperly used. Some people are also allergic to them. Find a licensed beautician who is aware of the dangers.

COMPLEXION.   When you are in the age bracket where pimples and acne attack without mercy, you are naturally highly concerned about how your skin looks. Dermatologists (skin specialists) have tried to find the cause and cure for acne, but haven't been very successful. Acne may be connected with hormone changes in the body or it may be a matter of heredity. Diet and exercise don't seem to affect acne directly, but they may be indirectly related as they are to other areas of health and good looks.

Since relatively little is known about treating acne, it is foolish to believe ads that claim that expensive preparations can cure it. It is better to compare the products by reading the list of active ingredients. The chemical names may not mean much to you, but maybe there are more active ingredients in one than in another. Or perhaps you will recognize an ingredient that was in a preparation you used in the past and found helpful. But don't expect miracles from any of the acne soaps or salves.

For all of us, acne or no acne, proper cleaning of the skin goes a long way toward a good complexion. Begin with a nice, warm, sudsy wash, and follow it with a cool, tingling rinse. Most books which talk about skin care give hints based on whether your skin is oily or dry. However, your skin can be oily in one place and dry in another, so you can't treat your whole face the same way. Areas that accumulate oils may call for a special cleanser or astringent. Dry areas may need lotion or cream.

Before you go on a wild sun-tanning spree, you should know that too much harsh sunlight on your face and body over a prolonged period of time can age your skin very early. In extreme cases, overexposure to sun can cause or aggravate serious skin diseases.

SMILE! YOU'RE ON CANDID CAMERA.   How much do you notice other people's mouths? Quite a lot, probably. The mouth is the most important element in a smile. The mouth does the talking, drawing attention to itself.

Your teeth matter a lot, both in terms of your overall health and in terms of your appearance. Not many of us are blessed with beautiful lines of straight, dazzling teeth. In fact, physical anthropologists have noted that the size of the human jaw is decreasing while the number and size of teeth remain pretty much the same. We can't do a lot about that, unless we have lots of money for orthodontia (teeth straightening). But all of us can keep our teeth clean and healthy.

Once you are past 25, you won't have to worry so much about tooth decay, but right now you are at a very vulnerable age. Good, old-fashioned brushing with a good quality brush is still the approved way of maintaining the health of your teeth and gums. Most dentists also encourage the use of dental floss to clean the tight spots between teeth. Try to make it to the dentist at least once a year. Even if you have to give up something else in order to be able to afford it, the dividends in beauty and health will be worth it.

Your gums are important too. If teeth aren't properly cleaned, residues build up and cause infections under the gums. Some gum disease can cause the gums to pull away from healthy teeth, leaving them exposed and unsupported, and perhaps even allowing them to fall out. If your gums bleed a lot when you brush your teeth, get to a dentist as soon as possible.

One thing that is easy to overlook in oneself is bad breath. Our sense of smell lessens after a few minutes of exposure to a scent. You may walk into a room where onions are cooking. After a few minutes, you will not notice the smell nearly as much as you did when you first walked in. Since you are around yourself all day, you may not notice if you have an unpleasant smell. It's best to work out a teeth-brushing, mouth-washing routine that insures that most of the time there will be no problem. Bad breath is especially serious for people whose work brings them in close contact with others, such as salespeople, dental assistants, doctors, and teachers. Jana found that out.

OUT OF THE MOUTH OF BABES.   Jana worked as a volunteer at a local community center. Her job was to babysit children a lot of whose parents were at family counseling or doctor appointments. She loved her job. But it seemed strange to her that the children drifted away when she tried to play with them. She tried to be more friendly and talkative, but nothing seemed to help. Then one day she sat down to help a four-year-old boy with a jigsaw puzzle. He had asked her to, and she was very glad to help out. They worked a few minutes, then the little boy said, "Whew, you has bad breath!"

At first Jana was offended. Children can be very honest sometimes. When she thought about it, though, it occurred to her that maybe that *was* her problem! She took precautions from then on. She had always brushed her teeth mornings, but now she knew that wasn't enough for her. She began carrying breath mints with her. She also kept a little bottle of mouthwash in her desk drawer at work with her other emergency supplies.

SHAVING: HIS AND HERS.   One of the books we consulted brought up the fact that there are hundreds of products for women's faces, but very few for men who wreck their skin shaving everyday. That situation is being remedied as a trip to a good drugstore will show. But still the age-old shaving problem exists. It isn't a particularly pleasant part of most men's lives.

Some grooming experts claim that electric razors are much less hard on the skin than safety razors which can nick and scratch. Men who have tried both, however, often prefer the closeness of the safety razor shave. You will probably want to try both and decide for yourself. In any case, a five-o'clock shadow at 8 a.m. in the morning doesn't give a picture of an alert, with-it man!

Men often enjoy having beards or mustaches. Should you? The Esquire book we refer to at the end of the chapter has some good advice on this. Again, you have to think about what really looks good on you, and again the matter of upkeep becomes crucial. A scraggly beard creates the same effect as scraggly hair. If you think having a beard or mustache is less work than shaving everyday, you may want to consult someone who has one before you begin. A good well-trimmed beard or mustache can be worth the trouble, though.

Most American girls wouldn't be caught dead without shaving their legs, especially during the swimming suit season. But in Europe many sophisticated women do not shave their legs or under their arms. There's no law that says you must or must not. If your hair is fine and light, you may prefer not to. Girls with dark hair on light-skinned legs may feel too conspicuous in our culture. Shaving under the arms can help cut down perspiration odor problems. You have the option of shaving or not shaving, so do whatever makes you feel the most comfortable.

GET A WHIFF OF HIM OR HER.   Now we're talking about pleasant smells. Aftershave or cologne are pleasant additions to one's preparation for the day. It's a nice touch to have a little scent about you. Good taste decrees, however, that you know when enough is enough. If you leave a wake of perfume lingering behind you as you walk down the hall, chances are you've overdone it. Just as an herb or spice you use in a recipe should not overpower the dish, so your scent should not knock anyone over. It should be a subtle suggestion of nice things.

HANDS AND FEET.   Hands can be a very expressive part of the body. Ragged nails, overgrown cuticles (skin around the nails), and rough skin detract from your general appearance. You should acquire your own little set of manicuring tools. Perhaps you will also need cuticle conditioner and remover. However, gently pushing back the cuticles after you have showered goes a long way toward keeping your nails looking nice and your cuticles soft and pliable.

If you work where your hands get stained, oily, extremely dry, or sensitive, you may have to use stronger soaps and lotions. Someone in your shop may be able to recommend the best substance to combat a particular problem encountered at your workplace. If your hands develop rashes easily, you should see a doctor. Some people are allergic to certain substances, and constant irritation can be very bad. Gloves may be the solution, or a prescription from the doctor may be necessary.

Some people have special problems with foot odor. If you have to wear heavy shoes that are tightly laced or if you like to wear tight boots, you should check your feet and your boots every day. Clean feet and socks or stockings are necessary, of course. You may also want to use foot powder. Airing out your shoes or boots after wearing them helps too. If you can afford to buy two or three pairs of shoes and change off wearing them, the foot odor problem will be considerably reduced.

POSTURE: BODY LANGUAGE.   A person who spent 14 months in a concentration camp during World War II told me that you could always tell which prisoners had given up and would soon die. They'd begin to hang their heads and shuffle along without lifting their feet, shoulders sloping forward. This is an extreme example, of course. Yet even in everyday life, people get hints about you from the way you carry yourself.

To some extent, your body weight and build influence the way you stand and walk. You have to accept your basic build as a fact of life, but you don't have to accept excess fat and flabby muscles. If you want to slim down or tone up, crash programs of dieting or exercise are not the way to do it. In fact, some of these crash programs and reducing pills can actually be dangerous. Overweight or out-of-shape people need to change their patterns of eating and exercise slowly and carefully. Many people can lose 20 pounds quickly, but few can keep the pounds off unless they have also gotten rid of some bad habits. Any of the books at the end of this chapter can help you set up a sound physical self-improvement program.

Some unpleasant postures: tummy sticking out, chest backing away; sitting sprawled out and slack in a chair; shuffling along without any sense of purpose, without energy; holding the head down so that you don't look anyone in the eye. Physical inactivity contributes to bad posture. If you have a desk job, you may have to make a special effort to avoid premature middle-age spread. There are some exercises (isometrics) which you can do sitting right in your chair!

THE SKELETON IN YOUR CLOSET

If you are like many high school students, your wardrobe is probably a skeleton collection. Many parents just can't afford to give their sons or daughters the best and newest in clothing, especially if they have several children to put through school. You probably haven't been earning money long enough to have done much about your wardrobe either. How can you go about fleshing out that skeleton in your closet?

Daryl Littlefield

We are presenting a three-point program for doing so. Take a look and see what you think of it.

1. When you get home today, take an inventory of your clothing. Make a list of the slacks, skirts, suits, dresses, sweaters, shirts, blouses, shoes, underthings, and accessories you have.

2. Make a list of the kinds of places you go, including work, the places you might go on a date, church or other organizations you belong to, sports and outdoor activities you're interested in. Consider what kind of clothing would be best for each of these.

3. Now compare 1 and 2. Match up the things you already have with the kinds of places you go. Determine what you are lacking. Make a list of things you would like to buy as soon as you can afford them, ranking your choices in terms of priority. What do you need the most? What can wait a little longer?

When you first start earning your own money, it is a temptation to buy things simply because you like them. It's certainly wise to like what you buy. After all, you have to wear it! But there are other considerations, too. You must think about what you already have. Do you own things that will go with the item of clothing you want to buy? Do you have the proper accessories (shoes, jewelry, scarf, etc.)? If not, isn't there a better choice you could make? You don't want a closet full of odds and ends!

Color is another important consideration. You will want to buy clothes in colors that look well on you. Also, for a person trying to build a good wardrobe, clothes in the basic colors should come first. Why?

Because they can be worn with so many things. Plain browns, grays, and blues go with other colors, plaids, and prints. Clothes in these colors are versatile. That means they can be made to look dressy or casual and can be worn on many kinds of occasion. Bright-colored clothes are nice to have, but they are less likely to be appropriate for various occasions. For the same reason, very dressy clothes should be lower on your list than basic outfits.

What about quality? Most of us would enjoy buying the best quality clothes at the finest stores. Few of us can afford to do so, though. We compromise and get the most for the money we have to spend. Inspect the garment you intend to buy. Look for faulty zippers, poorly sewn seams, messy topstitching, lost buttons, flaws in the material. Read the labels. See if the care instructions are such that they will fit into your time schedule and budget. For example, a light-colored garment that must be dry cleaned is not very practical. It can cost you a couple of dollars everytime you wear it. A wise shopper also tries to become familiar with different fabrics and brand names.

If you know how to use a sewing machine you can do all kinds of interesting things. Some sewing machine shops and department stores offer sewing lessons at quite reasonable rates. A number of good books on designing and making your own clothes have also been published. Your clothing budget can be stretched immensely if you can make some of your own clothes.

Caring for your clothes is another big factor in building a wardrobe. Clothes that are carefully laundered and not just dumped helter-skelter into an automatic washer and dryer will last much longer. They will hold their colors and shapes better.

Should men be responsible for making minor repairs on their own clothes? Why not? Many swinging bachelors with nice wardrobes have mastered the fine art of sewing on buttons and pressing slacks. Many of the finest tailors are men!

THE MIRROR TEST.   Before leaving for work or a date check yourself out in front of a mirror:

Hair clean and shiny? Part straight?
Right amount of make-up?
Jewelry and other accessories match and complement clothing?
Pants pressed?
Stockings without runs?
Shirt clean and pressed?
Do I look neat?
Do I feel comfortable and confident?
Is this outfit in line with what I'm going to be doing today?
How's my posture? Do I look like a winner?

How to Dress for Success
by Edith Head with Joe Hyams
(New York: Random House, 1967)

Edith Head has designed many of the clothes stars have worn in movies. She has won Oscars for her costumes. Her book is full of down-to-earth suggestions for the sophisticated woman.

Esquire Good Grooming for Men,
by the Editors of *Esquire Magazine*
(New York: Grosset and Dunlap, 1969)

This book goes far beyond what a young worker needs at the beginning, but is still very useful. Lots of good suggestions ranging from diets and exercises to diagrams showing how to tie ties and shape mustaches and beards.

Leslie Uggams Beauty Book,
Leslie Uggams and M. Fenton
(New Jersey: Prentice Hall, 1966)

An attractive book full of good ideas which sound like they are coming from your favorite big sister. A good book for helping girls develop poise and social grace as well as good looks.

Yoga for Young People,
Michaeline Kiss
(New York: Bobbs-Merrill, 1971)

Yoga, as you may know, is an ancient system of exercise designed to improve both physical and mental health and stamina. Many people have used it to learn both how to relax and how to concentrate. Good for keeping in shape, too. This book is for both young men and young women.

Exercise for Sports,
Hannelor Pilss-Samek
(New York: Sterling, 1973)

Although designed for people who want to participate in sports, this book will be highly useful for anyone who wants to get into top physical condition. The exercises can be done almost anywhere and do not involve special equipment.

What Do You Think?

Write a one-paragraph description of how you would like other people to see you. What kind of an impression would you like to make? Which of the following words best fits your idea of your appearance? Interesting, flashy, neat, simple, feminine, individual, masculine, fresh, outgoing, mysterious, clean, stylish, unusual, in good taste, classy.

Working Cooperatively

Plan a fashion show of *working* clothes. Everyone could wear clothes particularly suited to the kind of work he or she is doing or planning to do. These might include uniforms such as those worn in hospitals, restaurants, or laboratories; outdoor clothing such as a construction worker or bus driver might wear; snappy looking clothes such as a salesperson might wear; fairly dressy clothes to be worn to the office; clothes that would be safe and comfortable in a factory. If it is

December and you are a lifeguard, you have a problem!

Choose a committee of three to serve as commentators. Their job will be like that of the broadcast team commenting on the Rose Bowl Parade. Each model should submit a brief description of what he or she is wearing and for what sort of work it is used. The commentators will then be able to prepare something to say.

Is there another class you could invite to your Fashion Show, for example, a home economics class? Could it be part of your spring banquet plan?

❀ Chapter Eighteen ❀

APPROPRIATE AND INAPPROPRIATE WORK BEHAVIOR

Mutual of Omaha

STYLES OF DOING BUSINESS— FORMALITY AND INFORMALITY

Working situations differ greatly. In some places, people dress up more than in others. In some offices, everyone is on a first-name basis, while in others it is "Mrs. So-and-So" and "Mr. What's-His-Name." Actually, though, it seems that more and more places are going informal these days. Dress codes are not rigidly followed. People are expected to know what kind of behavior is appropriate without having to be given a rule book. In a way, things are easier because there aren't all kinds of little rules to worry about. In another way, things are harder because people have to be responsible for their own behavior. For the workers who have spent years being told how to behave, this can sometimes be a problem. They may feel awkward or unsure of what is expected.

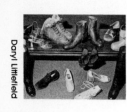

Daryl Littlefield

Perhaps the best idea is to look the situation over to see how formal or informal the workplace is, then try to fit in as best you can. Observe what people in positions of respect or people who are well-liked do. If you start out on a fairly formal basis, you may be able to shift to a less formal manner once your observations and experiences tell you the time is right. By then you will have a feel for the people and the place. Others will have had a chance to get to know you, too.

A lot of bad things have been said about conformity, but not all conformity is bad. Conformity means doing as others do. Some conformity makes sense and is necessary if we are to live together in a decent society. As a far-out example, imagine that you and six friends are lost in a woods in Alaska. You can hear wolves moving in on you. You quickly decide to build a fire and dance around it, making wild noises to scare off the animals. You all realize that if you join in doing this, you will be safe. So everyone does a crazy dance, yelling and howling, and the wolves go away, or at least keep their distance. Because you all conform to the behavior agreed on, you live to tell about it.

As a more ordinary example of conformity, think of people using a municipal swimming pool. They conform by paying the required admission fee and obeying the safety rules that have been set up. In return they get a safe and pleasant place to cool off on hot days.

Now for the wrong kinds of conformity. In years past Jewish people were disliked and feared in many countries. Non-Jewish people would try to drive them out of the country or kill them. Sometimes they would even wear buttons identifying themselves as Jew-haters. They would hold pogroms, which means they banded together to commit acts of violence against defenseless and innocent people. Maybe you have seen scenes of this kind in the movies. Members of such hate groups conform all right but to standards that are thoughtless and wrong to begin with.

There is another bad kind of conformity. Conformity can mean taking things as they are and never trying to better anything. It can mean living in front of a TV set, leading a humdrum existence, not really hating life but not really loving it either. It can mean doing as the Joneses do, rather than thinking up your own goals and following your own interests. It can mean going through the same old routines everyday and thinking the same thoughts your elders thought.

Now let's go back to formality and informality. We said that it is better to conform to whatever style is in at your place of employment, at least until you get established and know what the place is really like. Try not to be put off by either the formal or informal approach. If you can be alive to each situation, you will build up a background of experience. You will come to feel at ease in either kind of situation, and you will learn to shift easily between the two. With a little experience most of us can learn to be quite comfortable eating in a very nice restaurant or in a fast-food place.

Compare notes on the cooperative education jobs you are now holding. Below is a list. How many of these things would be okay to do on your job? How many would not be okay? Which would be okay but you'd just prefer not to do them?

1. Would you call your boss by her/his first name?

2. Would you say, "Yeah" or "Un-huh" to your boss? Your co-workers? Customers?

3. Would you drink coffee or eat at your desk?

4. Would you chew gum?

5. Would you smoke?

6. Would it be okay to wear jeans?

Can you think of other things you feel you can or cannot do? How many of you would say your place of work is formal? Informal? Do you have to shift between formal and informal during the course of a day? (Perhaps if you have contact with customers, patients, or clients?)

NEW FRIENDSHIPS

Try to imagine for a moment that you are a primitive man or woman. It is thousands of years ago, and there is no civilization as we know it today. You are going through the forest one day. Your eyes are cast down watching the barely visible path. Suddenly you glance up and see another human being coming toward you. You don't recognize him. He isn't one of the males of your tribe. All you know about him is that he, too, is a human being. Which of these would you feel as you approached each other:

Fear: is he going to hurt me?
Mistrust: what's he doing in our forest?
Curiosity: where did he come from? does he talk my language?
Anxiety: what does he want?
Excitement: what's he like?

Now bring yourself back to the present day. We think of ourselves as more civilized. We have developed ways of meeting and greeting strangers. But underneath these conventions (patterns of behavior), we still experience these feelings when we meet new people. Joe meets Paul for the first time. He isn't really afraid that Paul will hurt him physically, but he does have some fear that Paul will ignore or reject him. Joe doesn't know much about Paul except for how he looks, so he doesn't trust him. He can't help being curious, though. He wonders where Paul is from, where he's going, what he is doing here. Joe waits with some anxiety to find out what Paul wants and whether he will give a welcome sign or a keep out signal. It is exciting to both of them because something new is happening. If the meeting is between people of different sexes, there is often even more electricity in the air.

If all of the above are true, then no wonder the first day on a new job is both tiring and exciting. Sometimes people are in too much of a hurry to make friends and settle in, and they make mistakes. Or they fear they won't be liked, so they act very nonchalant as if they don't care. If people have had some bad experiences in meeting others, they might be defensive. They might make a point of rejecting others before others have a chance to reject them. (Maybe no one was even intending to reject them!) In any case, many of us have some problems in meeting new people.

Here are a few things to avoid doing:

1. Being gushy—complimenting everyone, calling everyone "honey" and "dearie," falling all over people. This kind of behavior scares people off and appears insincere.

2. Being clannish—picking out one person or one small group of people rather like yourself and ignoring everybody else.

3. Bragging—trying to tell people in words what would be much better said by actions.

4. Calling attention to yourself—wearing spectacular clothing or doing spectacular things to call attention to yourself.

5. Moving in too fast—this is related to the first point. It means taking friendship for granted before a friendship has even had a chance to grow and flower.

6. Being obsequious—agreeing with other people all the time, being overly submissive and humble. Trying to flatter others into accepting you as a friend or as a good worker.

Write three paragraphs about a new friend you have at your cooperative work training station. Develop the paragraphs as follows:

Paragraph One: Tell what attracted you to this person. Who made the first move toward friendship? How did things develop?

Paragraph Two: Tell how you would like this new friend to treat you. Tell some of the qualities you expect a friend to have.

Paragraph Three: Tell what your friend has the right to expect from you.

Do you feel confident when you are being introduced to someone or when you are introducing a friend to someone else? Choose members of your class to demonstrate the following introductions:

1. Introducing a new friend to your father or mother.

2. Introducing a new co-worker to your boss.

3. You are a sales representative introducing yourself to a purchasing agent you haven't met before.

4. A friend is introducing you to his girlfriend.

5. A friend is introducing you to her grandfather.

ON-THE-JOB BEHAVIOR BETWEEN MEN AND WOMEN

Our sexuality runs through everything we do. It is an important part of our wholeness as human beings. At certain ages expression of our sexual selves is more naturally showy and forceful. Then, and also later, there is a warmth and excitement that comes when working with persons of the opposite sex. It is naturally there and not something we consciously try to bring about. It may involve such little things as cologne and aftershave, and such deep and valuable things as a refreshing difference in viewpoint, sympathy and understanding, and a more general participation in being human.

If abused, this interchange between sexes ends up being a childish game. If valued, it adds pleasure and stimulation to the routine of daily living. A good rule is to try to express one's sexuality as naturally and unself-consciously as possible, keeping it in proportion so that those around you can see your other qualities as well.

Women and men who overplay their sexuality tend to make others uncomfortable. On the job, they can be disruptive. The woman who tries to be the femme fatale to express her femininity or the man who plays Mr. Universe to convince others of his masculinity is overdoing it. In fact, people who act this way may really be expressing feelings of inadequacy, both sexually and otherwise.

By this time in your lives, most of you have some idea of what kind of public behavior between the sexes is acceptable and in good taste. For the purpose of your job, just tighten those standards slightly, and you should be in tune. Rather than laying down a lot of rules, we will give two examples of situations we observed firsthand. The inappropriateness of both should be obvious.

A TOUCHY SITUATION   Gerald was the boss's son. He had gotten himself thrown out of two colleges in one year, so his father thought a year on the job might sober him up a bit. From the first day, though, Gerald showed that he didn't intend to do much work. He was much more interested in the girls than in his job. That was understandable enough at his age. But he had such childish ways of getting the girls' attention that everyone was annoyed.

Here's one example of the kind of things he did. He waited for one of the girls to go into the supply closet. He followed her in, closed the door, and flicked off the light. Then he tried to "find" her. None of the girls whom he "found" thought he was very funny. The slaps he got just seemed to add to his enjoyment. Since he was the boss's son, everyone just figured, "I guess he's our cross to bear."

Gerald gave attentions nobody wanted. It's almost as if he had just noticed girls for the first time, something you probably did at about ten years of age or sooner.

In our more tolerant moods we try to understand Gerald. We realize there's something wrong with a person who acts like a 10-year-old when he is 21. The fact remains that he is a pain in the neck. His story doesn't have a happy ending. His own father finally had to fire him, which was quite embarrassing.

ONCE TOO OFTEN   Alicia was a pretty girl, and she knew it. Shortly after she began working at the Fireside Company, people started asking her out. For some reason, Alicia felt the need to compete with all the other girls for dates. If she saw another girl making friends with a male co-worker she did something to call attention to herself. She often flirted with the man in question. Sometimes she succeeded in getting him to ask her out. Other times she made belittling remarks about the girl.

One day Rick asked Mary out. Mary, who was friendly toward Alicia, told her about it. Alicia said, "Oh, that's nice." But that afternoon she hung around Rick's drafting table, acting very interested. The next day she parked her car near his and timed everything so that they would come out of the office at the same time. She then pretended to be unable to start her car. Rick helped her get it going. She thought she was making progress. She didn't realize that Rick knew there was really nothing wrong with her car. Alicia continued to flirt in other ways, but Rick kept putting her off until she got tired of trying. She had been so obvious that all the people were making little jokes about it. Rick took Mary out and they had a good time. Alicia, on the other hand, was losing friends right and left. None of the girls trusted her, and the men thought she was foolish.

SHOULD YOU DATE SOMEONE WITH WHOM YOU WORK?

Yes. Your place of employment may be a good place to meet interesting people of the opposite sex. But remember, this isn't high school. Jazzing around with a girl or boyfriend during working hours could get either or both of you in trouble. Privately making an arrangement to meet for lunch or after work is the wiser thing to do.

Sometimes there are special circumstances which make dating a fellow employee a problem. Lola, for example, works for a large architectural-engineering firm. She and Tom make up the personnel department. All kinds of records and personal data are easily available to both of them. They are in a position of trust. It would be just as unethical for them to reveal what is in someone's file as it would be for a doctor or lawyer to do so. If either of them date other employees, the temptation to give out information might be very great. They would also have to be careful not to leak news about raises, promotions, or firings. They would have to use prudence and caution when dating people from work.

When you date someone from work, concentrate on each other and on your interests. Avoid talking about people you work with. Gossip can backfire and make you uncomfortable on the job. If you have confidential information about someone at work, keep it to yourself. No one gains status by telling such facts to others.

THE CUSTOMER

Any time your job causes you to have contact with the public, you represent your company. Whether you are the receptionist, a salesperson, an office nurse, or an executive, you are in a postion of trust. You must behave appropriately toward those people whom it is your job to satisfy. You are, in other words, a diplomat.

Some customers, patients, or clients are a joy to help. Others are considerably less than lovable. It's a big job to learn how to handle both kinds, but common courtesy goes a long way. Self-control is another valuable asset. When you have doubts about how to handle a certain customer, consult your supervisor. Sometimes you may have to do that immediately, while the customer waits. Other times you may want to describe the situation to your boss later and ask if there was a better course of action you might have taken.

In the following example, you may find it hard to believe that someone old enough to work would be so insensitive to the situation. But unfortunately, this is a true example. It really happened.

SHOPPING SPREE   Mr. and Mrs. York were visiting in Kansas City and decided to shop at a new plaza there. After browsing through many little shops, they found a wool shirt that Mr. York liked very much. The only salesgirl available was leaning against a counter, talking to someone on the telephone. She looked up when Mr. York approached and said, "Just a minute, honey," to the person on the phone. She reached for a bag and was about to stuff the shirt into it. But it was an expensive shirt and Mr. York wanted to try it on first. The girl sighed and pointed out the dressing room. Then she returned to her telephone call.

After Mr. York had tried on the shirt, he decided to buy it. He again went to the sales desk. The salesgirl was still on the telephone. This time she did not even lay the receiver down. She tucked it under her chin, reached for the shirt, and began tearing the ticket off. Then she held out her hand for the money. Mr. York was quite irritated by this time. "Do you want to wait on me or not?" he asked.

Finally the girl took the hint. She said, "Goodbye—I'll call you back later," and hung up. She made no apology to the Yorks. She completed the transaction and put the shirt into the bag.

Mr. and Mrs. York left feeling that they would not shop there again. "If I had time," said Mr. York, "I would call her boss and tell him what kind of service we got."

Some customers would not have been so patient. They would have left without buying the shirt. How long do you suppose this girl will keep her job?

THE USE AND ABUSE OF HUMOR

Many bad situations have been saved with humor. Humor relaxes tension. It gives people a breather, a time to calm down and get things in perspective.

Being able to laugh at yourself is also a valuable quality. It means you are truly human and know it. You become much more understanding of other people's faults when you realize your own shortcomings. You find you can like yourself even if you are not perfect. Others can like you *because* you aren't perfect. They feel easy at home with you.

Well, then, what do we mean by the abuse of humor? If humor is intended to pick out a person's weak spot and hold it up to ridicule, then it is being misused. It's hard to even call it humor at that point.

At the same time, all of us should avoid being too touchy. When a group is kibbitzing and having a good time, things can sometimes get out of hand. People try too hard to be funny, and someone may get hurt. Often, though, the hurt is small and unintentional. It should be forgiven and forgotten. It's a real mark of maturity to know when someone really intended to hurt you and when a person just got carried away.

Abuse can also be a matter of too much. There used to be an old radio program called, "Can You Top This?" The people on the panel took turns telling jokes. After each joke, a special laugh meter would measure how funny the audience thought the joke was. The next panelist would try to top that joke by telling one that registered even higher on the laugh meter. When people keep trying to top each other in real life, the jokes can get stale or out of hand. It gets like living in the land of Hee-Haw. Knowing when enough is enough is not always easy, but you can usually get some clues from other people's reactions.

Working Cooperatively

Make a class scrapbook of jokes which relate to the world of work. These could be cut out of old magazines and newspapers, or students could design and draw their own. Keep adding cartoons and jokes as you find them. Maybe you can bequeath your class joke book to the next class!

Chapter Check

1. Explain the difference between formality and informality.

2. What value does some conformity have? What undesirable kinds of conformity can you think of?

3. List a few things you would avoid doing when meeting new people.

4. In what sense are workers diplomats?

5. What does the phrase "overplaying one's sex" mean?

 Part Seven

Diagraph-Bradley Industries,

Herrin, Illinois

Understanding Economics

WHAT IS ECONOMICS?

You have just taken on a new role in our economic system. You have been a consumer since you were born. Now you are a producer, too. Most people play both roles in differing degrees during their lives. Their labor, services, or know-how are critical resources in our economic system. So is your consumption! But what exactly do we mean by an economic system?

Every time you buy a shirt, go to a movie, have a hamburger, go to the dentist, or in any way exchange money for goods or services, you are involved with the economic system. Goods are those things we purchase, tangible items such as clothing, food, cars or bikes, and the like. Services are intangible. That is, they are things done for us rather than material things. These might include haircuts, police protection, tooth extraction, car servicing, and a multitude of such things. An economic system might be defined as *the way a nation organizes itself to develop and use its resources to meet human needs and wants*.

What do we mean by resources? Many of us think first of iron and coal and soil. The term *resources* includes many more things. Economists (people who specialize in economics) classify resources into three groups: labor, capital goods, and natural resources.

Labor is what you do on the job to earn the pay you receive. The term includes both mental and physical work. It is the work done to produce all the material goods and to provide all the services people want or need. When people speak of human resources, they are referring to the men and women available to do various kinds of work.

Capital goods are those items used to produce other goods or to provide services. The big machine which stamps out the hood of a car, the high-speed drill which the dentist uses, the machinist's lathe, the printer's press, the serviceman's truck, the teacher's desk are just a few of the millions of pieces of capital equipment.

Natural resources are the raw materials that we need to make the things we use. They are found in nature, and man has learned to use them in many ways. Oxygen, water, trees, iron, and coal are natural resources. The book you are reading may have been a part of a pine tree in Georgia just a few months ago.

❋ Chapter Nineteen ❋

OUR ECONOMIC SYSTEM AND OTHERS

The Department of the Treasury

HOW ECONOMIC SYSTEMS WORK

Have you ever watched a juggler attempting to keep eight or ten balls in motion in the air all at the same time? The juggler had to have a system for putting the right direction and the right amount of pressure on each ball at the right time to keep the act from coming to a bouncingly embarrassing end. Societies also have to organize themselves in order to juggle all the elements in their economic systems successfully so that the people can benefit. They try different methods of doing this. In our world of today we can pick out three major kinds of economic systems: *capitalism, socialism,* and *communism.*

All economic systems must answer three basic questions:

1. *How much* should the economy produce?

2. *What kind* of goods and services should be produced?

3. *How* will the goods produced and services provided be *shared* by the members of the society?

We will define each system, then we will briefly look at how each goes about answering the above questions.

SOCIALISM   Socialism is a system in which the means of production and distribution are frequently owned collectively by the people and controlled by the government officials whom the people elect.

A document called *Aims and Tasks of Democratic Socialism,* published by the Socialist Party of the United States, contains a statement of the goals of socialism. Here are some of the main points:

- Public interest is to be considered more important than private profit. Practical aims include full employment, higher production, and a higher standard of living. Social security and a fair distribution of incomes and property are also vital parts of the socialist program.

- Production of goods must be planned. Such planning cannot be concentrated in the hands of a few, but must be democratically controlled by the people.

- Socialist planning can take several forms. The structure of the country concerned must help to determine how much public ownership and planning would be best for it.

- Public ownership can include nationalization of existing private industries, new enterprises under the control of the people, and consumers' and producers' cooperatives.

- Public ownership is not an end in itself, but a means of making production of goods more efficient and preventing monopolies which harm the public welfare.

- Socialist planning does not mean all means of production must be publicly owned. There is a place for private ownership in agriculture, handicraft, retail trades, and small and middle-sized industries. The state should both prevent private owners from abusing their powers and assist them toward increased production.

We might summarize by saying that socialists feel there should be public ownership of most of the means of production and strong governmental control of all privately owned businesses. They feel that private ownership and the desire for profit often work to the disadvantage of the people in general. Modern socialists also strongly believe that democracy must be an integral part of the planning and controlling process. Those who assume these functions must be duly elected officials.

How would an economic system designed and controlled by socialists answer the three questions? The elected representatives would make the decisions on what items should be produced and in what quantity they should be made available and kept on hand. They might decide that there should be one car for every four citizens, one bathtub for every eight people, and so on until the basic needs of all the citizens were met. Then the government officials would see to it that manufacturers tooled up to produce the proper quantities of goods, and they would plan a way to distribute the goods to the people who need them.

That is a very brief, and far from complete, overview of what socialism means in practice. Now let's take a brief look at communism.

COMMUNISM   First let's try to define it. Communism is a system of government in which the means of production and distribution are owned by the government, and the goods produced are to be shared by all citizens. If you look at this definition and compare it to that of socialism you can see that they look very much alike. Communism, however, also includes a set of doctrines which underlie a revolutionary movement. One aim of the movement is to abolish all capitalistic systems and establish societies in which all goods produced and services provided are owned, planned, and controlled by the people collectively. The production and distribution of the goods and services are supposed to be in accord with this rule: "From each according to his capacity, to each according to his need."

Socialism, on the other hand, involves a slower and more gradual change. It is not revolutionary in the sense that communism is. It depends on constitutional and democratic processes. Communism often involves totalitarianism. Totalitarianism means that the government is controlled by one political group and that its power is absolute. In some communist countries only a small percentage of the people as a whole belong to this ruling party. Citizens do not democratically elect their officials, at least not as it works out in practice. Sometimes there is only one candidate to vote for. Sometimes voting is not by secret ballot. In theory, though, the people should be getting more and more say-so under communism as the system matures. The more you study all three systems, the more you realize that ideas on paper do not always work out just as they were supposed to in practice. We'll be discussing this more fully a little later.

CAPITALISM—THE FREE ENTERPRISE SYSTEM   The economic system in which you are a worker and consumer has been called by many names: capitalism, free enterprise, the market system, and the profit system.

E. I. duPont de Nemours & Company

Capitalism is an economic system based on private ownership, competition, and the production of goods for the purpose of gaining profits. Profits are defined as the selling price of a product, minus the cost of production, distribution, and marketing of that item.

It should be emphasized at this point that there isn't any such thing as pure capitalism, pure communism, or pure socialism. Governments are classified according to the major philosophic ideals under which they operate. They can have features of other systems too, on a smaller scale. The United States is basically a free enterprise system. Free enterprise involves the right of private citizens to own and control the means of production. It also includes the right of privately owned businesses to operate in a free and open economy in which competition sets the prices charged for goods and services.

There are exceptions to these general rules. Goods and services which may be vital to the welfare of the country are regulated and sometimes even owned by the government. For example, controls have been placed on telephone service, electrical power, and water supply. Competition between utility companies might mean constant fluctuations in the prices charged, unreasonable raising of rates, and wasteful duplication of expensive equipment. Our laws do allow our government to intervene in cases where the public welfare is at stake.

How, then, does the free enterprise system answer the three questions with which every economic system must deal—what, how much, and for whom? There are many forces which operate in a free enterprise system which we must consider. Since this is the system under which we live, we will spend much of the next chapter exploring it more fully. Meanwhile, you will be the main character in the following example of economic activity in the United States.

FISHING FOR BASS—AND?   Over twelve million bass fishers live in the United States, and you happen to be one of the most enthusiastic of them. The excitement of getting out on the lake and casting a lure toward the bank with the high expectation that a tackle-busting black bass will take it is your idea of pure pleasure.

You get up early one Saturday morning and get out on the lake. You have three types of lures which have time and again proven to be the most productive lures on the market. But after two hours of casting, you don't have a single fish! Not even a strike! Mom's words, "If you have to waste time, I guess you might as well waste it fishing," are no consolation to you now.

On the very next cast, your favorite lure comes a little too close to the shoreline and smashes on the rock bluff jutting out into the water. There are two pieces of lure which bounce into the air after they hit the rock. "Another $2.75 down the drain," is going through your mind as you slowly retrieve the lure. You notice that the mangled lure is darting every which way in the water as you pull it in. Then all of a sudden the rod is almost yanked right out of your hand as a trophy-sized bass strikes.

After what seems like the battle of the century, you gingerly lift into the boat what later proves to be the largest fish ever caught on the lake. What a coincidence that that beautiful bass hit your worthless lure!

As you are about to replace the broken lure, the thought occurs to you to cast the dilapidated lure just once more. Wonder of wonders, another bite! Thinking, "Well, the bass have finally decided to start biting," you quickly change to a new lure. Fifteen minutes go by, and not one bass has been lured. It suddenly dawns on you that the reason for your success with the big bass might have been that weird-looking, wiggly, broken lure. Your hunch is confirmed by the frantic action which develops after you put that lure back on your line. By a freak happening, you have discovered a lure which is more productive than the three commercially-produced lures in your tackle box.

On the way home you decide to have that big lunker weighed on an official scale at the local sports shop. And, wouldn't you know it, the

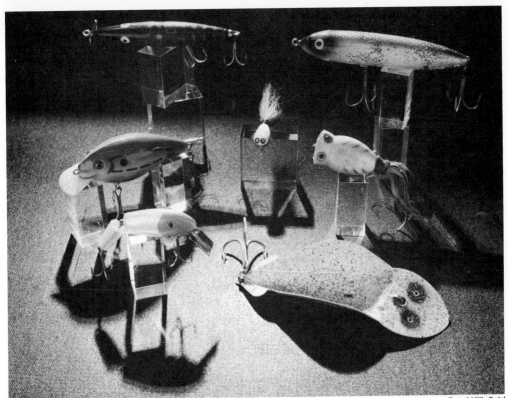

Daryl Littlefield

sports editor of the local newspaper comes and takes your picture with the prize catch weighing a cool 14 pounds, 6 ounces. As the editor takes notes for a feature article to be called, "The Biggest Bass Caught in Bundy County," the question of which lure you used to catch the monster comes up. Not wanting to give away your secret just yet, you tell the editor that the fish was caught on a lure which you had a hand in designing. It's called the "Wonder Wobbler" or "WW" for short. Without fully realizing it, you are setting certain economic wheels in motion.

Your father is excited when he sees the size and number of fish you caught. He is especially interested when you tell him the lure story.

The two of you take the lure out to the workshop in the garage and look at it closely. He sketches the exact shapes of the parts of the weird-looking lure. You measure the length, width, and height of it, paying careful attention to the shape and weight of the various parts. You decide to make another lure exactly like this one. It takes a lot of time, but eventually you finish it. Then you test it by dragging it through water in the bathtub to make sure it performs just like the broken lure.

Next morning, at the first light of dawn, you go out to the lake to give the lure a real test. Your highest expectations come true! The fishing action is fast and heavy. Bass after bass is boated. Now you are more than reasonably sure the lure works better than any lure you have previously used.

The afternoon after the article appears in the paper your phone begins ringing. Everyone wants to buy a WW lure. So you and your dad decide to manufacture lures in the garage after work each day.

In order to do so, you need some capital goods: hand tools, drill press, disc sander, paint sprayer, and hand sander. You have these items on hand already, so luckily you don't have to invest much to produce the limited number of new lures you want to make to begin with. You do need some materials, however. You need balsa wood, plastic, steel tube hooks and screw-eyes, acrylic paint, sandpaper, and electricity. You and your father provide the labor.

By the Friday following your first week of production, you and your father have produced 45 lures. The cost of production was:

Labor: 30 hours at $4.00 per hour = $120.00
            This represents you and your father each working
            15 hours and earning $4.00 an hour.
Materials (balsa, paint, hooks, etc.) = $30.00
Heat, lights, power, etc. = $5.00

It cost you $155 to make 45 WW lures. That would be about $3.45 each. You decide to sell them for $5.00 each, giving you a profit of $1.55, some money to invest in making more lures. Eventually you might even rent or build a small factory to mass-produce lures. What you and your father have done is to take the productive resources of labor, capital, and natural resources (which have been made into products you need to make the lures), mix them with technical know-how (technology), and make a product designed to meet the needs of the people. You have developed a lure that is in popular demand, and you have set up the shop to meet that demand. In a free enterprise system you have the right to earn a profit from your work, and you did so.

THEORY VERSUS PRACTICE

Did you ever try planning a day carefully in hopes of getting more done? Maybe you even wrote a list of things you hoped to accomplish. Like many of us who have tried this, you may have finished the day without finishing the list. Things didn't work out as you had planned. A friend dropped in on you. You had to go to the store because you didn't have something on hand that you needed. One task took much longer than you expected.

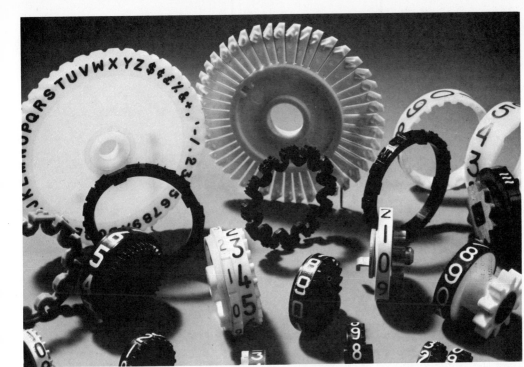

E. I. duPont de Nemours & Company

Something similar happens when economic systems are worked out on paper and then put into practice. The theories are carefully developed, and they look fine on paper. When applied to real life, though, they often fall short of the perfection they had in the minds of their creators. If a system is flexible, many flaws in it can be corrected. If the environment or the society or the situation changes, a flexible system can accommodate itself to these changes.

Perhaps that is why in the world of today we see very little that we could call pure socialism or pure communism or pure capitalism. As these major systems try to meet contemporary conditions, they borrow from each other. For example, there are privately-owned businesses in some communist countries. There is government regulation of some industries in capitalist countries.

Each system tries to provide the highest degree of human fulfillment and happiness, not only in terms of what citizens can have materially, but also in terms of how they are expected to spend their lives. Most of us feel that our system is the best so far and has resulted in a comparatively high standard of living for many people. This is not to say that our system is perfect, however. Every system needs constant changing and improvement.

We have made a beginning by learning a little about economic systems in the world of today. In the next chapter we will look more closely at the mechanics of the free enterprise system as it operates in our country on a day-to-day basis.

Working Cooperatively

Using the blackboard, list as many natural resources that go into the making of a car (or a house) as you can think of. List some of the capital goods involved. List types of labor that are needed.

What Do You Think?

How do you interpret the statement, "From each according to his capacity, to each according to his need"? How do you think it would work out in daily life? Who would determine an individual's capacity and/or need? How would this person go about it?

Chapter Check

1. Make a list of 15 natural resources found in the United States.

2. What are the three key resources which we need to produce goods or provide services?

3. What three questions does every economic system try to answer?

4. What is the main difference between socialism and communism? What is the main difference between socialism and communism on the one hand, and the free enterprise system on the other?

5. Why aren't there any examples of *pure* communism, *pure* socialism, or *pure* capitalism in the world today?

6. What elements of the free enterprise system did you see in the bass fishing story?

✿ Chapter Twenty ✿

MORE
ECONOMIC
CONCEPTS

C. William Horrell

KEY ELEMENTS OF OUR ECONOMIC SYSTEM

Over two centuries ago, Adam Smith described the five main elements of capitalism in his book *The Wealth of Nations*. You may run across it again someday. These elements are:

1. Private ownership of property
2. Profit motive
3. Free enterprise
4. Competition
5. Free market

Let's look at a few basic ideas behind these concepts.

C. William Horrell

PRIVATE PROPERTY.   Citizens of some countries have the legal right to own property on an individual basis. Furthermore, they are allowed to own natural resources such as capital goods, facilities for manufacturing products, offices, or stores.

PROFIT MOTIVE.   Motivation refers to a person's reason for wanting to do something. When people want to use their resources primarily to earn money, we say they operate on the basis of the profit motive. The profit motive has received much of the credit for the great economic development of capitalist countries. If people can profit by what they do, they may be more eager to do it and do it well.

FREE ENTERPRISE.   The saga of the Wonder-Wobbler in the last chapter gave you a good idea what free enterprise is. In a capitalistic system, an individual or a group has the right to start a business and reap profits from it.

COMPETITION.   The same concept (free enterprise) which gives you the right to manufacture your lures, or anything else, for a profit also works to make sure you don't rip off the public by making too great a profit. Since anyone has the right to organize a business to make something, you can rest assured that many lures very similar to the Wonder-Wobbler will soon appear on the market. There will be competition for your lure. Buyers will have a chance to choose between several lures. If you price your lure way out of sight or start cheapening the quality, people will buy someone else's lure. Your competitors will make a better profit than you will.

FREE MARKET. In a capitalist country, the market is generally not under government control. It is a free market. That means that people can decide to produce whatever they think they can sell. If they forecast the demand for an item correctly, they make a nice profit. If they misjudge the demand and make too many of an item, they suffer losses. In a socialist or communist economy, the government would determine what should be produced and in what quantities.

C. William Horrell

What Do You Think?

Call to mind five things you own that you really like. How do you feel about letting your brothers and sisters use them? How about friends?

It is nice to be generous with things you own. But if you have reason to believe that someone will damage, lose, or not return something of yours, do you have the right to refuse to lend it? What does ownership mean to you?

Name one thing you would like to buy and own during your first few years of employment. Can you think of some things it might be too much trouble to own? One person might say, "A dog would be too much trouble." Another might feel that way about a house. Why?

ECONOMIC INDICATORS

In the last chapter, you were introduced to some general concepts of economics and to some basic ideas about three economic systems. You learned about labor, capital, natural resources, communism, socialism, captialism and bass fishing.

It would be difficult to find a 30-minute newscast which did not include at least one of the following terms: GNP, CPI, inflation, monopoly, wage/price spiral, or cost of living, just to mention a few. Yet the average person on the street doesn't understand them well enough. Since these economic concepts do indeed have a major impact on our daily lives, we need to know as much as possible about them.

A person who goes to the doctor for a check-up will have his temperature taken, his weight and blood pressure recorded, and his heart checked. Various laboratory tests might be made. Economists have to keep an eye on the health of the economy much the same as a doctor keeps an eye on a patient's health.

Economic indicators are figures which economists study to see if the economy is healthy. They want to know how much is produced and consumed in a year's time, how much things cost, how the stock market is doing, how much the heavy industries are producing, how many people are unemployed, and what the current cost of living is. By watching trends, economists can help to correct bad situations before they become worse, saving the country from recession or serious inflation. We are going to take a look at some of the economic indicators economists use.

GNP (GROSS NATIONAL PRODUCT). GNP! Sounds like a sports car, doesn't it! Well, it may include the car you bought last year.

GNP stands for *gross national product.* The gross national product is the total amount of goods produced and services provided (in dollars and cents) in the United States during any one year. This figure generally runs in excess of 1,500,000,000,000 dollars! That 15 followed by eleven zeros is one trillion five hundred billion dollars! That amount reflects all of the cars, boats, homes, clothes, appliances, tools, toys and everything else that was manufactured and sold, plus medical, personal and other services that were provided.

Now, how does that figure stack up against the $2.50 you earn each hour? If you worked 8 hours a day, 50 weeks each year, it would only take you 300 million years to earn an amount equal to the yearly GNP in the United States of America.

The Gross National Product is made up of:

1. Goods and services purchased by individuals (about 63% of the GNP)

2. Business investments in new facilities and tools (about 15% of the GNP)

3. Goods and services purchased by the government (about 21% of the GNP)

4. Net export of goods and services (usually about 1% of the GNP)

Checkpoint

Try to get an idea of what you, personally, had to do with the gross national product for last year. Make a list of items you purchased. This can be anything from a bike to a set of drums to clothing or jewelry. What services did you pay for during the past year? Dental? Car repair? Shoe repair? Entertainment?

Did you contribute anything to the gross national product by:

1. Helping to manufacture any items? (Your contribution shows up as part of the price of the item, since the sale price includes what was paid out in wages in order to have the item manufactured.)

2. Providing any services for which people paid?

CPI (CONSUMER PRICE INDEX). An increase in the Gross National Product does not automatically mean that the country's economic base is healthy and increasing. Other factors have to be looked at as well. For example, economists look at the prices consumers had to pay for products and services. The economic indicator used to keep track of prices is called the Consumer Price Index (or the Cost of Living Index).

The following example will give you an idea why the CPI is important. Suppose that in one year $1,000,000,000 worth of new houses was bought. The next year $1,000,000,000 worth of new houses was again bought. But in checking further, you find that the average cost per house the first year was $30,000 while the second year it was $35,000. So you can see that actually fewer houses were sold the second year. Prices had gone up.

The idea of keeping a record of what different items cost each year sounds simple, but the way the CPI is arrived at is a bit complicated. Statisticians record the prices of items that are thought essential to maintaining a good standard of living. Each item is weighted according to its supposed importance. The statisticians then figure out how much it takes the average family of four to live in any one year.

The CPI affects how much you can buy for the money you earn. In 1967 the CPI was established at a base of 100. (This is a statistical device which is quite complex to explain, and we won't try.) In just five short years (1967-1972), the CPI rose from a base of 100 to 125. This meant that the portable television set which you bought in 1967 for $100 cost $125 in 1972. Also, that $2.50 per hour you were earning in 1967 had less buying power in 1972. You could only buy $1.88 worth of goods with it. The situation in which prices keep going up and buying power of the dollar keeps falling is called *inflation.* Inflation is a bad word to economists and to consumers. If people can buy three bags of groceries for $10.00 one year and only one a couple of years later, they are feeling the inflation crunch.

Many laborers in this country work under contracts which have guaranteed cost-of-living clauses. Their wages automatically go up if the consumer price index shows a certain increase. If the CPI rises, this wage increase helps them meet the increase in the cost of basic necessities.

It is probably becoming clear to you why people who live on fixed incomes have such a hard time when there is a general rise in prices, or inflation. Fixed income means that they receive a set amount each month. For example, people who receive pension checks are on fixed incomes. When the prices go up, the purchasing power of the dollar goes down. People on fixed incomes receive the same amount of money as they are used to receiving, but they can't buy as much with it.

You have probably had the experience of hearing your parents say, "When I was your age, I made 50¢ an hour and had all the spending money I needed." That is probably a true statement; however, that 50¢ may have had four times the buying the power it has today. You may want to lay the CPI on them the next time—cautiously, of course.

THE WAGE AND PRICE SPIRAL.   The wage and price spiral is another important indicator of rises in prices and services. Here's how the spiral works. Workers in one industry, let's say steel, want higher wages. They get their increase. The steel companies then raise their prices to pay for the increased wages. Other manufacturers who use steel for their products have to pay more for it, so they raise the prices of their products. Pretty soon other workers, who of course are also consumers, begin to notice the higher prices being charged for a lot of things they buy. So they ask for more wages to cover these increases. If they get raises, even more prices will probably go up. You can see why this is referred to as the wage and price spiral!

What Do You Think?

It has been said that prices in Germany during the nineteen-twenties were so inflated that people had to take wheelbarrows full of money to the market to buy just a small amount of food. That may be something of an exaggeration, but the situation was very grave.

How do you think inflation affects: People's attitude toward working? Family life? Whom people vote for?

?

PURE CAPITALISM?

As you no doubt realize by now, an economic system is a very complex business. A good system should be flexible. To refuse to make changes or add new ideas or to be unable to do so because a system is too rigid could mean the end of a system. Our system has run into many problems, and many changes have been made in it from time to time. Some of the solutions worked out for these problems have caused a change from a purer form of capitalism to a somewhat less pure form. Let's look at a few sample problems.

A PROBLEM WITH THE PROFIT MOTIVE.   What if people get so money hungry that they lose all sense of proportion? Maybe they overcharge their customers, underpay their employees, or make shoddy and unsafe products. The profit motive can corrupt people, just as power can corrupt them. Today, if they start victimizing others, they can be hauled into court. If we lived in a pure form of capitalism, the government would keep hands off and not interfere with the workings of the profit motive no matter what bad effects were felt. In our country, however, various laws have been passed to stop unfair practices that result from the profit motive getting out of hand. The thinking behind these laws is that people should be free to pursue profits but within reasonable limits.

A PROBLEM WITH THE LAW OF SUPPLY AND DEMAND.   If we had a totally pure form of capitalism, supply and demand would be the base of the free market. One problem is that it is not so easy to tell what the demand for a product is or will be. Businessmen can guess wrong, end up overproducing a certain item, and then get stuck with large quantities of unwanted goods. Sometimes nature or other forces interfere. A killing frost hits South America and the price of coffee doubles or triples. Or unscrupulous people can fake a shortage by warehousing an item and putting only a small amount out for sale. This creates an artificial shortage. The public rushes out to buy the product before it disappears from the shelves altogether. People will even pay higher prices for an item that appears to be hard to get. This is taking unfair advantage of the consumer, and in some cases the government steps in to stop such practices. But, generally speaking, in our economic system the government is expected to intervene only when there is a real problem. Ours is not a planned economy such as we might have if we were a socialist nation.

COMPETITION PROBLEMS.   A giant company with lots of money behind it can buy up all the little companies that are manufacturing the same product. It can corner the entire market, completely stifling competition. Or it can buy up other kinds of small companies so that it owns all the necessary resources and transportation facilities it needs thus making a product for much less, and selling it for less, than can smaller competitors who have to buy power and resources from others. The smaller companies then go bankrupt. The giants have the market all to themselves. They have formed a *monopoly*. They could conceivably start charging whatever prices they want. This actually has happened in our country from time to time. Laws relating to monopolies have been passed to curb such abuses.

LABOR PROBLEMS.   In the past, workers have been exploited. They have been overworked, underpaid, and forced to work in unsafe conditions. They often have not been well taken care of in terms of disability and retirement systems. In a purely capitalistic system, the government would again keep hands off and just wait for employers to be converted to a better way of treating their employees. But since that has often been slow to happen, the government has sometimes stepped in and made laws to stop unfair labor practices. Unions have also gained the right to organize. They in turn have needed to be regulated at times.

From this little survey of problems, you can see that we have to make our system work better by changing it to meet various needs as they arise. We have to realize that not all people do what is expected of them. Not all are fair and considerate. So through our government we try to regulate problem areas, stop abuses, and yet preserve as much freedom for business and labor as we can. Having a fair and workable system of **capitalism** is much more important than having a pure form of it.

In a group session, discuss the two following positions:

1. The profit motive in the United States economy is necessary for growth and stability.

2. The profit motive is good for little more than bringing out the greed in humanity.

We have covered a lot of ground in this chapter. You can check how well you understood the material by matching the terms below with their correct definitions.

1. GNP

2. CPI

3. Inflation

4. Profit Motive

5. Free Enterprise

6. Free Market

7. Competition

8. Monopoly

9. Law of Supply and Demand

10. Economic Indicators

a. The manufacture of things because the public demands them.

b. The right to establish your own business.

c. Complete control of a certain product or business.

d. The amount of goods and services purchased in the U.S. in one year's time.

e. Prices up, buying power down.

f. Record of price changes over a year's time; cost of living index.

g. Running a business or working in order to make money.

h. A market that is not regulated much by the government, but only by the law of supply and demand.

i. Many companies making the same product thus giving the consumer several options in quality and price.

j. Signs that economists use to get an idea of the state of the health of the economy.

❋ Chapter Twenty-One ❋

THE WORKER IN OUR ECONOMIC SYSTEM

THE UNION MOVEMENT

Before the industrial revolution, people were important in the manufacturing of things because they were skilled. Care and pride in their work made the products useful, durable, and often beautiful. The factory system was part of the industrial revolution. Machines were invented to do much of the work. Laborers were not individually so important anymore. They often only played a small part in the end product, and their skills meant little. Almost anybody could be taught to tend a machine all day or do one simple small part of an operation. The idea was to make more merchandise at lower prices. A worker aided by a machine could, perhaps, make several hundred shoes in one day. How many do you think he could make by hand?

Since employers no longer had to rely on workers' skills, they tended to look on their employees as beasts of burden. Some factory owners felt justified in paying very poor wages, and they gave workers few, if any, benefits. A normal working day was often from sunrise to sunset, 12 or more hours. Time for eating was very short, and the coffee break had not yet been invented. Children and women were made to work in dangerous and tiring conditions. Men didn't have it any easier. Health insurance? Sick leave? Retirement plans? Vacation days? These were not part of the picture for most workers.

If you had been a worker under such conditions, you probably would not have gone to your employer and complained. First of all, you needed the small wage paid you. If you complained, he could fire you on the spot and blacklist you as a troublemaker. The list of "bad" workers (the blacklist) could be passed from one factory to another, making it extremely difficult to get a new job.

Independence is not such a great thing if one is drowning in the middle of the Atlantic Ocean. The plight of the workers in the 19th century was about this grim. It appeared that the only way labor could be heard was for workers to organize themselves. They could then elect leaders to represent them with the owners-employers. They could campaign for government officials and politicians who would support their cause. The union movement began to gather momentum.

At first, owners and employers felt less than happy about their workers joining unions. They realized that by organizing, the workers would gain power. They preferred to keep things as they were. Many attempts were made to stop the growth of union membership, both by owners and by the public at large. Many people felt that if laborers got more power, they would get completely out of hand and try to run things. Also, of course, people wanted more goods at cheaper prices. Low wages would keep prices down.

To keep unionization from coming about, employers and others put pressure on lawmakers and judges. Unions were frequently banned as conspiracies. It was only in 1847 that a courageous judge, Lemuel Smith, of the Massachusetts Supreme Court, declared that unions were not conspiracies any more than organizations of stockholders were. His decision set the precedent which many other states were to follow. It finally became legal to belong to a worker's union.

In the early days there were many violent clashes between workers and management and between union and non-union sympathizers. Little by little, though, unionization came to be accepted as part of the economic picture. Unions have grown enormously. The United States Bureau of Labor Statistics has reported that approximately one out of every four workers belongs to a union. Will you be that one in four?

The growth of unions seems to be leveling off. If unions have done such a great job, doesn't it seem surprising that they are not still growing at a rapid pace? Several factors account for this. Workers today are not generally faced with the deplorable conditions that existed at the turn of the century. Some of the needs for which unions were established have been met. More laws protecting workers' rights have also been passed. Furthermore, private businessmen and corporations have come to realize that satisfied workers are more productive, are absent less often, have more loyalty, and stay with the company longer. All these things add up to increased profits. In other words, it pays to be fair.

Many people have lost faith in unions because of corruption among union officials. Various scandals have come to light. Fights for control of the big unions have often been bitter and violent. The question is, do these features outweigh the good things unions have done and can still do? Can the unions do a good job of cleaning their own houses? The quantity and quality of participation by union members in union activities may help to decide this question.

Unions can still do many things to help workers. They can continue to press for just wages and benefits. They can influence legislation relating to labor and fair trade. Unions may be able to work with government leaders to develop imaginative plans for curbing inflation and cutting down the possiblity of recession or depression. They can help workers whose jobs are threatened by automation to retrain for other jobs. Unions can also put pressure on employers and government agencies to see to it that health and safety measures are strictly enforced.

Working Cooperatively

Over several weeks' time, clip and bring to class newspaper items that have something to do with unions, strikes, labor affairs, etc. Have a committee of three choose the five most interesting articles. After someone has read a clipping out loud, determine what the main issue being reported was. Then, as a class, discuss the pros and cons of each issue.

SHOULD YOU JOIN A UNION?

Many of you might be faced with this question. In some states you may have to join in order to work in certain factories or businesses. When one condition for getting a job is joining the union, that factory is said to run a *closed shop*. An *open shop* is a workplace where you have a choice of joining or not joining the union. Closed and open shops are a matter of state rather than federal law. Many states have outlawed closed

C. William Horrell

AFL-CIO

shops. If you want to know if closed shops are legal in your state, you can check with your state department of labor.

If you have a choice about whether to join a union or not, how will you decide? First of all, it is a good idea not to be guided by generalities about unions as a whole. Investigate the specific union you will be joining. Find out what it has to offer you. Find out how and when it was formed, and what it has accomplished so far. See what kind of a program it has for the future.

The size of the place where you work may have some bearing on the question. If you work in a smaller place where access to the boss or owner is fairly simple, you may feel no need to be represented by a union. There are many employers who operate a fair and reliable shop without pressure from outside.

If you work for a big corporation, however, chances are it is run by a board of directors and owned by thousands of stockholders. The board of directors may be officed nearby or 1,000 miles away. In the gigantic organizations which exist today, you may not find it easy to make your needs known. The only possible way to negotiate may be through elected labor representatives.

You may also want to consider the cost of union membership. A person gets very little for nothing in this world. Unions need money to maintain their organization, inform the membership, affect legislation, support members on strike, and a host of other things. To pay for these services, each member is charged a fee. Usually you pay an initial charge when you first join the union. Then monthly (or weekly) dues are withheld from your paycheck. Sometimes your money will go to help other workers. Other times their money will be used to help you and other union members at your workplace. What do you think of this arrangement?

Something else to think about in advance is how you feel about going out on strike. Strikes that go on and on can be very hard on workers. The union has some monies set aside to pay striking workers, but there are limits to this. If the issue is important enough, you might consider striking a good move in the long run. But even if you think the issue is not that important, you may have to go along with the union's decision to strike.

Do unions lessen the independence of individual workers? Any time you join any such organization you give up some independence in order to work cooperatively with others. You hope to achieve goals together that you couldn't achieve on your own. But all persons should have some idea of how much independence they are willing to give up. Unions often endorse candidates for president and for other offices. If you blindly vote for these candidates just because they are union backed, you give up some of your independence. The same is true about political recommendations from other organizations as well.

You can also lose independence by joining a union and then not participating in any of the activities except to pay your dues. In effect, such people are saying, "I'm satisfied to let someone else speak for me and make decisions without me." These people don't lose their independence, they give it away.

To participate fully you would attend meetings of your local union and keep an eye on what's happening in the national organization. You would vote thoughtfully on issues that are brought up. You would find out as much as you can about candidates running for union offices. Someday you may even want to run for office yourself or serve on a committee.

THE LABOR MANAGEMENT RELATIONS ACT

We have come a long way since the days when there were almost no laws protecting workers. Earlier we looked at health and safety laws and equal opportunities legislation. Elsewhere in this book we will be covering laws that regulate child labor, and wages. In the remainder of this chapter we are going to concentrate on the law that gives workers the right to organize. It also attempts to keep a balance between the power of labor and the power of management.

The *National Labor Relations Act* was originally passed by the Congress in 1935. In 1947 the name of the act was changed to the *Labor Management Relations Act.* Further amended in 1959 and 1974, the present law defines and protects the rights of both employees and employers. It encourages collective bargaining and helps eliminate harmful labor or management practices.

One of the most powerful tools used to call attention to problems is the strike. A strike occurs when the workers walk off the job and production comes to a halt. The strike is an action of last resort because it can be very hard on all parties concerned—owners, workers, and frequently, the general public.

In an effort to avoid strikes, representatives from labor and management sometimes meet together before a crisis is reached. In some cases, negotiations are carried on almost continuously even when there is no immediate crisis. When labor and management leaders get together to work out their differences it is called *collective bargaining.*

Before the passage of the Labor Management Relations Act, a person could be fired for belonging to a union or attempting to bargain collectively. This Act spells out the workers' right to:

Organize and bargain collectively.

Elect their own representatives to bargain for them.

Start, join, or assist a labor organization.

It stops employers from:

Firing or threatening employees for joining unions.

Keeping workers from starting unions.

Threatening to close or move a plant to keep a union from forming.

Showing favoritism for one union over another.

The Labor Management Relations Act not only deals with the rights of workers and labor organizations, but it also spells out their responsibilities. Workers and unions are forbidden to:

Physically prevent non-striking employees from entering the work place.

Commit acts of violence in a strike situation.

Try to restrict employment of non-union members.

Practice discrimination.

Try to control which companies the employer can do business with.

Force employers to pay for services which are not really provided.

The Act was instrumental in setting up the National Labor Relations Board (NLRB). This Board has the power to take action in labor-management problems when the two parties are involved in interstate commerce. Interstate commerce includes any trade, service, traffic, transportation or communication across state lines. That includes the majority of the commerce of our country. The NLRB has the responsibility to see to it that unfair practices are corrected. To do this, the NLRB has nearly 50 regional offices located throughout the United States. Complaints are channeled through these offices.

Since the passage of the Labor Management Relations Act, many other laws dealing with strikes and arbitration have been passed. The Labor Management Relations Act is like the cornerstone of a building. It has been frequently added to and improved in order to enhance the life of the worker in our economic system.

What Do You Think?

Do you feel that workers necessary for the common welfare such as nurses, policemen, and firemen, should be allowed to strike? Do you think they can get fair treatment if they don't strike? If you were the mayor of a city and the police force struck, what would you do about it?

Working Cooperatively

Hold a mock arbitration meeting, using the following situation:

A company has 250 full-time workers. It lays off 25 of them during a slack period, and when things pick up the employer gives the remaining 225 employees overtime.

The union wants the company to re-hire some of the full-time workers who had been laid off rather than giving overtime to others. The union tells the company that unless it changes its policy by a certain date, the workers it represents will go on strike.

Choose three people in the class to represent the union and have them explain their side of the story. Choose three others to represent the company's side. Finally, choose three to be the arbitration team.

The arbitration team listens to both the union and the company sides. It then meets by itself to discuss what it has heard. Returning to the others, it makes compromise suggestions.

These suggestions are then discussed by all nine people. Then a vote on the compromises is called. (The arbitration team does not vote of course.)

Chapter Check

True or False:

1. The industrial revolution led to increased craftsmanship.

2. Mass production led to more goods at cheaper prices.

3. The blacklist was a device used to keep people at an economic disadvantage.

4. At one time it was considered illegal to belong to a union.

5. A *closed shop* is the term used to refer to a place of employment in which the employee must join a union.

6. The Labor Management Relations Act deals only with workers' rights.

7. Arbitration is the working out of a solution to a disagreement between workers and employers.

8. A closed shop is a shop whose workers are out on strike.

9. If you belong to a union you should always vote for the presidential candidate your union endorses.

 **Part Eight**

H. Armstrong Roberts

You and Your Money

BARTER VS. MONEY

Money is one of our more useful inventions. If you don't believe it, imagine life without a money system. How would you get the things you couldn't make or grow yourself? You would have to trade or barter.

Some trading can be quite simple and painless. Suzette has a paperback murder mystery she has just finished. Gary has a different one which he has read. They live down the block from each other and often talk together. The subjects of books comes up, and they decide to trade. Even Steven.

What happens when you have a book and the other person has a sack of potatoes. That's fine, if you need a sack of potatoes. Even so, how would you decide on the value of the book? How many potatoes equals one book?

Now think of a new red tractor. The farmer needs it and has cows, chickens, wheat, corn, and other farm products to trade for it. Imagine the quantity of these trade items that would have to be taken to the factory. What would the factory owners do with them? They may be able to use some of the farm products to pay their workers. But what the owners really need is more metal and rubber to build more tractors with. If they were lucky maybe they would find a steel producer who needed the farm produce. But, by that time, what would have become of the poor chickens, and pigs? Would they survive?

It's easy to see that except in a very small and simple society direct trade and barter are out of the question. Money as a medium of exchange has made it much easier for people to do business.

Experts have said that someday money as we know it will be obsolete. People will be using checks, credit cards, and computers to perform their transactions. Still, that won't relieve us of responsibility for managing their financial affairs. That's what the next four chapters are all about.

❀ Chapter Twenty-Two ❀

MANAGING
YOUR MONEY

Know All Men By These Prints that Daniel
Boone hath Deposited Six, vi, beaver Skins
in my keep in good order and of the worth
of vi shillings each skin and i Have took
from them vi shillings for the keep of them
and when they Be sold i will pay the balance
of XXX shillings for the whole lot to any
person who presents this certificate
an delivers it up to me at my keep Louisville
falls of ohio May 20 1784
John Sanders

Terry Mauzy

WHERE DOES IT ALL GO?

George and Jenny and two other couples were talking and playing
cards one evening. The subject of buying a house came up. From that the
conversation shifted to how much money they had already made in their
lifetimes. "Gee, whiz!" said George, leaning back in his chair. "I'm 33
years old. I've averaged about $10,000 a year since I was 20. Do you
realize that means that more than $100,000 has passed through my
hands? And what do I have to show for it?"

That was a sobering thought. He and Jenny each had a car, but they didn't own a house. They owned their furniture, but no appliances. They had no stocks or bonds, only a small bank account. After their visitors left, they talked about their financial situation some more. "Why don't we do something about it," suggested Jenny.

They were too tired to do anything about it that night, but the next day Jenny got some books on financial planning at the library. In the evening, they sat down together and made some drastic changes in their money management. "Better late than never," said George. "But I do wish we had started sooner. Well, honey, maybe we can still get that little dream house someday."

Many people make a considerable amount of money during their working lives and yet have very little to show for it. They have to admit that a good part of their resources has been wasted. This chapter might help you avoid such a fate.

Where are you financially right now? Take a piece of paper and write down what you can remember spending since your last payday. Does the list come close to the total amount of money you had to start with? Or is there a sizeable amount you can't account for?

It's important to see where your money is *really* going. Keep a spending log between paychecks. You may want to set it up like this:

Spending Log

Day of Month	Item	Amount
1	hamburger & coke	$1.30
1	movie	$2.00
2	birthday card	$ .50
3	french fries and coke	$ .80
4	date	$8.00

After doing this for a couple of weeks, you will have a good record to use in evaluating your financial situation.

FINANCIAL PLANNING—HOW TO

What have you been doing right, as far as managing your money is concerned? What would you like to do differently? Answering these questions involves setting goals. Your short range goals deal with taking care of your immediate needs. If you live at home, these would include clothes, transportation, and entertainment. Many young workers give their parents money to cover their share of food and housing expenses, or at least part of it. This seems fair, since it would cost you a lot more to live on your own somewhere. Of course someday when you move into an apartment of your own, you will have to allow money for rent, utilities, and, of course, food.

You may have other needs that you may be unable to meet out of one paycheck. Suppose you have to pay car insurance. If you are male and under 25 or female and under 21, you will have quite a chunk to pay. So when you are figuring your monthly expenses, you will have to prorate that yearly insurance figure. Prorate means that you will divide the premium by twelve months and figure out how much you will have to set aside each month in order to have enough money to pay that bill when it falls due.

Now you are ready to set up a budget system for yourself. Set it up in any clear and convenient way. A small notebook would be ideal. Use one page for each pay period.

Here is an example of how a budget works. Alan works 20 hours a week at Hernando's. This is his second year there, and he makes $3.10 per hour. His budget notebook looks like this:

April 1979

Gross pay: $248.00   Withholding Tax: $26.00
Net pay: $204.00   Social Security: $ 18.00

Estimated Regular Expenses	
Room and board (paid to his parents)	$40
Motorcycle expenses	$ 12
Clothing	$20
Entertainment	$25
	$97

Special Expenses	
Vacation Fund	$10
Insurance-Motorcycle (for three months coverage, due April 15)	$30
Graduation Picture	$ 18
	$ 58

TOTAL INCOME	$204.00
REGULAR AND SPECIAL EXPENSES	155.00
SURPLUS	49.00

Notice that Alan still has $49.00 left. What should he do with it? If he doesn't make plans for at least part of it, chances are it will "disappear." He won't know what he spent it for and will have little to show for it.

Planning what to do with this extra money involves his long range goals. He would be wise to put some of it where it can work for him. We'll talk more about that in the next chapter on banking services. It so happens that Alan would also like to buy a good used car someday. He doesn't want to get stuck with big monthly payments because he figures it will be hard enough to afford just to keep the car running. So he decides to start a car fund.

Look at Alan's expenses again. Some of them are *fixed expenses*. They are regular, set payments and can't be juggled too much. Can you tell which those are? The *variable expenses* reflect money he spent on things that were not absolute necessities. Alan can change these around as he sees fit. For example, he might go to fewer movies and spend the money on a shirt instead.

What Do You Think?

What would be the best way for a married couple to set up a budget? Should the man or the woman handle the financial matters? How many marital problems do you think are complicated by money matters? Do you think some of this is avoidable?

YOUR GOALS

By this time you no doubt have some idea of what kind of budget notebook you want to keep. Let's spend a little more time on setting goals. You can break goals down into three categories: immediate, intermediate, and long range.

If a life is directed entirely toward long range goals, it can be a drag. Immediate goals which we can satisfy fairly easily allow us to taste some of the fruits of our labor on a day-to-day basis. Immediate financial goals are those you can reach when you get your next paycheck, after you have paid for your basic necessities. You may have in mind clothing, sports equipment, dating, a gift, a charitable contribution, a magazine subscription.

Intermediate goals take a little longer to achieve. You may want to put enough aside to buy a new fishing tackle or a blow-dry hair styler. Or you might want to try saving enough money to go to Disneyland in a year or join an athletic club or buy a fancy sewing machine.

Checkpoint

Make a table of your goals. Are all the goals in each of the columns equally important to you? Probably not! After you have made each list of goals, rank those goals from one to whatever in order of their importance to you. Here is a sample table:

Rank	Immediate Goals
2	knit dress
3	food (not meals)
1	concert tickets

Rank	Intermediate Goals
1	traveling case
2	camera
3	trip to visit boy-friend in San Antonio

Rank	Long Range Goals
1	cosmetology course
2	used car
4	trip to Italy
3	apartment furnishings

After you have made such a chart, you may want to copy it into your budget notebook. You will then be able to keep track of how well you do in meeting your goals. Don't be disappointed if you don't reach all of them as soon as you expected to. If you manage to put some of your resources into the top items in your intermediate and long range columns, you are doing very well. Remember after you have established yourself in the world of work you will receive better wages. Then you can begin accomplishing those intermediate and long range goals more quickly and easily. There may also be many times when you give up an immediate goal in order to be able to afford a long range item.

Each time you get a raise or move to a better job, reconsider your financial plan. Otherwise you will find your additional income melting away, as we mentioned before. Good luck with your planning! Your first budget will be a matter of trial and error, but you'll eventually settle into a plan that gives you satisfaction and security.

Do you believe many people buy things they really don't want? How do you think this happens? Do you think lack of financial goals might partially account for this?

SOME PITFALLS TO AVOID

You will run into many people with financial difficulties. In fact, most of us have some problems with money from time to time. Some people are able to keep their problems under better control than others, however. It would be unfair to say that all poor people are poor because they don't know how to manage their money. This may not be the case. They may have had hardships and bad health. They may have many dependents to care for. We are not talking about these people. We are referring to people who are constantly struggling financially when they could be living comfortably if they knew more about planning and managing.

What are some of the reasons for financial failure? First let's consider *deficit spending*. Deficit spending is spending more money than you have. People who don't have plans or budgets spend freely after they get paid. Then they end up not being able to meet their obligations. Each pay period they fall farther behind because they are actually spending more than they make. For instance, they dip into their transportation money, or they use a charge account to avoid paying cash immediately. Sooner or later disaster strikes. All of the bills that have been put off suddenly come due.

Another pitfall is *financial competition.* Many people get involved with a certain circle of friends and feel forced to keep up with them. James and Wilhelmena get a new car, so Pat and Hubert do, too. Tamara and Frank buy a house; Jill and Jerry buy one, too. It's very easy to be drawn into an unending cycle of such competition. The end result is a lot of worry over meeting obligations and maybe some family quarrels as well. All this time these people could be quietly enjoying a style of life that suits them better and doesn't involve all that strain and fuss.

In this country we may be a little spoiled. For example, the other day some people were complaining because they were too broke to take a winter vacation. They own a house, a boat, two cars, and many other such items. Would you call them poor? When people start taking ownership of things for granted, they quite often stop appreciating them. It gets harder and harder for them to distinguish between necessities and luxuries. If a person puts luxuries before necessities, trouble is sure to strike.

A more difficult thing to control is *hidden cost*. Sometimes it takes experience to pick out extra costs, although forethought and research can help. Suppose you want to buy a car. The price of it is only one part of the cost. You have to pay license fees and purchase insurance, buy gas and oil, and allow for repairs. All the time you have the car it is depreciating in value. That is, its value is going down. You are putting wear and tear on it, too, even though there is no exact way to measure the rate. Maybe you are paying interest on a car loan. These are all hidden costs.

Working Cooperatively

Make a blackboard list of all the hidden costs you can think of in connec- tion with buying a house.

CONTINGENCY PLANNING

Life has its ups and downs. Sometimes things go exactly as planned and sometimes things go wrong. It is good to enjoy the pleasant, and very important to be prepared for the unpleasant.

What would happen to your financial plan if you broke your arm and couldn't work for three weeks, or the transmission on your car blew up? Would these emergencies completely derail your financial plan?

A contingency plan is an alternative plan to use in case your original plan does not work out exactly as you had hoped. Suppose you have planned to pick up your sister at the bus station when she comes home for Thanksgiving. The weather turns very bad and you call her and say, "Listen. If the roads are at all passable, I'll meet you at the station. If I'm not there, wait an hour or so. Then call Joe and Jessie. They'll come get you, and you can stay the night with them. I'm sure I'll be able to get through in the morning after the roads are plowed." That's a contingency plan, and you can see the wisdom of making it.

In financial planning, a contingency plan means putting aside a little money each payday to build up an emergency fund. Financial experts suggest that an emergency fund should equal at least two months' wages. If you earn $300 a month, your rainy-day fund should eventually be $600.

Of course, you can't build your emergency fund up to that level in a month or two. It may take a year or more, and it will take self-discipline not to dip into it when a mini-emergency occurs. If you do use part of it, you have to replace it as soon as possible. Your contingency plan will pay off in terms of having emergency cash, but it will also give you a more secure and positive feeling about the future than if your original plan had to be scrapped altogether.

Match the terms on the left with the proper response on the right.

1. Immediate goal   a.   When expenses exceed income

2. Intermediate goal   b.   Food

3. Long range goal   c.   A new stereo

4. Deficit spending   d.   A plan used when things don't go as expected

5. Fixed expense   e.   Entertainment

6. Variable expense   f.   A new album

7. Contingency plan   g.   A new home

1. How does setting goals help a person achieve financial independence?

2. Compare a budget to a road map.

3. How important do you think a contingency plan is?

4. Do you think your financial plan will change much over the next 5 years? 10 years? Why or why not?

❁ Chapter Twenty-Three ❁

Banking
Services
and Credit

SHOULD YOU HAVE A CHECKING ACCOUNT?

Pay day! You get your check, cash it, and put the money in your dresser drawer, right? Wrong! Why wrong? It's your money, isn't it? Precisely. But maybe there is a better way of handling it. Let's go back and consider what happened before you received your check.

Your employers knew they would owe you a specified wage on pay day, so they put some cash aside. In a drawer? Not likely! Rather than keeping enough cash on hand to meet payroll obligations, they put it in a bank. When your employers pay you, they write the banker a note telling him to give you some of their money. The note is, of course, a check.

The banker wants to make sure he and the employers agree on how much money is in the checking account. So once a month, the bank sends the employers a list (*statement*) of all the checks written during the past month for which money was paid out. Each sum of money paid out is called a *debit.* The statement also shows how much was deposited into the account during the past month. These deposits are referred to as *credits.* The amount left after subtracting the debits from the credits is called the *balance.* The bank also encloses all the checks listed on the statement. They are stamped *Paid,* and are referred to as *cancelled checks.*

Let's go over a few of these banking terms as we will be using them over and over again:

Check—a note written to the bank which says, pay so-and-so this amount of money out of my account.

Account—record of monetary transactions between an individual and a bank or between a company and a bank.

Check record—a record of the checks you have written kept in your checkbook or a record the bank keeps of the checks you have written.

Deposit record—a record in your checkbook of the amounts you put into your account or a record which the bank keeps of the amounts you deposit to your account.

Statement—a record of credits and debits to your account which the bank sends you to make sure their records and yours agree.

Cancelled check—a check that has been cashed and processed by the bank.

Balance—amount of money you have in your account.

It may be wise for you to put some of your pay in a checking account, just as your employers do. You may have bills to pay by mail, such as an out-of-town record club. Sending cash through the mail is risky business. Keeping large amounts of cash in your dresser drawer or anywhere else at home isn't a good practice either.

If you are considering opening a checking account, ask yourself:

1. Would I write enough checks each month to justify a checking account?

2. How many checks would I probably average a month?

3. How much money am I likely to have in the account at any one time?

4. Will I be able to make fairly regular deposits?

J. R. & J. M. Huck
1432 Danbury Avenue
Hucksville, Illinois 60606

Huck National
Bank of Illinois Member FDIC

Checking Account Statement

Date	Check No.	Amount	Deposit	Balance	Previous Balance	Comment
10/01/77					246.11	
10/03/77	304	18.75		227.36		
10/09/77	305	1.60		225.76		
10/12/77	306	7.40		218.36		
10/17/77	307	5.00		213.36		
10/20/77	308	6.56		206.80		
10/23/77	309	11.42		195.38		
10/25/77	310	6.87		188.51		
10/28/77	311	3.10		185.41		
10/31/77	312	8.04		177.37		
11/10/77	313	50.00		127.37		
11/10/77			340.27	467.64		

Check No.	Date	Check issued to or Description of Deposit	√	Amount of Deposit	Balance Forward
					$ 251.58
303	10/1/77	TO The Record Album	√	Check or Dep.	5.47
		FOR Record + Tape		Bal.	246.11
304	10/2/77	TO Bill's T.V. Stereo Pay	√	Check or Dep.	18.75
		FOR Repair of stereo		Bal.	227.36
305	10/6/77	TO School Lunch	√	Check or Dep.	1.60
		FOR		Bal.	225.76
306	10/7/77	TO Teen Times	√	Check or Dep.	7.40
		FOR 1 yr subscription		Bal.	218.36
307	10/7/77	TO Cash	√	Check or Dep.	5.00
		FOR		Bal.	213.36
308	10/19/77	TO Bob's Bike Repair	√	Check or Dep.	6.56
		FOR New Front Wheel		Bal.	206.80
309	10/20/77	TO Sally's Donut Shop	√	Check or Dep.	11.42
		FOR Going away party - Pat		Bal.	195.38
310	10/24/77	TO Ajax Cleaning	√	Check or Dep.	6.87
		FOR Suit Cleaned		Bal.	188.51
311	10/26/77	TO Francies's Flowers	√	Check or Dep.	3.10
		FOR mom's birthday		Bal.	185.41

There are many kinds of checking accounts. We will look at two of the most common to give you a basic understanding of the possibilities. You can then investigate the possibilities where you are.

Generally you can choose between two types of checking accounts, depending on the number of checks you think you will be writing each month. The first type is one for which the bank charges you a monthly fee called a **service charge.** You pay that fee, and you can write as many checks as you please without any additional charge. The bank sets a minimum balance for this type of account, usually around $200. If you needed to write $50 worth of checks, you would have to deposit $250 so that your balance would not go below $200. If you let it get below $200 there will be an additional service charge.

The other kind of checking account requires no minimum balance to be kept in the bank, as long as you keep the account open with a few dollars. With this kind of account, a fee is charged for each check you write. For instance, you may get a book of ten blank checks. You pay per check instead of a set fee. You can see that if you write many checks this could get expensive. If you write only a few, though, it is less expensive than paying a set fee. Students often use the per-check type of account since they write only a few checks per month. This is the less expensive way for them.

KEEPING YOUR CHECKBOOK IN ORDER

In order to use a checking account effectively, you must do a small amount of record keeping, just as your employers do. The following items of information go on the face of each check:

name of the bank
date on which the check was written
number of the check
your account number
the name of the person or company to whom you want the money paid
the amount of money to be paid (It is written as a number first, then spelled out in words on the next line.)

Sometimes your name, address, and phone number are already printed on your check by the bank.

When you write a check, immediately record the basic information on your check stub (the part of the check you keep) or in the check register which came with your book of checks. Then record the balance brought forward (the amount you had in the account before writing this check), and the balance left (the amount in your account after writing this check). You may also want to note your reason for writing the check.

To make this all very clear, let's take a look at Jane's checkbook. She ordered a pair of leather boots by mail from Wyoming. She has to enclose a check with her order. She writes the check. She makes a record of it in her checkbook. Now, at the end of the month, when her statement comes from the bank, there will be no confusion. Jane will have a good record in her check register and she can compare it with the record the bank sends her.

Once you open a checking account, the bank will send you a statement at regular intervals, usually once a month. The statement lists all the

checks you have written and all the deposits you have made. Enclosed in the envelope with your statement are all the cancelled checks from the previous month. A cancelled check has gone through the whole process and we sometimes say it has "cleared." The transaction has been completed, and the cancelled check proves it. It is a good idea to save your cancelled checks for two or three years, in case you should ever need them to prove that you paid for something.

That balance in your checkbook and the balance on your bank statement may not always be the same. Can you see why? The statement reflects the checks which have been cashed, cleared, and returned to the bank. For example, when Jane wrote that check to Danfan Western Store for her boots, it took a few days for the store to receive it. Then the store owner held it a few more days, until she was ready to go to the bank. Then it had to be processed and sent back to Jane's bank. Meanwhile, her monthly statement had been prepared and sent to her. The check to Danfan will therefore appear on the next month's statement.

Here are the steps you would follow to balance your checkbook. *Balancing* means checking to see that your figures and the bank's figures agree. Some statements have space on the back in which you can work out your balance.

1. Put your checks in order by check number.

2. Mark off in your checkbook those checks paid by the bank and appearing on your statement.

3. Make a list of the checks you have written but which, according to your latest statement, have not yet been paid and cleared by the bank. They are your outstanding checks. These checks will be on your next statement. You will also have to look back a month or so to see if there are any other outstanding checks. Perhaps that check you sent to Grandma for her birthday two months ago is still in her dresser drawer.

4. Add up all the outstanding checks you found in Step 3.

5. Subtract the total of the outstanding checks from the balance on the statement. The bank doesn't know it yet, but you've spent that money.

6. You will also have to check and see if a service charge shows on the statement, and be sure to subtract that amount from your checkbook balance.

7. If you have made any deposits since this statement was prepared they won't show on it. Add them to the balance shown on your statement.

8. If you and the bank have figured correctly, your checkbook balance and your statement balance should come out the same. If they aren't equal, first, carefully review your checkbook, making certain that you have recorded everything and that your math is correct. If the two still aren't equal, take a trip to the bank and ask them to help you find the error. Even with all their computers, banks, too, can make mistakes. If both you and the bank check and re-check, the error is sure to become obvious.

SPECIAL KINDS OF CHECKS

A very convenient and safe way to carry money on a trip is to use traveler's checks. If you travel out of state, you may have trouble cashing a personal check. Many businesses don't want to take a chance on an out-

of-state check. Traveler's checks, however, are accepted by banks and businesses in most places, including foreign countries. When you buy traveler's checks, you usually pay one dollar for each one hundred dollars worth of checks. For example, if you gave the banker $101.00 in cash, you could get 10 checks worth $10 each, or 5 checks worth $20 each, or 2 checks for $50 each, however you want the amount broken down. You will be asked to sign the checks right there in front of the teller. You will be asked to sign them again on another line when you cash them. The second time you must always sign in the presence of the person you are making the check out to. If you sign the second time up in your hotel room or on the airplane or train, the check won't be any good. When you sign it the second time, in the presence of the person who is cashing it, that person can be sure that you really signed it since he saw you do so. He can also compare this second signature with the first one which you wrote at the bank, and in that way he can verify that the check is really yours. Quite often you will also be asked for identification. Traveler's checks have another important advantage. They can be replaced if they are lost or stolen.

Money orders can be useful in certain situations. You can purchase them from the post office, American Express, or Railway Express. Certified checks and cashier's checks are similar and can be purchased at a bank. With this type of check you give your money to the agent or teller, together with a small fee to cover the charge for the service. The teller fills out the amount on the check with a special machine and gives it to you. You then fill in the rest and send it to the person or company you want to pay. Usually, if you have a checking account, you won't use this kind of check. But the occasion may arise when the person or company you are paying has a policy of not accepting personal checks. This kind of check insures them that the express office or bank has collected the money from you.

SAVINGS ACCOUNTS

Your employers are in business to make a profit. When they earn more money than they need for running expenses, they could spend the extra money on luxuries. But successful businessmen don't do that. They put some of their extra money to work for them. Sometimes they invest in stocks and bonds. Other times they put their money in the bank, but not in their checking accounts. It wouldn't draw interest there. So instead they place some of their extra money in a savings account. The banker then keeps some of it in the bank and invests the rest. The bank might lend some of it to a company or an individual at interest. Since the bank is using the employers' money, the employers are entitled to some of what is earned in interest on it.

This is how a savings account works for you, too. You take some of your money each pay day and put it in the bank. The bank puts it to work by investing it. You would then get some of the interest that money earns.

You have to keep records with a savings account just as you do with your checking account. How do you do this? It differs from bank to bank, and also with the type of savings account you have. Basically, though, you are given a small booklet, called a *passbook,* at the time you open the account. Each time you go to the bank to make a deposit in your savings account, you take your passbook with you. While you are

standing at the bank counter your deposit will be recorded. Check your passbook after the teller hands it back to you. You probably won't get a statement each month on your savings account. Your passbook is your record. Usually twice or four times a year the interest will be computed, and you will then receive a computer printout showing how much interest your money has earned. Some banks send you a report on your savings account for the previous year just after the first of the new year so that you will have the necessary figures to use for your income tax return. (You have to report the interest you have earned as income on your federal income tax form.)

In deciding at which bank or savings and loan association you want to have a savings account you will want to find out where you can get the best rate of interest on your money. You will want it to earn as much as possible. You can simply call different banks and ask them what the current rate of interest on savings accounts is. You will also want to ask how often interest is computed. Sometimes it is computed daily, and you earn interest up to the day you withdraw your savings. Other places compute interest quarterly, four times a year. If you take money out just before the end of a quarter, you lose the interest your money earned during that quarter. You will also want to know in advance how hard it is going to be to get your money out if you need to, and how long it will take.

BORROWING MONEY AND ESTABLISHING CREDIT

Credit comes from the French word for belief, trust, or confidence. Banks and other financial institutions extend credit (lend money) to people they feel they can trust. Credit card companies and various retail businesses issue credit cards to people they trust.

Credit is very important in our society. How can you get a good credit rating? You may need one to buy a large item such as a car or home or to start a business. You get a good credit rating by paying off a loan you have made. This seems to be going in circles. How do you get a loan if you have to have paid off a loan to get a good credit rating in the first place?

That's a good question. The best way, some bankers say, is to borrow a small amount first, while you are young. Perhaps your first loan is $50 to help buy a bicycle. The conditions of the loan require a number of monthly payments for a set number of months. All you have to do is to make each payment on time. Keep your part of the bargain, and you have a good start toward establishing good credit. You must, of course, make sure you will have sufficient income to make the payments before you decide to get a loan. You will have to carefully consider the amount of loan you can easily handle.

A number of credit bureaus across the country keep files on how well people fulfill their financial obligations. Say you do buy a bike with a loan from the bank. You make your payments without fail. The bank sends your record of payments to the credit bureau with which it is cooperating. The credit bureau gives you a good rating every time this happens. You become known as a good risk. A company considering making a loan to you or issuing you a credit card checks with the bureau to find out if you are worthy of trust. By the way, you have a legal right to know what information about you a credit bureau has in its files. You can ask for a copy of it.

Exactly the opposite happens when people don't meet their obligations. They get the reputation for being poor risks and not people who are likely to pay up without a lot of hassle. When these people try to buy something on time or get a loan, the answer is quite often, "No."

First we'll talk about borrowing money, then about buying on credit. Suppose you have saved half the amount you need to buy the car you want. If you have a budget plan such as we discussed in the last chapter, study it to see how large a monthly payment you can *comfortably* afford. Leave yourself some leeway.

Credit is expensive. The institutions that lend money do it to make a profit. You do not get credit for nothing. You pay interest. The first rule is to borrow no more than you need. The second is to shop around for the best deal at various banks and loan associations. See who offers the lowest interest rates.

Watch out for the fast-talking loan agent who tries to rush you to complete the deal. If someone says, "I can only offer you these terms today. Sign now, or you will lose your chance," be wary. Don't be pushed into anything. Deal only with well-known, reputable agencies. Trust has to flow both ways.

Make sure you understand all the terms of the contract or agreement before signing it. You should know the total cost you will be paying, including how much of that cost is a credit charge or interest. Most reputable places will automatically break it down for you.

You can borrow from several types of institutions. These are among the most common:

Commercial banks, such as the bank where you have a checking account.

Savings and Loan Associations do not have full banking services. Usually they don't handle checking accounts. They concentrate on arranging credit, quite often for home loans.

Credit unions are organizations of people who decide on a cooperative effort to save money and make loans among themselves at very low rates. This could be a group of employees of a firm, members of a church, or people in a private association of another kind.

Personal Finance Companies are usually smaller loan companies which take bigger risks but also charge more interest, often considerably more. It may be easier to get a loan from one of these, but chances are it will cost you more.

In addition to loans from banks and other savings institutions, a person can use credit cards. Easy money, right? Well, credit cards do make it easy to purchase things, but the credit they represent is very expensive. The company which issues the credit card allows you to borrow the money to pay for your purchases. You pay interest (rent) on that money. Many credit card issuers charge 1 1/2% interest per month, or 18% per year. On a $100 purchase you pay $18 if you take the full year to pay it back. Credit cards might make it easier to buy things, but they certainly don't make it any easier to pay for them!

Several kinds of credit accounts are popular. The **regular charge account** usually doesn't involve interest. Whatever you charge in one month, you pay for in full as soon as you receive your monthly bill. A **budget account** gives you a little more time to pay, usually three months. You pay a service charge, but it is generally much less than the interest would be on an installment plan. **Installment buying** means that you buy a set of tires for $200, and you agree to pay $20 a month plus interest for 10 months.

Revolving credit accounts are being used more widely now. This is a very flexible kind of credit. The company sets a credit limit for each of its revolving credit customers. If a customer spends $100 for a watch, there is a bill at the end of the month just as with a regular charge account. However, there are two options. The $100 can be paid in full, or a minimum payment, say $15, can be paid as specified on the bill. If the lesser amount is chosen, there will have to be several payments and interest on the unpaid balance. More items can be charged while the watch is being paid off, providing the credit line or credit limit is not exceeded.

You also have credit with the telephone, electricity, gas, and water companies. Each month you pay for the services used during the previous month. They trust you to do so because there is no way to tell in advance how much of their service you will require.

Many debates have centered on whether buying on credit is good or bad. Some of the arguments in favor of it are:

1. You can use the product or service while you are paying for it.

2. Credit can force you to develop good budget habits. Your money is committed for one larger purchase rather than just being spent little by little for knick-knacks.

3. It helps you develop a good credit rating, and that is very important.

Some of the arguments against credit buying are:

1. You may wear out or use up the product before you even pay for it.

2. Credit makes things cost more.

3. You can get into the habit of buying on credit. Then if you become sick or lose your job, you have all the payments hanging over your head.

4. People tend to buy at stores where they have credit rather than shopping around for the best deal.

5. People tend to buy more expensive items than they normally would because the cash doesn't come right

out of their pockets. It almost seems as if it's free—until they get the bill.

What do you think of these pros and cons?

JACK AND MARGIE. Jack and Margie were just married. Margie told Jack that because she had had to wash dishes all the time she lived with her parents, the first thing she wanted to buy was a dishwasher. Jack didn't tell her, but he had had to wash dishes, too, and he wanted to get a dishwasher just as much as she did. However, he hadn't been working long, and his salary wasn't great. Besides, there were many things they needed more, such as dishes.

Margie wanted the dishwasher, so she did her homework. The best deal in town was a Panbender Model 702, and the price was only $225. The salesman told her that a down payment of $40 and 12 monthly payments of just $18.75 would deliver it to her kitchen tomorrow.

Well, Jack may have been young, but he knew that "payments of just" was a phrase to look at closely. He told Margie that he knew how to get the dishwasher for less. He said, "What if we put $18.75 per month into a savings account that pays 6% interest?"

Margie didn't like the idea of waiting a year, and they had the first argument of their marriage.

That night, Jack did some calculating. The next morning he had a new strategy. He asked Margie if she would be willing to wait a year if he gave **her** $40 right now, rather than giving it to the salesman. And, they would still get the dishwasher for less. Margie's curiosity was aroused. Jack explained it like this:

Savings Plan
12 months × $18.75 /month = $225.00
Interest (compounded quarterly)
  for one year = $8.56

Total amount out of Jack and
  Margie's pocket = $225.00

Credit Plan
12 months × $18.75 /month = $225.00
Down Payment = $40.00
Total cost of dishwasher and credit
  charges = $265.00
Cost of credit = $265-$225 = $40.00
Total amount out of Jack and Margie's
  pocket = $265.00

So Jack can give Margie $40 in cash now, put $18.75/month in the savings account, and pay out of pocket only $225.00 for the dishwasher. Furthermore they have $8.65 they earned in interest as well.

Lights dim. Hero exits stage left. Hmmmmmm. The savings habit may have some real merit!

You need some arithmetic to protect yourself and to get the best deal! Here are a few typical computations you need to know how to do in order to be a wise credit shopper. We will work through the first example together. For the other four, you're on your own.

1. Joe buys a suit priced at $90. He makes a down payment of $25 and agrees to make seven installments of $10 each. How much is the credit costing him?

$90 cost of suit
$-$ $25 down payment
$65 balance left to pay

7 payments of $10 each = $70

$70
$-$ $65
_____
$5 for credit

2. Amy buys a set of stainless steel pots and pans priced at $95.00. She agrees to pay $10 a month for one year. How much interest is she paying?

3. Joe and Rich bought a small stove for their apartment. It was priced at $200. They made a down payment of $50 and agreed to pay the rest in 9 monthly installments of $20 each. What is the credit costing them?

4. Earl and Farah want to buy a clothes dryer which costs $300. They have a $25 down payment. The agent they want to borrow money from says, "I'll tell you what. You can pay $25 a month for a year. Or, if you want smaller payments you can pay $20 for 15 months." How much would the credit cost each way?

5. Jana received a $100 Christmas bonus. She wants to put it to work, so she puts it in a savings account at a savings and loan company where it will earn 7% interest providing she leaves it there for at least one full year. At the end of that year how much will her $100 have earned for her?

Working Cooperatively

Divide the class into pairs. Using 3 x 5 index cards or slips of paper, make flash cards of all the banking and credit terms that appeared in this chapter. Make one set for each two people. Put the word on one side and the definition on the other.

Quiz your partner, sometimes giving the word and letting the other person define it; other times give the definition and see if the other person can come up with the word. Then have your partner quiz you in the same way.

CREDIT TERMS EVERYONE SHOULD KNOW

Interest—amount a person pays to use money that belongs to somebody else. Also, the amount a person can earn by allowing his money to be used by somebody else.

Principal—amount being borrowed.

Installment—one of several payments made over a period of time to pay up a loan or to buy something on credit.

Contract—agreement one signs to borrow money or buy something on time.

Collateral—something valuable a person puts up to guarantee he will pay a loan. If he fails to pay, the collateral (car, camera, stereo, or whatever) becomes the property of the company which gave him the loan.

Repossession—the seller takes back merchandise sold on the installment plan when the buyer fails to make the payments.

Credit line—the amount of credit a company is prepared to extend to an individual.

Credit rating—a person's standing as a good or bad credit risk.

Chapter Check

1. When you write a check, what items of information do you record in your checkbook or on your check stub?

2. How does the number of checks you will be writing each month help you decide what kind of checking account to open?

3. What does balancing your checkbook mean? Is it difficult?

4. Why are traveller's checks handy when you take a trip?

5. How can you put money to work for you?

6. What does the word credit mean in a general sense?

7. Why is it important to establish a good credit rating and how do you go about doing that?

8. Name three kinds of places you might go for a loan.

9. Explain the difference between a regular charge account, a budget charge account, and a revolving credit account.

10. Give three reasons for and three reasons against buying merchandise on credit.

❀ Chapter Twenty-four ❀

MEETING YOUR INSURANCE NEEDS

Mutual of Omaha

INSURANCE

What do all of these have in common: your grandmother's ruby ring, your aunt's French poodle, your Volkswagen, the modern painting your friend has hanging in her apartment, your dad's power tools?

They can all be insured. People pay an insurance company so much a year to protect their belongings. The amount paid to the insurance company is called the *premium*. If anything happens to the insured property, the owner will receive compensation so that he can replace it, if possible.

Not only objects can be insured. You can insure your health and life. That doesn't mean that you can arrange to always be in good health and never die. It means that you can arrange things so that in case of an accident, ill health, or death, you or your family will be able to get help and financial catastrophe will not occur.

Why would any company want to insure people? We meet the profit motive again. Say that you ran an insurance company. You sell health insurance policies (contracts) to 100 people. Each of them pays you a premium of $20 a month. Some of them get sick and you pay their doctor bills. Others don't get sick. You take the extra money and invest it. Your assets grow because this extra money is working for you.

How do you decide what premium to charge each of your health insurance clients? Insurance companies collect many kinds of statistics. They have a good idea how many illnesses or accidents people average a year and which kinds are most common. From this information they determine how much of a risk they are taking and charge accordingly. In the case of your health insurance clients, you would study health statistics. Then you would charge each person a rate based on your estimate of what it will cost to cover their possible medical expenses. You also take into consideration your expenses in running your business. You collect the premiums from your insurance clients. Any money that is not actually needed to pay medical bills would be invested so it could earn more money for you.

Insurance is such an important part of your financial planning that it pays to know as much as you can about it. We asked an insurance agent, Mr. George Nadaf, to explain some of the ideas and terminology relating to the four basic types of insurance: health, automobile, property, and life insurance.

AUTOMOBILE INSURANCE

John Huck: Why don't we begin with car insurance since that's probably the one we're most familiar with. What protection does automobile insurance buy?

G. N.: Basically there are four kinds of protection: liability, medical expense, collision, and comprehensive.

J. H.: Liability insurance has to do with financial responsibility laws.

G. N.: Yes. That's right. All states have laws saying that if you are at fault in an accident you are responsible for any injuries to others and any damage to their property. Liability insurance covers the insured person for such expenses. Very few of us could pay for a serious accident out of our pockets or bank accounts. That's why state laws require car owners to have liability insurance. Quite often the amount of such coverage will be specified by a figure such as 10/20/5. That means the insured person has bought coverage for $10,000 for any one person injured in an accident; $20,000 for all bodily injuries in one accident; and $5,000 in property damages for the same accident. These figures could vary. For instance, they could be 20/40/5 or 25/50/5.

J. H.: Liability insurance would cover you for those injuries you cause someone else. What about your own injuries? How would they be covered if the accident was your fault?

G. N.: That's where the second kind of coverage comes in, medical expense. You, members of your family, friends, or guests who are riding in your car are all protected. That is, if you have this kind of coverage, medical bills resulting from the accident would be paid.

J. H.: Collision insurance has to do with payment for damages to your own car. Right?

G. N.: Yes, that's correct. An important thing to know about collision insurance is what *deductible* means. The premiums you pay for protecting your own car are higher than those you pay for liability protection. If you want to, you can get full collision coverage insurance for your car. When you damage your car, your insurance will cover the repair costs completely. But here's the catch. Full coverage car insurance is very expensive. If you want to avoid paying such high premiums, you can take out a policy with a deductible clause, which means you pay an agreed-upon amount of each repair bill. Say you have a $100 deductible policy. You have an accident that costs you $250 in repair bills for your car. You pay the first $100. Your insurance company pays the rest. If you had full coverage collision insurance, the insurance company would pay the entire amount, but it would also charge you a much higher yearly premium.

J. H.: Let's see. We've covered liability, medical expense, and collision coverage. What about comprehensive?

G. N.: Comprehensive car insurance protects you in case your car is damaged by such things as wind, fire, lightning, vandalism, etc. It also protects you against theft.

J. H.: If your car is quite old maybe it's only worth $100 or so. Would it pay to carry comprehensive or collision insurance?

G. N.:	Maybe not. If you're a young driver, chances are your yearly premium would be very high just for liability insurance. With collision and comprehensive, your premium may end up being more than the car is worth. There are also many options when you are considering collision and comprehensive insurance, and a good agent will help you understand them and get the coverage that is best for your particular case.
J. H.:	George, why are auto premiums so expensive for young drivers?
G. N.:	Purely statistics. Insurance companies study and analyze accidents and they know that male drivers under 25 are involved in more accidents than any other group, at least right now. Because it costs more to handle the accidents of this group, they have to pay more to be insured.
J. H.:	Could you explain a little bit about what having an insurance policy cancelled means?
G. N.:	Yes, that's important, too. Insurance companies think of some drivers as poor risks. These are the people who have one accident after the other. Often they have serious traffic violations, too, such as citations for drunken driving or speeding tickets. If such drivers become too much of a risk, or cost the insurance company too much money, their policies will be cancelled. That means that the company will notify them by mail that after a certain date they will no longer be insured. Such people then have to find another company willing to insure them. That might not be easy. Many people who have their insurance cancelled end up with companies that specialize in poor-risk insurance. Naturally these companies have to charge a great deal more to insure these bad drivers, and the poor risk driver ends up paying a very high premium.
J. H.:	How can the young driver get the best possible car insurance rates?
G. N.:	The best thing to do is to hurry up and get past the age of 25! No, seriously, rates are affected by several factors. One is whether you live in a rural or urban area. Accident and theft rates are higher in cities, generally speaking. Repair costs are lower some places than others. Accident rates are lower in some areas of the country. Still another factor is that some companies will give you a small discount on your premium if you have an A or B grade point average. Building up a record of safe driving will help you get the best rates later on.

Checkpoint

We have already covered a number of important insurance terms. See if you can match the following terms with the correct meanings.

1. premium

2. $100 deductible

3. poor risk driver

4. liability

5. comprehensive coverage

6. insurance policy

7. medical expense

8. cancelled policy

9. collision insurance

a. a person who has had many accidents or serious traffic violations

b. money a person pays an insurance company for protection

c. insurance coverage for damage to your own car in case of an accident

d. a clause in your collision insurance by which you agree to pay the first $100 damage costs, and the insurance pays the rest

e. an insurance company notifies a client that after a certain date he or she will no longer be insured by that company.

f. a contract between an insurance company and a person buying insurance

g. auto insurance that pays your medical bills if you are injured in your car, even if the accident is your fault

h. financial responsibility for an accident

i. auto insurance that covers your car in case of theft, vandalism, damage from lightning, wind, and flood

---

HEALTH INSURANCE

J. H.: How important do you consider health insurance?

G. N.: Extremely important. Even small illnesses or injuries are very expensive now and getting more so. A prolonged illness can quickly wipe out savings and put you in debt for years.

J. H.:	What kind of a health insurance policy should a person look for?
G. N.:	Well, health insurance should give two basic kinds of protection. The first kind is help with paying medical bills. It is called major medical insurance. The second is protection against loss of income. That is, if you have major surgery and are unable to return to work for six months, you won't be earning any money. Your loss of income insurance will give you at least some income during such a time.
J. H.:	What is hospitalization insurance? Is it the same as major medical?
G. N.:	No. It generally covers only illnesses or injuries that require hospitalization. Hospitalization policies vary a great deal. Some cover surgical costs as well as hospital expenses, others do not. One disadvantage of them is that you may have a prolonged illness and have to have medical care, but not in a hospital. You may recuperate at home, and then your hospitalization policy wouldn't do you much good. Your doctor bills probably would not be covered by most hospitalization policies.
J. H.:	What would you recommend, then, for a young worker as far as health insurance is concerned?
G. N.:	First, people should find out if any group insurance is available to them where they work.
J. H.:	Could you explain the difference between group health insurance and individual insurance?
G. N.:	Many people can get health insurance as part of a group plan where they work. Insurance companies can often give good rates to large groups because so many individuals are taking their health insurance from that one company. In very large offices and factories there may be two or three different group plans from which workers can choose. Group insurance is almost always a good investment. Take it if you can get it. If you are self-employed (have your own business) or if your company is small and has no such health insurance plan, you will have to see about getting health insurance on an individual basis, working with a reliable insurance agent.
J. H.:	Should you try to get a policy that will pay all your medical expenses?
G. N.:	Not necessarily. When we were talking about automobile insurance we said that a $100 or $200 deductible policy will mean a lower premium for you. A similar situation exists

with health insurance. You can have a policy that requires you to pay a certain amount of your medical expenses. This amount is usually low enough that the average person can manage it. If you have such a policy you will pay a lower premium than if you have a policy that stipulates that the insurance company will pay all of your medical bills. The more protection you get, the more expensive your premium will be.

J. H.: Say your health insurance covers you, your wife or husband, and your children. How will you know how much of the expense of having another baby will be covered, or how much the insurance company will pay on a child's illness that requires hospitalization?

G.N.: Your policy lists the maximum fees your insurance company will pay for each specific surgical or hospital procedure. It also lists expenses that will not be paid.

J. H.: Is it true that self-inflicted injuries such as a drug overdose are not usually covered by health insurance?

G. N.: Yes, that is often true.

J. H.: Okay. I think we are ready to move on to property insurance.

PROPERTY INSURANCE

J. H.: Is property insurance just for homeowners?

G. N.: Basically, yes, although now there are also policies for people who rent a house or apartment.

J. H.: What does a renter's policy cover?

G. N.: It protects the renter's personal property—clothes, stereo, furniture, etc., against fire, theft, and other catastrophes. It does not, of course, protect the building. The owner has to insure the actual structure.

J. H.: What about the homeowner? How does his insurance differ from the renter's?

G. N.: Homeowners have more to think about. They need protection for their belongings just as the renter does, but they also need to protect the house itself, plus other structures such as garages, sheds, and barns. And homeowners should have liability insurance.

J. H.: Is fire still the biggest threat to the homeowner?

G. N.: Yes, fire is still a very serious problem. It is the first kind of coverage homeowners usually get. Then there are natural disasters such as tornadoes, wind storms, and floods. You can get homeowners protection for many of these. Theft and burglary insurance is also important.

J. H.: Most of us have some idea of the importance of getting protection from these possibilities you just mentioned. But could you go into a little more detail on the importance of liability insurance?

G. N.: For homeowners liability is a serious matter. If your dog bites a visitor, that visitor can sue you. If you have a throw-rug and someone slips, falls, and breaks an arm, you may have to pay his or her medical expenses. People can sue the homeowner for many such accidents. If a lawsuit is big enough it can ruin a person financially unless that person has liability insurance.

J. H.: When homeowners set up their insurance, how should they go about it? Do they just tell the agent what kinds of coverage they want?

G. N.: Well, that's one way to do it. But probably not the best way. It's too hit-and-miss. Insurance companies have set up what is called a homeowners' policy. Such policies are designed to cover the most serious and common problems of the homeowner, some of which the new homeowner may not even be aware of.

J. H.: Is there only one kind of homeowners' policy?

G. N.: No. There are several. But all of them are fairly good. Few of them offer absolutely complete protection. Again, the more your premium is, the more protection you have.

J. H.: My homeowners' policy has a list of exclusions. Can you explain what an exclusion is?

G. N.: An exclusion is an exception. In the policy the insurance company spells out anything that it will not cover. These are the exclusions. Anything not specifically mentioned is covered.

J. H.: So you know what your property is insured against by reading the policy carefully.

G. N.: Yes. You should read any insurance policy just as you would read any other contract. If you don't understand something, ask questions. If you feel a policy doesn't really meet your needs, it can be reworked and tailored to your specifications. A good agent can also give you an idea of the alternatives available to you.

LIFE INSURANCE

J. H.: We've talked about car, property, and health insurance. I've saved life insurance till last because it seems more complicated to me. How can insurance protect against the calamity of dying?

G. N.: There is more than one calamity in death. The first is, of course, the physical death of a person. The second is the impact on the immediate family. If it is the breadwinner who dies, in addition to the sense of loss and grief the family suffers, its financial future can be grim. How will the remaining spouse provide for housing, food, education, etc.? Life insurance can provide some security at such a time.

J. H.: Would you explain the difference between term and whole life insurance?

G. N.: Term insurance is the cheapest form of life insurance you can buy. It insures you for a specified number of years, often 20 years. Sometimes you can renew at the end of that time, although the premium will be higher since you will be older.

J. H.: Some people say that buying life insurance is a good way of saving. Is that true of term insurance?

G. N.: No. Term insurance is not a savings plan. It is a protection plan. There is no cash value to your policy, you can't borrow money on the basis of it, and when the term is up and you stop paying the premium you get nothing from the insurance company. But during the term such insurance is in effect, your family has protection. Your beneficiary would get the amount of money the policy specifies if you should die. This is the least expensive kind of life insurance you can buy.

J. H.: You mentioned the word **beneficiary**. I don't think we defined that word so far.

G. N.: The beneficiary is the person you designate as the one who is to receive the insurance money if you die. On most life insurance policies there is a place to record your primary beneficiary and your contingent beneficiary. Your primary beneficiary is the first person to receive money if you die. But supposing something happens to that person, too. Then the contingent beneficiary would receive the money. If a husband and wife are both killed in a car accident, and the wife was the primary beneficiary of any life insurance policies, then the insurance company would not know who to pay unless a contingent beneficiary was named. The contingent beneficiary might be the man's brother, or the eldest of the deceased couple's children, or a very close friend.

J. H.:   If you have life insurance and then get married, can you change your beneficiary to your new husband or wife?

G. N.:   Yes. You should do that. Some people seem to think that happens automatically. But of course there is no way an insurance company can legally change a beneficiary on someone's policy unless the policy owner tells him to do so. So if you need to make such a change, you must write to your insurance company or pay a visit to your insurance agent.

J. H.:   Okay. So term insurance is for a specified amount of time, it is a protection rather than a savings type of insurance, and it is the least expensive. Now what about ordinary life insurance? How does an ordinary life policy work?

G. N.:   Ordinary life policies are often also called cash-value life insurance. As you pay your premiums, your policy is building up cash value. By contrast, a term life insurance policy doesn't ever build up any cash value.

J. H.:   How long do you pay on an ordinary life policy?

G. N.:   Here again we can break ordinary life policies down into two different kinds. Straight or whole-life and limited payment life. In straight life policies you pay your premium your entire life, or in many cases, until you are 95. However, you do have the option of discontinuing payment when your children are grown and you no longer feel the need for so much insurance protection. If you want to, you can then stop paying premiums and take the cash value of the policy, which ends the coverage. Another option is to take a paid-up policy for a reduced amount of protection for life.

J. H.:   How does that differ from limited payment policies?

G. N.:   Limited payment policies differ in that the insured person pays premiums for a specified number of years. After that, no premiums are paid, but the person is still completely covered.

J. H.:   It sounds as if the limited payment policy would be the most expensive of these two types of policies.

G. N.:   Yes, it is. And there are several kinds of limited payment policies. The most expensive of these is called an endowment policy. It gives the holder life insurance protection and also provides for putting money aside for the

	future. We won't spend much time on it because it isn't a recommended policy for most young people.
J. H.:	Why not?
G. N.:	Because it's so expensive and young wage-earners would probably not have money enough to pay endowment premiums and still provide adequate regular coverage for their families during the years they need it most. But it's important to know that such policies do exist.
J. H.:	I think we've covered a lot of ground. Thank you very much, George.
G. N.:	I'm glad to help. Yes, we've covered a lot of ground, but there are still many points that would be helpful for people to know about. In closing I'd like to suggest that each young person should work with an established company and a competent agent. If insurance needs are quite special, they may want to check with a lawyer as well.

Finding Out for Yourself

If your class is interested in going into more detail on various kinds of insurance, you may find the following book very helpful:
AM I COVERED?
by Gayle E. Richardson
Indianapolis:
Unified College Press, 1973

If this book is not available to you, try looking under **Insurance** in the library card catalog.

GUIDELINES FOR BUYING INSURANCE

Insurance can provide security for the young worker. To fully realize this, just sit back and imagine what pre-insurance days were like. What happened when someone's house burned down? What happened to families when the breadwinner died? What did a family do if their car was totalled and they weren't insured?

On the other hand, some people get carried away with the idea of security through insurance. They insure everything in sight and end up being "insurance poor." That means that so much of their income is going into insurance payments that they can barely meet their ordinary monthly expenses, let alone enjoy any of their income as they go along.

Prudential Insurance Comapny of America

Here are a few guidelines that might help you make insurance decisions:

1. Decide what kind of protection you need right now. Consider your health, your car, your property, and your life. Think in terms of **why** you need each kind of coverage.

2. Find a reputable insurance agent. Ask your parents or friends, or your teachers. Established companies usually have good agents.

3. Decide how much you can afford for insurance each year.

4. If you are thinking of insurance as a way to save money, compare it with other savings plans. Find out where your money will earn the most for you. And consider your other assets. Do you have social security? A retirement or pension plan?

5. Find out what kinds of insurance programs are available where you work. Try to get group insurance if possible.

Keep your insurance policies in a safe place. Some people rent a safe deposit box at the bank and keep such important items in it. They then keep a list of their policies at home, showing the name of the company, the policy number, the type of insurance, and the amount. If you don't use a safe deposit box you would still be wise to keep a separate list in one place and your policies in another.

FILING CLAIMS

The time may come when you will have an accident, an illness, or a loss of some kind. If you are insured, you will need to know how to collect from your insurance company. You will have to **file a claim.**

The first thing that needs to be stressed is that you must act promptly. The more time that goes by the harder it will be for you to prove your case. Many policies specify a time limit. For example, if you have an illness and fail to notify your insurance company within 20 days, your insurance company may not pay your medical costs. If you have suffered loss by fire, you also have a limited time to notify your company. If you don't contact your company within that time period, you may forfeit your right to payment.

Who should you notify? If your agent is in your town, call. If not, you may have to write your company. Quite often, though, your insurance agent may be able to handle the smaller problems without help. In the case of more serious claims, the company may have an **insurance adjuster** handle the case. An adjuster finds out if the loss actually occurred and gets all the important facts about it. The financial loss the client has suffered must then be determined. Next the adjuster reaches an agreement with the person making the claim as to how much compensation should be paid by the insurance company. Meanwhile the insurance company checks its records to see if the policy was actually in effect at the time of the loss and if it did indeed cover the type of loss involved. After all the facts have been determined and evaluated, the insurance company settles the claim by paying the agreed-upon amount.

Generally speaking, insurance settlements are fair and somewhat routine. Most companies are not out to cheat their clients. Besides, your policy is as valid as any legal contract. You can hold your insurance company to the terms of your policy if that should become necessary.

What about the clients who hope to make a fast buck from their insurance? Insurance policies are not designed to help people make profits from their losses. An insured person is entitled to be repaid for loss—no more, no less. People who make false or unfair claims can easily be spotted or checked out. Insurance companies can cancel the insurance of anyone who makes a fraudulent claim.

Mutual of Omaha

In closing, we will list just a few pointers to remember when you need to use your insurance protection:

In case of theft, report your loss to the police as well as to your insurance company.

Don't argue with anyone at the scene of an accident. Don't admit or deny guilt. Don't complicate your problem with hostile words or actions.

If someone is going to sue you, don't try to settle it on your own. Call in the experts (your insurance man or a lawyer) right from the beginning. Don't discuss the facts with anyone except these two people.

Keep a list of your household and personal belongings. Many people think they will be able to remember what they own, but it's not that easy. (To test this, try to list all the things in your suitcase the next time you arrive home from a short trip. Then open your suitcase and see how well you did.) Keep your list in your safe deposit box or in a metal file box.

Trust your insurance agent. But, also, don't give up being responsible for your own best interests. Read your policies when you are going to file a claim or before trouble even arises.

What Do You Think?

Much has been said about suing people. It has become so common that some people sue whenever they possibly can.

If you fell on a loose step in your friend's house would you sue her?

If your friend fell on a loose step in your house, would you expect her to sue you?

What do you think of the argument "I'm not suing the person, I'm suing the insurance company"?

What if the person only has $10,000 worth of liability insurance and you sue him for $20,000? What if **you** have only $10,000 worth of liability insurance and someone sues you for $20,000?

Chapter Check

1. **A premium is**

    a. the highest priced insurance policy you can get.

    b. a regular amount you pay to the insurance company for coverage.

    c. the money the insurance company pays you to cover damages when you have an accident.

2. **If you do not have collision insurance,**

    a. the car you hit won't be covered.

    b. damage to your car won't be covered.

    c. any person you injure in a car accident won't be covered.

3. **To be liable means**

    a. to be responsible for an accident.

    b. to be able to tell lies.

    c. to have someone tell lies about you.

4. **Your beneficiary is**

    a. a person who does you a good turn.

    b. your insurance agent.

    c. the person whom you designate to receive the money from your life insurance policy if you die.

5. George has a **$100 deductible** auto insurance policy. That means

   a. that if he has an accident he must pay the first $100 worth of damage on his car.

   b. that he can have his auto insurance premium deducted from his paycheck.

   c. that his insurance agent can deduct $100 from his annual premium if George has no accidents during that year.

6. On a homeowner's policy, **exclusions** are

   a. government regulations affecting the policy.

   b. a list of items, circumstances, or catastrophes that won't be covered.

   c. people in your home who aren't covered by your homeowner's policy.

7. The advantage of a **term life insurance policy** is that

   a. it covers you for more years than a whole life policy.

   b. you get more money when you retire.

   c. it is less expensive than whole life.

8. If you have a **straight whole life policy,**

   a. you usually pay premiums your whole life.

   b. you can't get any cash value from your policy.

   c. you can consider your policy paid up after 20 years.

9. **Limited** life insurance means

    a. you are only protected till the age of 60.

    b. you only pay premiums for a specified number of years.

    c. you are limited to $10,000 coverage.

10. **Comprehensive** car insurance

    a. covers only the worst accidents.

    b. insures against flood, theft, and other catastrophes beside accidents.

    c. is the least expensive car insurance.

❊ Chapter Twenty-Five ❊

YOU AS
A CONSUMER

Daryl Littlefield

ADVERTISING, HARD SELL, AND FRAUD

Hey, independent person! Want to buy the Washington Monument? Want to own some nice land that will be worth a million dollars in a few years? Want a practically new car for practically nothing?

Watch out! Something in the nature of many human beings likes the idea of making a sharp deal or getting something for nothing. No matter how old people are, they still fall for con jobs. Con job: someone gains your *con*fidence and then does a job on you.

Truly independent people think for themselves. They know some facts, and they know how to find out others. They ask questions. They act only after carefully analyzing the situation. They learn to know a con job when they see one. In this chapter we are going to concentrate on consumer protection. We will briefly look at advertising, hard sell, and fraud. We will discuss some of the techniques used to get people to buy products or services.

Do you know why television entertainers including athletes get so much money? Manufacturers pay millions of dollars to advertise their products on television and radio. Networks and stations can then afford to pay performers big money. Why are manufacturers willing to pay so much for television time? Because they know that television advertising is one of the surest ways to increase their profits. They hire skilled and creative advertising specialists to devise ads that will get people to buy. Advertisement specialists study characteristics of buyers, their buying habits, and their reasons for buying. They then come up with ads that will catch people's attention and make them want the product.

Hard sell is usually a face-to-face technique. Say you are trying on a suit. The salesperson is constantly at your side, keeping up a running commentary. He tells you how great you look in the suit, what a bargain you are getting—the material is indestructible yet the price is low. When you say you'd like to think it over, he replies that someone is sure to buy the suit by tomorrow. Perhaps his last attempt to sell you is confidential. Something like, "Listen. I'll even give up my commission. You can have the suit for $60 instead of $70. That's rock bottom. I can't go any lower."

Here's another example of hard sell. The other day a young man stopped by Eleanor's house and asked her if she had children. When she said yes, he insisted on showing her his product. It turned out to be a set of books for young children. She explained that her children were all in high school or older. He then tried to say that even high school people would be interested in these wonderful books. She looked at them and knew that wasn't the case, and said so. He then took a "hard line," saying he was experienced in children's books and knew much more than Eleanor about what her children wanted and needed. Once upon a time such a put-down would have worked with her. She would have listened in subdued silence. This time she didn't. She quietly insisted that he leave. At last he did, but only after delivering a speech something like this: "Well, if that's all you care about your children's education, fine. Two of your neighbors have shown great interest. I just thought you might share their concern and want to give your children an educational advantage." You can see how he was trying to use Eleanor's feelings about herself as a parent to sell his product.

Advertising and hard sell do not usually involve fraud. Advertisers may try to manipulate you into wanting what they have, but most of the time they do not lie about the products. For one thing, they know that false advertising is against the law and can be stopped. Also, they know that a poor product can't be sold for very long even with the slickest advertising. Many companies, of course, truly believe in their products and have no need to misrepresent them. Hard sell can involve being pushy and annoying, but it usually doesn't involve misrepresentation.

Fraud goes beyond merely trying to persuade you to buy a product. It tries to get you to buy a worthless product, or one that cannot possibly live up to the claims made for it. Fraud requires **intent** to deliberately swindle, trick, deceive, cheat, or misrepresent. There is always the possibility of human error and honest mistakes. Fraud only occurs when there is intent to mislead.

Perhaps some of you have had firsthand experience with fraud, as did Bob Eddles. He was a senior in high school. He had always been skinny and wanted very much to be bigger and stronger. He saw an advertisement in a magazine which described a body building course. The ad promised amazing results in just 60 days. The price for the course was "only" $10.

Would you have sent for the course? Bob did. What do you think he got for his $10? All he got was a list of several exercises and instructions on how and how often to do them. There were almost no illustrations. The library could have provided him the same information—and more of it—free of charge. Girls run into the same kind of problem with ads for figure development or modeling courses. If you feel you only got $1 worth of information for your $10, you're probably out of luck. It wouldn't be easy to get your $10 back. Such cases are borderline fraud. That is, it would be hard to prove in court that you were the victim of fraud. You did get something for your money, even if it didn't live up to your expectations.

There are also many cases of out-and-out fraud. One category is very old, yet it continues in various forms. It is the home improvement con game. Some home improvement companies offer free inspections of electrical wiring or roofing, for example. Through these inspections they "discover" that your house needs whatever they are selling. Then they overcharge for services performed, perform services you don't need, or don't even do the work at all. Old people are often the victims of such swindles. The con artists work on the fears of these people, telling them the furnace might blow up or termites might eat the house out from under them. In the next few years, as the impact of the energy shortage is more fully felt, fraud involving insulation, solar heating, and other energy conserving materials will probably be on the rise again.

Home improvement is only one area that a consumer needs to be wary of. Used car sales, land sales, health products, and even job training courses can involve fraud. How can you protect yourself? The first rule is always to read any contract before you sign. Don't agree to anything you don't fully understand. Over and above that, you can protect yourself by being aware of manipulative techniques. We will look at some of these techniques next.

MANIPULATIVE TECHNIQUES

To manipulate people means to manage them so that they do what you want them to. It might be getting them to vote for you, or to learn something, or to buy something you are selling. Manipulation does not necessarily imply evil intent. But there is a real problem here. Manipulative techniques discourage independence of thought. Facts are slanted or simplified in such a way that only one conclusion seems possible. The person being manipulated can be taken off balance. Maybe he or she will do something and later regret it. Being able to spot some of these techniques will keep you from jumping to the conclusions the manipulator wants you to jump to.

The common manipulative techniques that follow are used in various areas of our lives. But since we are concerned with the consumer in this chapter, we will concentrate on examples that involve getting people to buy things.

THE BIG PROMISE. "Buy our food processor. Only $250. With it you will be able to prepare dishes of the famous chefs right in your own home." Maybe so. But first you'd have to have training, money to buy expensive ingredients, time, cookbooks, and probably a real flair for cooking, too. And looking at it from another angle, if you do have a flair for cooking, you might be able to do some gourmet cooking without the costly food processor. In fact, some famous chefs might not even recommend the use of such equipment.

BANDWAGON. "Use Smile-O Toothpaste. Everyone does!" Get on the bandwagon. Don't think about why. If other people are doing it, it must be good. But, is it good *for you?* The number of people using it has very little to do with *your* evaluation of the product. Your preferences are valid whether a great many people agree with you or not.

TESTIMONIALS. "Herbert Hellman, star of the recent motion picture *At Home On Mars,* says: I get a better shave with the Sensoria Electric Razor." Or, June Johnell, the famous dress designer, tells the TV audience, "With fine clothes, you need a fine perfume. I wear only *Evening in Istanbul #15.*" One of the appeals of testimonials is that the audience can identify with a famous person. But when you think about it, these famous people are getting paid to say they like a certain product. They aren't saying so free of charge. So how reliable is their "testimony?" Maybe they really like the products they present. Maybe they don't. Even if they do, though, that doesn't automatically mean the products will please you, too.

STACKING THE DECK. "The Dune-Boggler 350 CC is the best trail bike on the market: automatic shin guards, three forward gears, non-skid tires, and the sleekest styling to date." Any possible bad points you might have thought of are wiped out by a steady bombardment of the product's wonderful qualities. Give yourself time. Think about important features that weren't mentioned. Consult a buyer's guide.

SNOB APPEAL. "Only a discriminating few can appreciate the Easy-Writer Ballpoint Pen. The way it writes is pure poetry. You pay more, but you get the finest." All of us like to imagine ourselves as wealthy, distinguished, possessing good taste. We can be tricked into buying things simply because they will supposedly give us special status. But do they?

PLAIN FOLK APPEAL. "Folks, I'd like to tell you about Nutberry Nibbles. For breakfast or snacks. I like my food plain and simple. No frills. And Nutberry Nibbles make no pretensions. Just plain old-fashioned flavor and goodness in every bite." This is the opposite of the snob appeal technique. Many of us can easily identify with people whom we see as being very similar to us. If they use a product, it must be something we'd enjoy too. Maybe!

PHONY SCIENCE. "Laboratory tests prove that goldfish live ten times longer when fed with Grow-Grain Fish Particles." Such statements try to put the seal of scientific truth on the claims made for the product. Look for loopholes. In this case you don't know if any such tests were really performed. If they were, you don't know whether they were properly designed and executed. What were the conditions under which the tests were made? Was there a control group of fish that was fed some other brand of fish food? What does the advertiser mean by "ten times longer"? Longer than what? The manipulator hopes you will be so impressed that you won't stop to ask such questions.

In addition to these techniques, manipulators make use of all kinds of appeals that involve our self-images. Most of us would like to be beautiful or handsome and have sex appeal. You can probably think of dozens of ads that promise to help us do that: ads for face creams, makeup, girdles, bath oils, scents, hair conditioners, low-fat foods, etc., etc., etc. Ads can appeal to our desire for good health. These could include ads for vitamin supplements, exercise apparatus, health foods, etc. Ads can appeal to our sense of romance: a moonlit bay, a beautiful man and woman, a sleek new car shining in the moonlight. It's the car that's being sold, but the atmosphere is doing some of the selling. There are ads that appeal to our desire to make more money, get smarter, and improve our personalities.

The first thing to think about in all of these cases is, "Can the product deliver the goods?" Can the product really bring about the improvement it promises? The next question is, "Could I get the same result without buying the product?"

What Do You Think?

Copy the following story on a sheet of paper. Then underline any part of it which you think influenced Lorraine's decision to buy the product. What feelings did the salesman arouse in her? What facts did he give her on which to base her decision?

Lorraine was looking for an acne preparation. The salesman was very pleasant and good looking. He showed her a cream and explained that it had a special new ingredient in it. He told Lorraine that she had very nice features and that with a little help for her complexion, she would be beautiful. He gave her a demonstration of how to use the cream. Lorraine thought it was much too expensive. Still she felt somewhat obligated because he had spent so much time with her. Besides, there was the possibility that the cream really might help. She longed to have clear skin more than anything. So she bought it. After using it a few times, she discovered it was much less effective than a less expensive cream she had used before.

Working Cooperatively

Each member of the class brings in one ad from a magazine. Divide into groups of four or five and discuss the ads. Try to answer the following questions:

1. Is this an appealing ad? Does it make a person want to use the product?

2. Can you detect any of the manipulative techniques we discussed earlier?

3. Do you think the ad is misleading? Honest?

SMART SHOPPING

You already know a good deal about the advantages of designing your own budget and living within it. The question now is, how can you get the most out of your shopping dollar?

A good rule to begin with is to avoid impulse buying. Impulse buying is buying something on the spur of the moment. Henry drives by a used car place and spots a neat little sports car. He pulls into the lot, meets the sales representative, and the next thing he knows he has arranged to trade in his car and buy the sports car. Jane walks by the wig counter in a department store. A salesperson is showing a new kind of hairpiece. She buys one then and there. Ted and Alice are at a shopping mall one evening. An appliance store is having a special on air conditioning units. It's a hot night and the salesperson is persuasive. Alice and Ted go home with a new air conditioner.

Sometimes impulse buyers are lucky. Sometimes they aren't. Henry might find the sports car very inconvenient when he wants to take building materials out to the cabin he is building. Jane might wear the wig once or twice and then decide it's just too warm and tight. Ted and Alice might be perfectly satisfied with their air conditioner or they may wish they had waited until they had the money for a bigger unit.

As you can see, the problem with impulse buying is that it is over and done with before the buyer has thought through the pros and cons. Impulse buying can also wreck your financial plans. You spend money you had earmarked for another purpose. Often the other purpose had a higher priority. That is, you needed or wanted it more than the item you bought.

If you buy a product repeatedly, or if you are planning to invest in a relatively expensive item, you need adequate information about it. You can learn something about products from ads you see, but of course ads are designed to emphasize the good points of a product. You need to find some kind of reliable, objective information. Preferably it should be something that compares various brands of the same item.

You can find publications at the library which help you make good buying decisions. A few of these are: *Consumer Reports* and *Consumers' Research Magazine.* With help from your librarian you will be able to find excellent information on many items including major purchases such as insurance, cars, and homes. If you do your homework, you may save yourself money and trouble and end up with a good deal on a better product.

Comparative shopping is another way of making your money go further. It takes a little more time than simply buying the item at the nearest store, but the trouble can be worth it. Comparative shopping means that you check with several stores either in person or by telephone. The idea is to compare prices, materials, weight, guarantees, and any other important features. You probably won't have time to do this on every small purchase, but for some of your larger purchases it is a good habit to get into.

Comparative shopping requires you to use some arithmetic. If you can buy 10 pounds of x-brand flour for $1.00 and 20 pounds of z-brand for $1.85, which is the best buy? Many grocery stores today post signs on the shelves which tell you the unit price. The *unit price* is the price per ounce, pound, pint, quart, etc. It makes it much easier to compare prices from brand to brand. For instance, if you compare a 16-ounce bottle of catsup to a 22-ounce bottle, the arithmetic can be a little complicated to do right on the spot. When the unit price is posted, smart shopping is easier.

In some towns and cities different grocery stores and supermarkets advertise their specials for the week in the newspaper. In our city they do so every Wednesday. This is a good time to sit down with your newspaper and a marking pen and pick out the best prices on grocery items you need. It's a much more convenient way of comparative shopping than running from store to store to compare prices on a number of small grocery items.

Another important point of comparison when you are getting ready to purchase something like a typewriter, kitchen appliance, camera, or bicycle is the guarantee. When you buy a stereo or a washing machine you want to be sure that if it doesn't work properly the dealer will repair or replace it. Many of us tend to be somewhat careless about guarantees. We feel pretty sure nothing will happen to the item we buy and that it will work well indefinitely. That's too big a chance to take, though, if you are investing several hundred dollars in the item. When you are comparative shopping, make the guarantee one of the points of comparison. Some guarantees are good for a greater number of days and others give more protection. Guarantees generally cover defects in workmanship. No manufacturer can be responsible for items that are damaged by the neglect or abuse of the consumer.

Bring some product guarantees to class. Maybe you can borrow one from your parents, or maybe you have a copy of a guarantee from something you bought. Read them carefully, one by one, out loud. Have a member of the class list the conditions specified on one of the guarantees on the blackboard. The blackboard list will include such things as time limit, parts covered, and procedure for using the guarantee if you had to.

WHAT LABELS CAN TELL YOU

Whether you are buying food, medicine, clothing, a stereo, or other appliances, you can protect yourself by reading labels, packages, and cartons. Some of the things you would find out are:

1.   Type of material used in the product

2.   Grade or quality of the product

3.   Directions for safe use of the product (dosage, whether or not to dilute it, when to take it, etc.)

4.   Directions for care of the product. (Keep in a cool, dry place, etc.)

5.   How much a product weighs so you can calculate the unit cost

6.   What a product should be used for, what it is supposed to be able to do

7.   Freshness of a food item, or items such as films and batteries

8.   List of active ingredients in the product

9. List of ingredients in the order of quantity, starting with the ingredient of which there is the most in the product and working down to the ingredient of which there is the least

10. Health warnings (don't use habitually, keep out of the reach of children, provide proper ventilation when using, etc.)

Working Cooperatively

Save the label from an item you use. Using a large sheet of paper, make a blow-up (enlargement) of it so that the details can all be easily read, including the list of ingredients, warnings, etc. Make a display of all the labels the class has made.

WHEN IS A BARGAIN REALLY A BARGAIN?

You can go to end-of-the-month sales or clearance sales and save a lot of money—or waste a lot. If you buy something you can't use, it isn't a bargain no matter how inexpensive it was. If you buy something you don't really need, you may be using money that you could have spent on items that mean more to you. If you buy something on impulse, you may not like it later. You may get very little use out of it, even though it seemed like such a bargain at the time.

A smart shopper will also get to know the stores in the area. Well-established stores carrying good quality merchandise usually have better sales. Their sale items are usually leftovers or slightly damaged merchandise and are often well worth the sale price. Second-rate stores often buy large lots of merchandise for one big sale. These items are usually of cheaper quality to begin with, so the bargain hunter really doesn't get much of a bargain. In other words, the merchandise is worth no more than the sale price. Look out for the store that is always "slashing" its prices and offering gigantic savings.

In buying sale merchandise you would want to look the items over even more carefully than when you buy non-sale merchandise. A reputable store will clearly label damaged or flawed items. For example a bath towel that has a flaw in the weaving of the material will be marked as a "second" or "irregular." A dress which has a broken zipper might be marked, "As is, $15." If you know how to sew, such a dress might be a real bargain. But in any case you would want to be aware of the problem before buying it.

Also beware of the *bait and switch* technique. An advertised sale features certain items. But when you get to the store, you are told, "Sorry. We're all sold out on that. But over here we have. . . ." Then you will be shown a more expensive item. A reputable store won't do this. It will not advertise a sale on items it really doesn't have. If it has only a few of a certain item, a good store will say so in its ad. Some stores also give "rainchecks" for items they have run out of, or they substitute another brand of the same quality.

CONSUMER PROTECTION

Several times during this chapter you may have thought, "There ought to be a law. . . ." There is. The only rule for many years was, "Buyer beware." This put all the responsibility on the consumer. Then people began to realize the scope of fraudulent activities that adversely affected consumers. Consumer protection laws were formulated and passed by Congress. Some states also passed special laws relating to consumers.

In 1972 the Consumer Product Safety Act was passed. It is designed to help protect the public from product-related injuries. The Consumer Product Safety Commission established under this act investigates the causes of injuries and fatalities which occur as a result of using a product. The commission also develops and enforces uniform safety standards, banning products that are proven dangerous. For example, a chemical process was used to make clothing for babies and small children fire-resistant. It was a good idea, but later it was found that the chemicals used could cause disease. So manufacturers were no longer allowed to use that process. Parts of cars or motorcycles might be defective, and the manufacturer is required to recall them. That means he has to contact people who bought them and ask them to bring the vehicles in for replacement of the defective part at the expense of the manufacturer.

Two other federal agencies are much in the news. The Food and Drug Administration (FDA) tests drugs before they are placed on the market, inspects fish products, and enforces part of the Fair Packaging and Labeling Act of 1956. This act requires that a product's label must give the name and location of the manufacturer. The label must not have misleading statements of quantity on it either.

The Federal Trade Commission (FTC) enforces another part of the Fair Packaging and Labeling Act. It also helps control false and misleading advertising.

Over 30 federal agencies provide consumer services. In addition,

Daryl Littlefield

many states have their own consumer service departments. Consumer protection requires teamwork. The team includes:

an educated and responsible group of consumers,

a concerned body of producers and retailers,

private non-profit agencies which perform comparative tests and make the results available to the public,

and government agencies to provide leadership in developing and enforcing consumer protection laws.

A great deal remains to be done to provide consumer protection. The best protection for you as a consumer is still accurate information and hard, critical thinking.

Chapter Check

1. Give an example of hard sell.

2. What does fraud involve?

3. What does to manipulate someone mean?

4. Give examples of five manipulative techniques.

5. Explain what impulse buying is.

6. What is comparative shopping?

7. Explain how unit pricing works.

8. List several things you can learn about a product by looking at a label.

9. What is the bait and switch technique?

10. Name three agencies of the government involved with consumer protection.

 Part Nine

C. William Horrell

You and the Law

FREEDOM AND THE LAW

When you were a child, your parents' word was law. That seemed restrictive. You couldn't get into the cookies and eat all of them. Your brothers and sisters couldn't either. Therefore, everyone got a fair share, and no one got left out. The law of your parents was both restrictive and protective.

The best laws of our country are like that. It would be nice to think that every boy and girl would just naturally leave enough cookies for the others. It would also be nice to think that all people would just naturally treat others fairly. But it would be unrealistic to do so. Most of us try hard not to mistreat others, but we have our needs, desires, and goals to consider. The law sees to it that we treat others reasonably well, and that others treat us well.

Have you ever heard or read about someone who was sent to jail for a crime he or she didn't commit? Did you ever hear of a person in high office who broke the law and went unpunished? All human institutions are imperfect. The law is no exception, and neither is our court system. Mistakes do happen. Unjust laws are passed and have to be changed. Good laws are abused or misinterpreted. Yet the overall picture is that we are much better off with law than without it. Our laws are an attempt to provide freedom and justice for all citizens, and these laws have come to the rescue of many people who otherwise would have suffered unjustly. The law provides both protection and control.

In the novel *The Trial* by Franz Kafka, the main character, called K, is arrested one day without really knowing why. He is never directly accused of anything or told what crime he is supposed to have committed. Day after day the investigation goes on until his life becomes a quiet nightmare of mental suspense and fear. In a more recent book, *Freedom and Beyond* by John Holt, the author says, "In a free society you can find out where the limits are; in a tyranny, you can never be sure." That means that if no legal limits are set by a society, then no individual is really very free to act. No matter what he does, he has to wonder if he will be punished. By contrast, when you know what you *can't* do, then you can go ahead and do the other things that aren't against the rules. If a government really wanted to snare its citizens, it could do so simply by not telling anyone what the limits are.

In this section we will be looking at many aspects of the law. First, we will see how law relates to everyday life. Next we will look at laws that are especially important to young workers. Then we will review the process of making and changing laws.

❋ Chapter Twenty-Six ❋

THE LAW
IN
YOUR LIFE

THREE KINDS OF LAW

Almost all adults come in contact with the law more than once during their lives. You can't drive a car—or get married—without a license. Paying taxes is a matter of law. And you may have to look to the law for help when some wrong is done you.

Laws are developed so that we can live in peace and harmony with other members of our society. Some laws are designed to prevent problems; others are passed to correct problems. Basically laws fall into three categories: civil, criminal, and constitutional. We will spend just a little time on each one. Knowing something about the system of laws under which you live can help you take advantage of and preserve your rights and freedoms.

CRIMINAL LAW.   Crimes are acts from which society feels it needs protection. Criminal law is designed to regulate public behavior so that people can live in peace and security. Criminal laws spell out those acts which are not allowed and the penalties for committing these acts.

Crimes differ in degree. The most serious crimes are called *felonies*. They include murder, arson, kidnapping, narcotics sales, and other such offenses. This class of crime is punished by heavy fines and long jail sentences. *Misdemeanors* are less serious crimes, such as speeding or breaking the peace. The penalty for committing a misdemeanor is usually a small fine or short jail sentence. Each state has its own set of laws. What might be a felony in one state could be a misdemeanor somewhere else, and vice versa. It is up to individuals to find out what the law is in their own states. If you commit a crime and then say you didn't know it was a crime, you will not be excused from the penalty. In most societies the rule is, "Ignorance of the law is no excuse."

The idea behind criminal law is that if people know they will have to pay a price for committing a crime, they might think twice about doing it. Of course many people have another reason for not breaking the law. They consider hurting another person or damaging or taking another person's property morally wrong. And they want to do anything they can to live at peace with their neighbors. So they obey the law.

CIVIL LAW.   Civil law is the kind of law you are most likely to come in direct contact with. Civil law involves private disputes between two people. If a person or company fails to live up to the terms of a contract, the other party can take legal action. Supposing there is a contract between you and a company which states that the company will fix a bad leak in your roof for $350. They work on it while you are at the office. You come home and inspect it and it looks okay, so you pay them the money. Then the next rainstorm comes. The leak is as bad as ever. If you contact the company and they refuse to do anything about it, you could take them to court.

A contract is really a law you and the other party make yourselves. Civil law helps you to get what you expected to get out of the contract. What you expected to get has to be clearly spelled out in the contract itself. That's why it is so important to read a contract carefully before signing.

A tort is a wrongful injury. It is a specific wrong that a person feels has been committed against him by another person or an organization. There are intentional torts and negligence torts. If someone fully intends to hit you and takes a swing at you, that is an intentional tort. (If the person misses, the charge is assault; if not, it is assault and battery.) On the other hand, if you don't clear your walk in bad winter weather and someone is injured in a fall, you may have committed an unintentional or negligence tort. You didn't intend to hurt the person, but you could have kept the accident from happening.

A tort can also be a crime. For example, if Joe punches you in the nose you can bring a civil suit against him to recover your medical expenses and to be compensated for your suffering and loss of work hours. The state can also bring a criminal suit against Joe, because he broke a law as well as committed a tort.

You can also injure a person by what you say. Maybe you go around telling everybody that Dr. Peterson has performed many unnecessary operations. He can bring a civil suit against you for slander or because you have damaged his reputation and hurt his business.

Divorces, debts, property sales, and business deals can all come under civil law. Most of us prefer to avoid legal entanglements as much as possible. But when you really need help, the civil law is there for your protection.

CONSTITUTIONAL LAW.   Constitutional law deals with the rights guaranteed to us by the Constitution of the United States and the Bill of Rights. We take the Constitution pretty much for granted, much as we take for granted the furniture in our homes. Yet many of the privileges and rights we enjoy result from the fact that the basic law of our land is sound.

The Constitution does not, of course, deal with specific issues and smaller concerns. It deals with fundamental rights. No state or local laws or ordinances are to be passed which conflict with our Constitutional rights. If such laws do get on the books they can be challenged in court. If they are declared unconstitutional they cannot be enforced.

Chances are, most of you will not have close contact with Constitutional law. Yet it is the framework upon which our whole way of life depends.

BREAKING THE LAW

If you were to ask people why they break the law, they might give one of these answers:

Everyone else does it.
The laws aren't any good.
I didn't know I was breaking the law.
I did it out of frustration.

Nobody cares about me, so why should I care about anyone?
They have more than I have, so I'm just equalizing things.
I don't know.

What do you think of these ideas? Can you find some truth in each one? Can you find flaws?

Most of us tend to rationalize our behavior some of the time. We find reasons or excuses for our actions. We mistreat a loved one and then tell ourselves it was partly their fault. We park in a no parking zone and convince ourselves that it was an emergency. Rationalizing is a bad habit to get into because it keeps us from seeing situations as they really are.

Breaking the law involves consequences for the individual and for society. When people break the law, they have made a choice and must be prepared to accept the consequences. The most obvious consequence is the possibility of arrest and jail or a fine. But what about the worry and fear under which the lawbreaker has to live? Also, a criminal record isn't easy to live down. Lawbreakers can find it very difficult to get and keep a job. Some lawbreakers are tough customers, but others are very sensitive people. They can lose respect for themselves and eventually give up once they have gotten into the petty crime routine. Patterns are hard to break.

Crime affects society adversely, too. It fills city streets with mistrust, fear, and hate. It prolongs the battle for equal rights for all citizens. It makes society harsher in meting out punishment to lawbreakers. People who otherwise might be in favor of prison reform and rehabilitation programs become hostile and refuse to vote the necessary funds. Businesses suffer because people don't want to shop in downtown areas they don't feel are safe. To some people crime appears to be a form of freedom. But in reality, crime often causes voters to vote for the enactment of even more laws and stricter law enforcement. Indirectly, crime cuts down the amount of freedom a society enjoys.

What about the victims of crime? Imagine yourself in one of the following situations:

1. Your three-year-old boy has just been run over by a drunken driver.

2. You have been on the job for three months. You saved much of your pay and bought a fine stereo, something you have wanted for a long time. It disappears.

3. You give your elderly neighbor a lift to the grocery store. The store is held up and your neighbor is wounded by gunfire.

4. You are playing pool and a person you don't know comes up and challenges you to a game. When you begin winning, he doesn't like it. He's been drinking, and the next thing you know he's hitting you with

Terry Mauzy

the cue. You end up with head injuries and have to be taken to the hospital for stitches.

5. Your mother is on her way home from work when two people knock her down and take her purse.

To get crime under control, we will have to attack it on many fronts. New methods and ideals for law enforcement will have to be developed. We will have to work on the underlying sociological causes of crime. We will have to try to make life more meaningful for ourselves and others. Most of all, each of us will have to take individual responsibility for our own actions.

What Do You Think?

In some states people in jail can take high school or college courses. Some have even earned college degrees while serving a sentence. Some people say that giving convicted criminals an education after they have let society down is rewarding them for their crimes. The money spent on such programs could be used to give people who are more worthy an education. Do you agree?

Other people say society in various ways contributed to the downfall of criminals and therefore should help rehabilitate them. What do you think about this?

How many chances do you think a person deserves?

THE COURTS OF OUR LAND

In our country there are two different systems of courts: the federal and the state. The federal court system is like a pyramid. At the bottom are the *trial courts.* In the middle are the *appellate courts.* These are courts of appeal for those not satisfied with the outcome in a lower court. At the top is the *Supreme Court of the United States.* It is the highest court in the land.

Each state has a court system very similar to the federal system. At the lowest level are the trial courts: the justice of the peace courts (usually in rural areas) and the municipal courts (urban areas). We call them "lower" courts because that is where most cases begin.

Larger cities sometimes have several kinds of municipal courts: traffic, small claims, marriage and divorce, criminal courts, and juvenile courts. The traffic and marriage and divorce courts are self-explanatory. Criminal courts handles cases involving breaking of the law. Juvenile courts are courts in which youthful offenders are tried. It is thought that minors should not be punished in the same way or to the same degree as adult offenders. With the continuing rise in juvenile crime, however, people are beginning to reconsider this whole issue. Juvenile courts may be undergoing various changes in the next decades. Right now they are designed to give the judge more flexibility in dealing with youthful offenders.

Small claims courts handle civil cases that involve comparatively small amounts of damages. For example, if a dry cleaner ruins a suit of yours through negligence and refuses to do anything about it, you might sue for the price of the suit, say $90. The amount of damages that can be recovered in a small claims court is usually limited to $200 or $300. Generally speaking you don't need a lawyer in small claims court, although you can usually have one take care of the matter for you if you want to. If your grievance involves a great deal more money, it will be handled in regular court and you will probably need a lawyer. The idea behind the small claims court is to take care of smaller cases in the most efficient and quickest way possible. If they had to be placed on the regular court calendar, it could take months and months for them to be settled. Also they would be taking up court time that could be used to take care of the heavy burden of criminal cases and other cases in which a jury is necessary. Most of our courts are overloaded these days.

Each state also has a number of appellate courts. People who are not satisfied with the judgment in a lower court case can appeal the decision. Their cases will be reviewed in an appeals or appellate court. The original decision can be confirmed or overturned. If the original judgment is confirmed (upheld), the person may still not be satisfied. They may still be able to take the case to the supreme court of the state. Every state has a supreme court of its own.

The question of jurisdiction is a complicated one. Jurisdiction is the lawful right to exercise authority. Over which cases do the federal courts have jurisdiction, and over which cases do the state courts have jurisdiction? The federal court system handles questions of constitutionality. It also takes care of cases involving interstate commerce or disputes between states. It tries cases in which federal laws have been broken. State court systems deal with legal problems that occur within the state. But sometimes a matter can be of concern to both the state and the federal government. Or a state law can be in conflict with the Constitution of the United States. When conflicts arise between different laws or different courts, the Supreme Court of the United States can be appealed to for a decision.

The ins and outs of our court systems can be very complicated, but fascinating. If you would like to know more about them, you might wish to refer to this book:

Court in Session, by Jethro Koller Lieberman (New York: Sterling, 1967)

FINDING A LAWYER

Many people who know a great deal about our legal and judicial system discourage people from trying to defend themselves in court when a serious charge is involved. There are some matters many people take care of without legal help, such as making a will or drawing up a simple contract. When your reputation and future are at stake, however, it is best to get professional help. Compare this situation to fixing your car. You could take care of certain maintenance problems yourself. More intricate or serious repairs require a good professional mechanic.

How would you go about finding a good lawyer? You could call several attorneys and find out what their fees are for the type of service you need. But the least expensive lawyer may not be the best. You can't tell the quality of the lawyer by the fee charged. Again, the seriousness of the problem can help you decide. The more complicated the case is, the harder you should try to get a lawyer who has handled such cases before.

You could ask a trusted friend, member of your family, or teacher to suggest a lawyer. In some states, the State Bar Association has a *Lawyer Referral Service.* Please keep in mind that State Bar Associations are not government agencies, but private organizations of lawyers. For states that have referral services you can find the toll-free number in the yellow pages. (In our phone book there is a listing under "Attorneys" which reads "Illinois Lawyer Referral Service.") When you call, someone will listen to you state your problem and try to determine whether you really need a lawyer or not. This person may suggest a government agency or someone else who might be able to help you. But if necessary, a competent lawyer near you is then suggested. It is up to you to contact the lawyer. For a modest fee, the lawyer will arrange a half-hour initial interview with you to go into your problem in more detail.

What if you can't afford an attorney? In criminal matters, the state appoints a public defender for accused persons who don't have the money to hire lawyers. In general, public defenders are highly competent people committed to seeing justice done. In our country, a person is considered innocent until proven guilty. Everyone is entitled to a defense.

If your problem is a matter of civil law, you may qualify for help from the legal aid office nearest you. Such offices are funded by the federal government and run by skilled paralegal workers (people who are not lawyers but have legal training and experience) and lawyers. These offices might help a person who was evicted from her home. They handle divorces. They defend minors whose rights have been violated at school. They help with violations of the Equal Employment Opportunity Act. They tell you what some of the options are for handling various kinds of civil law problems

Eligibility for legal aid depends on your gross annual income (or that of your parents if you are a minor) and the number of people in your family. To find out if you are eligible, you would have to contact the office nearest you. You must live in the county in which the office is located.

In cases involving constitutional rights, some organizations may be able to offer advice or help. For example, the American Civil Liberties Union (ACLU) or the National Association for the Advancement of Colored People (NAACP) have legal branches. You can find the addresses of such groups and a brief description of what they do at your library.

LEGAL TERMS EVERYONE SHOULD KNOW

Paul is arrested at the scene of a robbery. He is taken to the police station and *booked.* He is allowed out on $1000 *bail.* He consults an *attorney.*

A few weeks later he is *arraigned* in court. The *indictment* against him is read, and he *pleads* guilty or not guilty. A date is then set for his trial. Before the date of the trial Paul and his attorney may meet with the judge for a pre-trial conference.

The day of the trial arrives. Paul and his attorney appear in court. Paul is the *defendant.* The state is the *plaintiff.* Paul's attorney, the *counsel for the defense,* presents his evidence. The *state's attorney* presents evidence for the state's case. The *witnesses for the defense* are questioned (*examined*) by Paul's attorney and then *cross-examined* by the state's attorney. *Witnesses for the prosecution* are examined by the state's attorney, then cross-examined by Paul's attorney. After all witnesses have presented their *testimony,* final arguments are presented on both sides.

If it is a *jury trial,* the jury deliberates. That is, the members of the jury discuss the case among themselves in a private place set aside for that purpose. A *verdict* is reached. Paul is declared guilty or not guilty.

If he is not guilty, he goes home and stays out of trouble from then on. If he is declared guilty, a date is set for *sentencing*. When that date comes, Paul again appears in court. His sentence is read to him. He may have to go to prison and/or pay a fine. Or he may be placed on *probation*.

If he goes to prison and is a model prisoner, he may become eligible for *parole*. If he lives up to the terms of his parole, he will stay free and begin life again.

You will have gotten the general meaning behind most of the underlined words from the context. Here are some more exact definitions:

Book: to make a record of arrest and charges against a person.

Bail: money put down as surety that an accused person will appear in court. All but a small percentage of this money is returned if the accused keeps his word and appears in court.

Attorney: lawyer. Also called counsel.

Arraigned: an accused person appears in court, is identified, and formally charged with a crime.

Indictment: a formal statement of what the person is being accused of.

Plead: to make a formal claim that you are guilty or not guilty.

Defendant: the person accused of committing the crime.

Plaintiff: the party bringing the complaint that a law has been broken or an injustice done.

Counsel for the defense: the accused person's lawyer.

State's attorney: the lawyer handling the state's case against the accused.

Witnesses for the defense: people testifying on behalf of the accused.

Witnesses for the prosecution: people testifying on behalf of those making the accusation.

Testimony: information given by the witnesses under oath in court. If they lie under oath, they commit perjury. If they refuse to give important information, they can be held in contempt of court.

Jury trial: a trial in which a group of qualified people deliberate on the facts in a case and bring a verdict of guilty or not guilty. A grand jury is a group of qualified people chosen from the list of registered voters who decide whether or not a person should be indicted. It usually consists of 23 people, so it is called a grand, or large, jury.

A petit jury is also called a trial jury. A group of qualified people chosen from the list of registered voters listens to the evidence in a case and decides if the person or organization is guilty or not guilty. It consists of 12 people, so it is called a petit, or little, jury.

Verdict: a judgment or decision for or against the accused.

Sentencing: reading in court the penalty for a crime a person has committed.

Probation: practice of letting a convicted person go free but under the supervision of an officer of the court and only as long as good behavior continues.

Parole: early release from a prison sentence for good behavior under the supervision of a parole officer and only for as long as good behavior continues.

Working Cooperatively

Divide into groups of four or five. Have each group make up a story about going to court, something like Paul's story. Use as many of the legal terms above as you can. When each group has finished its story, read them aloud to the whole class.

ARE THERE ANY UNIVERSAL LAWS?

In our country, and in the world, for that matter, there seems to be a lot of confusion over what is right and wrong. Is there a set of laws that applies to everyone, everywhere? We aren't referring to the kind of laws we've talked about earlier, laws that have been written down and can be enforced by the police and the courts. Rather, we are talking about rules of conduct which help us decide what to do in situations that aren't covered by written laws. You might run up against a situation at work that will throw all the responsibility for a good decision on your shoulders. No one will be there to say, "that's okay" or "that's wrong." How will you handle such situations? Let's look at a few examples.

LOVES ME, LOVES ME NOT.   Lily and Marshall work in the same factory. Marshall always has a little joke for Lily when he comes in in the morning, and she likes him. In fact, she hopes he will ask her out sometime. After they work together for several weeks, they eat lunch together. Later that week, Marshall waits for Lily after work one afternoon. "Hey, Lily," he says. "Tomorrow I may not come in on time because an army buddy is in town and we're going to make a night of it tonight. Would you punch in for me in the morning if I'm late?"

"I can't do that," said Lily.

"Sure you can. I'll give you my card and number. Punch yourself in a little early. The guard always changes at nine. Punch me in after the new guard comes on duty. My record will show me being a little late, but at least I won't lose a whole hour or so."

Lily is not very happy about the whole deal, but she doesn't want to say no to Marshall. She takes his time card and goes home. That evening she worries about the whole situation. She decides to think it over carefully because she can still call Marshall and tell him she doesn't want to do it. But she must call him before he goes out for the evening, so she has to begin thinking immediately and come to a good decision.

First she considers the *advantages* of clocking in for Marshall:

1. If I do it, Marshall will like me more.

2. He'll know he can trust me.

3. Marshall would have a little leeway in coming to work.

Then she lists the *disadvantages:*

1. I might get in trouble if anybody finds out.

2. Marshall could get fired.

3. I'll be doing something I really don't want to do.

Next she thinks about the *short-term* and *long-term results.*

Short-term results: If it works out okay, Marshall will have what he wants, and I will be even better friends with him.

Long-term results: Marshall may expect me to do this over and over again. It would get harder and harder to say no. A friendship based on my doing these kinds of things for Marshall could turn sour in a hurry. If I act like I don't mind doing it when I really do mind, I'm doing something bad to myself. And I'll probably get more and more worried about getting caught.

Lily gets that far, then she says to herself, "Well, what else could I do?" She tries to think of *alternatives:*

1. I could call Marshall and tell him I have the flu and won't be going in tomorrow.

2. I could ask someone else to do it, one of Marshall's male friends at work.

3. I could call Marshall and tell him the truth, that I simply don't want to.

Last of all, Lily has to be willing to accept the *results* of her decision. If she chooses alternative #3, she has to face at least three possibilities.

Marshall might get angry, slam down the phone, and stop speaking to her. He could even try to make her sound like a goody-goody at work. He could be angry for the moment, but later, when he had had time to think about it, he might realize that he had put Lily in a bad position. He could even like Lily more for it in a long run.

STEPS IN DECISION MAKING

Weighing advantages and disadvantages
Measuring the immediate results against the long-term results
Considering as many alternatives as possible
Being ready to face the consequences of a decision

ALICE IN MARKETLAND. Alice has a job as a supermarket detective. She pushes a grocery cart up and down the aisles as if she were shopping, but really she is watching for shoplifters. Her manager trusts her. He doesn't know that she is bragging to her friends that she doesn't report many people. Just enough to fill her quota.

What do you think of Alice's way of doing her job? How do you think a person would feel if he or she were one of the few Alice happened to report? Would it be fair?

If you were the boss and found out about it, what would you do?

What long-range outcomes may Alice have failed to consider?

WHY TRUST TO LUCK?. George would like to get a promotion. Bill, the man just above him, is leaving the company, and George sees this as his big chance. It is so important to him that he doesn't want to trust to luck. When a co-worker comes to him for help with a report he is working on, George thinks to himself, "Maybe this guy is eligible for the promotion, too!" So George purposely gives him the wrong information.

What is the first problem you can see in George's approach? Can you see other, more long-range problems that might come up for George in terms of relationships with his co-workers and even with the promotion itself?

OUTER SPACE. You get a job with an aircraft company, working on an advanced design bomber. A few years go by. The project is evaluated, and the President and Congress begin to doubt its value. It now appears too expensive for the amount of protection it will be able to offer. Besides, existing equipment can do almost as good a job. If the project is scrapped, you lose your job. How would you feel about that?

If you feel the decision to halt the production of the plane is right, but your co-workers put pressure on you to join a group to save the project, what would you do?

Do you think the public good should always come before the private good? What about in this case?

"AND THEY LIVED HAPPILY EVER AFTER. . . ."

Is the good person always rewarded? That's a little like asking, "Is the bad person always punished?" Sometimes we wish for a system of rewards and punishments that would be consistent and reliable. That's usually when we're thinking about it, though, not when we're actually living it. Almost all of us want exceptions to be made for us and for others now and then. For example, if a traffic officer is about to give you a ticket and you explain the circumstances, he may decide to just give you a warning this time, although you probably deserved the ticket.

Even though our system for rewarding good and punishing evil isn't hard and fast, it does have a certain pattern to it. Here are some of the rewards we reap from making good decisions in the area of right and wrong:

1. Most obvious of all, we keep ourselves out of trouble.

2. We make it easy for others to trust and like us.

3. A society in which we can count on each other to do the right thing most of the time is a better place to live than a society that is just one big free-for-all.

4. We feel better about ourselves when we feel we have done the right thing.

All of us have the right to glow with pleasure at the good things we accomplish. Most of us want others to recognize these things, too, but we can't always expect that to happen. Sometimes your good deeds will be complimented and appreciated. Other times no one but you will know about them. Our final standards of right and wrong have to be independent of praise from others. At such times our reward is a quiet inner satisfaction.

Chapter Check

1. What is the difference between a felony and a misdemeanor?

2. Name some situations that are covered by civil law.

3. What is an intentional tort? A negligence tort?

4. What three levels of courts are there in both the federal system and the state systems?

5. List four kinds of municipal courts.

6. What are small claims courts for?

7. Explain what it means to appeal a case.

8. What is the difference between a grand jury and a trial or petit jury?

9. If you are bringing a complaint or accusing someone of something you are the: a) defendant b) the plaintiff c) the counsel.

10. If you are defending yourself against an accusation you are the: a) jury b) defendant c) plaintiff.

11. If you lie while you are under oath you are guilty of a) assault b) perjury c) contempt.

12. What are some of the things you would consider in making a decision about whether to do or not do a certain thing?

Chapter Twenty-Seven

WHAT THE LAW SAYS ABOUT YOUNG WORKERS

HOW LAWS PROTECTING YOUNG WORKERS CAME INTO BEING

In the late 1800's and early 1900's, factories were as dangerous as battlefields, yet children worked in them. They often spent as many hours a day there as adults did, and their wages were much lower. They had virtually no rights as workers. Some factories even had whipping rooms for children who could not keep up with the work quotas expected of them. Few people gave any thought whatsoever to the education of working children. Sometimes both the physical and mental growth of young laborers were stunted.

Today the situation has changed dramatically. Young people under the age of 16 can work, but only under certain conditions. The hours they may work and the wages they receive are matters of law. Occupations considered highly dangerous are closely regulated, and people under 18 are not allowed to work in them. The law that helped bring about these sweeping changes was the *Fair Labor Standards Act*.

By the turn of the century, some state governments had passed laws protecting the young worker. But getting good labor laws on the federal books was slower. Public interest in the problem came and went. Still, work quietly proceeded on a comprehensive law. Finally, in 1938, the Fair Labor Standards Act was passed. Since then, it has been amended several times. The provisions of it have proved to be of great importance to workers of all ages. Let's look at what this law says.

WHAT BUSINESSES ARE COVERED BY THE FAIR LABOR STANDARDS ACT?

Generally speaking, two main criteria are being used to determine if a company comes under the Fair Labor Standards Act. One, is the business involved in interstate or foreign commerce? Two, does it gross over $250,000 a year?

Commerce means the buying or selling of goods. Interstate commerce is the term used for trade that crosses state lines. You can manufacture corncob pipes in Missouri and sell them there, and that would not be interstate commerce. If you also sold your pipes in Illinois, Indiana, and Maine, you would be engaging in interstate commerce. If your product goes to Argentina or Tasmania, you would be involved in *foreign commerce*.

Interstate commerce covers more workers than you might imagine. If you work in radio or television broadcasting, your "product" usually crosses state lines. People who maintain highways, railways, or airfields come under the Fair Labor Standards Act, as do those who service vehicles that cross state lines. Employees of banks, insurance companies, and advertising agencies often transact business across state lines, so they, too, are engaging in interstate commerce.

In addition to all those businesses which fall under the act because they carry on interstate or foreign commerce or because they gross more than a quarter of a million dollars a year, other businesses have recently been declared subject to the provisions of the act. These include hotels, motels, restaurants, hospitals, laundries and dry cleaning establishments, homes for the care of the sick or aged, service agencies, some government agencies, and schools. The trend has been to gradually bring more and more types of businesses under the coverage of this law. Now most businesses except small, family-operated businesses are included.

WHAT DOES THE LAW SAY ABOUT AGE?

It seems as if young people are always waiting for something. You have probably thought ahead to your graduation from high school, your eighteenth birthday, your marriage, or some other important milestone in the not-too-distant future. In terms of youth employment laws, there are three such milestones: when young people reach the age of 14, when they turn 16, and again when they are 18.

If you are 14 or 15 years old, you may legally hold a variety of jobs in retail sales, food services, and service stations. You may not work at every task done in such places, but you may work at these:

1. Office and clerical work

2. Cashiering, selling, modeling, art work, work in advertising, window trimming, and comparative shopping

3. Price marking and tagging, assembling orders, packing and shelving

4. Bagging and carrying out customers' orders

5. Errand and delivery work by foot, bicycle, and public transportation

6. Clean up work and maintenance of grounds, but not including use of power-driven mowers or cutters

7. Kitchen work and work involved in preparing and serving food and beverages

8. Work in connection with cars and trucks including dispensing gas and oil, courtesy services, car cleaning, washing, and polishing

9. Cleaning vegetables and fruits, and wrapping, sealing, labeling, weighing, pricing, and stocking goods

Fourteen- and 15-year-olds have restrictions on when and for how long they may work. They may not work during school hours or before 7 a.m. or after 7 p.m., from Labor Day through June 1. They are not allowed to work more than 3 hours on school days or more than 18 hours during school weeks. They may not work more than 8 hours per day on non-school days, or more than 40 hours during non-school weeks.

Your sixteenth birthday opens up many more work possibilities for you. You may work at any job except those which have been declared dangerous by the Secretary of Labor. These jobs are often referred to as the *seventeen hazardous orders*. Because of your special status as a vocational student, certain exceptions may sometimes be made. We will discuss both the hazardous orders and the exceptions a little later.

Eighteen is the magical age. You are then considered an adult and can work at almost any occupation you wish. You are credited with enough experience, self-control, and common sense to work sensibly and safely and to avoid most accidents.

In order to work, high school students have to be able to prove they are legally old enough. You may be asked to obtain a document that will verify your age, such as a work permit or proof of age certificate. Employers want to make sure of your age because, if they violate the law, they can be fined up to $10,000. Age certification is also a protection for you. It keeps employers from placing you in dangerous occupations.

THE HAZARDOUS ORDERS

If you were to study accident statistics, you would see that workers on some jobs suffer more injuries than workers in other occupations. When government officials were setting up the hazardous orders, they had a great deal of information upon which to base their decisions. The following occupations were designated as too dangerous for workers under 18:

1. Manufacturing and storing of explosives

2. Outside helper on motor-driven vehicles

3. Coal mining

4. Logging and sawmilling

5. Operating power-driven woodworking machines

6. Occupations involving exposure to radioactive substances or ionizing radiation

7. Operating power-driven hoisting apparatus

C. William Horrell

8. Operating power-driven metal forming, punching, and shearing machines

9. Mining other than coal mining

10. Slaughtering, meat packing, processing, and rendering

11. Operating power-driven bakery machines

12. Operating power-driven paper products machinery

13. Manufacture of brick, tile, and related products

14. Operation of power-driven circular saws, band saws, and guillotine shears

15. Wrecking, and demolition

16. Roofing

17. Excavation

In addition to these, you may not work at any agricultural job that is highly dangerous if you are under 16 years of age.

Look again at order numbers 5, 8, 10, 12, 14, 16, and 17. You are allowed to work in these 7 hazardous occupations if you meet certain conditions. The first is that you must be enrolled in a cooperative education program that is recognized by the state or local educational authority. The second is that you must be working under a written agreement with special provisions. You have already satisfied the first condition. As far as the written agreement is concerned, your training agreement can be stated in such a way that it would meet this requirement. It would have to include the following provisions:

That the work in a hazardous occupation is incidental to your training.

That such work would be intermittent and for short periods of time, under the direct supervision of an experienced person.

That safety instructions would be given by the school and correlated with on-the-job training.

That a plan must be prepared showing that you will be moving from one task to the next in an organized way, moving from one level of skill to the next.

What does all this mean? Let's say that you have enrolled in the cooperative education program so that you can learn to become a printer. You will be learning to do layout work, operate the offset printing machine, and you will become skilled at other tasks spelled out in your training program. There is a machine in the printshop called a guillotine shears. It is used for cutting large stacks of paper. A powerful blade drops down from overhead and cuts through many sheets at once. Generally, a person who is under 18 is not permitted to operate this machine. You may be allowed to operate it occasionally because you are in a cooperative education program and you need to learn this skill. But operating it cannot be your only job in that printshop. Learning to use it would be a sideline, not a main job. You would operate it now and then (intermittently), not on a regular basis. You must have thorough instruction beforehand and supervision during the time you operate it.

MONEY MATTERS

The Fair Labor Standards Act sets up minimum wages that workers must be paid, including young workers. The minimum wage is the lowest wage employers are allowed to pay workers. They can pay more if they want to, and some do so in order to attract the best workers to their businesses. A company may be covered by both federal and state minimum wage laws. The law which is most beneficial to the worker applies.

The minimum wage is periodically changed by Congress. The reason for this is that the cost of living goes up and the minimum wage isn't enough for workers. The best place to check on the current minimum wage is the nearest Department of Labor Office. If you can't find one in your community, consult the public library.

From time to time objections to the minimum wage law have been raised. Some people say employers could provide jobs for more people if they didn't have to pay such high wages. Others who have worked for substandard wages say that many people don't realize how hard it is to exist on less than the minimum wage, especially when there is a family to support. Some economists have argued that having some income, even a substandard wage, is better than not working at all. Other economists say that lowering or abolishing the minimum wage law would lead to the same old wage abuses of the past. What do you think of these arguments?

At one time some members of Congress considered setting two minimum wages, one for young workers and one for workers over 18. The thinking behind it was that then employers would hire more young workers. They thought this would be good for the country because teenagers are one of the groups with a high unemployment rate. Do you think the plan would have worked?

EXCEPTIONS TO THE MINIMUM WAGE LAW

Some exceptions are also made to the minimum wage law. Many of you may be learning quite complicated jobs. The employer is allowed to pay you less if you are working in an occupation having a long training period, several months perhaps. The reason for this exception is that while you are learning you will be less productive than other workers. Such training could be too expensive for your employer if he had to pay the full minimum wage. Therefore he may apply for permission to pay trainees 75% of the minimum wage. He fills out a special form with the Wage and Hour Division of the Department of Labor. He must do this at least 30 days before you begin working. His application to pay you less will not be approved if:

1. The occupation does not really demand special skills that require long learning periods.

2. A regular worker is being displaced.

3. Wage rate or the quality of the work environment would go down.

4. The community or industry doesn't really need more workers in that occupation.

5. There are already violations of the Fair Labor Standards Act on the employer's record.

6. The number of student-learners working at a reduced rate is too large.

Overtime You should also know about the overtime provisions of the minimum wage law. An employee who works more than 40 hours in any one work week must be paid 1 1/2 times the normal rate for the hours over the regular 40 hours. For example, Toni works at an hourly rate of $2.90. One week she works 50 hours. She would receive $159.50 for her efforts, rather than the $145.00 she would have gotten had the extra hours been figured at the usual rate.

Total Hours Worked = 50
Hours worked at regular pay = 40
Hours worked at time-and-a-half = 10
Money received for the first 40 hours = $116.00
     (40 hours × $2.90 = $116.00)
Time-and-a-half rate = $4.35 an hour
     ($2.90 + $1.45 = $4.35)
Money received for the 10 hours overtime = $43.50
     (10 hours × $4.35 = $43.50)
Total amount earned = $159.50

     ($116.00 + $43.50)

Checkpoint

Make sure you understand how to figure overtime. Try this example.

John Jamerson works at the telephone company and is paid $3.20 per hour. What is his gross (total before deductions are taken out) pay if he works:

a. 17 hours in one week?

b. 43 hours in one week?

c. 46 hours in one week?

d. 50 hours in one week?

1. Below are three important labor laws we have studied in this book so far. See if you can match each law with its provisions.

a. Occupational Safety and Health Act

b. Fair Labor Standards Act

c. Labor Management Relations Act

X. Sets minimum wage for various types of work, designates hazardous orders

Y. Sets up health and safety standards for workers in many industries

Z. Assures workers of their right to organize, provides guidelines for collective bargaining

2. Explain what the hazardous orders are and give two or three examples.

3. What restrictions does the Fair Labor Standards Act place on the hours a 14- or 15-year old may work?

4. At what age can you do any kind of work you choose?

5. Explain the minimum wage concept.

6. If a state and a federal law cover the same ground, which law applies to the young worker?

❧ Chapter Twenty-Eight ❧

OUR
TAX LAWS

Portland Cement Assoc.

WHO TAXES AND WHY

Most modern countries have a taxation system. If people didn't pay taxes, they would have to go without many of the services they now receive. We have been talking about independence throughout this book, but independence has limits. Some things we can't easily supply for ourselves. Police and fire protection, public education, building and maintaining our roads, welfare, and other such services fall into the category of public needs. The government takes care of these for us, but it needs money in order to do so. That's what taxes are all about.

Taxes are enforced contributions of money. A person's income, property, purchases, and inheritance can be taxed. The money collected is used to run the government and to take care of public needs. In this chapter we will be looking at various kinds of taxes, finding out how to figure our tax, and seeing where the tax dollars go.

FIVE KINDS OF TAXES

Although there are many kinds of taxes, we are going to deal with only the most common ones. To get them in some kind of order we are classifying them according to what is being taxed. Let's begin with income tax.

TAXES ON WHAT YOU EARN—INCOME TAX.   Your income is the money that comes into your pocket as a result of your labor. You decide how you want to spend much of it. However, a certain percentage has to go for taxes. It is your contribution to the public good. You are part of the public, so you will receive some of the good.

In January or February after the first year (or part of a year) you work, you will need to fill out a federal income tax form. You will need to know about two forms—the *1040* and the *W-2*. These forms change from time to time. In recent years the trend has been to simplify them. However, certain basic concepts and terms stay pretty much the same. We will concentrate on these.

If you have been paying taxes for a while, you will automatically get a 1040 form in the mail each year. If this is your first year of paying taxes, or if for some other reason you don't get one in the mail, you can pick a 1040 form up at your post office. City halls and banks also sometimes have them. These forms come from the Internal Revenue Service (often referred to as the IRS). The IRS is responsible for all the paperwork that goes into the collecting of taxes. IRS offices are located all over the country, and you can call them if you don't understand something on your tax form. The IRS also checks tax returns as they are sent in. Sometimes it finds mistakes and notifies the taxpayer. Sometimes they also find income tax evaders, people who try to avoid paying their taxes. The IRS is a very busy agency.

Once you have your 1040 form, you are ready to begin. One of the first items of information you will need is your *gross income.* That term has come up several times already, so by now you know that it means the entire amount you earned before any deductions were made. For a young worker, gross income generally consists only of wages earned for the year. For some people, however, it might include money made on stocks and bonds, interest earned on savings, rents collected, and so forth.

Determining your gross income is easy if you are on a payroll. After the first of the year, your employer sends you a W-2 form. This form tells you exactly what you earned in the past year. The largest figure on it should be your gross income. If you have saved all your check stubs, you can add them up and make sure the figure on your W-2 form is correct.

The diagram that follows will give you a preview of the steps you will be going through to complete your income tax form.

Gross Income	minus	Adjustments	equals	Adjusted Gross Income

Adjusted Gross Income	minus	Deductions	equals	Taxable Income

Adjusted Gross Income If you had moving expenses or other outlays of cash in connection with your job, you really didn't have as much money to spend as you thought. So you are allowed to subtract a certain amount for each such expense. Exactly what expenses can be included is spelled out in the booklet of directions that comes with the 1040 form. At first you will probably not be entitled to any such adjustments. Later on you may be, so it is important to be aware that they exist. After any such expenses are deducted from your gross income, the figure remaining is your *adjusted gross income.*

Deductions. Each person is allowed a certain untaxed amount of money for living expenses. People can take advantage of this allowance in two ways: they can *itemize their deductions* or they can *go directly to the tax table.*

Itemizing Your Deductions. To itemize your deductions, you must use what is known as the long form. It is another version of the 1040, and on it there is space to list what expenses you had which were tax exempt. Here are some of the items you can subtract from your adjusted gross income if you choose this longer way of figuring your tax:

medical and dental expenses
some medical insurance premiums
state and local taxes you paid
gasoline and sales taxes
real estate tax
interest you paid on your home loan, other loans, charge accounts, etc.
contributions to your church, synagogue, or other non-profit charitable, educational, or research organizations

You can see that itemizing such deductions means that you would have had to keep good records. You should have receipts to prove you actually made such expenditures. It takes more time and effort to fill out the long form.

Why then do some people itemize? If they have had large medical expenses or have paid out large amounts in interest or taxes, they can subtract a large amount from their adjusted gross income figure before figuring their taxes. The more you can deduct the better, because you are taxed on the amount left after deductions of this kind are made. For some people, it's worth it to file the long form.

Going Directly to the Tax Table   If you don't want to itemize, you can simply accept the standard amount which the government has figured to be about what the average person needs for the items listed above. It is a fair figure, and it certainly makes filling out your income tax form much simpler. If you haven't had much medical expense or high interest payments or something of the kind, there isn't much point in itemizing.

Previously people had to subtract the figure for living expenses (then called the *standard deduction*) from their adjusted gross income. Then they had to multiply the amount allowed for each dependent times the number of dependents they had and subtract that figure from their gross income, too. Then they were ready to go to the tax table.

Now that has been changed to make filing your income tax even more simple. The set amount for living expenses and the allowance per dependent are both built right into the tax table. All you have to do is turn to the tax table which applies to you. Run your finger down the page until you come to the line with your gross income on it, then move across the page to the right until you come to the column that applies to you. The figure you find there will indicate the amount of tax you owe.

Which column applies to you? The columns are numbered at the top —1, 2, 3, 4, etc. These numbers represent the number of exemptions you are claiming. An *exemption* is a fixed amount you are allowed for yourself and each dependent. The instructions that come with the 1040 form tell you whether or not someone in your family qualifies as your dependent. Basically, a dependent is someone you support: a wife, a husband, an invalid member of your family, children, brothers, sisters, etc. If you were married and had two children you would have four exemptions. These would include yourself, your wife or husband, and the two children. Once you have moved to the correct column on the correct income level, your finger should be on the amount of tax to be paid.

Next you will have to decide if you owe the government anything or if it owes you something! Why would the federal government owe you anything? Well, your employer *withheld* a certain amount each payday for taxes. Look again at your W-2 form and you will see that it tells you exactly how much was withheld from your paychecks during the year. If

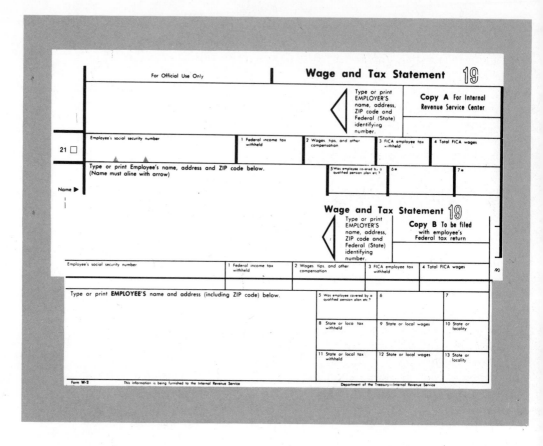

too much was withheld, you get a refund. If the amount of tax you owe according to the tax table is less than the amount withheld from your checks you will get some money back.

You can guess why the federal government requires the employer to hold out some money for taxes each payday. Many of us would hate to put out $1000 or more all at once. In fact, most of us wouldn't be able to do so. Having money withheld from each check is a less painful way of paying taxes, and it assures the government that it will get the necessary funds to keep going.

One other feature of federal taxation is that it is a graduated or progressive income tax system. The more money you make in a year's time, the higher the percentage of tax you pay. If you fall into the income bracket of people who earn between $10,000 and $15,000 a year, you will pay a smaller percentage than people in the $30,000 to $35,000 a year bracket.

If we didn't have this type of system, then all people would pay the same percentage of their salary in taxes, regardless of their annual income. If everyone, say, paid a straight 10%, this is what would happen.

Josephine, who earns $8000 a year, would pay $800 in taxes, leaving $7200. At the same, Marietta, with an $80,000 annual salary, would pay $8000, leaving her $72,000.

However, this is not how our system works. The percentage of annual income that goes for taxes gradually increases as the person's earnings increase. Thus, the heavier tax burden falls on the shoulders of the person earning the higher wages. Josephine's income falls in the 10% tax bracket, so she would still pay $800, with $7200 remaining for her to spend. Marietta's much higher income falls within the 25% tax bracket. Now she pays $20,000 and has $60,000 left to spend.

Most states have a state income tax. It is much less than the federal income tax. A person files state income tax forms each year at the same time he files the federal form. The state income tax form is sent to your state capital, not to the Internal Revenue Service, after you have filled it out.

Checkpoint 1.

We've introduced a number of terms so far in this chapter. See if you have mastered all of them by matching the following:

1. file a return

2. IRS

3. Form 1040

4. gross income

5. W-2 form

6. itemize

7. taxable income

8. graduated income tax

a. to list deductions one by one

b. a form your employer sends you stating your gross income and the amount of tax withheld for the past year

c. to send in your filled out income tax form

d. tax form individuals use for paying federal income tax

e. the amount on which you actually pay taxes

f. the total amount you earn before any deductions are made

g. the more you earn, the higher percentage of taxes you pay

h. Internal Revenue Service

What Do You Think?

At times in our lives we look at others and say, "I wish I had as many clothes as that person." Or, "I wish I had as nice a house." We look at people with big incomes and think, "Well, they ought to pay more taxes. They can afford to." That's true, to some extent. But how much more is fair? This isn't an easy question to answer. Look at the following two situations.

Pete is 18. He likes nice clothes. Now that he is working and can afford to buy the kind of clothes he likes, he builds up a good wardrobe. Then one day Pete's father comes and says, "Hey, you really have a lot of clothes. Frankie doesn't have so many. We'll just give him five of these shirts and a couple pairs of your slacks." Frankie's your younger brother. What would your reaction be?

Or take this case. Sally is 25. She and her husband have worked hard and saved enough money for a down payment on a house. They find just the house they want, buy it, and move in. What if the government came and said, "There are many families who only have a few rooms to live in. We're going to move one of these families in here with you. After all, you have more space than you really need for just the two of you." How would you feel about it?

In modern societies we need to take better care of each other. The rich should not get richer at the expense of the poor. But on the other hand, it isn't fair to be penalized because you have more than your neighbors, providing you earned it honestly. Do you think it would be possible or practical for the government to see to it that everyone had the same amount of wealth?

TAXES ON WHAT YOU SPEND—SALES TAX.   When you buy a pair of scissors, a deck of cards, or a stuffed animal for your baby brother, you pay tax on it. Almost anything you buy can be taxed, even entertainment. Taxes on what you purchase are *sales tax.*

There is no federal sales tax as such. State and local governments levy taxes on what you buy so that they can provide money for local services and programs. The amount of sales tax varies from place to place. It can be 4% in one city and 5% in another. Usually stores and other places of business have a tax table available at the counter so that they can look at it quickly rather than having to calculate the amount of tax to charge for each purchase.

Remember that we said federal income tax is graduated or progressive. The upper income brackets carry a heavier load of the income tax burden. Sales taxes, however, are regressive. That means they place a greater burden on people with small incomes because they pay the same amount of sales tax per dollar as do people with larger incomes.

If your state sales tax is 5% on the dollar, how much tax will you have to pay on a sweater which costs $14.95?

$$\begin{array}{r} \$14.95 \\ \times\ .05 \\ \hline .7475 \end{array}$$

Your tax would be $ .75. The total cost for the sweater would be $14.95 + $ .75.

With a sales tax of 5%, how much would you pay for the following items:

1. A bottle of after-shave for your boyfriend costing $3.75

2. A liquid silver necklace costing $15.50

3. A mini-refrigerator for $225.00

4. A Moped for $580.00

5. A car for $3,250

J I Case

TAXES ON WHAT YOU OWN—PROPERTY TAX.   Whatever you own is your property. Taxes on such possessions are called *property taxes.* Basically, there are two types of property tax: personal property tax and real property tax. In earlier days, the word *real* when associated with property meant the property was not movable. Houses and land thus became known as *real property*. The term is still used today in such words as real estate. Although we now have the equipment to move buildings from one location to another, we still consider them real property.

Personal property includes such items as cars, trucks, and household goods. In most localities you are required to pay tax on real property, that is, your house or land. You may also have to pay a tax on your personal property in some cities and states.

Real estate tax is based on the assessed value of houses and/or land. To assess a piece of property means to estimate its value. This is usually done by a local government official working in the assessor's office. Taxes are then levied on a percentage of that assessed valuation. In most places you get your real estate tax bill in the mail. You will be told when and where to pay it, and in some cases you will be allowed to divide the amount due into several payments if necessary. Real estate taxes are largely used to support the local public schools.

American Iron and Steel Institute

TAXES ON WHAT YOU USE. A use tax is levied on those who use a service or facility that requires money for upkeep. The most common examples of this kind of tax are the gasoline tax and licensing fees for automotive vehicles. The money collected from these sources is primarily used for the construction and maintenance of roads.

Taxes on gasoline may be levied by local, state, and/or the federal government. Licensing fees are normally a state-level responsibility.

TAXES ON WHAT YOU LEAVE—INHERITANCE TAX.   Assuming that you are successful in the career you choose and that you amass a fortune (or, like most of us, a mini-fortune), upon your death you will leave an estate to your family or friends—or cats. An estate in this sense is all the property, real and personal, that you own at the time of your death. Your will says how you want your assets disposed of, but whoever inherits your wealth will not get the full amount. They will have to pay an inheritance tax on the amount you bequeath to them.

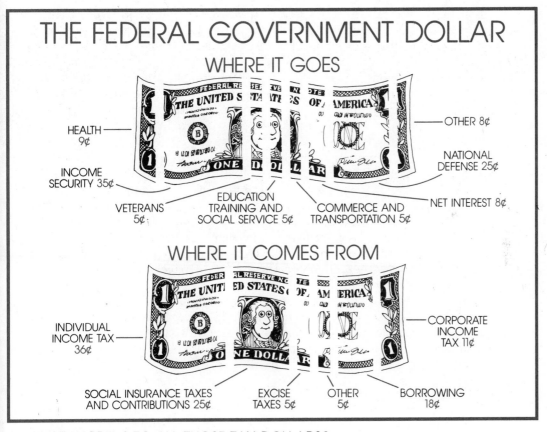

THE FEDERAL GOVERNMENT DOLLAR
WHERE IT GOES

HEALTH 9¢

INCOME SECURITY 35¢

VETERANS 5¢

EDUCATION TRAINING AND SOCIAL SERVICE 5¢

COMMERCE AND TRANSPORTATION 5¢

OTHER 8¢

NATIONAL DEFENSE 25¢

NET INTEREST 8¢

WHERE IT COMES FROM

INDIVIDUAL INCOME TAX 36¢

SOCIAL INSURANCE TAXES AND CONTRIBUTIONS 25¢

EXCISE TAXES 5¢

OTHER 5¢

BORROWING 18¢

CORPORATE INCOME TAX 11¢

WHAT HAPPENS TO ALL THOSE TAX DOLLARS?

Chart One gives an idea of where the federal government gets its money. It has various sources of revenue. Income tax, although it represents a sizable chunk of the federal government's funds, is only one source.

Chart Two shows what the money is spent for. This changes, of course, depending on the needs of the country. Maybe there has to be more military spending at one time and more welfare spending at another.

The President works out the federal budget and proposes it to Congress. Members of Congress make the changes they feel are necessary and then okay it. Any appropriation of funds must be approved by Congress.

TAX EVASION

As you might have guessed, some people try to get out of paying their taxes. We call this tax evasion. If you were living with a group of four or five people and you had all agreed to share expenses, how would you react to a member who didn't keep the agreement? The IRS has a similar problem with tax evaders except on a greater scale. So penalties for not paying your taxes have been set up. Penalties have also been established for lying and cheating when you make out your income tax form or for being late in filing it. Tax information is now screened primarily by computer, so there isn't much chance of a person getting away with cheating.

Each year a number of income tax returns are randomly selected to be audited. You might say they are pulled out of a hat. Then they are carefully checked. If the IRS has any questions about a particular return, the taxpayer who filed it is required to meet with a representative of the IRS. The taxpayer must answer any questions and help resolve the problem. It is, of course, a great help if that taxpayer has receipts and records to prove the information on the tax form is correct. If the person and the tax official can't agree, either the IRS or the taxpayer can begin court proceedings to have the problem resolved.

Penalties for tax cheating are severe, including large fines and prison sentences. A person can, however, make an honest mistake. In that case, an adjustment can usually be made to everyone's satisfaction. Most United States taxpayers are honest people and have nothing to fear from an audit of their income tax returns.

Chapter Check

1.   What are the five basic taxes in terms of what is being taxed?

2.   What is a progressive tax? Is it fair? Why?

3. What is a regressive tax? Who is most affected by it?

4. True or False. State income tax is usually much higher than federal income tax.

5. True or False. State and local governments are usually responsible for collecting sales tax.

6. True or False. A tax evader is a person who accidentally makes a mistake on his income tax form.

7. Explain what the 1040 and W-2 forms are.

8. Why do many people take the standard deduction rather than itemizing their deductions? When would it be better to itemize?

9. Name some of the services your tax dollars help to provide.

❧ Chapter Twenty-Nine ❧

SOCIAL SECURITY

H. Armstrong Roberts

WHY SOCIAL SECURITY?

If you are like many high school students, you do not like being dependent on others. You don't like asking your parents for every nickel you need. You want to be on your own, independent.

Old people feel the same way. Once they can no longer work and earn a living, they do not like having to ask their sons or daughters for help. (Maybe they don't even have sons and daughters to ask.)

That's what social security is all about. It is a way of saving money now so that when you retire you will still have some money coming in every month. Retirement is a long way off, of course, but it takes years to build up such a fund.

Also, you may need to know the basics about how social security works even while you are still young. You may have to take advantage of the disability provisions of the social security law. You may have to help others in your family get their benefits. For example, suppose ten years from now you are married and have two small children. Your parents reach retirement age. You want to help them financially, but you really aren't in a position to do so. Perhaps they do not know what they are eligible to receive under the social security laws, or even how to go about finding out. After studying this chapter, you will know how to get them started.

Some 1300 social security offices are spread across the country. If your city or town has one, it is a simple matter just to look in the phone book and call when you have a question. Try the white pages under "United States Government." In checking phone books from various cities, we found that sometimes the listing was under, "United States Government—Social Security Administration;" other times it was under, "United States Government—Department of Health, Education, and Welfare, Social Security Administration." There may be other variations, and you may have to look all through the United States Government listings.

Representatives working out of these social security offices make frequent visits to nearby towns and cities which have no offices. You could arrange by phone to meet with such a representative if necessary.

HOW SOCIAL SECURITY WORKS

During your working years a small amount will be taken out of each paycheck. Your social security deduction will show on your check and on your W-2 tax form as "F.I.C.A." contributions. F.I.C.A. stands for Federal Insurance Contributions Act, the act which specified that people expecting to benefit from the system must also contribute to it. Your employer contributes the same amount as you do to your social security account. You can call your social security office to find out exactly what percentage should be deducted from your check each month. If you are self-employed, a somewhat different kind of calculation is used to determine how much you should pay into the fund. The money is held in trust funds and cannot be used for any other purpose except to pay benefits to eligible people.

Each person must earn his right to social security benefits by working and contributing for 40 quarters, which is the same as ten years. This does not necessarily have to be ten years in a row. For example, a woman might work 20 quarters, then take time out to have a family, then work 20 more quarters. She would be eligible for benefits at retirement age. There are exceptions to the 40-quarters rule, but we want to give you an overview here. You can always inquire at the social security office about the fine points or special circumstances.

When it first became law in 1936, social security dealt only with retirement income. Since then, the law has been changed and new provisions have been added to it so that it now includes more people (almost everybody) and deals with more problems. The four important areas of coverage are: retirement income, survivors' benefits, disability insurance, and Medicare. Let's look at each of these more closely.

RETIREMENT INCOME.   When you turn 65, you can begin receiving monthly social security checks. The amount of these checks varies from person to person because it is based on the person's average income during the working years. A wife (or dependent husband) may also be eligible to receive a check. If you want to you can retire at 62, but then your monthly check will be less than if you had waited till the age of 65, and it will remain less for the rest of your life.

SURVIVORS' BENEFITS.   When a worker dies, certain members of the family can receive money from his or her social security account. Usually this means that a surviving wife can receive what would have been her husband's retirement income had he reached the age of 65. Or if a man loses his wife and she was working and had been providing at least half of the family's support, the husband may receive benefits from her social security account. Dependent children are also eligible for social security support under some conditions. The remaining parent can begin receiving checks to help support children almost immediately after the death of the other parent.

DISABILITY INSURANCE.   When people are badly injured or become seriously ill and can no longer work, they can receive money from their social security accounts. To be eligible, they generally have to have worked 20 quarters out of the last 40. Younger workers who haven't had time to accumulate a sufficient number of quarters are still able to receive benefits. A different scale is used in figuring what those benefits should be. There are also special provisions for blind people and for people who have been disabled from childhood. Sex makes no difference. Women workers have the same benefits as male workers.

MEDICARE.   When people are over 65, they often cannot afford expensive medical treatment. Their regular social security checks just cover their living expenses in most cases. The Medicare part of the social security program gives them hospital and medical insurance. Medicare also covers people who are disabled or have severe kidney disease which requires the

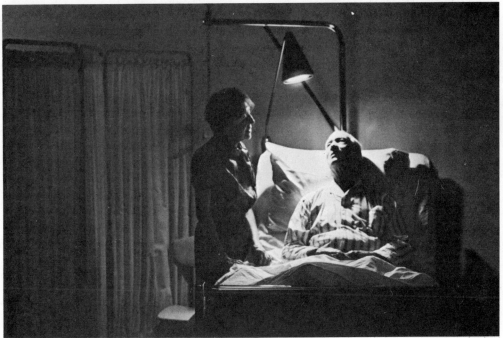

Blue Cross-Blue Shield Chicago-Based

use of a kidney machine. Medicare is a relatively new part of the social security program, and it is being studied and improved as the years go by.

What Do You Think?

It has been said that a society's attitude toward the poor, the old, and the handicapped reflects the level of civilization that society has reached. It has also been said that helping and supporting people makes them less and less able to help themselves.

What do you think of these differing viewpoints? Can you think of some good compromises between them?

KEEPING THE SOCIAL SECURITY SYSTEM FLEXIBLE

One of the big problems with all savings programs (that's really what social security is) is that $10 today may be worth only $9 fifteen years from now. Our economic system has its ups and downs, as you know if you listen to the stock market and financial reports on the evening news. It could happen that when you are ready to retire, the country might be suffering from inflation. That would mean that your money would be worth less and buy less. You would be in a bind because your social security check wouldn't be enough to live on. This problem was foreseen by lawmakers, too, and in 1972, they passed legislation that allows social security benefit checks to go up automatically every time the cost of living goes up three percent or more within a year's time. This is called a *sliding scale of benefits.*

Another principle that is basic to the social security system is that when a condition that made a person eligible for cash benefits changes, that person may no longer be eligible. For example, if a retired person earns more than a certain amount by working part time or on a non-official basis, he must give up his right to social security checks. In 1977 he could earn up to $2,520 and still receive his social security payment. If he earns more than that for a while and doesn't get social security checks, he can always begin getting them again, once his earnings go below the set amount. If a disabled person's condition improves so that he can work again, he no longer receives checks. If such guidelines were not followed, the system would become too costly and would be unfair.

YOUR SOCIAL SECURITY CARD

Most of you already have your social security cards, so you have made a start on planning for the future. Your social security number is yours and yours alone. It is also your tax number. It's not a bad idea to memorize it. Put your duplicate card in a safe place. You can get a replacement from your social security office. Your number always remains the same so that there won't be confusion in recording your wages and contributions.

If you change your name because of marriage or for another reason, you should report it to your social security office as soon as possible in order to avoid any mix-up in your account.

CHECKING YOUR BENEFITS

If you are receiving social security benefits and have some questions about the amounts you have been receiving, you should contact the social security office. Try to do this as soon as you suspect something is wrong. If you go to your social security office with a problem it helps to take records of your earnings, doctor's forms, anything you have among your papers that helps to explain your case. If, after you have visited your social security office you feel the decision made there was wrong or unfair, you can take the following steps:

1. You can ask the Social Security Administration to reconsider your case. The social security office you go to will provide the address.

2. Then, if you hear from them and you are still not satisfied, you can request a review by the Bureau of Hearings and Appeals.

3. Still not satisfied? Ask for a review by the Appeals Council.

4. At this point, you can take your case to the federal courts. This is difficult but not impossible.

Usually such procedures will be unnecessary, but it is important that you know your rights and have some idea what to do about a situation you feel is unfair.

THE FUTURE OF SOCIAL SECURITY

Maybe it is fair to say that people should try to take care of themselves and not rely on the government for help any more than they have to. The fact remains, though, that without social security, many of us would not get around to saving on a regular basis even though we had good intentions. Some of us, through no fault of our own, might be unable to provide for ourselves under some severe conditions, even though we hadn't been careless or thoughtless with the money we had. A prolonged illness of one member of the family could bring such a situation about. Death of the breadwinner in a family with several small children could be catastrophic.

Whenever social legislation is passed it seems there are people who are very much in favor of it and people who strongly oppose it. One side shouts, "Too much!" The other side shouts, "Too little!" Sometimes people feel that a certain social program bends over backwards to help one group and ends up being unfair to another. Sometimes a social program is good, but there isn't enough money to have it reach all the people who need it. Some critics have also said that social programs can be set up to interfere with a person's privacy. That is, the forms a person fills out to participate in a certain program require personal information. Critics of the critics then say that you can't just hand out money to whomever thinks he needs it.

Social security has had its share of critics and problems. Mistakes are made, funds are short, coverage is sometimes inadequate, people cheat and don't get caught. Some people respond by saying, "Let's junk the whole system." That would be like throwing the baby out with the bath water. We need instead to make the best, most honest use of the system, and, through our lawmakers, improve it.

LIMITATIONS OF SOCIAL SECURITY

Social security provides a basic income. It does not provide money for luxuries. After you have graduated and worked a few years, you may want to start thinking of additional kinds of retirement income. Perhaps there is a retirement plan where you work. If you belong to a union, it may have a plan. You might also want to consider private retirement insurance plans and various kinds of investments.

Imagine that Mr. and Mrs. Gray have just retired. Discuss their retirement budget. What expenses will lessen now that they have stopped working? What expenses might increase? What will their high priority items be? What is the minimum amount of money you think they can live on each month?

Chapter Check

1. What four important programs are part of our country's social security program?

2. Who pays for social security?

3. True or False. The number and kinds of workers covered by social security have increased greatly since the system began in 1936.

4. Explain what a sliding scale of benefits is. Why is it important?

5. Do you think you will need any other retirement plan in addition to social security? Why or why not?

❧ Chapter Thirty ❧

KEEPING LAWS CURRENT

Daryl Littlefield

HOW NEEDS BECOME LAWS

Laws are passed to meet the needs of a society. This simple statement is complicated by the fact that not all of us have the same needs. A person living in rural Montana has different needs than someone living in New York City. Often two people living in the same community do not even have the same needs. You can imagine how many factors the people who make our laws have to consider! For example, look at the following situation.

Beef shipped to the United States from South America costs less than American beef. The American shopper buys the cheaper South American beef to cut down on the expenses of feeding the family. As more South American beef is purchased, less of the beef produced in the United States in consumed. This forces down the price of U.S. beef. The beef producers in this country then feel they can no longer make a decent living. They want the prices on imported meat to be raised to a competitive level. The consumer, however, wants beef at the lowest possible price. The needs of the beef producers and the consumers are definitely at odds.

In order to get the price of foreign beef up to that of American beef, the American beef producers organize. Eventually, they get a law passed which puts a tariff (tax) on all beef shipped into the United States. The price of foreign beef is then comparable to that of American beef and consumption of American beef rises again.

You might think that, while such a law meets the needs of the 100,000 beef producers, it works to the disadvantage of the millions of people who purchase beef, since they must pay higher prices at the market. However, before you conclude that the law is completely bad, please consider the following questions:

1. Is beef production important to the American economy?

2. Is the South American beef as good as the North American beef?

3. If the beef producers of the United States are forced out of business, will the South American beef remain inexpensive?

4. Do we wish to be completely dependent on a foreign nation for our beef?

5. Does the government have a responsibility to protect the domestic market?

6. What if a foreign competitor threatened *your* job?

These are just a few of the concerns the lawmakers have to grapple with before they can make a reasonable decision. Framing a law is more difficult than it looks!

Working Cooperatively

People in your neighborhood get together and decide they would like to start a tool pool. They will buy a number of home and garden tools jointly, and then take turns using them. This will give the participants access to many more tools, and probably better tools, than they could afford on their own.

To make the idea work you would have to do something besides just pile the tools in a shed and let everyone help himself. There would have to be rules.

Work out the details for setting up such a plan. You will have to think about such things as:

Which tools your group needs the most

How much money each of you will need to contribute

Rules for borrowing and returning

A check-out system

Repair and maintenance procedures

Fairness in the amount of time people keep tools

HOW LAWS ARE MADE ON THE FEDERAL LEVEL

When we say *the* government, we usually mean the federal government in Washington, D.C. Laws which apply to all of us are made there. Laws made by individual state governments apply to people living in those states. We will look at the steps by which a bill becomes law on the federal level. Most state governments function along similar lines, but there can be many variations in the details.

STEP ONE.   A citizen, committee, or organization makes a strongly-felt need known to an elected senator or member of the House of Representatives. For our purposes, let's make it a member of the House.

STEP TWO.   This legislator, working with a staff, drafts a bill to meet the need.

STEP THREE.   The bill is introduced into the House of Representatives.

STEP FOUR.   The bill is referred to a committee. (Over 20,000 bills are introduced into Congress in each two-year session, but only about 700 make it all the way through the process to become laws. Most of the bills that don't make it are stopped at this stage.)

STEP FIVE.   The committee studies, discusses, and holds public hearings on the bills which pass their first screening. The committee listens to testimony from the bill's sponsor, public officials, experts in the field to which the bill relates, and from any special interest goup which may want to speak for or against it. The committee may then kill the bill, adopt it as written, or amend it (make changes in it).

STEP SIX.   Bills approved by the committee go to the House Rules Committee. The Rules Committee decides how much time will be allowed for debating the bill and whether the bill can be changed or whether members will only be allowed to vote *yes* or *no* on it.

STEP SEVEN.   The bill is read, discussed, and voted on in the House of Representatives.

STEP EIGHT.   If approved, the bill is sent on to the Senate. There it goes through much the same procedure as it did in the house.

STEP NINE.   The Senate can approve the bill as is, vote *no* on it or vote *yes* but with changes. If changes are made, a joint committee of senators and representatives meet to work out the details of the proposed changes.

STEP TEN.   The bill goes back to both the Senate and the House for a final vote.

STEP ELEVEN.   If the bill passes both the Senate and the House, it goes to the President for signature. Once it is signed by the President, it is the law of the land and takes effect on the specified date. If the President wants to, he can *veto* it. That means he refuses to sign it. Back it goes to the Senate and the House for another vote, only this time it needs a 2/3 majority to pass rather than a simple majority.

ADMINISTRATIVE LAWS

In addition to the laws made by the Congress of the United States, there are also many boards, commissions, and agencies which are empowered to make rules and regulations. They are granted this power by the federal government. The actions of these agencies can affect the clothes you wear, the car you drive, the house you live in, the food you eat, the water you drink, and the air you breathe. Here is a list of some of these federal agencies:

The Food and Drug Administration (FDA)
Equal Employment Opportunity Commission (EEOC)
Nuclear Regulatory Commission (NRC)
Interstate Commerce Commission (ICC)
Federal Communication Commission (FCC)
Federal Aviation Administration (FAA)
Consumer Product Safety Commission (CPSC)
Environmental Protection Agency (EPA)
Securities and Exchange Commission (SEC)

If you want to find out more about any of the above agencies, or any others, you can get addresses, basic information, employment information, etc., from:

The United States Government Manual
Office of the Federal Register
National Archives and Records Service
Washington, D.C. 20408
Most public libraries have this manual.

STATE AND LOCAL LAWS

The relationship between the federal, state, and local governments is quite complex and has long been a matter of debate. Even when the Constitution of the United States was first being framed, there was disagreement on which government, the federal or the state, should have greater authority. Generally speaking, Americans have felt that the federal government should be responsible for foreign policy, for matters that need to be uniform throughout the country, and for constitutional matters. Many people feel that everything else should be left up to the state and local governments. People can then have more say-so about the rules that govern their daily lives, and they can be in closer contact with their own lawmakers. State and local governments cannot, however, make any laws which are in conflict with the basic human rights guaranteed by the Constitution of the United States.

CHANGING LAWS

Do laws ever need to be changed? Look at the following:

In California, you aren't supposed to set a trap for a mouse without first obtaining a hunting license.

You must have a doctor's prescription to take a bath in Boston.

You are breaking the law in Minnesota if you hang men's and women's underwear on the same clothesline at the same time.

In Baltimore, it is against the law to mistreat oysters.

You may not carry ice cream cones in your pocket in Lexington, Kentucky.

These and many other strange laws appear in Barbara Sealing's *You Can't Eat Peanuts in Church and Other Little-Known Laws.* (New York: Doubleday and Co., 1975). How do such laws get made? Perhaps in a few cases someone was trying to be funny. Quite often, however, people were reacting to what they saw as a problem. They didn't like something or felt uncomfortable with it, so they tried to get rid of it or regulate it. As the years went by, people forgot all about the law that had once seemed so important. Times changed. Still, it was a lot of trouble to get a law off the books officially, so there it stayed. Many such laws are just not enforced after a few years have passed.

These strange, quirky little laws probably can't do anyone a lot of harm. Some laws are a more serious matter, however. State, local, and/or federal laws can be passed without enough thought or with too little input from the people expected to obey them. Sometimes unfair laws are passed in a moment of great national fear. For example, when World War II broke out and the United States entered it, Japanese Americans had their property confiscated (taken away from them) and they were moved to special detention camps. Few people stopped to think that these people were American citizens whose rights were being grossly violated.

When a law or an order is unfair, unwise, incomplete, or outdated, it has to be changed. How is this done?

A LAW CAN BE CHALLENGED IN COURT. Sometimes a law seems fair enough when it is passed. But when it is put into practice flaws are found in it. If these flaws are serious enough to damage an individual's constitutional rights, that individual can take the matter to the courts. If the court rules that the individual's rights have been violated, the law is regarded as no longer effective. Sometimes we say it has been struck down.

A LAW CAN BE IMPROVED BY LATER LAWS, OR BY AMENDMENTS. As an example of this, look at the social security laws and how they developed to include more people and more benefits.

A LAW CAN BE REPEALED. To repeal a law means to "call it back." This is usually done by passing another law that states clearly that the old law is no longer in effect.

A REFERENDUM CAN BE INITIATED. A law can be referred to the people for final approval. Perhaps a law-making body has written a law, but there is strong feeling for and against it. Voters can get up petitions saying they want the law to appear on the ballot at the next election. Say a city passes an ordinance that no massage parlors may operate within the city limits. Some citizens feel this is an infringement of their rights. They want to make their own moral decisions. They get up a petition saying that they want the issue on the next ballot. If they can get enough signatures, the question has to be put to the voters at the time of the next election. If the feeling that the individuals should be able to make their own moral decisions prevails, the ordinance may be struck down. If the majority of the voters feel that massage parlors are a bad influence on the community, they may vote to keep the ordinance which forbids them.

Working Cooperatively

Look up the 18th and 21st Amendments to the Constitution of the United States. (You can find them in an encyclopedia under "Constitution" or in a government or history book.) These amendments relate to both the sale and the consumption of alcoholic beverages.

Amendment 18 forbids anyone to buy or drink any alcoholic beverage. At the time it became law (1919), there was a strong feeling that alcohol was ruining lives, destroying families, and causing untold suffering.

What do you think was wrong with

this law? Was it practical? Do you think it got to the root of the problem? Do you believe people stopped drinking as a result of the amendment?

What did the 21st Amendment do about it?

Some social problems can be helped by good legislation, but laws aren't always the answer, or the only answer. Some problems must be attacked on many different levels and in many different ways.

PEOPLE POWER

Southern Illinois University / Photographic Service

To some extent we are living in an era of pessimism. A pessimist is a person who believes that if things can get worse, they will. A pessimist doesn't believe much can be done about problems and difficulties in society. Pessimism is like a contagious disease. It can infect an entire society.

The optimist is the opposite of the pessimist. Optimists see the bright side of things and are confident that improvement is possible. They realize that there is no magic wand that can be waved, thus bringing about the righting of all wrongs. Instead, they work at bringing about gradual change and improvement.

Neil Postman and Charles Weingartner have written an interesting book called *The Soft Revolution.* (New York: Delacorte Press, 1971) It is really a handbook for changing things you don't like at your school, but many of the principles in it could apply to other areas of life as well. One of the first points the authors make is to *think small.* Don't try to change the world overnight or believe that what you are doing is going to alter the course of world history. To get what you want takes thought, humility, patience, and cleverness. A sense of humor helps, too!

Good government demands flexibility and change. The most obvious way we participate in our government is by voting. We can't all go to our state capitals or to Washington, D.C., so we choose representatives to go for us. We try to pick persons who will reflect how we feel on certain issues.

Picking the best candidate implies that you will have to do some homework before you can make the best use of your voting power. You can find out what the candidates stand for by listening to them and reading the literature they distribute. You can also listen to what responsible people say about them. In many communities you can also get some facts about the candidates from a nonpartisan group. A nonpartisan organization backs neither candidate, but tries to make available unbiased information about the candidates. Unbiased means free from prejudice or favoritism. It takes time and effort to be a smart voter. If we don't take the time to vote wisely, we must share the responsibility for the bad government we may end up with.

If your candidates state certain views before the election and then don't follow through, you can help put them out of business the next time around by not voting for them again. Keep track of their record on various issues by reading the newspaper or watching the news on television. You can also write to your Congressmen and ask them how they voted on certain issues or how they plan to vote on an upcoming bill.

A few hints for writing to your representatives follow.

1. Be sure you know what you want to say and state it clearly and simply. Don't feel you have to use big words or fancy English. Concentrate on clearness.

2. Try to suggest what you want, as well as criticize what you don't like.

3. If you don't like the way your letter sounds, ask a friend to read it over with you and make suggestions. Your ideas are important, even if

you have trouble expressing them. Everytime you try, it becomes easier.

4. You can find out from your public library who your state and federal lawmakers are, and where to write to them.

5. Short, crisp letters to your newspaper can also be very effective since they reach a wider audience and put pressure on lawmakers.

6. If the issue is very important to you, get friends who feel as you do to write letters, too.

OTHER FORMS OF PARTICIPATION

Another form of participation in government is jury duty. In our system of justice those who are accused of wrongdoing may be judged by a panel of their peers. This panel is referred to as a *jury,* and those who serve on it are called *jurors.* Each citizen of legal age (18) has a chance of being chosen for jury duty. Different states have different ways of choosing jurors. One common method is to select people from the registered voters list. The names are chosen at random. Then those chosen are notified by registered letter. About 50 people report to the courthouse on the specified day. The attorneys for the opposing sides and possibly the judge ask them questions to find out if they are acceptable jurors for the particular case coming up for trial. If a man has recently been mugged and robbed, he may not make a good juror if the case he is going to help judge has to do with a mugging. If a person's religion forbids drinking alcoholic beverages, that person may be prejudiced against someone accused of injuring a pedestrian while driving in a state of intoxication. The first twelve members who are acceptable to both the prosecuting and defending attorneys become the jury and hear the case. Serving on a jury means that you will have to be absent from work. Often there is compensation for the time you lose.

On the local level, you can go to town or city hall meetings. You can run for a place on the liquor commission or school board or whatever. You can circulate petitions. You can organize a committee to get a certain project done. It just depends on how many ideas you have, and how much energy you are willing to spend on a specific issue.

Some people view elected officials as masters, but essentially they are servants of the public. In old movies you have seen the butler or servant appear, saying, "You rang for me, sir?" The master then tells the servant what he wants done, and the servant does it. Public servants do not respond so quickly, and because they have many people's needs to consider, they cannot respond as fully as a servant can who has only one master. Still, there are ways you can "ring" for your public servants. A lot of people "ringing up" their public servants helped bring about the end of the VietNam War, encouraged civil rights and equal opportunity legislation, and influenced many other political decisions.

How much do you know about voting in your community? If you can find the answers to these questions, you should be all set to vote when the time comes. You may be able to get someone from the League of Women Voters, the poll workers, or the voting registrar's office to come to your class and discuss some of these questions.

1. How old do you have to be to vote?

2. Where do you go to register to vote?

3. How far in advance of an election do you have to register?

4. Do you have to register to vote before each election or just once?

5. What is a precinct?

6. How do you know what precinct you are supposed to vote in?

7. How long do you have to have lived in your community in order to be able to vote?

8. How do you get an absentee ballot? (An absentee ballot is a ballot that makes it possible for you to vote even if you are traveling or away from home for the year.)

KEEPING THE LAW: ANOTHER WAY TO PARTICIPATE

Living up to the laws of our land is another important way in which we participate. Each of us must to some extent fit into the society in which we live. Many arguments for and against conforming have been raised during recent years. Let's look at a few of them.

FOR: Society can only survive when people are responsible and law-abiding.

Life is a matter of give-and-take. Society has benefits to offer in return for the freedoms it takes away.

Insisting on personal freedoms is unrealistic in our crowded and complex world.

AGAINST: Our society is corrupt, so fitting in only means corrupting yourself.

Society doesn't deliver the goods. It's supposed to give protection, security, and a livelihood, and it doesn't.

Insisting on smoothing down our personal differences and making us all alike so that we will fit in is unrealistic in a world as varied and fascinating as ours.

Which of these statements seem true to you? If you look carefully you will probably see some truth in each as well as some "blind spots." Now let's make a third list which we will call "Half-Way House." It will consist of ideas from both of the above groups.

HALF-WAY HOUSE. If people are to live together in peace and harmony, they do have to give up some of their freedom and independence. But they cannot afford to give up too much. The Constitution of the United States spells out what freedoms an individual should have. When these personal freedoms are disregarded by society, society itself has to be corrected. This can be done through our legal and court systems.

Our society does have its share of corruption, yet it is a mistake to think of it as totally corrupt. Even if we started all over again, any new system would also have its flaws. We must be willing to accept imperfections while striving toward the bettering of human life.

Insisting on personal rights is a must today as our world grows more crowded and our governments grow larger and more powerful. True, we don't want to become robots doomed to a puppet existence. When we say *human being,* we should be able to imagine a great many different kinds of people.

If we are giving up more than we are getting, we have to make changes in the structure of our society and government. We have to cooperate in forming rules or laws we all agree to follow. Tearing our society apart with words and deeds doesn't do the trick. It only puts us farther behind. Taking our society apart with our minds and hearts means we can thoughtfully put it back together again in better order than we found it. If your watch breaks, you can dash it to the ground and stomp on it. Or you can slip a pocket knife under its back cover, open it up, and see what's the matter. You can also get help from the jeweler.

What Do You Think?

Many of our forefathers came here from other lands: Italy, Africa, England, Poland, Russia, etc. One famous immigrant, a man from Germany named Carl Schurz, came to the United States in the 1840's because he wanted political and personal freedoms he could not get in his native land. He loved his newly adopted country. But it wasn't long before he saw that it wasn't perfect. Slavery existed. He worked hard against it and tried to help get Lincoln elected president. After the Civil War, he was against harsh treatment for the southern states which had left the union. This is one of Schurz's famous statements:

"My country, right or wrong: If right, to be kept right; if wrong, to be put right."

What if he had stopped at "my country, right or wrong"? That would have meant that he thought his country was always right, no matter what. But he knew better than that. He knew things would go wrong from time to time, but he also felt that wrongs could be righted.

Do you think it is disloyal to realize that your country and your government make mistakes? In other words, can you be both loyal and critical?

Chapter Check

1. Why is it difficult to make a law that can satisfy everyone?

2. Outline the steps a bill goes through to become law. (Assume that it doesn't run into trouble.)

3. What are some of the reasons a law might need to be changed?

4. Name some of the ways in which laws are changed.

5. How can you participate in your own government? What can you contribute? What's in it for each of us?

 # Part Ten

Habitat

ROOM TO LIVE

Animals and plants have a natural habitat. For some organisms, the habitat where they thrive best is a specific river or a certain desert area. Others range over a wider area. An organism survives and prospers when the climatic and geographical conditions are right for it or when it has become biologically adapted to an environment.

What is our natural habitat? We have so many ways of overcoming the problems of climate, food supply, and shelter that we can live almost any place on the face of the earth. People can create their own habitat to some extent.

Each of us has a habitat. Are you pleased with yours? Many people would answer no. In this century, we have allowed city slums and country slums to develop. Between them, we've placed belts of suburbs which are often neat and modern, but sprawling and unexciting. What about the countryside? Even there, the natural environment has been damaged, sometimes beyond repair. We suffer from various kinds of pollution and litter, as well as from crowding and congestion. It isn't too late to act. There are plenty of steps we can take both individually and on a community basis.

Let's begin by thinking about what kind of a habitat we want and need.

❀ Chapter Thirty-One ❀

PROTECTING
OUR
LIVING SPACE

HUD

LIVING WITH TECHNOLOGY

Technology has brought about some wonderful advances in civilization. We have an easier life because machines do much of the drudgery. Computers eliminate some of the repetitious, dreary mental work associated with certain jobs. Thanks to technology, we have more material goods, because they can be manufactured more quickly and easily. We live more comfortably in some respects; many of us have central heating and air conditioning and modern plumbing. We travel and communicate faster and more widely than at the turn of the century. Medical technology has improved our chances for living longer, and we can be patched up better if something goes wrong.

Technological advances have also brought trouble. We use up many more resources than before the industrial revolution. One book estimates the amount of resources used up per person in one year at about 13 tons! (D. S. Halacy, Jr., *Now or Never: the Fight Against Pollution,* New York: Four Winds Press, 1971.) And in using more resources we create more waste. The results: shortage and pollution. Blaming technology is a shallow response to this problem. Lack of understanding and wisdom in using technology is the real problem.

Every technological advance has side effects. Few environmental decisions can be made that affect only one small part of the environment. It is as if you are traveling on a busy street. Your car is in the right lane. Suddenly you remember that you want to pick up your clothes from the cleaner's. You need to turn left in a hurry. Does your decision to turn affect anyone else?

The same is true about many environmental decisions. The effect of them ripples out and touches many other people and areas of life. We can't anticipate all the effects any one decision will have, but we can do much better than we have in the past. We have a great many mistakes from which to learn!

A famous environmental mistake occurred in China. Sparrows were eating too much grain in the fields. A notice was sent out to the people to kill the sparrows. Destroying them was considered a patriotic act. A few years went by. Sure enough, sparrows were scarce. Bugs weren't, however. Many of the insects the sparrows had formerly eaten were alive and well, eating grain, leaves, whole plants! The decision to get rid of the birds had wider ranging results than anyone had imagined.

China is far away. What about our own mistakes? On an island in the United States rabbits were multiplying so fast that they were using up more than their share of vegetation. They were also becoming a nuisance. Someone suggested that some foxes should be imported and let loose on the island. They could eat the rabbits. But it turned out that that particular kind of fox did not care to include rabbit in its diet. However, the foxes did find plenty of other food, with the result that they thrived. Then the people on the island found themselves faced with an over-population of both rabbits and foxes.

Sometimes just the reverse has happened. Predators such as coyotes, wild cats, and eagles, have been killed off, while the species they had preyed on, such as deer, got too numerous for the food supply available to them.

Some decisions can be even more hazardous. Take crop-dusting, for example. Farmers want to protect their crops against insects. They realize that if they dust crops from the air there is going to be some fall-out.

They try to take into account such factors as wind and precipitation. Yet it took scientists and ecologists a number of years to fully realize all the problems involved with crop-dusting. Many crop-dusting chemicals found their way into the water supply. Rain drained into a creek after it had picked up some of the chemicals on the plants and on the ground. The creek drained into a river. The researchers started to wonder if the fall-out could contaminate animal food supplies miles away, if it could then get into the human food chain, if fish could be affected by these waste chemicals. In many such environmental problems we end up being faced with many more doubts and fears than we started out with!

Now let's move on to industrial pollution. A factory dumps its manufacturing wastes into the little river at its back door. These wastes contain known toxic substances (substances that can be poisonous). But the reasoning is that these waste materials will be so diluted by the water that they won't hurt anything. However, suppose there is more than one factory on that river, maybe even in the same town? If the water level is down in the summer, the concentration of the chemicals will be greater. Or fish could start dying and decaying along the river. Children might swim too near the dumping place before the chemicals are dispersed or diluted.

Keeping in mind the interrelatedness of environmental decisions, let's look briefly at some of our more pressing pollution problems. We consider a problem pressing if it affects our health and safety or offends our sense of beauty and well-being.

If you were looking for garbage, would you look up or down? Your first response would probably be, "Down, of course," and you would probably be thinking of garbage cans, gutters, alleys, and dumps. We don't often stop to think that we walk through airborne garbage almost everyday. You can see it as a brownish-yellow haze over an industrial area. You can sometimes smell it. The linings of your throat and nose can sometimes feel it. Your lungs don't like it. Studies on the relationship between respiratory diseases and air pollution have come up with rather grim findings. Where does all this aerial junk come from?

We like to use big industry as the main scapegoat. Actually, big industry is only one of the three big contributors. Different modes of transportation account for approximately four times as much pollution as does heavy industry. We have come to accept such pollutants as sulphur, lead, hydrocarbons, arsenic, mercury, fluorides, and many others, as part of everyday life. We have also come face to face with the devastating threat of radioactive contamination. Many of us have gotten into the habit of thinking, "Oh, well, if we want to live in our present state of high technological development and have lots of materials goods, we will just have to take the bad with the good." But, *do* we have to? Or is such an attitude really short-changing people? Maybe we are capable of lessening the bad effects.

Many people are acting to stop the devastation of our habitat. They have put pressure on themselves to be more deeply aware, less careless, and more appreciative of even small environmental successes. They have put pressure on their lawmakers to do something about nationwide environmental problems. Some have even put pressure on industry and transportation companies to clean up their part of the environment.

Checkpoint

Pick out five of the following adjectives that best descibe your dream community, the kind of place you would most like to live in. Write your choices on a piece of paper and use it as a bookmark for this section.

busy	dramatic	lively
sunny	shady	slow
quiet	clean	planned
colorful	crowded	green
open	safe	fresh

THE GOVERNMENT TO THE RESCUE

Lawmakers have long been aware of threats to the environment. A Clean Rivers and Harbors Act was passed as long ago as 1899. Below are some other acts that deal with ecological matters:

1924   Oil Pollution Control Act
1952   Water Pollution Control Act Extension
1965   Clean Water Act
        Clean Air Act
        Solid Wastes Act
1970   National Environmental Policy Act

The 1970 Act was the most comprehensive, covering many facets of the pollution problem. The Environmental Protection Agency (abbreviated EPA) was set up as a result of this act.

Federal laws are important because of the ripple effect we mentioned before. What is done in one state can affect another state miles away. What is dumped into a river moves down the river to pollute water supplies. Pollution is often a matter of interstate commerce. Federal laws take the whole picture into account.

In some cases, however, federal standards may not be adequate for the needs of individual communities. Then state and local governments take over where the federal government left off. Laws and ordinances that they make relate to problems of a specific locality. Perhaps a city is surrounded by mountains and can't tolerate the burning of high sulphur coal.

(High sulphur coal pollutes the air. The mountains form a barrier and keep the pollution hovering over the city.) It passes a law prohibiting the use of such coal. Another town on the coast may have stiff regulations for oil refineries on its shores in order to cut down on the risk of spills. If a factory is causing environmental damage, the city officials might step in to regulate it if no federal laws cover it. It takes a combination of good federal, local, and state laws to deal with all the problems.

We must also have enforcement of environmental laws. The earlier laws didn't add up to much action because few people really cared whether these laws were enforced or not. The crisis stage hadn't been reached. As an old saying goes, "You don't miss the water till the well runs dry." How much protection we get from the newer laws depends to a large extent on how much we insist on having.

How do you as a citizen insist on enforcement? Awareness of problems precedes everything else. Once you are aware, then you must be concerned. Then comes your voting power. If your representatives consistently vote down environmental measures let them know that you don't like it. If the issues are particularly important to you, don't vote for those representatives again. Another tactic is to write to your city's newspaper stating a problem or drawing attention to helpful action that has been taken. You could also write a letter exposing carelessness or unconcern in a matter that affects your whole community.

Finding Out for Yourself

Have a committee of three go to the library and ask for *The United States Government Manual.* Bring back to class a list of some of the duties of the Environmental Protection Agency (EPA).

For one week watch for newspaper or magazine articles about activities of the EPA. Bring any you find to class for discussion.

What Do You Think?

In a city on the West Coast, a certain paper pulp mill was causing heavy yellow smoke and odor to hang over the community, especially when there wasn't much wind. People got tired of the air being stagnant, smelly, and sometimes unhealthy. They wanted something done about it. The city council contacted the

factory. The company agreed to sit down in a meeting with representatives of the citizens and of the environmental agency. The city officials proposed an ordinance that would have forced the paper mill to erect a modern, less polluting smokestack. The company then said that if it was forced to put that much money into a new smokestack it would have to close down. It couldn't afford to comply.

Citizens realized that if the mill closed, several hundred people would lose their jobs. If you lived there and had to vote on the ordinance requiring the new smokestack, how would you vote?

What if your job was on the line? What if you had emphysema or some other respiratory disease? What if you wanted jobs for your community *and* clean air? Can you think of alternative plans?

We have come to realize that developing fair and helpful environmental laws is no easier than writing any other kind of laws. Many aspects have to be considered.

ANTI-POLLUTION-AND-SHORTAGE TACTICS FOR THE INDIVIDUAL

So often we say, "Why doesn't the government do something about it?" The "it" might be unemployment, fraud, environmental protection, or any number of things. Since we elect our government we have the right to expect it to carry out our wishes. However, we must realize the government's limitations. It doesn't have an endless supply of money. In fact, most of its money comes from us, the taxpayers. So when we say we want something done, we have to be ready to help pay for it.

People who want the government to regulate everything are almost asking for a police state. Most of us don't want to be hemmed in on all sides by laws, rules, regulations, people telling us what to do and not do. We can avoid that by taking more responsibility for our own actions. We could ask the government to do only those things which we cannot do for ourselves. How, then, should we approach the problem of personal responsibility for ecological standards? One thing we can do is try to understand modern attitudes, our own included. We said that the advance of technology has changed our environment. It has changed us, too.

For example, the industrial revolution changed our pattern of living. We've come together in cities in bigger numbers than ever before. That means crowding and congestion. Crowding and congestion contribute to a faster, more hectic pace of living. We rush to work through the city streets with very little awareness of the weather, the air, the buildings, the trees. We've almost stopped noticing our habitat. Our environment need not be something we "ooh" and "ah" over everyday. But we've gone so far in the other direction that we barely notice when something is wrong with it—or right!

Isn't it harder to care about something far away than something close at hand? For example, if you hear that people are starving in a distant place, you feel mildly upset, but it doesn't seem real enough to take seriously. If you see a starving person firsthand, though, it is hard not to be upset and concerned. You are much more likely to take action.

Many of us have gotten out of touch with nature. We know more about concrete than we do about grass. *Nature* seems like a far away, romantic idea that poets write about. If we were to experience our natural world more intimately, we would probably end up caring more about what happens to it. If you sunbathe or hike in your city park, you are more likely to want it kept beautiful. You are less likely to litter or injure it. If you and your friend like fishing in an unpolluted stream, you are going to fight to keep it that way. In other words, the more we enjoy our habitat, the more willing we will be to defend it.

Individuals can join such organizations as the National Wildlife Federation, the Sierra Club, the Audubon Society, and many others. They will find their ecology consciousness being raised. These groups also work for good legislation in ecological matters, and they support research. Your interest in saving and bettering your habitat might take the form of joining such a group.

C. William Horrell

Another kind of fall-out from the industrial revolution is that we've gotten more acquisitive. That means we want more material things. We earn more money, and more goods are available to us. Some thinkers have said that highly technological societies tend to be based on the concept of waste. Make, buy, use, throw away, get a new one.

In this country we have become accustomed to thinking BIG. If it's BIG, it's beautiful. If it's BIG, it's good. If it's super or colossal, it's even better. The designer/philosopher F. Buckminster Fuller feels we have to do an about-face. We have to think about how we can do more with less.

Someday you may be able to see an exhibit of Dr. Fuller's inventions and plans. He has designed buildings, cars, even cities. In our town we have a house featuring his famous geodesic dome. The geodesic dome is based on a more-with-less idea. It uses less material to enclose more space. Furthermore, the enclosed space is more exciting than in many conventionally designed buildings.

What Do You Think?

Do you believe that we have to waste things, manufacture things of poor quality that will have to be replaced, and buy as many luxuries as possible in order to keep our economic system in order? Do you believe that unemployment and breakdowns in the law of supply and demand will occur if we decide to try to use less?

Checkpoint

How does the more-with-less principle apply to you?

For two days keep a list of any appliance, tool, means of transportation, or other item you use that is not powered entirely by you. After that time is up, look over your list. Are there any operations you could have performed without using a source of energy outside of yourself? Could you have walked or ridden your bike a few of the times when you drove a car instead? Could you have hung the laundry out instead of using the dryer? If you used an electic knife or scissors, could you just as well have used the musclepowered kind instead?

How could your little savings of energy be important? That may be hard to see. However, multiply it by the other individuals in your community. In your state. In our country. That's what we call a cumulative effect.

Also, did you know that the energy we save brings about a lower rate of pollution? That's because about 14% of our pollution is caused by the generating of power.

Working Cooperatively

As a class, put together a "Favorite Outdoor Places" bulletin board. Have each person do one of the following:

  —Write a one-page description of a favorite outdoor place.

Make a drawing of one.

Take a photograph of one.

Arrange these three kinds of items into an attractive bulletin board display.

Chapter Check

1. What features of our advanced technology mean most to you in your daily life? Think in terms of what things you would be doing differently if certain inventions hadn't been made.

2. What are two of the biggest problems concerning our habitat that the industrial revolution helped to create?

3. Give an example of a decision that has far-reaching effects on the environment.

4. Can the government do the whole job of cleaning up our habitat and preventing shortages?

5. What is a "cumulative effect"?

6. Explain what is meant by the more-with-less concept.

Chapter Thirty-Two

SUCCESS STORIES

HUD

URBAN HOMESTEADING

In pioneer days, homesteading was common. It meant being given a parcel of land out on the frontier, moving there, and trying to make a go of it. Many people were successful at it and ended up as independent farmers. They had a head start since they didn't have to pay much—or anything—for the land.

Not long ago, someone came up with the idea of urban homesteading. Many old homes in the heart of big cities are still basically sound in structure even though they become the property of the city when the owners refuse to or are unable to pay the taxes on them. There they stand, vacant and neglected. What if these homes were given to people who were willing to renovate them at their own expense?

Wilmington, Delaware, was one of the first cities to try the idea. The mayor, Thomas C. Maloney, was anxious to solve some of the habitat problems in his city. It was decided that 10 of these old, abandoned homes would be offered for urban homesteading. More than 100 people applied for them! The agreement was that those who got one of these homes would have 18 months to bring it up to normal housing standards. They were required to live in the home for three years before receiving a clear title to it. By comparison, if they had had to buy such a house, they would probably have had to pay for it over a period of 20 or 30 years. Perhaps they would then not have had the money to do much fixing up.

The plan has worked very well and has now been tried in many other cities. Not only did the families who got such houses benefit, but the community habitat was greatly improved.

C. William Horrell

STRIP MINE SHOWCASE

We need all the coal we can get to supplement our supplies of natural gas and oil. Does that mean that we should allow strip mining to total out whole areas of farm lands? In the past that has happened. Sometimes the topsoil was not only removed, but actually sold by the truckload. When the coal had been stripped, there was no topsoil to put back. Imagine how long it took to get vegetation going again on such land.

Sometimes the topsoil was not sold, but was dumped indiscriminately in heaps with other layers of soil and rock. The coal was harvested with huge draglines, then the place was abandoned as it was. Pools of water formed in the hollows between heaps of dumped soil and rock. The water sometimes turned toxic from materials that had been turned up nearer the surface or had seeped out of broken bedrock. Wildlife couldn't use the water. In some parts of our country you can still drive through desolate regions that almost look as if they had been hit by a bomb.

Does strip mining have to be devastating? No. The first strip mine photograph shows an orderly replacement of the disrupted soil. The second shows land left in good shape so that it can recover much more quickly than in the old days. Cows are grazing peacefully on land that was strip mined less than a decade before.

Some laws read that not only must the landscape be restored after strip mining, but the layers of soil have to be put back exactly the way they were, with the topsoil on top so that plants can begin growing immediately. Such regulations cost the mining companies money and may even push the price of coal up. However, the alternative is far worse. One thing we can't produce more of is land!

C. William Horrell

CLEANUP PARADE

Little Rock, Arkansas, cut down its litter by 35% in 9 months; Indianapolis, Indiana, 29.7% in 6 months; Hayward, California, 10% in 1 month.

How did they do it? They tried the Clean Community System. This system was developed on the basis of research done to find out what attitudes encouraged litter. Researchers found that litter tended to be worse where:

1. There was already a lot of junk accumulated.

2. There were lots of people gathered and it seemed like someone else's job to clean up after the crowd.

3. The property was public, such as a beach, and no one felt there was an owner, so no one was careful.

The three cities mentioned above attacked their litter problems using these findings. Can you think of some of the things these cities did to counter the attitudes that help cause litter? If you wanted to conduct a "litter awareness program" in your community, how would you go about it?

COMMUNITY GARDENS

In many places people don't have enough—if any—land around their dwellings to plant much of a garden. Yet city people need a chance for contact with the soil and plants and nature. They also need the fresh fruits and vegetables they can grow. The idea of community gardens therefore becomes very appealing.

A community garden is a plot of land which the city or town allows residents to use for gardening. The plot is divided up so that everyone who wants to gets to use some of the land.

Two college students got the people in a neighborhood of Sacramento, California, excited about the idea of a community garden. They went to city hall and got permission to use three acres of land. They also went through all the red tape of applying for funds to get started with. The land was weed-choked and filled with junk, but everyone pitched in and helped clear it. The two college students took the lead in doing so.

Many people said the plan would never work. The people, coming from widely differing ethnic backgrounds would probably fight. There would be vandalism and stealing. Once the idea was no longer new, people would lose interest. But none of these things happened.

Instead, people who had sat cooped up in their tiny low-rent houses now had a place to work outside. The satisfaction of growing plants was theirs. They had more and often better vegetables to eat all summer and fall. Many of them became acquainted with their neighbors for the first time, and there was less hostility between different groups than ever before. The endeavor was an ecological and social success.

PLANNING THAT PAYS

City planning is not a new idea. Many European cities are built on plans that were made centuries ago. In this country many cities grew more or less haphazardly. In the early days, this wasn't so much of a problem. Communities were small, and there was at least a center of interest and a well laid out central section. Since then, however, our cities have grown rapidly and with very little planning. The results: urban sprawl, dying central districts, abandoned buildings left to crumble and rot while new ones are built still farther out from downtown.

Now the federal government, as well as local and state governments, realize that city planning will have to play a part in saving our cities. Various urban renewal plans have been tried. Problems turn up, but planners are learning. People who live in the blighted areas are being asked for their ideas and help. We need to find new ways of blending the old and the new, keeping the basic integrity of each neighborhood while improving it. Keeping the integrity means letting it keep its traditional character, preserving the flavor of it, keeping it a distinct community rather than just tearing everything up and replacing the old with a bland, tasteless, cleaner new community.

There will be chances to plan entirely new communities, too. Alaska is working on a new city to house its capital. In planning new communities we need to keep in mind the "more with less" idea. We need to provide more living space, more opportunity to enjoy our surroundings, more natural beauty, more excitement.

For example, in St. Louis several housing projects had become so unfit for living that they had to be pulled down and bulldozed. The people who lived there had become irresponsible and even destructive, the buildings were poorly managed, upkeep was haphazard, and crime and delinquency were out of hand. Some people said, "See what happens? You give people nice housing, and they tear it all up and make a mess of it."

That may have been true of a certain element of the people who lived there. But how many families there wanted to live under such conditions? Very few! A great many innocent people were suffering.

The tenants of these particular housing projects went on a rent strike. During the negotiations, they asked for the right to manage the projects themselves. Things were worked out so that people from among the tenants were chosen and trained to be managers. The expense of the training was partially covered by the Ford Foundation. The new managers reorganized the administration of the housing complex. They took over the job of determining the qualifications of the renters, collecting the rents, making repairs, and making the area safer and more beautiful.

Things improved dramatically. People in the project felt that someone was in control who really understood their problems and complaints. Even more important, people felt responsible for themselves and their dwellings as never before. Perhaps this success is again tied up with the idea of independence. Being taken care of by your parents or the government or charity may be acceptable if there's no alternative. But it certainly doesn't seem like a comfortable or healthy way to live in the long run. It makes people lose both initiative and hope.

CITY TREES. Trees are natural air conditioners. Trees cut down noise and provide homes for wildlife. Trees are part of the natural water filtering system. That is, they help purify the water that eventually gets into our water supply.

That's why the Pinchot Institute was formed. The institute is named for the first Chief of the United States Forest Service, Gifford Pinchot. Usually when we think of forestry, we picture a wilderness, lumber country, a whole mountainside of trees. But the Pinchot Institute deals mainly with urban trees. We have come to realize that city forestry is just as important as wilderness protection. Researchers at the Institute study the problems and the successes of different methods of keeping city trees alive and healthy.

GLASSPHALT

What can you do with old bottles? Probably many more things than have yet been imagined! For example, the Owens-Illinois Corporation paved a parking lot with a mixture of asphalt and glass.

Check your community to see if there are any recycling facilities. Are there places to take used bottles and cans? Clubs and other organizations in some communities raise funds for their treasuries by collecting materials for recycling.

Divide into the committees suggested below. You are now ready to plan a community, at least on paper.

STREETS AND TRAFFIC COMMITTEE. This committee has the final responsibility for laying out the street pattern and traffic system after other committees submit lists of their needs and wants. Pedestrian malls, bike routes, bus routes, etc., should be considered.

HOUSING COMMITTEE. The committee determines what kinds of housing are needed. Will your town have high rises? How many? Where will the private one-family houses be placed? Will there be different price ranges in housing?

SOUL OF THE CITY COMMITTEE. This committee will decide what will be the heart of the city, the center of interest. Will it be on the river flowing by, a lake in the middle, a public plaza? What will this center of interest be used for? How many age groups will be able to enjoy it?

PARK AND RECREATION COMMITTEE. The responsibility of this committee will be to see to it that no one in the new community will be able to say, "There's nothing to do in this town." It will decide on the number and kinds of parks, perhaps including some mini-parks, and it will decide whether or not there should be a community center with activities for various age groups.

MERCHANT AND BUSINESS COMMITTEE. This committee will work out a plan for an ideal business district as well as plans for smaller neighborhood business clusters. It might also design a cooperative plan between city government and business owners to provide for a safe and beautiful business area.

PUBLIC BUILDINGS COMMITTEE. What public buildings should the city have? This committee will have to decide. City hall, governmental offices, hospitals, schools, day care centers, etc., are some of the possibilities.

ENVIRONMENTAL PROTECTION COMMITTEE. This committee decides where any factories or heavy industry will be located. It will also determine the kind of sewage plant the city will need, where the water for use by the people will be processed, how refuse and garbage will be removed, etc. It will also set up a small group of environmental protection laws.

Appoint any other committees you think you will need. When all committees have met and made their plans, the whole class can meet as a group.

Cover the blackboard with paper. Make a map of your proposed city. Each committee adds to the map the structures, roads, and areas for which it is responsible. Your first try at making a map will probably be a rough draft. Have three people do a good, final version of the map.

Part Eleven

C. William Horrell

Planning for
the Future

TEN YEARS FROM NOW

Where would you like to be ten years from now? We hope this book has been a good source of new ideas for you in terms of occupational possibilities. Now, everything is up to you. When you enter the world of work, you will be considered a bona fide adult. You will have more privileges and you will have a greater degree of independence than ever before. Along with that, you will become totally responsible for yourself. What will you do with your life?

If you had a crystal ball that really worked, what would you like to see in your future? A good job? A car and maybe a house? Most of us think in terms of material possessions, but we realize there are other important things we also want. Do you feel you might like to have more education or a different kind of education? Do you want to make a good name for yourself? How do you feel about marriage? Do you look forward to sharing your life with someone and starting a home of your own? Or would you rather be a swinging single for a while? What about your free time? What will you do with it? Dance, paint, build something, race cars? Many young people look forward to the time when they can more fully participate in their society, changing and improving it. A good plan for the future will involve many such issues.

What Do You Think?

Where would you like to be ten years from now? What would you like to be doing for a living? What educational goals do you have? What recreational pursuits would you like to have time for? What volunteer activities might you consider? Knowing what you want is the first step toward getting there.

❈ Chapter Thirty-Three ❈

SELF-IMPROVEMENT

Bruce Wilcox

IMPRESSIONS

In the first chapter of this book we looked at a sample skills pyramid and talked about how a worker can advance from the lower levels up to the more highly skilled jobs. At that time we said there was nothing wrong with not wanting to reach the top. Doing a good job on whatever level you find yourself may provide plenty of satisfaction for you. Your steadiness and loyalty will be appreciated.

For some of you, that won't be enough. You will want to use more and more of your skills and special talents. You will expect deeper satisfaction in your work as you move along. What can you do to advance yourself in your chosen occupation?

Each young worker must establish a good work reputation. To do that you must make sure your employers get their money's worth. Do you show up for work regularly and on time? Do you concentrate on your work? Do you expect to be better at it in a year's time than you are now? Are you open to every opportunity to learn more? Give yourself a report card every so often.

The impression others have of your performance on the job not only involves how well you do the work, but the way you get along with others. If you build up the reputation for being someone who gripes a lot and can't seem to get along very well with anybody, the path to advancement may be blocked. Even very gifted people end up being a liability to their employers if they cause a lot of personnel problems. In many cases an employer would almost prefer having a less talented individual who gets along with others than a more talented one who makes trouble everyday and destroys all the team spirit so necessary to a business. Can you think of a similar case in the world of sports? What good does it do to have star players if they can't cooperate with the rest of the team?

To advance on the job you must not only improve your skills, but learn as much as possible about getting along with others. What else might be helpful? Look at some of your co-workers who have not advanced very much in all the years they've been working. Why not? Then look at a person who has experienced considerable success on the job, someone you like and respect. What differences do you see in terms of the following:

> How they talk to their co-workers
> What they say about others
> How many skills they have
> How they get along with their bosses
> How much they care about the business
> How much they care about themselves
> How knowledgeable about their work they are
> How their supervisors treat them
> How realistic they are about their own capabilities
> How many outside interests they have

Do you realize that sometimes things that happen to you outside of your working day have a strong influence on how your job goes? If you have problems at home, a health or drug problem, or too much financial responsibility, you may find it hard to turn off your worries and do a good job. But that is exactly what you must sometimes do. Life is full of changes, trouble, sadness, happiness, success, failure, conflict, peace. If you allow your feelings to overwhelm you, how much energy will you have to put into your work or into your daily life as a whole?

To gain some measure of control over your life you will have to deal with a great many situations in a cool and realistic way. Isolating yourself now and then in order to have some time to think and plan is one way to help yourself. Another way is to seek help when you need it. For some reason people will willingly go to a medical doctor if they feel sick, but they pull back from going to a minister, priest, rabbi, teacher, parent, psychologist, counselor, or the county Mental Health Department. So many agencies are there for people who want to use them, yet it seems there is some kind of stigma involved with admitting you have a special problem.

The more you think about it, the more you realize that admitting you have a problem is a sign of maturity. It is the first step toward solving it. There is no place for shame or fear or holding back. Reach out for help and take whatever you judge to be useful for you in your particular situation. If you try something and it works, remember the elements that benefitted you. If you try something which fails to help, consider the elements that weren't so good for you and avoid them in the future.

What you are as a whole person, both on and off the job, will often affect your advancement on the job. When we speak of self-improvement we are thinking of you as a total person and not just as a worker.

CHANGING JOBS

If you are unhappy with your job, should you change to another one or should you just "grin and bear it?"

The first thing to realize is that no one is happy on the job *all* of the time. The same is true about friendships, marriages, belonging to organizations, etc. The immature person simply quits when a problem arises. That's maybe the easy way out in one sense. But, in the long run, it is no way out at all. It often only means a change from one bad situation to another.

Take the case of Jonathan. He gets a job in a newspaper office. He has to start at the bottom, working as a messenger and errand boy. After a few months he feels that he is being pushed around, made to do menial tasks when he had intended to become a cub reporter. He doesn't stop to think if he has the qualifications to be a reporter, or if he was promised more when he came to work there. He just quits.

He gets another job, this time in the office of a big department store. It is almost the same kind of job he had at the newspaper. Everything is fine for a few weeks, then a job one level above his opens up. He applies for it but doesn't get it. So, again he quits. He feels he has to because nobody appreciates his talent. If he does this three or four times in one year, would he have made any progress whatsoever in solving his problem?

When you change jobs, you should not do so on impulse. You must think about your reasons and decide what you hope to accomplish by making a change. Then when you move into a new job, you must try to avoid repeating mistakes that could turn the situation into one very much like that of the one you left.

For instance, when Jonathan left his newspaper job, he could have said to himself, "I don't like being at the bottom of the totem pole. But that's where I'm always going to be unless I do something about it. But what should I do? I know. I'll take another job just to keep myself in money. Then I'll decide which skills I could improve and enjoy using. Maybe I can go to school part time or learn on the job some place."

Such a self-evaluation would have enabled him to make a big step forward. He would have come to grips with the fact that he couldn't hope for a more prestigious job right away. Then he would have approached his next job more realistically, not expecting great things. He would have been on the lookout for new ideas to improve his employability. He would also be looking for a way of earning a living that would satisfy him more fully. His troubles wouldn't be over, but he would be making progress.

Job hopping can be a most damaging practice for a young worker. When employers were surveyed to find out the main reasons job applicants did not get hired, one of the main reasons was that the person had had too many jobs within a relatively short period of time.

If you put yourself in the employer's shoes, you might have questions about such a person. You might wonder if the person was somewhat immature and unstable. You might question an applicant's ability to get along with others. You would look at the application form and see what kind of reasons were given for leaving previous jobs. You might detect a pattern. It might occur to you to wonder if the person has any gumption or stick-to-it-tiveness.

Besides these considerations, employers have to face the fact that breaking in a new employee takes time, patience, and money. Why should an employer offer these to an applicant who may stay only a few months and who may be a problem on top of it all? A new employee is often not worth his wage the first month or so.

Now, the other side of the coin. There are many cases in which a person must have the courage to make a big move. Not everyone who wants to change jobs is unstable and irresponsible. People have legitimate reasons for feeling unhappy and dissatisfied. It would be wrong to try to convince them that they should stay put and be content with their lot. After all, that is like asking them to waste themselves—their time, their talents, their energy. Their value to society might be lessened as well.

When deciding whether or not to change jobs, you might ask yourself such questions as:

1. Have I given myself enough time on my present job to make a good judgment of the work situation?

2. Do I feel good about my job a good deal of the time? Do I have periods in which I get great satisfaction from my work?

3. Have I listened to other people too much? too little? Have I carefully sifted through all advice, pro and con?

4. If my occupational needs change, would there be a place for me in this company?

5. If my problem is a personality conflict with my boss or co-workers would it be better to see it through on this job than to imagine that things will be better on a new job? In other words, is there something in me that may be about the same problem all over again on a new job?

6. Do I have a chance to advance on my present job if I worked hard at it?

7. Am I ready for something better? That is, do I really have skills that aren't being used on this job?

8. Am I prepared to get more education and training in order to advance myself on the job?

To summarize, a change in jobs or in occupations should be a planned event with a definite goal in mind. It may involve making changes in yourself as well as in your job situation.

If you do decide to change jobs, the way in which you do so will be important. It is essential to leave a job with a minimum of friction or negative feelings between you and your employer. Quitting suddenly in a huff does little for any worker.

Your immediate supervisor should be the first to know if you plan to leave. Don't talk about it to your co-workers and friends, allowing your boss to find out second-hand. Go to him and tell him as politely and honestly as you can why you are leaving. Usually such notice that you intend to leave should be given at least two weeks in advance. That gives your employer a chance to find a replacement for you. If your job involves a great deal of detail, practice, or responsibility, you may want to give notice even further in advance. In some places you may be asked to write a letter of resignation. This should be formal and brief, stating when and why you are leaving. Remember that your reasons for leaving could play a part in your future employment. Don't put down petty grievances. Don't create the impression that you are someone who can't get along with others. Leaving because you want more opportunity to advance or you want to change locations or you now have training to do something else are all good reasons to put down. There are others.

What if you should get laid off or fired? That is a hard blow for anyone to take. Even executives in important companies have to face this possibility. When it happens, even the most self-confident person feels badly. Give yourself time to recover. Then you will have to go through a self-evaluation again. What did you contribute to the situation? What would you do differently the next time? Do you feel your employer was unfair to you? Were there financial or other reasons that made the move necessary? What would you have done had you been in your employer's place?

Such a self-evaluation might be very painful. But if you don't do it, you won't really know exactly what happened. You won't have any way to protect yourself or to avoid future problems. Plenty of people have been through such crises. We don't have any statistics to tell you how many people have gotten fired and still gone on to successful careers. We do know quite a few who made such comebacks. We even know one woman who got fired for not getting along with her co-workers. She was so shocked by this that she underwent therapy. She later became a successful personnel manager!

Your work life may be compared to a ladder. Each job you have represents one of the rungs or steps. The strength of the entire ladder depends on how well each step is fastened between the uprights. A strong, firmly attached first step makes it much easier to work on the second. Each step contributes to the strength and usefulness of the whole ladder.

MORE EDUCATION?

Some of you may be saying, "More education I can do without!" And, no wonder. You've been in school a long time. But after you have been out in the world of work, you may change your mind. You may want to develop new skills that you did not realize you were interested in before.

In the past, many parents insisted on their children going to college because it was the thing to do if you wanted to be successful. Success was

C. William Horrell

often calculated in terms of how much money you could make. If education could help you earn more money, then it was a good thing. The idea that education could bring you other satisfactions was more or less overlooked.

Does a college education really help you earn more money? Authorities on the subject differ widely. Some of them point to the many college graduates who can't find jobs suitable for their level of education. Others point to statistics that show that the average college graduate does advance much more rapidly than the high school graduate, especially in certain fields.

Here are a few suggestions to think about. If you want a college education, try to pick a field that isn't already overcrowded. College counselors and placement officers can give you a good idea of what fields these are. The United States Department of Labor also makes forecasts of the future need for workers in many occupations. This is published in several handbooks, including *Occupational Outlook Handbook* and *Occupational Outlook for College Graduates*.

What if, more than anything else in the world, you want to prepare for a field which is already overcrowded? Then you must try it, in spite of the odds. If your feelings about it are that strong, you may very well end up being one of the graduates who gets one of the few jobs in that field. Of course, you would be taking a chance. If you are reasonably sure of your own capabilities in this area, you are taking about the same risk as a person who starts his or her own business.

If you don't achieve exactly what you want, you will at least have an education that can open up other alternatives for you. Besides, there is intrinsic value in education. Intrinsic means "in or of itself." Education can make you a richer person in a non-material sense, richer in what you have experienced and what you know about the world you live in.

When you think of education, keep in mind the great variety of possibilities.

- You can go to special training centers for paraprofessionals. Paraprofessionals, you may remember, are important assistants to professionals. A paralegal, for example, helps a lawyer prepare cases, does research, counsels people, etc., but does not defend people in court. Paramedicals do many things doctors do, but not surgical or other highly skilled treatments.

- Many states now have very good post-secondary technical schools. Often there is no tuition for residents of the state in which the school is located.

- Many private trade schools exist. One note of caution here, however. Some trade schools can be disreputable. You must find out whether or not they are any good before giving them any money or signing anything. Be very suspicious of big claims, such as that they can prepare you for a highly skilled job in a few weeks or that they can place every one of their graduates in a job. Your local Better Business Bureau may be able to help if you have doubts about a specific trade school. You may also want to refer to the book *Getting Skilled* by Tom Hebert. (New York: E. P. Dutton, 1976).

- Consider apprenticeship programs. You can talk to workers in the field about these programs and ask them how you go about getting into one. Some unions also have apprenticeship training programs. Your school counselor may be able to help you find out more information about these.

- Investigate your local community college, which probably offers a wide range of courses. You may have to get your education in the evenings, at least to begin with. Quite often evening students are mature and interesting people with much experience.

■ The Armed Forces also provide educational opportunities and training programs. You can look into the possibilities at your nearest recruitment office.

The next big question is how can you afford an education? It's not easy. The price of education keeps going up along with many other commodities. Many parents can't afford to help their children, even though they might like to. What are the alternatives?

You could work for a few years and save enough money to get started in college. You would probably have to work while you take classes, but many good jobs are available for students right on the campuses where they attend classes. In some cases there are special work programs for people from lower income families. You can find out by asking at the financial aid office or the registrar's office on most college campuses. You might be surprised at the number of possibilities.

Scholarships are another possibility. If your high school grades aren't so hot, you might attend junior college for a year first. If you do very well, then you can apply for financial aid. The government also makes low-interest loans available to students. These are paid back by the borrowers after they have completed their education.

Getting a college education may require knocking on a lot of doors and asking a lot of questions. It can be difficult, but it can also be an exciting, problem-solving adventure.

❊ Chapter Thirty-Four ❊

SELF-FULFILLMENT

Alan Carrier

MATURING TOWARD MARRIAGE

You are now ready to take care of yourself. Are you also ready to take care of someone else? Are you ready to be half of a lifelong partnership in which the caring goes both ways?

Although marriage as a sociological institution has had its ups and downs in the last decades, many young people still long for a lasting love relationship. Maybe you aren't one of these people, or at least you aren't one right now. Maybe you are. Knowing where you stand on this question can save you and other people a great deal of pain and suffering. It can also lead to a deep sense of fulfillment and happiness.

Let's look at a few reasons people give for not wanting to be married.

1. "I'm too young. I want to play the field a while." This is a perceptive remark. Many young people are unwilling to admit that age can be a real factor. The young person who fully realizes he or she isn't ready to settle down yet has less chance of making a serious mistake. Playing the field is a good idea if it means that you want to meet and find out about many different kinds of people. If it means that you just want to build up a reputation for being a big-time playboy or playgirl, that's a bit childish.

If you choose to play the field, each relationship should still be important to you. Don't treat anyone in a way you would not like to be treated. Let the other person know how you feel, and don't lead them to expect more than you are willing to give. Don't rush the other person, either. An honest, open friendship is much more valuable than a quick romance that ends up with one party feeling hurt and cheated. Common sense and courtesy are as vital in more casual relationships as in very serious ones.

2. "I want a career. Marriage would interfere with my getting where I want to go." At first, this sounds selfish, doesn't it? But isn't it better to realize this about oneself and to say so than to get into a marriage in which the other party is expected to do all the giving? Many a woman has more or less signed over her whole life to her husband. Some men's lives have centered around the career of a talented wife. But these are rather special arrangements, and not everyone is capable of success in such a relationship. However, many modern young couples are capable of combining two separate careers in one marriage and making it work.

3. "Marriage isn't necessary any more. I can get everything I want without it."

Yes, we are living in an era of new sexual freedom. If marriage means sex to you, then you are right. You can, in many circles today, have sex without marriage. One important fact is not to be overlooked, however. A good marriage is a matter of growing and building together. It provides a focus for your life, a living center for it. A lot of dates and sexual encounters can't do much for you in this respect. In fact, as Don Juan found out, they become boring because they are so shallow.

4. "I've seen too many bad marriages. I have no reason to expect my luck to be any better." If you really feel this way, you are probably setting yourself up to be a loser in this—and in other respects too. You need to build more self-confidence. Suppose you come from a family in which there was a divorce. You don't have to follow that pattern any more than you have to buy the same kind of car your mother or father drives. You can make your own world, up to a point. Your chances for a good marriage are greatly improved if you take the time to reflect on what you expect from a marital relationship. Don't be in a hurry, though. It takes time to sort these things out.

5. "No one will ever want to marry me." That may sound a little funny, but many of us have thought that at one time or another. One of the problems of a mass society such as ours is that it is often very hard to meet and establish close relationships with others. If you feel somewhat left out, what would you do about it? You might join a singles club, a church group, an organization that has a program of interest to you. There are choirs and other musical groups, sports teams, and many kinds of clubs. Enjoy casual friendships whenever you can. Don't push too hard for a permanent relationship. Otherwise you might make others feel uneasy or trapped in a relationship they didn't want. Be alive to each person, and be patient. Waiting is often the hardest part, especially when you're young.

Marriage doesn't really cause problems. Rather, problems exist in any love relationship. The same kinds of problems crop up in less conventional ways of living together. For some people, though, the commitment of a marriage provides a better basis and reason for working things out, for maturing together. Some people need the security of a marriage to give them the confidence and trust to solve problems in their love life. Any relationship, marriage or otherwise, that is entered into without commitment gives only a limited amount of such security.

Financial problems can be a serious threat to what might have been a good marriage or relationship. If you are thinking about marriage, you will have to pay even more attention to the kind of financial planning discussed in Part VIII. Worry about finances can make people very difficult to get along with. If children enter the picture, the young father and mother can feel completely overwhelmed. You can't avoid all financial worry. You can, however, watch your credit buying, save for a big down payment before making any major purchase, buy your groceries wisely and not just on a whim. In other words, people who live within their means have one less marital problem to worry about.

What Do You Think?

Do you think it is a good idea for all young people to live on their own at least one year before getting married? Would a wife who has worked and maintained herself for a few years be more appreciative of her husband's efforts? Might a husband who has bacheloried appreciate his wife's contributions more? Do you believe that a wife who has worked would have a better idea of what she wants career-wise?

BEING PARENTS

What can you do to prepare for parenthood? Most obviously, you must know how you feel about having children. You and your spouse should talk seriously about it *before* marriage. Do you both want children, or not? Do you share ideas on how to rear children? Your ideas need not be exactly alike, but they must be in agreement on basic issues. Accepting children as a normal and expected part of marriage is all to the good. But failing to realize the kind of wisdom and patience—and time—it takes to be a good parent is something else. It's important for a couple to learn to live together themselves first, then to think about children. Being a parent is no bed of roses. At times it is great fun and very rewarding. At other times it can be a very frustrating experience. Are you really ready for parenthood? Are you mature enough to behave like an adult when dealing with a child, rather than countering with childish behavior of your own?

If you run into marital problems or problems in raising children, what will you do? If you don't take any action at all, frustration and bitterness may begin to ruin the relationship. First try to iron out things between the two of you. You won't succeed if you come at each other in anger or accusingly. Think of yourselves as two nations at war who really want peace. Be as diplomatic, kind, and polite as you can be.

What if you make a sincere, all-out effort to solve a problem and can't quite manage it? Again, try your minister or priest. Go to a family counseling center. If there is a university or college in your town it may have a special counseling clinic. Sometimes time is the answer. Learn the art of patient waiting. Many people have done so and afterwards been glad.

Thinking in advance about what you expect of marriage and family life can be valuable in the same way that thinking and planning for your career is valuable. The library has many good books on marriage, family planning, child rearing, and other related topics.

YOUR LEISURE HOURS

Work is only a part of your life. It is like one note of a chord you might strum on a guitar. It consumes a good deal of your day but not all of it. The time that is left over can be just so many hours in front of a television set, or it can be time spent doing many other more satisfying things.

Structuring your leisure time does not mean that you have to plan something for every free hour. Hours spent swinging in a hammock or lying on a beach are good for everyone. Most of us wouldn't want a steady diet of inactivity, however.

You can use some of your leisure time keeping yourself in shape. That may take the form of participating in a sport, attending the Y, lifting weights, taking karate lessons, sailing, fishing, or running. Keeping yourself in shape can also be a way of meeting new and interesting people.

If you are cooped up inside most of the day, you may find outdoor activities appealing. Often we get a longing for some contact with the natural world. So we plant a garden or go camping. Maybe we even arrange to take a canoe trip with several friends, or hike on a wilderness trail in one of the state parks in the area or in a national park.

Maybe you expend a lot of physical energy at work, but you don't feel that your mind is kept sharp enough. You might use your free time

C. William Horrell

toning up your mind. That might involve reading or taking a night school class just for the pleasure of learning something you are interested in. You could plan a project for yourself that involves mental and physical skills, such as building a piece of furniture or making a model.

Many vocational education students miss out when it comes to contact with the performing and fine arts. Is there a whole sector of your life that has been neglected? The arts are for everybody. Would you be brave enough to tackle a drawing or sculpting class? How would you feel about acting with an amateur theatrical group? What about attending a lecture or slide show at the art museum near you? You could start a musical group of your own or join an established one if you have the skill. Park departments in various cities offer classes in all sorts of things, ranging from belly dancing to bird watching. Concert groups tour the country, stopping in big and small cities. Usually you can find out what is going on culturally in your town through the newspaper or by calling the museums, chamber of commerce, park department, etc.

A leisure time activity that never goes out of style is being with friends. Sometimes this means sitting quietly down to talk with each other. A little thought and planning can make this joint leisure time happy and meaningful. What about getting together a bridge club or a bowling team? Why not plan to eat out once a month with five or six friends, trying various interesting restaurants in your area? Could you form a volunteer group of some kind? For example, young volunteers visit the elderly and read to them or just sit and talk to them. Another volunteer group in our city helps physically and mentally retarded people. There are dozens of possibilities for wise and rewarding use of leisure time!

GIVING

Human beings have gotten a rather bad press, so to speak. You hear so much about meanness, cruelty, abuse, and dishonesty. Yet there are frequent occasions on which someone does something noble: saves someone's life, stops an unfair practice, befriends a friendless person, stands by a friend in a crisis, etc. We could go on and on. Why do you think people do kind things? What pleasure do they get out of giving?

Often young people are thought of as selfish. Is that really true? Self-centered might be more accurate. They need to spend a lot of time trying to get a focus on their lives, thinking about themselves and the possibilities open to them. When given the chance, however, many young people are very generous. It seems as if they were waiting for a chance to do something for others.

Giving often takes the form of loving one's own family more as one matures and trying to help them in various ways. Some young people have found that their main contribution to family life can be to avoid conflicts with younger members of the family, or to help solve them when they occur. Others try to help financially. The time comes when some young adults can suddenly give their parents' point of view a real hearing. Even though they may not agree with it, they listen and understand. All of these are ways of giving.

Then the circle widens out. It comes to include the joy of giving to someone you are in love with. From there it can spread out to people outside your immediate circle of relatives and friends. You look around you and see all that needs to be done, and you decide you can do some of it.

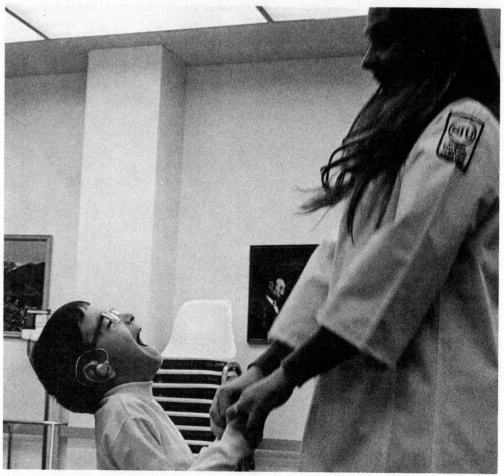

Terry Mauzy

LIFT OFF!

You have come a long way since the beginning of this book. Not only have you had a look at a variety of topics, but you have actually been experiencing the world of work firsthand.

Have you gotten some ideas about how to use your experience to the greatest possible advantage?

Do you believe that you now have the imagination and gumption to set goals for yourself and then proceed toward them?

Are you willing to seek advice and help when you need it? Do you know where to look for this?

If you can answer yes to these questions, you have gotten a great deal out of your cooperative education class. All we have to do now is wish you Bon Voyage!

Answers to Checkpoints ═══

Chapter 5

1. D
2. E
3. B
4. A
5. C
6. F

Chapter 9

1. International Periodicals Dictionary
2. World Almanac and Book of Facts
3. Scott Standard Postage Stamp Catalog
4. The Toll-Free Digest
5. Dictionary of Scientific and Technical Terms
6. Motor's Auto Repair Manual
7. Congressional Quarterly's Washington Information Directory
8. Consumer Complaint Guide
9. Book of Etiquette and Good Manners
10. Famous First Facts
11. Baseball Encyclopedia
12. Comparative Guide to Two-Year Colleges and Their Programs

Chapter 10
GAME ONE

Drinks	Deodorants	Vehicles	Magazines
Coke	Right Guard	Honda	Mad
Seven-Up	Ban	Ford	Seventeen
Bud	Secret	Harley Davison	Time
V-8	Sure	Corvette	Ebony
Dr. Pepper	Fresh	BMW	Newsweek
Sanka	Dial	Yamaha	People
Folger's	Arrid	Pinto	Playboy
Kool-Aid	Mum	Rabbit	Reader's Digest

GAME THREE:

injustice, sexist, disgraceful, fearful, nightmare, unthinking, lollipop, threatening, innermost, homemade, enrage, earrings, landmark, conformity, beekeeper, uphold, courageous, freeway, intersection, stereotype, stepbrother, resentment

GAME FOUR:

1. intersection: a place where streets or roads cross
2. stereotype: mental image one has of a certain group of people
3. sexist: favoring one sex over the other
4. enrage: to make angry
5. threatening: frightening, dangerous
6. uphold: keep, protect
7. courageous: having courage, brave
8. landmark: important, pace-setting
9. innermost: inside oneself

GAME SIX:

autograph: writing one's name

biography: written story of someone's life

graphite: a writing material, the lead in a lead pencil

illumination: the lighting up of something

luminous: glowing with light

television: vision from a distant place

telegraph: written message from a distance

telescope: instrument for bringing a distant object closer

Chapter 11

CHECKPOINT 1
1. $161.05
2. $70.80
3. $147.85

CHECKPOINT 2
1. B
2. D
3. E
4. F
5. A
6. C

CHECKPOINT 3
1. $ .55, 10.55
2. $23.14
3. $39.25

CHECKPOINT 4
1. $ 13.50
2. $142.50

CHECKPOINT 5
1. G
2. E
3. A
4. D
5. C
6. B
7. F

CHECKPOINT 6
1. kilograms
2. kilometers
3. meters
4. °C (degrees Celsius)
5. liter
6. grams
7. milimeters

Chapter 24
1. B
2. D
3. A
4. H
5. I
6. F
7. G
8. E
9. C

Chapter 27
a. $ 54.40
b. $142.40
c. $156.80
d. $176.00

Chapter 28

CHECKPOINT 1
1. C
2. H
3. D
4. F
5. B
6. A
7. E
8. G

CHECKPOINT 2
1. $18.75
2. $77.50
3. $236.25
4. $609.00
5. $3412.50

Index

D

Damage to property, 304
Data sheet, 203–205
Dating, 245
Deals, business, 336
Debit, 287
Debts, 336
Decision making, 346
Deductible insurance, 304
Deduction, tax, 131–132, 360, 361
Defendant, 342, 343
Defensiveness, 18–19
Deficit spending, 283
Dental hygiene, 232–233
Dependence, 1–2
Dependents, 131, 361
Detentions, 10
Devil's advocate, 115–116
Dewey decimal system, 112–113
Dictionary of Occupational Titles 160, 191
Diplomacy, 246
Diploma, high school, 108
Disability, 371, 372
Disagreements, 69
Discrimination, 52, 54–56
Dislikes, 189
Disrespect, 30–31, 32
Dissatisfaction, 76
Divorce, 336
Dress codes, 10, 229, 239
Drugs, 92–93

E

Ecology, 162
Economics, 248–258
Economic systems, 250–258, 259–261
Education, 6, 107–108, 208, 415–418
Emergency, 96
Emergency fund, 284–285
Employment history on resumé, 208
Employment offices, 196–197
Endowment insurance policy, 311–312
Energy crisis, 162–163
English, standard, 123
Environment, 390, 393
Environmental protection, 392–400
Environmental Protection Agency
   (EPA), 395

Equal Employment Opportunity Act, 342
Equal Employment Opportunity Commission
   (EEOC), 54
Equal opportunity, 54
Escalation, 69
Esteem needs, 185
Ethnic groups, 52–53
Evasion, tax, 359, 368
Exemptions, tax, 131–132, 361
Expenses, 281, 303
Experience, 20, 190
Expulsion from school, 10–11

F

Factory system, 144
Failure, 41–42, 44
Fair Labor Standards Act, 350–351, 354
Fair Packaging and Label Act, 329
Family influence, 2
Farrier, 147
Federal budget, 368
Federal Insurance Contributions Act
   (F.I.C.A.), 371
Federal standards, 395
Federal Trade Commission (FTC), 329
Felonies, 335
Femininity, 46
Finance companies, 296
Financial competition, 283
Financial difficulties, 283–284
Financial planning, 279–281, 303
Financial statement, 287
Financial stress, 62
Fine arts careers, 170–171
Fire insurance, 308–309
First aid, 96
Flexibility, 123
Food and Drug Administration (FDA), 329
Food distribution
   and processing
   careers, 177
Formality, 239–241
Fraud, 321
Freedom, 332–333, 388
Free enterprise, 252–254, 260
Free market, 261
Friendship, 36–37, 241–243
Future Planning, 408–426

G

H

I

J

K–L

Knowledge, lack of, 87–88
Labels, package, 327–328
Labor, 249
Labor Management Relations Act, 272–274
Labor problems, 266
Language skills, 123–128
Law, 53–54, 332–389
   breaking, 336–338
   challenging in court, 383
   changing, 382–383
   improving, 383
   keeping, 387–389
   keeping current, 378–389
   making, 380–381
   repealing, 383
Laws, types of
   administrative, 381
   civil, 335–336
   constitutional, 336
   criminal, 335
   federal, 380–381
   local, 382
   protecting young workers, 349–357
   referendum, 383
   state, 382
   unconstitutional, 336
   universal, 344–347
   tax, 358–369
Law suit, 316, 336
Lawyer, 341–342
Lawyer Referral Service, 341
Legal aid, 342
Legal terms, 342–344
Leisure time, 169–170, 423–425
Liability insurance, 303, 304, 309
Liberation, 48–50
Library, 112–113, 326
Life insurance, 310–312
Likes, 189
Litter awareness, 31, 404
Loan, 295–297, 418
Losing, 41–42, 44
Loss of income insurance, 307
Luxuries, 283

M

Magazines, 113, 197
Major medical insurance, 307

Manipulative techniques, 114–115, 322–324
Manual skills, 143–144
Manufacturing careers, 172
Market, free, 261
Market system, 253
Marriage, 419–421
Marriage and divorce courts, 339
Masculinity, 46
Math, 130–142
Maturing, 419–421
Media, 118
Medical careers, 168
Medical expense insurance, 304
Medical expenses, 303
Medicare, 372–373
Metric system, 138–142
Migrant workers, 162
Military service careers, 178
Minimum balance, 288–289
Minimum wage, 354–357
Mining careers, 176
Mining, strip, 402–403
Misdemeanors, 335
Money, 276–331
Money order, 293
Monopoly, 266
Motive, profit, 260, 266
Municipal courts, 339
Museum, 153–155

N

National Association for the Advancement of
   Colored People (NAACP), 342
National Endowment for the Arts, 152, 155
National Institute for Occupational Safety
   and Health (NIOSH), 100, 101
Nationality stereotype, 38–39
National Labor Relations Act, 273
National Labor Relations Board (NLRB),
273
Natural habitat, 390–391
Natural resources, 249
Needs, 184–185, 283
Negligence torts, 335
Neighborhood influence, 2
Net pay, 131, 132
Newspapers, 113
Nonpartisan group, 385

O

P–Q

R

Design and Production:
T.R & Associates — Phoenix, Arizona

Printing:
Von Hoffmann Press — St. Louis, Missouri

This book is set in Garamond 11/12. Heads are
set in Avant Garde Book 30 point.